AF631532

Circular Happiness

Circular Happiness: Building Sustainable Workplaces for the Next Generation

EDITED BY

PAWAN KUMAR
Lovely Professional University, India

PRETTY BHALLA
Lovely Professional University, India

RAJESH VERMA
Lovely Professional University, India

AND

SUMESH S. DADWAL
London South Bank University, UK

emerald PUBLISHING

United Kingdom – North America – Japan – India – Malaysia – China

Emerald Publishing Limited
Emerald Publishing, Floor 5, Northspring, 21-23 Wellington Street, Leeds LS1 4DL.

First edition 2026

British Library Cataloguing in Publication Data
A catalogue record for this book is available from the British Library

ISBN: 978-1-80592-908-6 (Print)
ISBN: 978-1-80592-907-9 (Online)
ISBN: 978-1-80592-909-3 (Epub)

Printed and bound by CPI Group (UK) Ltd, Croydon, CR0 4YY

INVESTOR IN PEOPLE

To every *thinker, dreamer, and doer*
who believes that happiness and sustainability can walk hand in hand.

To the *leaders who inspire with empathy*,
the *educators who nurture with purpose*,
and the *changemakers who build with conscience*.

To the *participants of Hapttitude sessions* across nations –
your voices, reflections, and optimism ignited the idea that joy can be circular,
renewing itself through every act of kindness, creativity, and care.

And above all,
to all those striving to make their workplaces – not just productive – but
humane, inclusive, and sustainable.

May this book remind us that the true measure of progress is not how much we achieve, but how deeply we thrive, together.

Contents

About the Editors *ix*

About the Contributors *xi*

Foreword *xxi*

Preface *xxiii*

Acknowledgements *xxv*

Chapter 1 Understanding Circular Happiness
Komal Diwakar and Pretty Bhalla *1*

Chapter 2 The Role of Marketing in Promoting Employee Well-being
Mridhu Rajput and Avtar Singh *23*

Chapter 3 Human Resource and the Happiness: Performance Link
Amrita Sidhu, Akanchha Singh and Pretty Bhalla *41*

Chapter 4 Purpose-driven Business Growth Through Sustainable Practices: Pathways to Employee-centric Circular Happiness and Organisational Competitive Advantage
Sumesh S. Dadwal, Pawan Kumar, Vipin Nadda, Imad Yasir Nawaz and Gordon Bowen *59*

Chapter 5 The Financial Implications of Well-being Investments in the Workplace
Monika Kalani and Tanima Dutta *93*

Chapter 6 Circular Economy Principles in Organisational Strategy
Ruchi Verma, Rashmi Mathur, Sandeep Singh and Surbhi Ghai *111*

Chapter 7 Measuring Happiness: Key Performance Indicators (KPIs)
Shikha Goyal, Tanima Dutta and Anushikha Sharma 131

Chapter 8 Leadership's Influence on Workplace Happiness
Jaskiran Kaur and Razia Nagina 151

Chapter 9 Creating a Culture of Sustainability and Happiness
Narinder Kaur and Shamily Jaggi 165

Chapter 10 The Happiness Loop: Circular Business Models Enhancing Customer Satisfaction and Empowering Employees Through Ownership
Abhishek Sharma, Pinnika Syam Yadav and Ankitha Sharma 183

Chapter 11 Diversity and Inclusion: A Pathway to Happiness
Pooja Agrawal and Omvir Gautam 203

Chapter 12 The Future of Work: Trends Shaping Happiness and Sustainability
Harsha Mishra 217

Chapter 13 Technology's Role in Enhancing Employee Experience
Minie Bhalla, Abhishek Pandey, Ruchi Verma and Sakshi Thakur 241

Chapter 14 A Framework for Circular Happiness: A Systematic Literature Review and Future Research Agenda
Manoj Bansal, Bharath S.and Asmita Choudhary 267

About the Editors

Pawan Kumar is a Professor of Marketing at the Mittal School of Business, Lovely Professional University, India, with 20 years of combined experience in industry (4 years) and academia (16 years). His research interests include sustainability, entrepreneurship, e-commerce, and consumer behaviour. He has published across *Scopus* and *Web of Science* journals and has supervised doctoral theses on topics such as social media influencers, consumer buying behaviour, and youth empowerment through rural self-employment initiatives.

Pretty Bhalla is a Professor and Hapttitude Coach at Lovely Professional University (LPU). She is an accomplished academic leader with 15+ years of experience in teaching, research, and consultancy. She holds an executive development certification in Women of Color Leadership from Harvard Business School (2024) and a PhD in management. A prolific researcher, she has authored *Scopus*-indexed papers and books, developed E-content, and secured copyrights. She pioneered Hapttitude, integrating happiness into leadership and workplace culture. She has conducted national and international workshops, faculty development programmes (FDPs), and consultancy projects, making significant contributions to academia, industry, and sustainable organisational well-being. https://orcid.org/0000-0003-0291-0748

Rajesh Verma is a Professor and Sr. Dean at Mittal School of Business (NIRF Ranked), Lovely Professional University (LPU), where he leads the academic and administrative functions of the business school. He has a PhD in Marketing from Himachal Pradesh University, an MBA from Utkal University, and an Executive Programme in Data Driven Product Management from IIM Lucknow. He is also a Wiley Certified Design Thinking Practitioner.

Sumesh S. Dadwal is a Senior Lecturer in Strategy at London South Bank University Business School. Since joining LSBU in 2022, he has led the BA (Top-up) cohort; taught Comparative International Management, Innovation and Technology Strategy, and SMEs Leadership; and supervised UG, PG, and PhD students. With 25 years of experience across UK institutions – including Northumbria, London, Birkbeck, Glyndŵr, and others – he previously worked as a project engineer and supply chain quality analyst. His research spans innovation strategy, entrepreneurship, and business in emerging markets, with numerous edited books and chapters, including *Corporate Cybersecurity in the Aviation, Tourism and Hospitality Sector* (2024).

About the Contributors

Pooja Agrawal is an accomplished academician in the Faculty of Commerce & Management at Vishwakarma University, Pune, with over 16 years of experience in academia and research. She specialises in human resource management, organisational behaviour, leadership, happiness, competency mapping, diversity, equity and inclusion (DEI), and general management. With a strong commitment to academic excellence, she has published more than numerous research articles in esteemed *Scopus* and *Web of Science*-indexed journals. She is passionate about fostering intellectual curiosity, professional growth, and industry-relevant learning among students and peers. Known for her collaborative spirit, she actively engages in multidisciplinary initiatives, integrating innovation in pedagogy with practical application. Her scholarly rigour, dedication to continuous learning, and ability to build synergies position her as a valuable asset to both her institution and the wider academic community, contributing significantly to the advancement of knowledge and professional practice in her fields of expertise.

Manoj Bansal is working as an Assistant Professor at the University School for Graduate Studies at Chaudhary Devi Lal University, Sirsa (Haryana), India. He has about 10 years of rich teaching experience with excellence in Commerce. He has a significant professional career in Commerce and Management with major qualifications such as MCom, MPhil, UGC-NET, and PhD. He has published more than 10 research papers in reputed national and international research journals. He published five research chapters in reputed edited books, including Taylor and Francis, IGI Publishing (*Scopus*-indexed). He has authored one textbook on Marketing Management. He also has the credit of editor of three edited books.

Minie Bhalla is an Associate Professor in Lovely Professional University. She embarked on her research career with a clear mission to bridge the gap between environmental sustainability and corporate decision-making. As a faculty member at a leading business school, she established herself as a trailblazer in the field of management, spearheading innovative research projects that explored the intricacies of environmental reporting and its impact on organisational performance. Her studies have illuminated the ways in which companies can integrate sustainability metrics into their reporting practices to drive strategic decision-making and enhance stakeholder value. She has attended more than 10 national and international conferences and has more than 10 research papers in the pioneer journals. She has guided three Capstone projects and completed one ICCSR project on 'Strengthening Punjab's Start-up Culture: Assessing Awareness, Challenges and Policy Interventions'. Recently, four research fellows have been pursuing a PhD under her.

Bharath S. is an esteemed academician and currently serves as the Director of MBA and Vice-Principal at Brindavan College. He holds a PhD from Presidency University (2024) and possesses an extensive academic background, including an MBA and MCom. With over 8 years of teaching experience, he has published 15 research papers in leading journals. His research interests encompass fintech, digital financial inclusion, and blockchain technology in banking. He is actively involved in academic conferences, faculty development programmes, and has contributed significantly to the development of research and teaching methodologies in higher education.

Gordon Bowen is an Associate Professor in Management at Anglia Ruskin University (Chelmsford) and Lecturer at Northumbria University London. With senior roles in telecommunications and corporate strategy previously, he now specialises in strategy formulation, digital marketing, SMEs, CSR, and international business. A DBA in strategy (University of Hull) and MBA (Sheffield Hallam), he has edited several books, authored research on social media's role in strategy and marketing, and served as doctoral supervisor, examiner, and external examiner. He holds numerous editorial and reviewing roles and has collaborated with academic and industry partners globally.

Asmita Choudhary working as an Assistant Professor at University School for Graduate Studies at Chaudhary Devi Lal University, Sirsa (Haryana), India, holds an MBA in HRM from The IIS University, Jaipur, and is pursuing a PhD in Human Resource Management. She is UGC-NET qualified in HRM and Labour Legislations. Her research focuses on work–life balance, training and development, strategic HRM, labour law, and organisational behaviour. She has published two papers in UGC care journals and presented at international conferences. With over four years of teaching experience, she also organises academic events and faculty development programmes.

Komal Diwakar is a Senior Research Fellow (UGC-NET JRF) at Lovely Professional University, Punjab. Her research focuses on transgender issues, entrepreneurial ecosystems, social entrepreneurship practices, and sustainable society development. She has examined inclusive entrepreneurial practices through innovative frameworks such as framing, convening, and multivocality. Her expertise includes qualitative research methodologies, primary data collection, and case study analysis. A key area of her interest is social entrepreneurship and the empowerment of marginalized communities. She has conducted multiple studies on the transgender community in India, exploring its evolution, ecosystem, social inclusion, opportunities, and the challenges faced by prominent transgender entrepreneurs. Driven by concerns about existing gaps in knowledge and limited opportunities for diversity, she is committed to fostering equity within entrepreneurial and academic environments. https://orcid.org/0009-0009-7557-2111

Tanima Dutta is a Professor of Economics at Mittal School of Business, Lovely Professional University, with over 24 years of teaching and research experience. She specialises in development economics, agriculture, banking, and policy, strongly focusing on gender and social entrepreneurship. She has led government-funded projects, including an ICSSR Viksit Bharat@2047 study, and supervised multiple PhDs. As Coordinator of the Innovation and Entrepreneurship Cell and Nodal Officer of the Punjab Entrepreneurship Mindset Program, she integrates policy and practice. An active researcher with 40+ publications, she bridges academia, policy, and practice to advance inclusive economic development. https://orcid.org/0000-0001-9695-5482

Omvir Gautam serves as Assistant Professor in Marketing & Strategy and Director – International Relations & International Student Centre at Vishwakarma University, Pune. Holding a PhD in Management and being UGC-NET/JRF qualified, he has made notable scholarly contributions, with over 170 citations and an h-index of 6. His research expertise encompasses marketing, strategy, digital marketing, and data analytics, with publications in reputed *Scopus* and *Web of Science*-indexed journals. He has significantly advanced the university's global engagement by representing India on multiple international academic visits across Asia and Europe, establishing cross-border collaborations, and enhancing institutional partnerships. He actively mentors PhD scholars, conducts faculty development workshops, and shares his expertise on global academic platforms. His blend of research acumen, strategic leadership, and international exposure positions him as a distinguished academic leader, contributing to the advancement of knowledge and fostering a culture of innovation, collaboration, and academic excellence.

Surbhi Ghai is an Assistant Professor. She teaches human resource management at Mittal School of Business, Lovely Professional University, Punjab, India. Her areas of interest include industrial psychology, digital transformation, consumer behaviour, among others. She obtained her Doctorate in the field of digital transformation and employee well-being from the Central University of Jammu, India. She has published in international journals. She has been a Research Assistant in the ICSSR research project. She has been awarded the best paper award at the international conference.

Shikha Goyal is currently working as Professor and Head at Mittal School of Business, Lovely Professional University, Phagwara, Punjab (India). Having extensive academic experience of 10+ years, she has served at various reputed institutes. She had been a face of number of events like HR Summit, Youth Parliament, and MUN. In her career span, she has counselled a diversified group of students for the well-being of individuals and academics. She has been invited as a resource person in various faculty development programme in the areas of case-based teaching, teaching pedagogy, creative thinking, stress management, interpersonal skills, innovation in classroom assessment techniques. Leadership skills, life skills for delightful life-mindfulness, research methodology. https://orcid.org/0000-0002-3964-0879

Shamily Jaggi is working as a Professor (Digital Marketing and Business Analytics) at Indus International University, HP, India. She has published 23 research papers in journals (*Scopus*/UGC listed) and research papers/chapters in refereed edited books. She has written two case studies that are published with the care centre. She has guided nine research scholars. She edited one book titled *Consumer Engagement & Marketing*. She was a resource on digital marketing, research methodology, and business analytics. She acted as a session chair at international conferences.

Monika Kalani is an Associate Professor of Finance at Mittal School of Business, Lovely Professional University, holds a PhD in management and has over 22 years of academic and 3 years of industry experience. Her research spans corporate finance, financial markets, and corporate social responsibility. She is a chartered financial analyst. She has supervised a handful of post-graduate students for projects in financial markets in the area of corporate finance.

Narinder Kaur is working as an Assistant Professor at Maharishi Markandeshwar University, Mullana, Ambala, Haryana, India. Her research areas are service marketing, online shopping behaviour, technology innovations, and marketing management.

Jaskiran Kaur is an Associate Professor at Lovely Professional University, Phagwara, with a strong academic and research background in management, human resource development, and marketing. She earned her PhD from CT University, Ludhiana, in 2023, following an MBA with distinction in HR and marketing, and a BTech in Electronics and Communication. She is also UGC-NET qualified and has consistently demonstrated excellence by securing top positions at Punjab Technical University during her academic career. Her professional journey includes progressive roles across reputed institutions, where she has taught a wide array of subjects, including marketing management, organisational behaviour, strategic management, human resource management, and creativity and innovation. She has also contributed extensively to e-content development and course coordination for Lovely Professional University (LPU) online, fostering innovative learning approaches. https://orcid.org/0000-0002-4452-1807

Rashmi Mathur is currently an Assistant Professor at Lovely Professional University, India, specialising in human resource management with 13 years of teaching experience. She has contributed extensively to the field through numerous publications in peer-reviewed journals.

Harsha Mishra serves as Associate Professor at Sant Hirdaram Institute of Management for Women, Barkatullah University, Bhopal, MP, India. She heads the Placement Cell and is the Institute's Nodal Officer for the Yi Bhopal Chapter. Additionally, she is the Regional Coordinator (Central Region – MP) for NCCIP–AICTE. Her professional journey includes over three years as HR and IR Officer at Vardhman Yarns (Vardhman Textiles Ltd.) and over eight years of academic experience. A silver medallist in MBA from MANIT, she earned her PhD in management from DAVV, Indore, and has qualified UGC-NET in management (2024) and commerce (2025). A prolific researcher, she has presented over 15 papers at national and international forums and published 10 papers in reputed journals. Her Mantra to Success is: 'Believe in yourself and happiness with success will follow you … as the best is yet to come'.

Vipin Nadda is a Senior Lecturer and Programme Manager (Tourism & Hospitality) at the University of Sunderland in London. He holds a PhD in Tourism Management along with MBA (marketing) and MTA (tourism), and brings over 15 years of combined academic and industry experience. He teaches programmes in International Tourism & Hospitality, Events & Entertainment, and supervises MBA, MSc, and PhD students. His research covers strategic tourism development, sustainable tourism, destination branding, service marketing, and CRM. He serves as an external examiner, editorial board member, and reviewer for international journals, and contributes extensively to consultancy and curriculum development for organisations, including the Bangladesh Tourism Board and Confederation of Tourism & Hospitality.

Razia Nagina is a Professor at the Mittal School of Business, Lovely Professional University (LPU), Jalandhar, Punjab, India, with over 16 years of academic experience. She began her career as a lecturer at LPU in 2009, later serving as an associate professor for more than seven years before assuming her current role as professor in 2025. Her expertise lies in commerce and management, and she has contributed extensively to teaching, research, and institutional development. https://orcid.org/0000-0002-0305-8393

Imad Yasir Nawaz is a Deputy Dean of Business and Arts, Design & Social Sciences at Northumbria University London. He is an HR Management practitioner and lecturer with extensive experience teaching undergraduate and postgraduate students from diverse backgrounds. A graduate member of the CIPD, he has worked across academic, commercial, and non-profit sectors in the United Kingdom and abroad. His research and teaching focus on continuing professional development, communities of practice, employee engagement, psychological contracts, psychometric assessments, and qualitative research methods. He also delivers corporate training, consultancies, reviews academic work, and acts as external examiner for doctoral work.

Abhishek Pandey is a dedicated academician and researcher with over 10 years of teaching experience, including 8 years at Lovely Professional University (LPU).

Holding a PhD in Commerce, he specialises in accounting, finance, and marketing, with expertise in teaching subjects such as financial modelling, business strategy, and research methodologies. A passionate researcher, he has published more than 20 research papers in reputed journals and presented at 10+ national and international conferences, earning 2 best paper presentation awards. His research primarily focuses on accounting and marketing, contributing to academic and industry discussions. As an active member of the Indian Commerce Association (ICA), he engages in scholarly collaborations and stays updated with emerging trends in commerce education. Additionally, he has participated in numerous faculty development programmes (FDPs) to enhance pedagogical skills. He is also committed to guiding future researchers, currently supervising two PhD scholars. His contributions extend to intellectual property, with one copyright registered and two patents applied for, reflecting his innovative approach to academia. Beyond teaching and research, he actively participates in institutional committees, workshops, and industry-academia initiatives, striving to bridge theoretical knowledge with practical applications.

Mridhu Rajput is a research scholar in marketing at Lovely Professional University and currently serves as a marketing faculty member and soft skills trainer at Amity University, Punjab. With over five years of experience in training, facilitation, and student engagement, she has guided diverse learners in developing professional communication, personality development, and interview-preparation skills. Her research focuses on sustainable marketing and consumer behaviour, with a special interest in pink marketing. She has also worked in the corporate and academic sectors, combining industry insights with educational leadership. Mridhu's interdisciplinary approach bridges marketing, ethics, and behavioural studies, aiming to empower individuals through both scholarly and applied contributions.

Abhishek Sharma is an Assistant Professor in the Department of Marketing at Lovely Professional University, Phagwara, Punjab, India. He earned his PhD in 2022 from the same institution. His research interests span digital marketing, consumer behaviour, Internet of Things (IoT), and public administration. He has published eight papers in *Scopus*-indexed journals, including works on virtual reality in HR, IoT personalisation, artificial intelligence in business strategy, predictive analytics in financial markets, and public policy. Additionally, he has contributed three papers in ABDC-C category journals and two papers in UGC CARE journals focusing on public distribution systems and women entrepreneurs. He holds four patents related to AI, digital marketing, branding, and global CRM technologies, along with a UK Design titled 'Robofly' and a copyright on industrial relations and work culture. His research and innovations reflect his commitment to advancing knowledge in marketing, technology, and management.

Ankitha Sharma is working as an Assistant Professor in the Department of Finance-Banking & Insurance, Lovely Professional University, Phagwara,

Punjab, India. She received her PhD degree from Lovely Professional University, Phagwara, Punjab, India in 2023. Her research areas include entrepreneurship, entrepreneurial orientation, and business performance. She has published two research papers in *ABDC-C* category journals, three papers in *Scopus*-indexed journals and one in the *UGC Care* journal. And she has also published nine book chapters in refereed edited books. He has one patent in her name, 'AI-Driven Chatbots for Marketing: A Unique Chatbot that Personalizes Marketing Pitches to Individual'. She also has one copyright on his name, titled 'Moderation effect of Incubation Support on Entrepreneurial Orientation, BUSINESS Performance Relationship for Women Entrepreneurs'.

Anushikha Sharma, with 15 years of experience in teaching, administration, and institutional management, she exemplifies the educator-as-innovator ethos. Her expertise in curriculum development, student performance management, and immersive pedagogy aligns seamlessly with design thinking principles. She has led multiple academic programmes, organised national conferences, and published extensively on topics such as employee empowerment, organisational culture, and AI-based systems. Her editorial lens is shaped by a deep understanding of human behaviour, strategic planning, and the transformative power of experiential learning. She works on bridge theory and practice, making her a vital voice in the conversation on design-led education. https://orcid.org/0009-0001-9554-3678

Amrita Sidhu is an independent researcher with six years of research and two years of teaching experience. She earned her PhD in Management from Lovely Professional University, Phagwara, and her postgraduate degree in Human Resource Management from Amity Business School, Noida. Her research spans HRM, psychology, statistics, and organisational behaviour, with publications in *ABDC* and *SCOPUS*-indexed journals. She has conducted pioneering empirical research on workplace romance in the Indian hotel industry, examining its relationship with emotional intelligence and employee performance. She holds two registered copyrights – one for developing a workplace dating policy and another for a tool assessing managers' perceptions of workplace romance. She has authored book chapters with Taylor & Francis, including topics on digitalisation in higher education and the influence of social media on organisational ethics. Her recent publication in Corporate & Business Strategy Review explores the interplay between social media, social capital, and business strategy.

Avtar Singh is a distinguished Associate Professor of Marketing at the Mittal School of Business, Lovely Professional University. Holding a PhD in Sports Marketing and an MBA, he combines rigorous academic training with extensive industry experience. His research focuses on the commercialisation of academic research and global R&D management, reflecting a strong commitment to bridging theory and practice. With over 13 years of experience in the marketing domain, he possesses profound insights into strategic marketing challenges and solutions. As a certified digital marketing professional, he expertly integrates digital tools and analytics to foster business growth. His core areas of specialisation include social media marketing, sports marketing, digital marketing, sustainability, and other related sectors. Renowned for his dynamic teaching approach and scholarly contributions, he consistently inspires and equips students with cutting-edge knowledge and skills. His expertise and leadership significantly enrich the academic and professional marketing communities.

Akanchha Singh is an Assistant Professor at the School of Business, Manav Rachna University, Faridabad, recognised for her expertise in human resource management and organisational behaviour. With over six years of academic experience, she is committed to shaping future leaders through knowledge sharing and practical learning. She earned her PhD from Khwaja Moinuddin Chishti Language University, Lucknow, and has authored two books. Her research portfolio includes over 20 papers and book chapters published in *Scopus*, *ABDC*, and *Web of Science*-indexed journals and edited volumes, with 1 chapter featured in the WHO COVID-19 research database. She has presented more than 18 papers at national and international conferences and actively contributes as a reviewer for reputed international publications such as the *Journal of Marketing Communications* and *IGI Global*. Her academic contributions reflect her dedication to advancing research and fostering excellence in management education.

Sandeep Singh is currently the Chief Operating Officer and Director-Training and Management at Designistic Group, Mohali, Punjab. He holds a PhD in Emotional Intelligence from Jaypee University of Information Technology, Himachal Pradesh; an MBA with specialisations in Human Resource Management and Marketing Management from the University of Jammu, Jammu & Kashmir, and has cleared the UGC-NET in Management.

Sakshi Thakur is an Assistant Professor in the Department of Accounting at Lovely Professional University, Punjab. She holds a PhD in E-governance with a focus on G2B initiatives in the textile sector. With over seven years of teaching and research experience, she specialises in e-commerce, business studies, and e-governance. She has published several research papers in *Scopus*-indexed journals.

Ruchi Verma is an Assistant Professor at Lovely Professional University, India, specialised in human resource management. Her PhD is in Human Resource Management from Himachal Pradesh University. With over 12 years of experience in teaching and research, UGC-NET qualified, she has contributed significantly towards academic research. She has also published numerous articles in peer-reviewed journals, focusing on HR evolutions. She is currently working on the book 'HR Analytics'.

Pinnika Syam Yadav is a distinguished academic and researcher specialising in digital marketing, emerging technologies, and business administration. His scholarly work significantly advances the understanding of digital intelligence and its strategic applications in the Indian retail sector. Holding a PhD, he combines rigorous theoretical inquiry with applied research, producing impactful contributions on digital platforms, consumer behaviour, and business innovation. His academic journey reflects growth and transition, beginning at Lovely Professional University (LPU) and more recently progressing to his current role as Assistant Professor at Christ University, Bengaluru. Thematically, his research emphasises the transformative role of digital platforms – particularly influencer marketing – on consumer decision-making, alongside studies on virtual reality, chatbots, sustainability, and pro-environmental consumer behaviour. He has built a strong collaborative network, frequently co-authoring with scholars such as Mithilesh Pandey, P. B. Narendra Kiran, and Monu Singh. His prolific research portfolio continues to provide valuable insights for academia and industry stakeholders.

Foreword

In a time when organisations are searching for balance between progress and purpose, *Circular Happiness* arrives as a deeply relevant and inspiring contribution. It reminds us that the future of work must be both sustainable and humane – where success is measured not only by profit, but by well-being, inclusion, and shared growth.

This book beautifully unites two transformative ideas – *Circular Happiness* and *Hapttitude*. The former builds a framework for renewing sustainability and purpose in every organisational act, while the latter brings emotional depth and human energy into that circle. *Hapttitude* – a fusion of happiness, attitude, and results – captures the essence of how inner positivity and resilience can translate into collective success. Together, these ideas move beyond rhetoric; they offer a pathway for organisations to flourish responsibly and compassionately.

Through its thoughtful chapters, interdisciplinary insights, and global perspectives, *Circular Happiness* demonstrates how empathy, sustainability, and innovation can coexist. It is a call to reimagine our workplaces as ecosystems where people thrive, communities prosper, and the planet heals.

I commend the editors and contributors for their vision and scholarly depth in shaping this book. May it inspire educators, policymakers, and leaders across the world to cultivate a new culture – one where happiness fuels sustainability, and sustainability sustains happiness.

Prof Gurwinder Singh Bawa
Dean
Guru Nanak Dev University (GNDU)

Preface

The pursuit of happiness has long been considered a personal journey, while sustainability has been viewed as a collective responsibility. *Circular Happiness* brings these two seemingly distinct pursuits together – proposing that true well-being in organisations and societies emerges when individual fulfilment and sustainable practices form a continuous, regenerative loop.

In an era defined by climate urgency, mental health challenges, and generational transitions in the workplace, the idea of Circular Happiness offers a timely framework. It envisions workplaces where happiness is not a fleeting emotion or a managerial slogan but a *strategic principle* that sustains people, profits, and the planet in harmony. Much like the circular economy that reduces waste and regenerates resources, Circular Happiness seeks to create systems that continually renew energy, motivation, and meaning at work.

The philosophy underpinning this book rests on the belief that *employee well-being and environmental sustainability are not parallel goals but deeply interconnected forces.* Organisations that care for the planet often care better for their people – and vice versa. When employees find purpose in sustainable missions, they bring energy, creativity, and loyalty that translate into stronger organisational performance. The circularity of happiness thus creates a cycle where caring leads to thriving, and thriving reinforces caring.

This edited volume explores how organisations can embed such circular principles into their culture, strategy, and daily practices. The chapters collectively demonstrate how sustainability can enhance workplace happiness – through inclusive leadership, ethical marketing, empowered employees, and innovations that respect both ecological and emotional ecosystems. Drawing on interdisciplinary insights from psychology, organisational behaviour, and environmental economics, this book provides models and evidence showing that happiness, when institutionalised sustainably, becomes a renewable resource rather than an exhaustible one.

Within this broader framework, the idea of *Hapttitude* – a blend of happiness, attitude, and results – serves as a behavioural dimension of Circular Happiness. Hapttitude emphasises how individual positivity, resilience, and proactive mindset transform into collective outcomes. Leaders with a Hapttitudinal approach cultivate optimism and inclusivity, translating inner balance into outward productivity. Together, Circular Happiness and Hapttitude offer complementary perspectives: the former builds the *systemic foundation*, while the latter provides the *human fuel* that sustains it.

Ultimately, *Circular Happiness: Building Sustainable Workplaces for the Next Generation* is a call to reimagine success – not as linear growth, but as circular progress. It is about creating organisations that replenish what they consume, restore what they impact, and renew what they inspire. The chapters that follow invite readers to explore how we can design futures where work becomes a source of well-being, purpose, and shared sustainability – one where happiness, in its truest form, completes the circle.

Acknowledgements

This book, *Circular Happiness: Building Sustainable Workplaces for the Next Generation*, is the result of a shared journey – one that brought together diverse voices, ideas, and inspirations from across disciplines and continents.

We extend our deepest gratitude to all the *editors and contributing authors* whose dedication, insight, and scholarship have shaped this volume into a meaningful dialogue on happiness, sustainability, and workplace transformation. Each chapter reflects the unique perspective and expertise of its author, yet together, they form a cohesive narrative that embodies the spirit of collaboration, compassion, and curiosity.

A special note of appreciation goes to the *participants of the Hapttitude sessions held across nations* – academics, practitioners, students, and leaders – who, through their thoughtful engagement and shared experiences, sowed the earliest seeds of this book. Your reflections and enthusiasm gave life to the idea that happiness is not only a personal pursuit but a collective responsibility – a foundation for resilient, inclusive, and sustainable work cultures. What began as conversations around Hapttitude gradually evolved into the concept of *Circular Happiness*, reminding us that joy and purpose can, indeed, coexist in continuous renewal.

We are also thankful to our *institutional partners, reviewers, and professional networks* whose encouragement and constructive feedback strengthened this endeavour. To the publishing team at *Emerald Publishing*, thank you for believing in the vision of integrating well-being with sustainability and for providing a platform to share this work with a global audience.

Finally, our heartfelt appreciation to every reader, thinker, and change-maker who believes in the transformative power of happiness and sustainability. May this book inspire you to build circles of happiness that extend far beyond workplaces – into communities, cultures, and futures that thrive in balance and purpose.

Chapter 1

Understanding Circular Happiness

Komal Diwakar[a] *and Pretty Bhalla*[b]

[a]*Sanjivani University, India*
[b]*Lovely Professional University, India*

Abstract

Circular happiness is explored as a way of thinking about well-being, organisational health, and environmental sustainability that work together. Based on the ideas of the circular economy, it shifts the definition of happiness from a straightforward pursuit of pleasure or material success to a dynamic, self-sustaining process. In this chapter, the authors look at how psychological drivers, such as autonomy, mastery, purpose, and environmental alignment, interact with corporate culture and ecological design to create feedback loops that support long-term health. Based on a literature review, using systems theory, organisational behaviour, and best practices from around the world, this chapter discusses how both happiness and business models are transitioning from linear to circular thinking. Real-world examples and evidence from Bhutan's Gross National Happiness (GNH) Index, along with companies like Patagonia and Interface, demonstrate how circular processes help people thrive, protect the environment, and maintain long-term employee engagement. Finally, the chapter highlights design tools like the happiness ecosystem canvas and the circular happiness flow model that can be used to implement these ideas in the workplace. This integrated approach encourages us to redefine success, not as growth at any cost, but as sustainable and inclusive growth across all human and planetary systems.

Keywords: Well-being; circular happiness; sustainability; corporate culture; systems thinking; psychological flourishing

Circular Happiness: Building Sustainable Workplaces for the Next Generation, 1–22

Published under exclusive licence by Emerald Publishing Limited
doi:10.1108/978-1-80592-907-920261001

1. Defining Circular Happiness: A Balance between Sustainability and Well-being

Instead of viewing happiness and well-being as a goal to achieve or a single emotional state, circular happiness sees it as an ongoing process that continuously renews itself and is connected to other processes. It incorporates ideas from the circular economy to understand happiness as a system loop that involves personal fulfilment, social connectedness, and ecological balance within a self-sustaining cycle where each element enhances and reinforces the others (Jackson, 2009; Murray et al., 2017). This perspective challenges the common linear view of well-being, which often equates happiness with wealth, status, or fleeting pleasures. Instead, circular happiness focuses on building lasting values, healing the ecosystems inside and outside of us, and minimising material, emotional, and relational waste.

At its heart, circular happiness is based on four ideas that are all connected:

1. Interdependence: this concept emphasises how the health of individuals, communities, and the world all rely on each other. It is similar to the ecological systems theory, which states that human development occurs within social and environmental contexts that are interconnected (Bronfenbrenner, 1979). Raworth's (2017) doughnut economics, which advocates for fulfilling human needs within planetary boundaries, supports the idea that no one does well alone.
2. Renewal: in this case, happiness means regularly caring for your emotional and mental health through activities like mindfulness, rest, self-reflection, and spending time in nature. Fredrickson's (2004) broaden-and-build hypothesis states that positive feelings help people heal and strengthen their mental resources so they can handle future challenges.
3. Sustainability: living by pro-environmental ideals is beneficial for your health and the health of the entire community. Gifford and Nilsson (2014) state that doing things that are good for the environment is not only the right thing to do, but it also makes people feel better about themselves. Hunecke et al. (2007) also observed that people who care about the environment often feel more fulfilled and have a greater sense of purpose in life.
4. Resilience: the ability to adapt and grow through tough times is central to circular happiness. This essential skill is especially valuable in today's world of climate change, social inequity, and economic uncertainty. Resilience is not just a mental trait; it is also a social and organisational skill that can be cultivated over time (Luthar et al., 2000; Masten & Reed, 2002).

There is real-world evidence supporting these ideas. For example, Binder and Blankenberg (2017) observed that people who live in environmentally friendly ways are likely to be happier with their lives, which suggests that caring for the environment benefits mental health. Brown and Kasser (2005) found that prioritising intrinsic goals like community, personal growth, and environmental conservation over extrinsic ones like consumerism leads to better mental health and less anxiety. These findings show that being aware of the environment and being happy are compatible.

From a systems perspective, circular happiness functions by creating feedback loops that reinforce each of the three main areas: the person, the organisation, and the environment. Flourishing on an individual level includes factors like mental health, independence, purpose, and emotional resilience (Ryan & Deci, 2001; Seligman, 2011). According to Cameron et al. (2003), cultures that promote psychological safety, inclusion, and shared values help both individuals and groups thrive. The environmental domain adds a third pillar, emphasising the need for clean environments, healthy ecosystems, and a connection between labour and ecological values (Norton et al., 2014).

The circular model differs from the linear happiness model, which suggests that people are motivated by cycles of consumption (acquire → use → discard). The circular model states that value is restored, relationships are rebuilt, and well-being continuously grows. This type of change aligns with the broader concept of positive organisational scholarship, which emphasises that people and organisations that thrive are rooted in a shared purpose, moral values, and environmental awareness (Di Fabio & Rosen, 2018).

The Happiness Research Institute in Denmark is a great example of how circular happiness can be applied in real-world settings. The institute integrates sustainable methods with mental health frameworks, encouraging staff to have positive experiences through activities like circular design workshops, mindfulness classes, and volunteering for environmental causes. These initiatives increase participation and help Denmark achieve its national sustainability goals. They demonstrate how businesses can implement circular happiness in ways that benefit the environment and culture (*The Happiness Research Institute | The Science of Well-Being*, n.d.).

Fig. 1.1 shows how sustainable well-being comes together at the crossroads of personal growth, organisational support, and environmental health. It emphasises that real happiness is a cycle, renewed through mindful living, responsible systems, and a balance with nature.

Ultimately, circular happiness is not just a different way of thinking about happiness that isn't based on individualism and consumption, but it is also a practical method to transform organisations and society. It advocates for using regenerative design, community-building, and ecological ethics to incorporate happiness into policies, workspaces, and systems. This shifts our perspective on happiness from having more to being more, together (Senge et al., 2008).

2. The Shift from Linear to Circular Thinking in Happiness and Business

Linear models have impacted modern ideas of happiness for a long time. In these models, well-being is linked to getting things, having status, or getting rewards, and success is linked to making money or getting things. The principle for this method is simple: get → feel wonderful → move on. This model may make people happy in the short-term, but it often leads to diminishing returns, emotional

Fig. 1.1. The Synergy of Circular Happiness. *Source*: Authors' creation.

exhaustion, and hedonic adaptation, which is when people quickly return to a baseline level of happiness even when things get better (Brickman & Campbell, 1971; Kasser, 2002). This cycle of doing things over and over again encourages consumerism without satisfaction and leads to mental exhaustion, especially when personal beliefs clash with the need to be productive and spend (Ryan & Deci, 2001).

Research shows that chasing external goals like money and status is often linked to lower life satisfaction, while chasing internal goals like personal growth, meaningful relationships, and community well-being is linked to higher well-being and emotional resilience (Deci & Ryan, 2000; Kasser & Ryan, 1996). Also, materialistic attitudes have been associated with anxiety, depression, and less social connection (Dittmar et al., 2014).

On the other hand, circular theories of happiness focus on regeneration, interconnection, and long-term viability. Circular pleasure is not based on fleeting highs, but on eudaimonic well-being, which comes from living in line with one's purpose, values, and social duties (Huta & Ryan, 2010). This paradigm says that happiness isn't something you buy; it's something you grow. It also says that having meaningful experiences, being part of a community, and living by your values may produce cycles of well-being that keep you going. Research in positive psychology backs up these views. It says that authenticity, mastery, and connection, not material achievement, lead to personal fulfilment (Csikszentmihalyi, 1990; Seligman, 2011).

The way people think about business has changed in the same way that philosophy has changed. The most common industrial model, which is built on taking, making, and throwing away, creates waste and uses up both human and natural resources. It sees value as a one-time event instead of a process, which makes employees less interested, production unsustainable, and the environment worse (Bocken et al., 2014). On the other hand, circular business models use a systems-based approach: products → process → people → planet → profits → products. This creates a regenerative loop where waste becomes a resource and the well-being of all stakeholders is the most important thing (Ellen MacArthur Foundation, 2015). These models stress creating long-term value, shared accountability among stakeholders, and closed-loop systems that connect economic operations with social and ecological goals (Geissdoerfer et al., 2017). These kinds of actions not only help the environment, but they also make organisations stronger and encourage new ideas.

Interface Inc., a company that makes modular carpets, is a great illustration of this. They went from a model that used a lot of resources to a business structure that is entirely regenerative. Interface wanted to have no impact on the environment by 2020 through its 'Mission Zero' programme. Biomimetic design, closed-loop production, and staff-led sustainability projects were all part of the effort. These projects greatly improved the company's environmental performance while also raising employee morale and market reputation (Anderson, 2009; Stubbs & Cocklin, 2008). In the same way, firms like Unilever, Danone, and IKEA have made circularity and well-being a part of their business plans by creating programs to improve employee health, using ethical sourcing, and encouraging stakeholder participation. These actions show how environmental, social, and emotional sustainability are becoming more and more important for long-term business success (Accenture, 2019).

To make pleasure a part of business, roles need to be redefined. Employees are no longer seen as cogs in a machine, but as important drivers of creativity, collaboration, and purpose. Companies that put their employees' well-being first by creating psychologically safe, inclusive, and values-based work cultures, as well as providing mental health support, tend to have higher retention rates, stronger commitment, and better financial performance (Harter et al., 2003; Robertson & Cooper, 2011). Also, research on positive organisational behaviour shows that organisations with a clear purpose encourage emotional commitment and make the group stronger. In these situations, the happiness of employees and the health of the environment are not separate from the aims of the business; they support each other (Cameron & Spreitzer, 2012). This change from linear to circular thinking in both happiness and business is not only a matter of ideology; it is a strategic and moral necessity because of the growing number of environmental problems, mental health issues among employees, and demands from stakeholders. By making circularity a part of their work, people and organisations may build ecosystems that are regenerative, open to everyone, and ready for the future.

Fig. 2.2 shows how organisations can combine purpose, employee well-being, sustainability, and community to create regenerative value. It stresses a never-ending cycle in which emotional, ecological, and economic aspects work together to ensure long-term success. To sum up, circular happiness and circular business models are two ways that well-being is built into everyday actions, choices, and policies. The shift from models based on consumption to systems based on value and self-renewal is a model for long-term success, not just for businesses and economies, but also for people and communities.

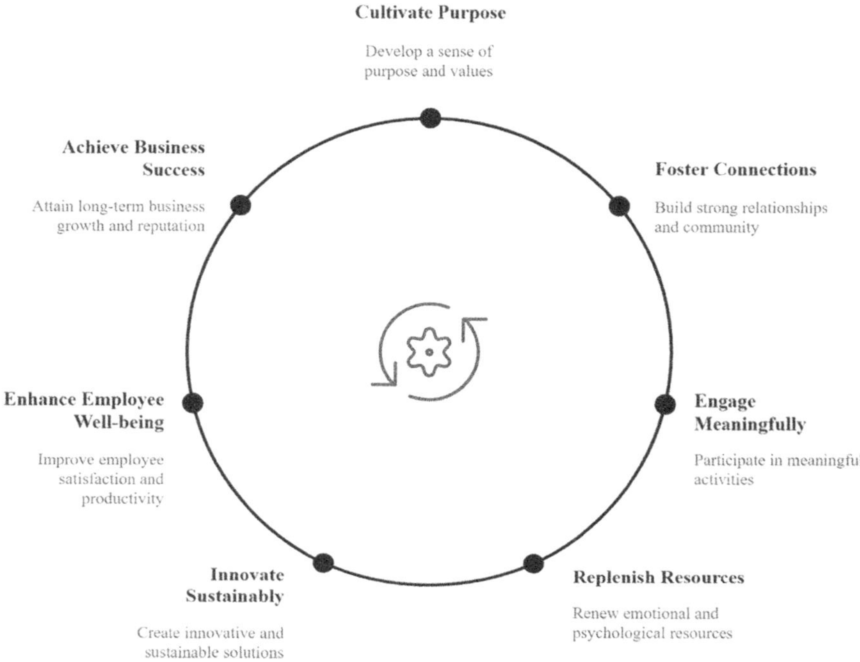

Fig. 2.2. Circular Happiness and Business Cycle. *Source*: Authors' creation.

3. Psychological and Organisational Factors of Well-being

In the context of circular happiness, well-being is not seen as a separate or only individual experience, but as a result of the dynamic interaction between psychological requirements and organisational settings. This systems-based view implies that long-term well-being comes from reciprocal reinforcement, which means that structural, social, and environmental aspects in the workplace constantly shape people's motivation and emotional needs. Self-determination theory (SDT), which was created by Deci and Ryan (2000), is at the heart of these psychological dynamics. It says that autonomy, competence (or mastery), and relatedness are all important psychological demands for motivation, engagement, and well-being. In the context of circular happiness, these basic needs are expanded to include purpose, which is the feeling of being part of something bigger than yourself, and environmental alignment, which is the harmony between personal values and institutional sustainability goals (Di Fabio & Rosen, 2018).

3.1. Autonomy

Autonomy is the feeling that you are in charge of your actions and decisions. Research has shown repeatedly and time again that workers who feel free to make their own decisions at work are happier, more motivated, more creative, and healthier (Deci et al., 2017; Gagné & Deci, 2005). In circular happiness, autonomy also includes being able to match your job with your values and being aware of the surroundings. This helps to create a sense of honesty and integrity in the workplace (Ryan & Deci, 2001).

3.2. Competence (Mastery)

Another important part of well-being is mastery, Competence or the desire to be good at something. It means always learning new things, improving your skills, and feeling like you can handle your professional tasks. As Seligman (2011) says in the PERMA model, feeling like you have control over your life boosts your self-esteem and protects you from burnout and disengagement. Companies that spend money on training, mentoring, and upskilling their employees not only make them more resilient and happy, but they also make them more creative (Luthans et al., 2007).

3.3. Relatedness (Connection)

For emotional health and organisational unity, connection or relatedness is very important. Baumeister and Leary (1995) say that the 'need to belong' is a basic human drive. They also say that having strong social ties makes people happier, less stressed, and better at their jobs. These ties grow stronger in cultures that are collaborative and open to everyone, where trust, empathy, and a shared goal are encouraged (Grant & Parker, 2009). Social capital in teams often leads to psychological safety, which lets people talk to one other, try new things, and get help (Edmondson, 1999).

3.4. Purpose

Purpose is the feeling of making a difference that goes beyond personal or business gain. According to Dik et al. (2013), workers who see their work as having a purpose are more likely to be emotionally committed to their jobs, engaged in their work, and happy with their lives in general. People are starting to see purpose-driven firms as strong and poised for the future, especially after the pandemic, when making sense of things is important for keeping employees happy and keeping them (Lepore & Greenberg, 2021; Pink, 2009).

3.5. Environmental Alignment

A rising body of research focuses on environmental alignment, which is how much employees' own views about sustainability are reflected in their jobs. Employees who think their companies care about the environment are more likely to feel like their values are in line with those of the company, be more loyal, and have better mental health (Norton et al., 2014; Robertson & Barling, 2017a, 2017b). This congruence helps people feel like they are doing the right thing and makes them more likely to identify with the organisation's mission.

3.6. Organisational Enablers of Circular Well-being

Individual psychological needs are what drive people, but the organisational framework either makes it easier or harder for them to meet those requirements. Organisations are very important for making the conditions right for circular happiness to grow.

3.7. Emotional Climate and Leadership

Real, caring, and regenerative leadership is very important for the health of a company. Leaders who value sustainability and put people's well-being first help create a good emotional environment and show others how to act ethically (Avolio & Gardner, 2005; Cameron et al., 2003). Transformational leadership is also associated with more trust, teamwork, and psychological safety, especially when it is used with tactics that focus on well-being (Kelloway & Barling, 2010).

3.8. Voice and Flexible Work

Policies that promote flexible work arrangements, management that supports autonomy, and open communication channels are very important for the well-being and engagement of employees (Kossek et al., 2011). Employees are more likely to feel ownership, intrinsic motivation, and mental clarity when they feel listened, appreciated, and empowered (May et al., 2004).

3.9. Physical and Social Design

The physical setting of the office has a big effect on how people think and feel. Biophilic design features, such as having access to natural light, plants, and open communal areas, have been demonstrated to improve cognitive performance, recovery from stress, and general health (Kellert & Calabrese, 2015; Nieuwenhuis et al., 2014). Social architecture, such as open governance, peer mentorship, and team cohesion, also makes people feel like they belong and gives them emotional support (Dutton & Ragins, 2007).

Google's Singapore office is a well-known example of this. It combines biophilic architecture, mindfulness areas, and eco-friendly infrastructure. Internal reports showed that staff satisfaction went up by 35% and stress went down a lot, which backs up what Nieuwenhuis et al. (2014) and others have said about the mental health advantages of green office spaces. This shows how purposeful organisational design can use environmental and experiential clues to boost circular pleasure.

Fig. 1.3 shows how psychological factors (such as autonomy, mastery, and purpose) and supportive organisational structures (like leadership and ecosystem design) work together to make employees happier, more committed, and more productive. It stresses how beliefs, policies, and the environment all work together to keep people healthy at work.

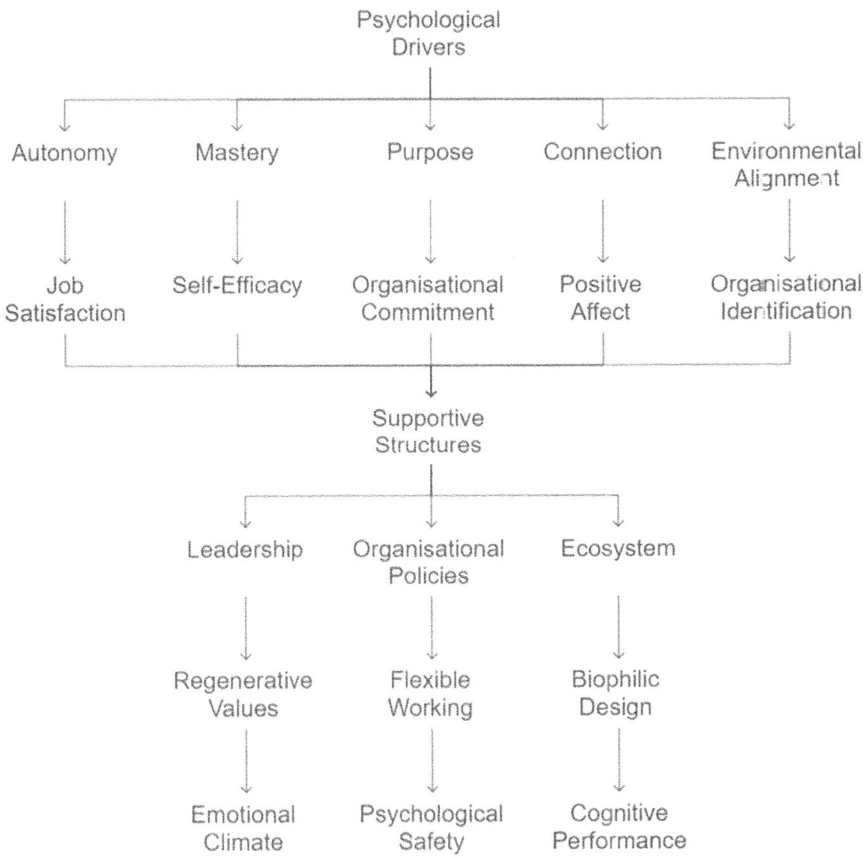

Fig. 1.3. Psychological and Organisational Factors of Well-being.
Source: Authors' creation.

Well-being in the context of circular happiness is multidimensional and comes from making sure that psychological demands are in line with organisational and ecological systems. Organisations may create a cycle of happiness that promotes both individual growth and social sustainability by meeting basic needs like autonomy, mastery, connection, purpose, and environmental alignment in workplaces that are open to everyone and good for the environment. As work cultures around the world change, notably after COVID, it becomes not only strategically important but also morally necessary to design for circular well-being.

4. Global Trends in Workplace Happiness and Sustainability

In today's fast-changing global economy, company models are changing from ones that focus on making money to ones that are more human-centred, ecologically friendly, and emotionally smart. As today's workers learn more about ethical, environmental, and social issues, companies are being asked to make well-being and sustainability a top priority in their operations and strategies (Deloitte, 2024; PwC, 2021). People no longer see combining employee satisfaction with caring for the environment as an optional advantage. Instead, they see it as a strategic must for long-term success, competitiveness, and resilience. Recent polls from throughout the world show that workers, especially Millennials and Gen Z, want jobs that give them a sense of purpose, make them feel safe, and make them care about the environment (Cone Communications, 2017; Deloitte, 2024). As a result, businesses are moving away from traditional economic measures and towards multi-dimensional well-being indicators. This is similar to the idea of 'circular happiness', where organisational practices support individual happiness and environmental renewal in ways that benefit everyone (Senge et al., 2008).

4.1. The Business Case for Happiness and Sustainability

Studies show that organisations that use sustainable and circular models have much greater employee engagement levels – often 30–40% higher than standard enterprises – and their turnover rates are up to 20% lower (Gallup, 2023). Not only are these results good for the environment, but they also improve the culture, trust, and emotional alignment of the firm. Companies that put sustainability first show that they are honest and share the same values, which makes employees more motivated and loyal to the company (B Corps, 2022; Robertson & Barling, 2017a, 2017b).

Also, the rise of environmental, social, and governance (ESG) frameworks has led businesses to make their well-being and sustainability indicators more official. Psychological safety, job satisfaction, workplace inclusion, and environmental impact are now common ESG criteria. This is because it is understood that employees' well-being is closely linked to corporate responsibility and resilience (Aggarwal & Dow, 2012; Eccles et al., 2014).

The World Happiness Report (Helliwell et al., 2020) backs up this trend by naming things like faith in workplace institutions, a sense of purpose, and job stability as important characteristics that make people and organisations happy. Companies with greater happiness scores consistently do better in terms of productivity, innovation, and financial returns (Achor, 2010; Diener & Seligman, 2004).

4.2. Regional Practices and Innovations

Not everyone in the world is on board with happiness and sustainability. This is because cultures, governments, and economies are different in different parts of the world. But a general trend is that workplace ecosystems are moving towards being more inclusive, regenerative, and aligned with values.

4.2.1. Europe

There is an increasing focus on the 'quadruple bottom line' – people, planet, profit, and purpose – across Europe, especially in Scandinavia, the Netherlands, and

Germany (Ehnert et al., 2016). Organisations regularly do well-being audits, put green human resource management (HRM) policies into place, and use environmental key performance indicators (KPIs) to rate how well employees are doing (Renwick et al., 2013). Denmark's 'Great Place to Work' programs and Sweden's 'Lagom' lifestyle policies show how cultural balance, sustainability, and happy workers are all connected (Anderson, 2015).

4.2.2. Asia

Mindfulness-based leadership, resilience training, and nature-integrated design are becoming more popular in Asia, especially in Japan, India, Singapore, and South Korea. Ikigai (Japan) and Ahimsa (India) are two classical concepts that these practices are based on. They stress harmony, purpose, and being aware of the environment (Chaskalson & McMordie, 2021; Singh & Singh, 2020). Companies in India, like Tata Group and Infosys, have started corporate sustainability programs that focus on mental health, community involvement, and environmental restoration. These programmes have helped employees feel more connected to their jobs and stay longer.

The Sustainable Workplace Alliance in Singapore combines biophilic office design, psychological safety rules, and carbon-neutral business practices to create a model for green and pleasant workspaces (Urban Redevelopment Authority, 2023).

4.2.3. South America

In South America, especially in Brazil, Colombia, and Ecuador, social cooperatives and small businesses are using community-led regenerative models to spread cyclical pleasure. These include eco-farming projects, participatory governance, and inclusive employment, especially for communities that are often left out (Utting, 2015). These models show that social solidarity economies can be good for the economy, the environment, and people's mental health (Coraggio, 2011; Razeto, 2010).

4.2.4. Bhutan and the Global South

Bhutan's GNH Index is probably the most well-known global project. It has led countries and businesses to rethink the problems with gross domestic product (GDP)-based development approaches. GNH says that mental health, community health, cultural preservation, and environmental protection are all important parts of a country's success (Brooks, 2013; Ura et al., 2012). Companies like Unilever, Danone, and Natura have said that Bhutan's GNH has influenced how they think about and plan their happiness-driven business strategy.

The United Arab Emirates has also started national happiness and well-being programmes, such as hiring a Minister of State for Happiness and starting a National Program for Happiness and Positivity. This shows how governments can make well-being a main goal of development (UAE Government, 2019).

4.3. Reframing the Definition of Success in a Global Context

The global push for workplace happiness and sustainability is part of a bigger shift in how we think about success. People no longer judge modern businesses only on how much money they make. They now look at how they help people, the earth, and ethical behaviour (Porter & Kramer, 2011). These changing standards not only meet the needs of stakeholders, but they also address environmental risks, a lack of skills, and social inequalities. Also, investors, policymakers, and customers are more and more making decisions based on ESG and well-being data. This makes it financially possible – and often necessary – for companies to use regenerative and emotionally intelligent ways of doing business (Clark et al., 2015). Fig. 1.4 shows five main factors that affect the long-term and meaningful well-being of employees around the world: GNH influence, ethical awareness, employee engagement, ESG integration, and regional adaptations. It stresses the necessity for methods that are culturally sensitive and morally sound in order to make employees happier around the world.

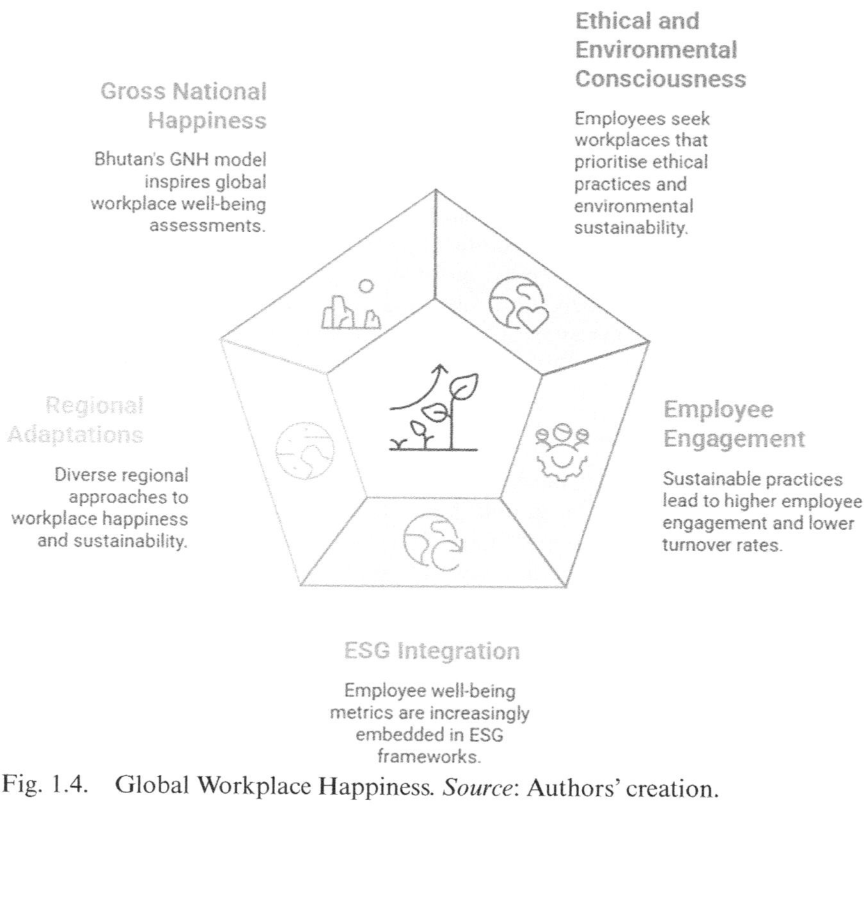

Fig. 1.4. Global Workplace Happiness. *Source*: Authors' creation.

There is a clear trend around the world towards making pleasure and sustainability two important goals in 21st-century organisations. Companies can create long-lasting, inclusive, and regenerative value by using models that put employee purpose, environmental awareness, and mental health first. These techniques not only help businesses keep their employees and come up with new ideas, but they also make sure that firms follow new global standards for ethical and environmental responsibility. This will help businesses stay relevant in a future moulded by conscious capitalism and sustainable development.

5. Creating a Happiness-sustaining Ecosystem

To promote circular happiness in businesses, it is important to create regenerative ecosystems that focus on both mental health and environmental sustainability. This method shows a shift away from separate well-being programs and towards design methods that are systemic, built-in, and planned to improve the resilience of people, groups, and the environment across time (Capra & Luisi, 2014; Senge et al., 2008). An ecosystem that supports happiness sees organisations as living systems made up of energy flows, feedback loops, and the ability to adapt. The goal is to make a place where people can grow, resources can be refreshed, and real connections can last. It requires a transition from linear efficiency models to circular thinking, in which interconnectedness, shared values, and regenerative practices are used to promote well-being (Di Fabio & Rosen, 2018).

5.1. Key Practices for Designing Circular Happiness

There are four interrelated activities that can help organisations put circular happiness into action:

1. Mapping the flow of energy, emotions, and resources
   To construct regenerative organisations, you need to know how energy, creativity, emotions, and materials move throughout teams and departments. Tools like organisational network analysis (ONA) and systems mapping can help you see where people don't communicate well, where they don't work well together, and where they aren't emotionally involved (McChrystal et al., 2015; Spreitzer et al., 2005). In this diagnostic phase, businesses can figure out where energy is flowing in a good way and where it is stuck or running out. For instance, studies on positive organisational networks have found that interactions that make coworkers feel good about each other lead to more trust, inventiveness, and engagement (Cross et al., 2003).

2. Identifying depletion points
   Depletion can happen in the mind, the body, or the environment. Employees burn out and lose interest when they are under chronic stress, don't know what their roles are, or when their work doesn't fit with the environment (Maslach & Leiter, 2008). Using too many natural resources or not caring about how

they affect the environment can also hurt the legitimacy of an organisation and the trust of its employees. Burnout inventories (like the Maslach Burnout Inventory (MBI)) and environmental audits can assist find depletion zones, which can be anything from team members who are too busy to procedures that waste energy (Tetrick & Winslow, 2015).

3. Closing the feedback loops
   Feedback loops are important for keeping learning going, encouraging good behaviour, and strengthening the ability to adapt. In regenerative cultures, feedback isn't just given during performance reviews. It's part of the daily work rhythm through things like after-action reviews, public recognition systems, and group reflection (Carpentier, 2020). Studies show that cultures of open feedback and shared learning make people feel safer and encourage new ideas (Edmondson, 1999). Rotating roles, participatory evaluation, and storytelling sessions are also good strategies to close feedback loops and build cultures that are open to everyone and focused on learning (Boyatzis et al., 2006).

6. Institutionalising Renewal

Rituals, policies, space design, and how leaders act must all support well-being. Here are some things you can do to help your mental and physical health: paid days off for mental health or reflection; access to green or biophilic areas; peer mentorship programmes and learning across generations; retreats that let you serve in your community and spend time in nature. Studies have shown that being in nature can help your brain work better, lower your stress levels, and make you feel better (Berman et al., 2008; Kaplan & Kaplan, 1989). Renewal activities that promote empathy, gratitude, and connection also have a favourable effect on corporate citizenship behaviour (Podsakoff et al., 2000).

6.1. Strategic Tools: The Happiness Ecosystem Canvas

The happiness ecosystem canvas is a visual planning tool that helps businesses figure out, plan, and improve their practices for health and sustainability. It shows: important people (workers, leaders, community, suppliers); support and energy flows (motivation, feedback, working together); areas of depletion and rejuvenation (places where people burn out vs places where teams do well); systems for measuring and learning (quantitative measurements + qualitative insight). The happiness ecosystem canvas is based on tools like the business model canvas and theory U (Scharmer, 2009). It may be used in many different types of organisations and promotes co-creation, openness, and ongoing improvement.

6.2. Measuring and Learning from Ecosystem Health

To make sure that everyone is on the same page and getting feedback all the time, multimodal evaluation is needed for strong well-being ecosystems. Some important ways to measure are:

Gallup Q12: this test looks at how engaged and satisfied employees are with their employment; the PERMA profiler (Seligman, 2011) looks at positive emotions, engagement, relationships, meaning, and achievement; ESG + happiness audits: this method combines measures of well-being with measures of the environment, society, and governance; Patton (2002) and Bushe (2012) talk about qualitative methodologies including storytelling, ecosystem health narratives, appreciative inquiry, and reflective journaling; measurement isn't just about being responsible; it's also about adaptive learning, which lets organisations change direction and build cultures of trust, empathy, and innovation.

6.3. Scaling Up with Partnerships and Pilot Programmes

Many successful regenerative projects start with small-scale tests, including making 'green teams', appointing well-being ambassadors, or trying out mindfulness-based leadership groups. These small changes act as learning labs, giving us information about how ready a culture is and where it could be improved.

As things pick up speed, companies can make a bigger influence by: integrating human resources (HR) policies, such as flexible scheduling and hiring for a reason; programmes for developing leaders that focus on empathy and renewal; working together across sectors with schools, non-governmental organisations (NGOs), and governments (Pretty, 2011); partnerships help spread circular happiness by including it in regional planning, public health programmes, and school curriculum. This has bigger social and environmental advantages.

6.4. A Real-life Example: Patagonia's Regenerative Model

Patagonia is a great example of how to make an ecosystem that keeps people happy. Patagonia is known for its radical transparency, empowering employees, and activist culture. The company incorporates environmental and social well-being into every part of its value chain (Haanaes et al., 2013). Some of the most important things to do are: taking time off to work on environmental issues; supply chains that are clear and fair; '1% for the Planet' gives money to grassroots groups; making decisions about climate strategy as an employee. These kinds of efforts to bring people together lead to more motivated employees, lower turnover rates, and a strong corporate identity based on collective well-being and environmental ethics (Crane et al., 2014).

Fig. 1.5 shows how businesses can map out their energy and resources, find spots of burnout, and set up feedback loops to encourage rejuvenation. It stresses the importance of ongoing learning and making well-being a part of the culture for long-term engagement and growth.

A system that keeps people happy is not a fixed collection of perks or benefits. Instead, it is a flexible system that gets input and respects the connections between people, organisations, and the environment that make work meaningful. Businesses can build strong cultures, give people power, and create sustainable futures by making circular ideas a part of their DNA, from leadership and policy to physical space and community participation. In this manner, pleasure

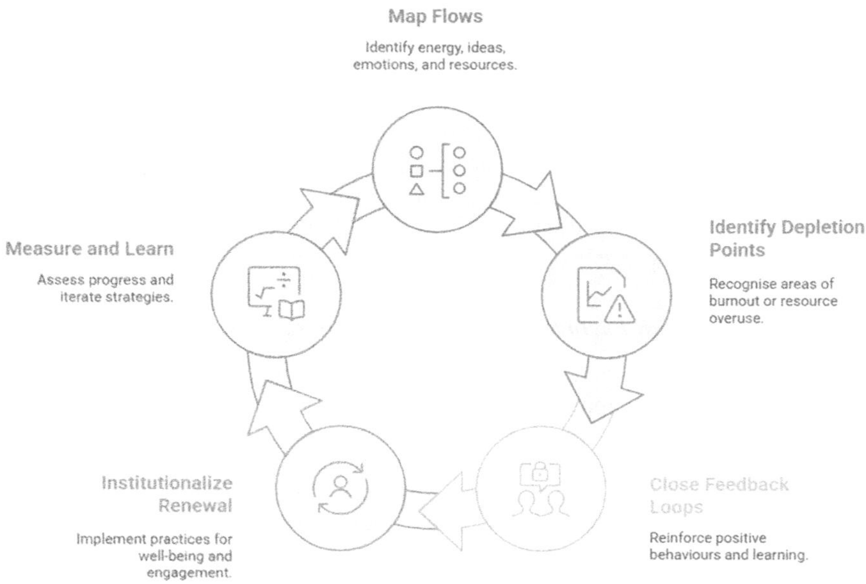

Fig. 1.5. Circular Happiness Ecosystem Cycle. *Source*: Authors' creation.

is not an end goal, but a process of co-evolution and renewal that goes on all the time.

6.5. Illustrated Model: The Circular Happiness Flow

The illustrated model of circular happiness shows how personal, organisational, and environmental areas work together in a dynamic and interrelated way to maintain long-term well-being. The concept is shown as a circular loop that shows feedback and regenerative cycles (Capra & Luisi, 2014). This is based on systems thinking and organisational behaviour theory. The loop is in the middle of the diagram. It goes from personal flourishing to organisational culture to environmental well-being and then back to personal flourishing. This flow shows that both the health of the environment and the structure of an organisation may affect people's happiness. In a regenerative cycle, one part feeds into the next, which is in line with the concepts of the circular economy applied to human well-being (Murray et al., 2017). Positive psychology research (Deci & Ryan, 2000; Seligman, 2011) backs up the ideas of autonomy, mastery, purpose, and emotional balance as parts of personal flourishing. People who are happy and healthy do better work. This, in turn, improves the culture of the organisation, which includes the way executives act, the rules they make, and the way the office is set up. A good culture encourages pro-social conduct, sustainable practices, and inclusivity (Cameron et al., 2003).

Access to green places, infrastructure that lasts, and design that blends in with nature are all part of environmental well-being. These kinds of environments lower stress, make thinking better, and make sure that employees' values match what they do every day (Nieuwenhuis et al., 2014). This alignment with the environment makes personal growth stronger, which closes the circle. Fig. 1.6 shows how the circular happiness model stays alive through the changing relationship between human growth, organisational culture, and environmental health. It stresses a cycle in which each part strengthens the others for overall enjoyment. This approach can be used to check how well an organisation is aligned and also to plan new policies and changes to the workplace. Meadows (2008) says that systems models like this one help people see where they can make changes and help different groups of people understand each other better.

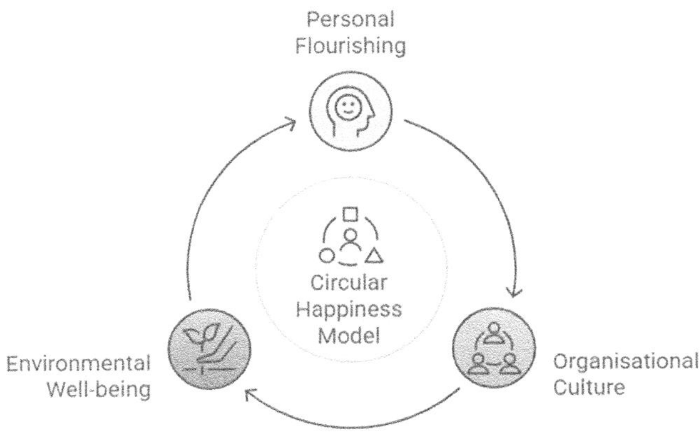

Fig. 1.6. Circular Happiness Flow. *Source*: Authors' creation.

7. Conclusion: Seeing Well-being as a Chance to Start Over

Circular happiness is not a set point; it is a dynamic and regenerative system – a process that is always changing and where human well-being, organisational vitality, and environmental sustainability are all integrally connected. The circular model, on the other hand, encourages us to adopt long-term, all-encompassing, and environmentally friendly definitions of success (Jackson, 2009). This is different from linear approaches to happiness that focus on short-term pleasure or expansion that takes a lot of resources.

This change in thinking means that well-being needs to be redefined as a shared experience that is supported by systems of reciprocal reinforcement, not just as individual pleasure or business success. Organisations that make sustainability a part of their culture – through leadership practices, physical work settings, and strategic decision-making – create spaces where happiness, purpose, and productivity can all thrive together (Senge et al., 2008). Values-based living, psychological resilience, and being in line with ecological consciousness are all ways to get new energy and motivation (Fredrickson, 2009).

When we use the ideas of the circular economy on emotional, social, and environmental capital, we go beyond short-term fixes and extractive methods. We instead build ecosystems that create new energy, build trust, and help everyone in society thrive (Di Fabio & Rosen, 2018; Raworth, 2017). These regenerative loops help people get back on their feet during tough times, help organisations come up with new ideas all the time, and keep communities ecologically healthy.

This chapter has given you both the ideas and the tools you need to create ecosystems where circular happiness can grow. The parts of circular happiness that can be put into action and are founded on research include work environments that are full of feedback, infrastructure that lasts, and leaders who are kind and think about systems. When these methods are put into action and grown, they could change not only how we work and live, but also how we define success.

Seligman (2011) says that true well-being is about thriving, not just getting by. Circular happiness extends on this paradigm, putting flourishing inside interconnected systems that value human dignity, organisational purpose, and planetary boundaries. In this way, it gives us an optimistic and realistic picture of how to achieve long-term growth and well-being for everyone.

References

Accenture. (2019). *The circular economy handbook: Realizing the circular advantage*. https://www.accenture.com

Achor, S. (2010). *The happiness advantage: The seven principles of positive psychology that fuel success and performance at work*. Crown Publishing.

Aggarwal, R., & Dow, S. (2012). Corporate governance and business strategies for climate change and environmental sustainability. *Corporate Governance: The International Journal of Business in Society*, *12*(5), 660–673.

Anderson, E. (2015). The Nordic model of welfare capitalism. *Journal of Economic Perspectives*, *29*(4), 77–98.

Anderson, R. (2009). *Confessions of a radical industrialist: Profits, people, purpose—Doing business by respecting the earth*. St. Martin's Press.

Avolio, B. J., & Gardner, W. L. (2005). Authentic leadership development: Getting to the root of positive forms of leadership. *The Leadership Quarterly*, *16*(3), 315–338.

Baumeister, R. F., & Leary, M. R. (1995). The need to belong: Desire for interpersonal attachments as a fundamental human motivation. *Psychological Bulletin*, *117*(3), 497–529.

Berman, M. G., Jonides, J., & Kaplan, S. (2008). The cognitive benefits of interacting with nature. *Psychological Science*, *19*(12), 1207–1212.

Binder, M., & Blankenberg, A. K. (2017). Green lifestyles and subjective well-being: More about self-image than actual behavior? *Journal of Economic Behavior & Organization*, *137*, 304–323. https://doi.org/10.1016/j.jebo.2017.03.009

Bocken, N. M. P., Short, S. W., Rana, P., & Evans, S. (2014). A literature and practice review to develop sustainable business model archetypes. *Journal of Cleaner Production*, *65*, 42–56.

Boyatzis, R. E., Smith, M. L., & Blaize, N. (2006). Developing sustainable leaders through coaching and compassion. *Academy of Management Learning & Education*, *5*(1), 8–24.

Brickman, P., & Campbell, D. T. (1971). Hedonic relativism and planning the good society. In M. H. Appley (Ed.), *Adaptation-level theory* (pp. 287–302). Academic Press.

Bronfenbrenner, U. (1979). *The ecology of human development: Experiments by nature and design*. Harvard University Press.

Brooks, J. S. (2013). Avoiding the limits to growth: Gross National Happiness in Bhutan as a model for sustainable development. *Sustainability*, *5*(9), 3640–3664.

Brown, K. W., & Kasser, T. (2005). Are psychological and ecological well-being compatible? The role of values, mindfulness, and lifestyle. *Social Indicators Research*, *74*(2), 349–368.

Bushe, G. R. (2012). Foundations of appreciative inquiry: History, criticism and potential. *AI Practitioner*, *14*(1), 8–20.

Cameron, K. S., & Spreitzer, G. M. (Eds.). (2012). *The Oxford handbook of positive organizational scholarship*. Oxford University Press.

Cameron, K. S., Dutton, J. E., & Quinn, R. E. (2003). *Positive organizational scholarship: Foundations of a new discipline*. Berrett-Koehler.

Capra, F., & Luisi, P. L. (2014). *The systems view of life: A unifying vision*. Cambridge University Press.

Carpentier, N. (2020). Engaging with participatory organizational cultures. *International Journal of Cultural Studies*, *23*(3), 395–411.

Chaskalson, M., & McMordie, M. (2021). *Mindfulness for coaches: An experiential guide*. Routledge.

Clark, G. L., Feiner, A., & Viehs, M. (2015). *From the stockholder to the stakeholder: How sustainability can drive financial outperformance*. Oxford University.

Cone Communications. (2017). *Millennial employee engagement study*. https://www.conecomm.com

Coraggio, J. L. (2011). Economía social y solidaria: El trabajo antes que el capital. *Editorial Abya Yala*.

Crane, A., Palazzo, G., Spence, L. J., & Matten, D. (2014). Contesting the value of "creating shared value" for CSR: A critical perspective. *California Management Review*, *56*(2), 130–153.

Cross, R., Baker, W., & Parker, A. (2003). What creates energy in organizations? *MIT Sloan Management Review*, *44*(4), 51–57.

Csikszentmihalyi, M. (1990). *Flow: The psychology of optimal experience*. Harper & Row.

Deci, E. L., Olafsen, A. H., & Ryan, R. M. (2017). Self-determination theory in work organizations: The state of a science. *Annual Review of Organizational Psychology and Organizational Behavior*, *4*, 19–43.

Deci, E. L., & Ryan, R. M. (2000). The "what" and "why" of goal pursuits: Human needs and the self-determination of behavior. *Psychological Inquiry*, *11*(4), 227–268.

Deloitte. (2024). *Global human capital trends*. https://www2.deloitte.com

Di Fabio, A., & Rosen, M. A. (2018). Sustainable development and psychology: An integrative proposal. *Sustainability*, *10*(7), 2410. https://doi.org/10.3390/su10072410

Dik, B. J., Byrne, Z. S., & Steger, M. F. (2013). *Purpose and meaning in the workplace*. American Psychological Association.

Dittmar, H., Bond, R., Hurst, M., & Kasser, T. (2014). The relationship between materialism and personal well-being: A meta-analysis. *Journal of Personality and Social Psychology*, *107*(5), 879–924.

Dutton, J. E., & Ragins, B. R. (Eds.). (2007). *Exploring positive relationships at work: Building a theoretical and research foundation*. Psychology Press.

Eccles, R. G., Ioannou, I., & Serafeim, G. (2014). The impact of a corporate culture of sustainability on corporate behavior and performance. *Harvard Business School Working Paper* (12-035).

Edmondson, A. (1999). Psychological safety and learning behavior in work teams. *Administrative Science Quarterly*, *44*(2), 350–383.

Ehnert, I., Parsa, S., Roper, I., Wagner, M., & Muller-Camen, M. (2016). Reporting on sustainability and HRM: A comparative study of sustainability reporting practices by the world's largest companies. *The International Journal of Human Resource Management*, *27*(1), 88–108.

Ellen MacArthur Foundation. (2015). *Towards a circular economy: Business rationale for an accelerated transition*. https://ellenmacarthurfoundation.org

Fredrickson, B. L. (2004). The broaden-and-build theory of positive emotions. *Philosophical Transactions of the Royal Society B: Biological Sciences*, *359*(1449), 1367–1377.

Fredrickson, B. L. (2009). *Positivity*. Crown.

Gagné, M., & Deci, E. L. (2005). Self-determination theory and work motivation. *Journal of Organizational Behavior*, *26*(4), 331–362.

Gallup. (2023). *State of the global workplace report*. https://www.gallup.com

Geissdoerfer, M., Savaget, P., Bocken, N. M. P., & Hultink, E. J. (2017). The circular economy – A new sustainability paradigm? *Journal of Cleaner Production*, *143*, 757–768.

Gifford, R., & Nilsson, A. (2014). Personal and social factors that influence pro-environmental concern and behaviour: A review. *International Journal of Psychology*, *49*(3), 141–157.

Grant, A. M., & Parker, S. K. (2009). Redesigning work design theories: The rise of relational and proactive perspectives. *Academy of Management Annals*, *3*(1), 317–375.

Haanaes, K., Michael, D., Jurgens, J., & Rangan, S. (2013). Making sustainability profitable. *Harvard Business Review*, *91*(3), 110–114.

Harter, J. K., Schmidt, F. L., & Keyes, C. L. M. (2003). Well-being in the workplace and its relationship to business outcomes: A review of the Gallup studies. In C. L. M. Keyes & J. Haidt (Eds.), *Flourishing: Positive psychology and the life well-lived* (pp. 205–224). APA.

Helliwell, J. F., Layard, R., & Sachs, J. (2020). *World happiness report 2020*. Sustainable Development Solutions Network.

Hunecke, M., Blöbaum, A., Matthies, E., & Höger, R. (2007). Psychological, sociodemographic, and infrastructural factors as determinants of ecological impact caused by mobility behavior. *Journal of Environmental Psychology*, *27*(4), 277–292.

Huta, V., & Ryan, R. M. (2010). Pursuing pleasure or virtue: The differential and overlapping well-being benefits of hedonic and eudaimonic motives. *Journal of Happiness Studies*, *11*(6), 735–762.

Jackson, T. (2009). *Prosperity without growth: Economics for a finite planet*. Earthscan.

Kaplan, R., & Kaplan, S. (1989). *The experience of nature: A psychological perspective*. Cambridge University Press.

Kasser, T. (2002). *The high price of materialism*. Cambridge: MIT Press.

Kasser, T., & Ryan, R. M. (1996). Further examining the American dream: Differential correlates of intrinsic and extrinsic goals. *Personality and Social Psychology Bulletin*, *22*(3), 280–287.

Kellert, S. R., & Calabrese, E. F. (2015). *The practice of biophilic design*. Terrapin Bright Green LLC.

Kelloway, E. K., & Barling, J. (2010). Leadership development as an intervention in occupational health psychology. *Work & Stress*, *24*(3), 260–279.

Kossek, E. E., Pichler, S., Bodner, T., & Hammer, L. B. (2011). Workplace social support and work-family conflict: A meta-analysis clarifying the influence of general and work-family-specific supervisor and organizational support. *Personnel Psychology*, *64*(2), 289–313.

Lepore, M., & Greenberg, M. (2021). Rethinking purpose in a post-pandemic world. *Harvard Business Review Digital Articles*, *99*, 1–5.

Luthans, F., Youssef, C. M., & Avolio, B. J. (2007). *Psychological capital: Developing the human competitive edge*. Oxford University Press.

Luthar, S. S., Cicchetti, D., & Becker, B. (2000). The construct of resilience: A critical evaluation and guidelines for future work. *Child Development*, *71*(3), 543–562.

Maslach, C., & Leiter, M. P. (2008). Early predictors of job burnout and engagement. *Journal of Applied Psychology, 93*(3), 498–512.

Masten, A. S., & Reed, M. G. J. (2002). Resilience in development. In C. R. Snyder & S. J. Lopez (Eds.), *Handbook of positive psychology* (pp. 74–88). Oxford University Press.

May, D. R., Gilson, R. L., & Harter, L. M. (2004). The psychological conditions of meaningfulness, safety and availability and the engagement of the human spirit at work. *Journal of Occupational and Organizational Psychology, 77*(1), 11–37.

McChrystal, S., Collins, T., Silverman, D., & Fussell, C. (2015). *Team of teams: New rules of engagement for a complex world.* Penguin.

Meadows, D. H. (2008). *Thinking in systems: A primer*. Chelsea Green Publishing.

Murray, A., Skene, K., & Haynes, K. (2017). The circular economy: An interdisciplinary exploration of the concept and application in a global context. *Journal of Business Ethics, 140*(3), 369–380.

Nieuwenhuis, M., Knight, C., Postmes, T., & Haslam, S. A. (2014). The relative benefits of green versus lean office space: Three field experiments. *Journal of Experimental Psychology: Applied, 20*(3), 199–214.

Norton, T. A., Zacher, H., & Ashkanasy, N. M. (2014). Organisational sustainability policies and employee green behaviour: The mediating role of work climate perceptions. *Journal of Environmental Psychology, 38*, 49–54.

Patton, M. Q. (2002). *Qualitative research and evaluation methods* (3rd ed.). Sage Publications.

Podsakoff, P. M., MacKenzie, S. B., Paine, J. B., & Bachrach, D. G. (2000). Organizational citizenship behaviors: A critical review. *Journal of Management, 26*(3), 513–563.

Porter, M. E., & Kramer, M. R. (2011). Creating shared value. *Harvard Business Review, 89*(1/2), 62–77.

Pretty, J. (2011). *Interconnectedness and the environment: Moral and spiritual dimensions.* In L. Zsolnai (Ed.), *Spirituality and ethics in management* (pp. 157–168). Springer.

PwC. (2021). *Workforce of the future: The competing forces shaping 2030*. https://www pwc. com

Raworth, K. (2017). *Doughnut economics: Seven ways to think like a 21st-century economist*. Random House.

Renwick, D. W. S., Redman, T., & Maguire, S. (2013). Green human resource management: A review and research agenda. *International Journal of Management Reviews, 15*(1), 1–14.

Robertson, I., & Cooper, C. (2011). *Well-being: Productivity and happiness at work*. Palgrave Macmillan.

Robertson, J. L., & Barling, J. (2017a). Corporate sustainability and employee well-being: A theoretical framework. *Journal of Organizational Behavior, 38*(8), 1240–1255.

Robertson, J. L., & Barling, J. (2017b). Toward a new measure of organizational environmental citizenship behavior. *Journal of Business Research, 75*, 57–66.

Ryan, R. M., & Deci, E. L. (2001). On happiness and human potentials: A review of research on hedonic and eudaimonic well-being. *Annual Review of Psychology, 52*(1), 141–166.

Scharmer, O. (2009). *Theory U: Leading from the future as it emerges*. Berrett-Koehler.

Seligman, M. E. P. (2011). *Flourish: A visionary new understanding of happiness and well-being*. Free Press.

Senge, P. M., Smith, B., Kruschwitz, N., Laur, J., & Schley, S. (2008). *The necessary revolution: How individuals and organizations are working together to create a sustainable world.* Doubleday.

Singh, J., & Singh, R. (2020). Mindful leadership for sustainable business: A study of Indian companies. *International Journal of Organizational Analysis, 28*(2), 451–470.

Spreitzer, G., Sutcliffe, K., Dutton, J., Sonenshein, S., & Grant, A. M. (2005). A socially embedded model of thriving at work. *Organization Science*, *16*(5), 537–549.

Stubbs, W., & Cocklin, C. (2008). Conceptualizing a "Sustainability Business Model". *Organization & Environment*, *21*(2), 103–127.

Tetrick, L. E., & Winslow, C. J. (2015). Workplace stress management interventions and health promotion. *Annual Review of Organizational Psychology and Organizational Behavior*, *2*, 583–603.

The Happiness Research Institute | The Science of Well-being. (n.d.). Retrieved August 21, 2025, from https://www.happinessresearchinstitute.com/

UAE Government. (2019). *National program for happiness and well-being*. https://u.ae

Ura, K., Alkire, S., Zangmo, T., & Wangdi, K. (2012). *An extensive analysis of GNH index*. Centre for Bhutan Studies.

Urban Redevelopment Authority. (2023). *Green and happy workplaces in Singapore*. https://www.ura.gov.sg

Utting, P. (2015). Social and solidarity economy: Beyond the fringe. *UNRISD/Pluto Press*.

Chapter 2

The Role of Marketing in Promoting Employee Well-being

Mridhu Rajput[a] *and Avtar Singh*[b]

[a]*Amity School of Business Administration, Amity University, India*
[b]*Department of Marketing, MSOB, LPU, India*

Abstract

The modern global marketplace demands organisations to support sustainability principles along with policies that include inclusivity and complete well-being in their operations. A progression in corporate culture now moves forward from empathic and emotional leadership which 'pink' symbolises towards environmentally responsible sustainability measures known as 'green'. Brand success in future business will emerge through the unification of human recipients with ecological stewardship and organisational direction. This study investigates methods which organisations can integrate sustainability as well as well-being into their fundamental corporate identity and workplace culture. Research based on purpose-driven companies identifies how the strategic value emerges when organisations develop cultures centred on employee emotional bonding and environmental sustainability, and workforce well-being. Research evaluates different organisational transformation frameworks, including circular economy principles, as well as the methods used for Environmental, Social, and Governance (ESG) integration and happiness-driven leadership models. The study reviews how organisations should leverage their internal brand culture because it serves as the primary force which produces external results. The collaboration of organisational strategies which gives employees valuable safety conditions and social alignment with corporate objectives helps create genuine brand messaging for stakeholder engagement. The chapter details organisational barriers that involve greenwashing risks together with employee resistance to change

Circular Happiness: Building Sustainable Workplaces for the Next Generation, 23–39

Published under exclusive licence by Emerald Publishing Limited
doi:10.1108/978-1-80592-907-920261002

and inconsistent action versus declared values. This chapter presents brands with a clear path to unite profitability with social purpose which creates both sustainable business success and responsible stakeholders' values.

Keywords: Sustainability; corporate culture; emotional branding; employee well-being; purpose-driven brands; ESG integration

1. Introduction

They say women are half of society, with the presence of women in different areas of life, focusing on them in preparing marketing strategies has become necessary because they play an important role in the life of a society, including in making important decisions at different levels, but from marketing point of view, women are not only half of society, but more than that, as marketing studies say that 85% of the purchasing decisions made by women or affected by them (Shehata & Fayyad, 2020). So, interest in the issue of women has become a fundamental issue in human social treatments (Al-Khasawneh, 2015). Freihat et al. (2021) mentioned that this great influence of women in purchasing decisions called on both marketing experts and practitioners to devise new marketing methods and techniques that suit their nature and fit their needs, desires, way of thinking, and purchasing motives. These marketing tactics geared towards women are called Pink Marketing, which is one of the marketing types that appeared in the 21st century, refers to women, and all marketing efforts directed to women. Since the behaviours of women differ fundamentally in many aspects from that of men, understanding the needs of women as a customer, who contributes to the process of purchasing and consuming decision-making, or as a marketer who own skills in the performance of her marketing tasks, becomes more urgent (Gharib, 2015). Colour is an important tool that delivers a brand image with stronger persuasive power than shape, and it appeals to emotions rather than rationality (Singh, 2006). Colour is also closely related to consumer behaviour (Nitse et al., 2004). As a result, colour also plays an effective communication role in situations where direct and specific verbal expression is difficult.

Women are also engaging towards sustainable lifestyles, as natural cosmetics and beauty care products are believed to harmonise their self-image, health risks and feminism which explain the growing demand for eco-friendly cosmetics and beauty care products. However, a few empirical studies have reported on the ecological behaviour of females and their perceptions for green cosmetics and beauty care products (Cervellon et al., 2010; Duff, 2007; Laroche et al., 2001; Manaktola & Jauhari 2007; Rahbar, 2004; Tsakiridou et al., 2008). The American Marketing Association (AMA) prescribed green marketing as the process of marketing products that are deemed to be safe and not harmful to the environment. Green marketing encapsulates a huge spectrum of topics under its umbrella. Green marketing is a 360° approach where manufacturing, marketing, utilisation, and discarding of the products happen in a manner that affects the environment in a very minimal or negligible manner (Kapoor et al., 2019). Electronic-word-of-mouth (eWOM), along with specific consumer-opinion and review platforms, such as bulletin boards, forums, blogs, social network sites, and online communities can exert a strong impact on members and their decision-making (Pollach, 2006). This holds a business and marketing benefit in the promotion of products and services, but also a community benefit in facilitating online participation and increasing membership through the sharing of information, knowledge and experience content between members (Cheng & Meihua, 2010; Jin et al., 2009; Okazaki, 2009).

1.1. Pink Marketing and Its Importance

According to Kaddumi, Pink marketing can be defined as applying the elements of a product marketing mix, pricing, promotion, and distribution in a manner consistent with and commensurate with the psychology and lifestyle of women to meet their needs and desires effectively, enabling companies to reach the stage of customer loyalty (Kaddumi, 2017). Pink marketing includes all activities and marketing efforts targeted at female clients, encompassing product, price, distribution, and promotion in a way that suits women. Organisations must address women unequivocally with their marketing messages because this approach is characterised by a pattern that no longer applies to women. Marketing messages must show understanding and conformity with the essence and needs of women (Ahmed et al., 2017).

Women occupy many areas of life, making them the focus of many organisations that develop and improve marketing strategies targeting women. The women's market grows and develops when institutions understand and meet the needs of women, thereby succeeding in developing and increasing market shares (Berletta, 2003). This field is characterised by how to design products and environments so that they are loved and desirable, achieve a great deal of happiness, and increase the love of acquisition. This field works to create positive experiences that the user remembers that enable him to boast about them, increase his loyalty to the product, and increase the interest of others in it (Huang et al., 2012). Mills has confirmed that the use of colours effectively increases comprehension and doubles attention, as a study conducted by the company (M3) revealed that colours are one of the main reasons why the display visuals have an impact that greatly exceeds the non-coloured offers, as colour ads attract the attention of a larger number of readers, up to 80%, and sales of advertised products rise by more than 50% when using colours, and the stability of the contents of the advertisement in the mind of readers increases from 55% to 80% in case of colour ads (Mills, 2001).

1.2. Power of Pink Marketing

The power of pink marketing is in its ability to tap into consumers' emotion and influence their emotional responses and their buying behaviour through the use of colour pink strategically. The pink colour earlier was associated with femininity, softness, and delicacy, but now it has evolved to become an all-purpose tool in modern marketing. Several brands utilise pink colour in order to create a sense of nurturing, calmness and warmth, which proves to be quite effective in the sectors of health, beauty and wellness (Koller, 2008). By associating pink with feminine gender, it serves as both a strength and a limitation; while it appeals to traditional gender norms, but also can strengthen stereotypes (Zotos & Landreth Grau, 2016). In the light of introduction of 'millennial pink', a range of soft or pastel pink shades, it has redefined pink as a unisex colour, which can appeal to a broader audience (Bideaux, 2019). Therefore, a shift in cultural evolution towards gender inclusivity and adaptability was noticed. Several effective campaigns by the brands like Nike and MAC Cosmetics have highlighted how pink can defy stereotypes and engage with modern consumers (Khan, 2017). Further, pink marketing has played roles in building powerful brand images, like that seen in the movie Barbie, and in raising populace awareness of diseases like breast cancer (Ma & Wang, 2024). Even though pink is criticised as 'pinkwashing', it remains to be one of favourite, relevant, and versatile tools in the marketing communication arsenal as it can capture and retain consumers' attention and loyalty.

1.3. Impact of Pink Marketing on Brands

Pink marketing has considerably impacted brand identity, consumer behaviour and positioning in different fields. The brands promoting pink marketing have been able to build extended emotional bonds with their clients. For instance, the use of pink throughout cosmetics packaging and magazine advertisements stimulates the feelings of youth and beauty to appeal to the females targeted by this industry (Koller, 2008). The examples of the brands following this are MAC Cosmetics and Fair & Lovely, which have helped them to set up a unique market presence and foster brand loyalty (Ataur, 2017).

Furthermore, pink marketing has created solutions for social causes and an improved brand image. The symbolic use of pink ribbon to market breast cancer awareness is a good example. Apart from being enhanced by associating with a cause, brands that align with such causes not only serve the greater societal benefit but also strengthen their corporate image and consumer trust (Ma & Wang, 2024). The integration of contemporary social issues in pink marketing has proven to be a powerful tool for creating a link between a certain brand and the socially aware consumer. The fashion industry also utilises pink marketing with brands like Nike as well as Adidas, which market pink products to the wider market. It has enabled these brands to break free from conventional gender role stereotyping and claim a position of social sustainability (Khan, 2017). These campaigns demonstrate that pink is not only effective in marketing products as a colour traditionally associated with females, but it can also be used for products that both male and female consumers of all age groups will appreciate.

In conclusion, pink marketing has had a powerful effect on brands as it has allowed them to create emotional connections, support social initiatives, and engage in discussions about gender non-conformity. The colour pink has become instrumental in promoting brands' market presence, building consumer loyalty, and portraying brands as socially sensitive (Ataur, 2017; Bideaux, 2019; Ma &

Wang, 2024). As consumer consumption patterns continue to shift, the versatility offered by pink marketing, with its ability to evoke emotional responses from consumers, will remain an advantage for many brands across sectors.

1.4. The Rise of Conscious Consumerism

Conscious consumerism is marking a major change where people prefer choosing brands that support the environment, are ethical, and are health-conscious. Drawing from Moldavska (2017), the author underlines the key role played by the organisational context, including leadership's commitment, reviewing sustainability strategies, and regular improvements in its implementation. People looking for transparency and responsibility in brands notice and appreciate these features. Fonseca et al. (2021) explain that corporate sustainability integration relies heavily on commitment, engagement, communication, and trust. These factors not only improve how the organisations' internal processes work, but also align perfectly with consumers' desire for authentic, responsible brands. Still, Delmas and Burbano (2011) point out that conscious consumers today can see through greenwashing, where companies make false environmental claims about their products, and hence, today's informed consumer expects companies to back up their environmental promises with factual actions.

This recent evolution in the behaviours of consumers brings both hurdles as well as new substantial opportunities for the brands. Though it is important to reduce greenwashing and uphold transparency, those brands that genuinely incorporate sustainability and wellness in their corporate environment can gain a competitive edge and foster long-term customer loyalty. Today's consumer actively demands attention in key areas of environmental responsibility, ethical conduct, and health aspects. The research findings point out that meeting the shifting consumer expectations depends greatly on strong leadership, meaningful stakeholder involvement, and genuine commitment. When brands put these ideas into practice, they can support what people care about and help make the environment healthier while doing well in business.

1.5. Sustainability as a Strategic Imperative

Initially seen as a secondary corporate social responsibility (CSR) goal, sustainability has grown into a main priority driving a company's brand value and competitive market standing. From the findings of Ioannou and Serafeim (2021), sustainability is now part of fundamental business strategies and leads to decisions in operations, new product creation, and how companies engage with their stakeholders. Examples like Microsoft and Adidas prove that putting sustainability first helps companies stand out, raises their brand awareness, and makes customers more loyal, through efforts like achieving carbon neutrality or adopting circular economy principles, that transcend simple ethical considerations. Since consumers, investors, and government bodies demand greater openness for more transparency, sustainability has now become a key decisive factor for any company's long-term success (Sheehy & Farneti, 2021). Adopting sustainability into company culture helps businesses reach goals like the United Nations Sustainable Development Goals (SDGs) and gain trust, which leads to better performance in the market.

Sustainable practices are now seen as the main contributors and significant impetus for innovation and improved business outcomes. Maintaining a unique and hard-to-replicate approach to sustainability practices enables companies to outcompete others and earn better financial returns (Ioannou & Serafeim, 2021). Green marketing campaigns and environmentally conscious product blueprints not only address environmental issues but also appeal to more consumers who prefer sustainable brands (Siminică et al., 2015). The addition of sustainability to business strategies gives companies an edge over their competitors, appeals to people who care about social issues, and lessens risks tied to evolving regulations or resource scarcity. According to Bosch-Badia et al. (2017), sustainability has evolved from being a mere footnote; it is now vital for a company's strategy as it helps increase value and guarantees its survival in an uncertain global market.

1.6. Integrating Well-being into Corporate Purpose

Organisations are now merging employee and community health with their corporate mission to fit in with the values of society, as people now see that well-being is essential in many ways, including improving performance; hence, more organisations are changing how they view well-being. In Sheehy and Farneti's view (2021), modern sustainable companies are now putting more emphasis on social responsibility, especially on employee care and active community involvement, as part of their overall effort to be sustainable. This process fits with the idea of 'corporate sustainability', which works to achieve economic, environmental, and social goals to satisfy both present and future stakeholders. Fostering well-being in employees encourages their satisfaction, increases their productivity, helps keep them loyal to the company, and also builds a trusting relationship with people in the local community. An example of this approach can be seen in employee wellness programmes, combined with community projects and partnerships with non-governmental groups, demonstrating how corporate strategies can create shared value.

Focusing on well-being is becoming a unique feature for companies competing in market of today. Studies by Siminică et al. (2015) indicate that businesses that place importance on social and environmental activities, such as well-being, have increased stakeholder involvement and brand loyalty. It is most crucial in industries where trust and what the public thinks matter greatly for the company's future. Participating in community health programmes or giving access to schooling is a good way for any organisation to increase its recognition as a responsible company. In this way, urban regeneration projects are in line with the United Nations SDGs, which involve inclusive growth and collective well-being. By placing well-being in the corporate values of companies, businesses not only share their positive influence on society but also stand out as key players in responsible and sustainable business practices.

2. Literature Review

2.1. Historical Context of Pink in Marketing

The origin of pink in marketing is indeed very interesting, especially with regards to gender and consumer preferences. At first, pink was considered a colour for boys, while blue was deemed to be a girl's colour. However, this trend was altered in the 1940s when marketing and cultural influences began to play a significant role. The feminisation of the colour pink was further compounded by the Nazis' use of the pink triangle during World War II to mark homosexual men. By the 1980s, the colour blue had almost become the complete opposite of femininity. This shift contrasted with earlier female-targeted marketing strategies, where women and girls were the primary audience for many products. This practice has also been reinforced through cultural and commercial practices to which consumers are socialised from a very young age (Pomerleau et al., 1990).

Furthermore, the depiction of pink and everything it represents was amplified by the cosmetics and fashion industries, which became the major markets for all things pink. While this trend was initially limited to Western cultures, it started to evolve, making pink a colour that could transcend traditional gender roles. The colour pink, once restricted to women, is now embraced by men as well. 'Millennial pink' is the latest colour to blend into the unisex range of colours. It is gender-neutral, making it appealing to a wide range of people.

A new term has emerged in the last few years which is referred to as 'millenial pink' which is a range of pale pink shades that are believed to be gender neutral and can be worn by both genders. This can be seen as a change in broader socio-cultural contexts in the society that seeks to be more gender inclusive and fluid (Bideaux, 2019). Similarly, Nike and MAC Cosmetics have employed pink as a marketing strategy in order to reach out to a more progressive audience (Freihat et al., 2021).

2.2. Consumer Perceptions on Sustainability and Their Motivation

The view of sustainability is influenced by a product or brand's impact on the environment, society, and the economy. Factors such as transparency and affiliation with sustainable practices (Gonzalez, 2021) also shape this perception. In other words, consumers' view of sustainability is shaped by how their values align with the brand's values, the general trust in environmental claims made, and the authenticity of the brand's sustainability efforts (Baum, 2012; Oyedele & Dejong, 2013; Yu et al., 2013). Assuredly, consumers trust and become loyal to companies with a reputation for being sustainable (Situngkir & Nuvriasari, 2024).

Factors such as health, environmental concern, and the desire to advance a good societal image serve as incentives for purchasing green products (Cervellon et al., 2010; Jaini et al., 2019). Consumers are motivated to make purchases in order to lessen their carbon footprint, ensure their purchases are ethical, and avoid actions that contradict their values (Cervellon et al., 2010; Jaini et al., 2019). Eco-friendly options are available to consumers, and the reason for choosing them is often linked to health concerns, reducing environmental harm, and supporting the cause of environmental preservation (Cervellon et al., 2010; Jaini et al., 2019).

2.3. Branding and Sustainability: Evolving Theoretical Frameworks

The theoretical frameworks, such as the triple bottom line (TBL) and stakeholder theory, have been responsible for guiding the interconnection between sustainability and social responsibility. The TBL, which was introduced by Elkington (1999), states the relationship between people, planet, and profit, and thus advises the brands to balance their company's financial health, along with taking environmental charge, which ultimately strengthens brand equity. This model has convinced brands to embrace sustainability, which consumers do expect and enhances brand quality. Similar to this, as stated by Carroll (1991, 2004), stakeholder theory encourages businesses to meet the expectations of several groups, including customers, staff, and local communities, using approaches that are ethical and philanthropic. With Carroll's Pyramid of CSR, these responsibilities are sorted into economic, legal, ethical, and philanthropic types, guiding businesses in adjusting their image to fit with public expectations. Altogether to these frameworks showcase how sustainability is important for a brand's strategy, which builds trust, fosters loyalty, and gives a company an edge over time (Flammer & Luo, 2017; Lu et al., 2020a).

2.4. Corporate Culture and Employee Well-being

Corporate culture plays a crucial role in influencing the satisfaction of employees, their well-being, and their efficiency. In their research, Mache et al. (2014) noted that people who are actively engaged at work are often more satisfied with their jobs and lives, and the initiatives that support wellness and time-friendly programmes increase performance and commitment. Research by Talukder et al. (2018) reveals that the productivity of employees is increased when companies offer strong supervisor support and a good work-life balance, which in effect reduces employee turnover. Likewise, Han et al. (2019) discovered that a company's environmentally responsible activities also make employees feel a sense of comfort and want to be loyal to the business. Furthermore, Ahmed et al. (2020) showed that ethical leadership and sustainability efforts reduce workplace stress and enhance job satisfaction. All in all, these findings reveal that combining wellness with company culture helps not only in overall employee health but also makes the organisation more successful by improving how employees work and feel.

2.5. Green Branding and Consumer Loyalty

Green branding has become a crucial strategy for building a lasting consumer trust, their loyalty, and maintaining long-term relationships. According to Elkington (1999), aligning brand messaging to sustainability strengthens the connection between brand identity and customer values, thereby increasing trust and loyalty. Flammer and Luo (2017) discovered that when CSR centres on environmental care, it improves how people think about a company and leads to loyal customers and promotion. Ahmed et al. (2017) also discovered that being clear about green initiatives encourages loyalty, makes customers believe in the brand and increases their involvement. Studies carried out by Lu et al. (2020b) pointed out that when companies embed sustainability with branding, it helps them to stand out in the market, appealing particularly to environmentally conscious customers. Moreover, Talukder et al. (2018) concluded that brands that promote sustainable practices effectively resonate with expectations of conscious consumers, enabling long-term customer loyalty. Together, this research demonstrates that the strategic importance of green branding helps businesses build trust and enjoy lasting customer loyalty.

2.6. Pink Marketing in Contemporary Context

The word 'pink marketing' has come to encompass something broader in recent years, becoming imbued in a culture that is being radically transformed with the growing influence of feminist and queer theories. A margin of Bideaux's (2019) paper has looked at the gradually developing pink-on-pink monochromatic range from which was birthed millennial pink, associated with many shades of pink almost prominently from the mid-2010s. The millennial pink trend, which was propagated largely by social media and fashion, attempted to strip pink of its age-old, intrinsic connection to femininity and present it instead as 'genderless'. 'This being one more example in a long, sometimes inspiring, history of the fluidity of colour symbolism and the power of colour themselves to cross yet challenge gender boundaries' (Bideaux, 2019). The motion picture industry has also really helped in doing curtail in modern times the reason behind pink. Typical examples are 'Legally Blonde' and the recent Barbie movie, which creatively utilise pink imagery as an empowerment- or independence-conveying kind of language. The use of pink by films like Dole's (2008) and Havrylenko's (2023) analyses infers how the two understand that most films employ pink to generate representations that are constructive and many-sided in regard to women, thus shaping perceptions and behaviours among the audiences of females. These successes have emphasised the power of pink in determining cultural narratives and consumer trends.

2.7. Sustainable Beauty Trends and Pink Marketing

The joint venture of pink marketing and sustainable beauty trends stands out with the promise it has of forging a greater environmental consciousness in the beauty industry. The aesthetics of these types of marketing will focus on educating consumers who have become increasingly aware of the environmental impact of their purchasing choices. This will, in turn, produce sustainable, eco-friendly beauty products that promote consumer awareness and engagement well into the future. This change has been a wake-up call to the people towards feminisation in marketing.

2.8. Social Responsibility and Ethical Practices

Sustainable beauty trends are not only about environmental sustainability; they also include social responsibility and ethical practices. The modern population cares more about issues like animal testing, fair-trade, and labour practices. Hence, Pink marketing can also be used to show that a particular company is engaged in practices that are ethical, showing images that convey messages of compassion and social responsibility. For instance, The Body Shop has long been at the forefront of beauty with conscience in ethical practices such as not testing on animals and fair trade. The brand strengthening its position on social responsibility through the use of pink in its marketing materials makes a difference to consumers who weigh ethical considerations when making buying decisions (Shehata & Fayyad, 2020).

2.9. Consumer Education and Engagement

Genuine 'pink' marketing campaigns embody the educating and engaging consumers regarding sustainability. Campaigns which have the pink colour and theme can also be used for campaigns towards environmental awareness and sustainability. The ability to reach social consumers will be amplified through the use of the imagery of pink to stimulate attention and action, social media miles beyond the reach of traditional mass media in terms of consumer engagement. The Pink Ribbon has shown how pink marketing can mobilise consumers around a cause were going by example such would be to continue inspiring consumers towards earth-friendly behaviour and marketable beauty products (Bideaux, 2019).

2.10. Challenges and Criticisms of Pink Marketing

Regardless of the positives, Pink marketing also has its disadvantages or reproaches. For example, Uncu and Calisir (2018) argue that using pink so much in marketing can reinforce gender stereotypes and limit the choices available to consumers. 'Pink bombing' is a marketing strategy where companies use the colour pink to sell products, trying to make people want things they might not actually need by focusing on the colour. This can create unnecessary desires and make products seem only for certain genders. This tactic can create unrealistic expectations and, at times, make gender differences worse by reinforcing stereotypes. In opposition, this idea can make femininity seem overly important, which might push away male consumers. As a result, it creates something called 'pink bias', where the colour pink is associated only with femininity, excluding or alienating men (Mileti et al., 2023). Therefore, pink marketing is actually superior to meaning into an inclusive and more dynamic approach. While pink can be a resource for targeted approaches, it must not limit the consumption preferences and identities of consumers and perpetuate gender stereotypes. Here, pink does culture transcend boundaries as well as sustainability values, thus becoming more inclusive and far-reaching in marketing strategies (Grisard, 2017). Therefore, pink's significance is a phenomenon narrowing in on the cultural and psychological evolutions of gender identity, empowerment, and sustainability. A wider audience can be reached while pushing for green behaviour if consumers have become increasingly concerned about the planet and if brands have aligned their pink strategies with trends in not just sustainable beauty but also ecologically friendly packaging, chemicals, ethical practices, as well as educating consumers.

RQ1. What role do cultural differences play in shaping consumer preferences and behaviours towards sustainable beauty products, and how can marketing practices adapt to these variations?

RQ2. In what ways can understanding colour psychology and cultural dimensions improve the design of beauty product websites to enhance consumer engagement and brand perception?

3. Methodology

When conducting this literature review, a professional and orderly process was used to spot and study relevant studies for our research. Around 50 high-quality journal articles were chosen, as each one focuses on different aspects of Pink Marketing, consumer behaviour, word-of-mouth (WOM) impact, and sustainable beauty products. To cover the subject in detail and stay updated, the review analysed studies published from 2012 to 2024. These research keywords were applied in academic studies via platforms such as Google Scholar, Springer, and IEEE.

The chosen articles were carefully reviewed to find valuable information and new theories. The findings were then grouped and summarised to show what was noticeable in the current literature. All the studies had the following themes: loyalty among consumers, how brands are perceived and the significance of WOM methods in Pink Marketing. By comparative analysis, it was possible to note that certain trends and similar opinions kept appearing which helped uncover the main factors that affect how people choose sustainable beauty products.

It was also found that Pink Marketing greatly affects how consumers think and act, mainly when it includes emotional and sustainability stories. People's experiences with a brand, shared with others, turned out to be a big factor influencing both trust and the decision to buy. This combination gave us a wider view of the developments in beauty marketing, mainly related to sustainability and ethical choices. Combining these ideas again highlights the importance of Pink Marketing and gives practical advice to professionals in the beauty business who wish to capture consumers' interest in sustainability.

4. Discussions and Conclusions

The review chapter summarises findings of research in various subjects in the beauty products industry and captures an exhaustive dimension of customer loyalty, marketing strategies, consumer behaviour, and social implications. Several important themes emerge from articles reviewed regarding how the beauty sector carries these insights for marketers as they navigate through this competitive landscape.

Customer loyalty remains a key proposition in the beauty industry where product quality, brand reputation, emotional attachments, personalised experiences, loyalty programmes, incentives, aggressive marketing strategies, and customer engagement factor into the overall issue. Therefore, such measures as developing sound relationships through the various components should build brand loyalty and advocacy among the consumers. Loyalty programmes and incentives, therefore, are critical to customer retention and immediately coming back to the same brands where value-adding experiences happen. Only a few factors such as product, brand image, trust, experience, and innovativeness in marketing strategies were identified as critical point drivers for customer loyalty and perception in the beauty industry.

The impact of WOM strategy on consumer behaviour and brand perceptions is yet another critical aspect brought into the focus of these research papers. It has been proven that e-WOM communicates powerful messages about product purchases, brand creditability and hence overall success. Positive WOM serves as a strong testament of brand reliability and creates customer devotion and advocacy in the beauty industry. The conventional as well as digital WOM strategies have been identified to significantly affect consumer behaviours, trust, credibility, and brand engagement. These certainly need to be heeded carefully to drive consumer loyalty and advocacy. Increasing competition, evolution of consumer taste, and adaptation to technology are some of the challenges faced by beauty brands. All these challenges actually present new ways of being innovative and diverse, along with the use of technology and social media, to create better customer experience and loyalty. Marketers need to keep up with changing consumer preferences, focus on what the customers want, and include WOM strategies in their marketing plans to make their brand successful and stay competitive. Research also pointed out important insights about being ethical in respecting cultural differences and using creative marketing approaches in the beauty industry. The discussions then focused on the need to align marketing practices with ethical values-discourse on such things as gender stereotypes, environmentally identified brands, and CSR-which most of their decisions found to be essential in having an environment that designs inclusion, gender equality, and sustainability in reflections of the rising demand by consumers for brands that are ethically responsible. Among other things, it highlighted the significant impact of cultural dimensions on the user preferences and behaviours on websites thus emphasising the importance of cultural differences with respect to web design and colour psychology to improve user experience as well as boost brand loyalty. On a broader strategy, some of the novel marketing tools such as experiential marketing, colour psychology, and the marriage between environmental sustainability and CSR practice were maximised as thrusts for consumer engagement and relationship building. All these are necessary ingredients in the recipe for sustainable growth in the highly competitive beauty market. Such differences also include gender-based pricing differences, like the pink tax, contributing to gender inequality in product marketing, as highlighted in the review. These underscored the need for continued generations of research, policy interventions as well as education of consumers for such inequalities to be addressed.

Cumulatively, all these findings led to the bearing of the idea that businesses need to move away from segmented marketing and all possible integrated approaches to successful brand marketing, including key drivers of the customer loyalty – WOM strategies and digital tools. Future research should investigate creative marketing ideas, find better ways to connect with customers, and use digital platforms to keep growing in a changing market. By learning from these areas, beauty businesses can create marketing plans that are inclusive, socially responsible, and focused on customers. These strategies can appeal to a wide range of people, build customer loyalty, and help the business succeed for the long-term in the fast-changing beauty industry.

5. Implications and Future Scope of the Study

The research on pink marketing has thrown further light on the often green potential that comes with this marketing tactic in sustainable beauty, as there are several implications for marketers and brands. The exploration of contemporary marketing's colour pink has significantly opened up new and promising avenues for the understanding of female consumer behaviour and the cinematic.

5.1. Strategic Takeaways for Sustainable Brand Transformation

Transforming a brand sustainably involves integrating a company's corporate culture, branding efforts with social and environmental values to ensure lasting success. Both Elkington (1999) and Carroll (1991) stress the vital role of embracing the TBL approach to be utilised by companies, which encourages a balanced focus on being profitable, ecologically responsible, and socially impact. Being clear and honest in the communication related to sustainability is paramount, as research by Ahmed et al. (2017) confirms that transparency reduces customer doubt and, in turn, fosters consumers' trust and loyalty. Flammer and Luo (2017) state that using sustainability in branding helps brands stand out and form closer relationships with their customers, and Lu et al. (2020b) found that sustainability draws in environmentally minded consumers.

Looking after employees' well-being is very important within the company. Mache et al. (2014) proposed setting up wellness programmes to help staff feel satisfied with their jobs and be more productive, while Talukder et al. (2018) emphasised the value of supportive leadership and work-life balance efforts, which play a key role. Additionally, Han et al. (2019) mentioned that following both ethical leadership and CSR practices helps employees become more engaged and motivated. Future practical recommendations include environmental considerations in the company's strategic vision, highlighting sustainable efforts for customers, and establishing programmes for employee health. Integrating sustainability and well-being in both their operations and brand messaging allows companies to earn customer trust, loyalty, and a competitive edge while aligning with the world's environmental and social needs.

5.2. Implications for Policy, Practice, and Future Research

Corporate sustainability carries important consequences for policy making, how companies operate, and educational research. For policy purposes, adopting the TBL (Elkington, 1999) and similar tools ensures the organisation considers economic, environmental, and social concerns. Making transparent disclosure of sustainability efforts, as explained by Ahmed et al. (2017), leads to greater accountability and increases the trust among all stakeholders. In accordance with Flammer and Luo (2017), tax breaks, discounts on purchases, and certificates from the government can speed up people and companies adopting green choices. Also, focusing corporate actions on international platforms such as the United Nations SDGs promoted by Sachs (2012) can help address environmental and social matters better.

Integrating sustainability into both the organisational culture and the processes of an organisation is very important for managers. Leaders need to put ethical leadership and employee engagement as a priority, using initiatives such as work wellness and a healthy work-life balance (Talukder et al., 2018). Using environmentally friendly branding plans can create a stronger bond with buyers and make a company differentiate itself from its competitors (Flammer & Luo, 2017). Models such as the Integrative Sustainable Intelligence (ISI) make it possible to integrate sustainability targets into how a business is run. Future research should examine the use of emerging technologies like artificial intelligence (AI) and blockchain to improve clear and accountable reporting in sustainability. There is also a need for longitudinal research to assess how sustainability initiatives affect consumer preferences, helping to fine-tune global sustainability approaches.

References

Ahmed, R. R., Štreimikienė, D., Abrhám, J., Streimikis, J., & Vveinhardt, J. (2020). Social & behavioural theories and physicians' prescription behaviour. *Sustainability*, *12*(8), 3379. https://doi.org/10.3390/su12083379

Ahmed, R. R., Vveinhardt, J., & Štreimikienė, D. (2017). Interactive digital media and impact of customer attitude and technology on brand awareness: Evidence from the South Asian countries. *Journal of Business Economics and Management*, *18*(6), 1115–1134. http://dx.doi.org/10.3846/16111699.2017.1400460

Al-Khasawneh, A. (2015). *The use of women in TV advertisements: Jordan TV and Ruya Channel as a model* [Master's thesis]. University of Petra, Amman, Jordan.

Baum, L. M. (2012). It's not easy being green … or is it? A content analysis of environmental claims in magazine advertisements from the United States and United Kingdom. *Environmental Communication: A Journal of Nature and Culture*, *6*(4), 423–440. https://doi.org/10.1080/17524032.2012.713073

Berletta, M. (2003). *Marketing to women: Understand, reach and increase your share of the world's largest market segment*. Dearborn Trade Publishing.

Bideaux, K. (2019). Millennial pink: Gender, feminism, and marketing. A critical analysis of a color trend. *Cultura e Scienza del Colore – Color Culture and Science*, *11*(1), 82–89. https://doi.org/10.23738/CCSJ.110110

Bosch-Badia, M.-T., Montllor-Serrats, J., & Tarrazon-Rodon, M.-A. (2017). Efficiency and sustainability of CSR projects. *Sustainability*, *9*(10), 1714. https://doi.org/10.3390/su9101714

Carroll, A. B. (1991). The pyramid of corporate social responsibility: Toward the moral management of organizational stakeholders. *Business Horizons*, *34*(4), 39–48. https://doi.org/10.1016/0007-6813(91)90005-G

Carroll, A. B. (2004). Managing ethically with global stakeholders: A present and future challenge. *Academy of Management Perspective*, *18*(2), 114–120. https://doi.org/10.5465/ame.2004.13836269

Cervellon, M. C., Hjerth, H., Richard, S., & Carey, L. (2010). Green in fashion? An exploratory study of national differences in consumers' concern for eco-fashion. In *Proceedings of the 9th international marketing trends conference* (pp. 20–21). Venice, Italy.

Cheng, X., & Meihua, Z. (2010). Study on the effect of e-WOM: A literature review and suggestions for future research. In *International conference on management and service science (MASS)* (pp. 1–6). IEEE Xplore, and Research Gate. https://doi.org/10.1109/ICMSS.2010.5576422

Delmas, M. A., & Burbano, V. C. (2011). The drivers of greenwashing. *California Management Review, 54*(1), 64–87. https://doi.org/10.1525/cmr.2011.54.1.64

Dole, C. M. (2008). *The return of pink: Legally Blonde, third-wave feminism, and having it all*. Routledge.

Duff, M. (2007). Niche marketing for cosmetics. *DSN Retailing Today*, *38*, 29.

Elkington, J. (1999). *Cannibals with forks: The triple bottom line of 21st century business*. John Wiley & Sons Ltd.

Flammer, C., & Luo, J. (2017). Corporate social responsibility as an employee governance tool: Evidence from a quasi-experiment. *Strategic Management Journal*, *38*(2), 163–183. https://doi.org/10.1002/smj.2492

Fonseca, A., Abreu, I., & Silvestre, W. J. (2021). Investigating context factors in the strategic management of corporate sustainability integration. *Journal of Cleaner Production*, *314*, 128002. https://doi.org/10.1016/j.jclepro.2021.128002

Freihat, S. M. S. S., Alotoum, F. J., & Homsi, D. M. A. (2021). Pink marketing and women's purchasing decision-making. *Multicultural Education*, *7*(4), 47–56.

Gharib, M. (2015). *Understanding marketing directed at the pink market*. Hsoub Academy. Retrieved September 3, 2015, from https://www.hsoub.com

Grisard, D. (2017). "Real men wear pink"? A gender history of color. In R. L. Blaszczyk & U. Spiekermann (Eds.), *Bright modernity: Color, commerce, and consumer culture* (pp. 77–96). Palgrave Macmillan.

Han, H., Kim, S. S., Chiriko, A. Y., & Quan, L. (2019). Environmental corporate social responsibility and the strategy to boost the airline's image and customer loyalty intentions. *Journal of Travel & Tourism Marketing, 36*(3), 371–383. https://doi.org/10.1080/10548408.2018.1545119

Havrylenko, V. (2023). *The art of marketing: How the Barbie movie became a brand and cultural event*. World Scientific Reports.

Huang, Y., Chen, C.-H., & Khoo, L. P. (2012). Products classification in emotional design using a basic emotion-based semantic differential method. *International Journal of Industrial Ergonomics*, *42*(6), 569–580. https://doi.org/10.1016/j.ergon.2012.08.002

Ioannou, I., & Serafeim, G. (2021). *Corporate sustainability: A strategy?* Harvard Business School Working Paper.

Jaini, A., Quoquab, F., Mohammad, J., & Hussin, N. (2019). "I buy green products, do you...?" The moderating effect of e-WOM on green purchase behavior in the Malaysian cosmetics industry. *International Journal of Pharmaceutical and Healthcare Marketing*. https://doi.org/10.1108/IJPHM-02-2019-0022

Jin, X. L., Cheung, C. M., Lee, M. K., & Chen, H. P. (2009). How to keep members using the information in a computer-supported social network. *Computers in Human Behavior*, *25*(5), 1172–1181. https://doi.org/10.1016/j.chb.2009.05.006

Kaddumi, B. (2017). *New marketing*. Hammed for Publishing and Distribution.

Kapoor, R., Singh, A. B., & Misra, R. (2019). Green cosmetics: Changing young consumer preference and reforming the cosmetic industry. *International Journal of Recent Technology and Engineering*, *8*(4), 2277–3878.

Khan, S. A. (2017). Pink and blue: Crossings. *A Journal of English Studies*, *8*, 120–127.

Koller, V. (2008). Not just a color: Pink as a gender and sexuality marker in visual communication. *Visual Communication*, *7*(4), 395–423. https://doi.org/10.1177/1470357208096209

Laroche, M., Bergeron, J., & Barbaro-Forleo, G. (2001). Targeting consumers who are willing to pay more for environmentally friendly products. *Journal of Consumer Marketing*, *18*(6), 503–520. https://doi.org/10.1108/EUM0000000006155

Lu, J., Ren, L., Zhang, C., Rong, D., Ahmed, R. R., & Streimikis, J. (2020a). Modified Carroll's Pyramid of corporate social responsibility to enhance organizational performance of SMEs industry. *Journal of Cleaner Production*, *271*, 1–18. https://doi.org/10.1016/j.jclepro.2020.122456

Lu, J., Ren, L., Zhang, C., Wang, C., Ahmed, R. R., & Streimikis, J. (2020b). Corporate social responsibility and employees' behavior: Evidence from mediation and moderation analysis. *Corporate Social Responsibility and Environmental Management*, *27*(4), 1719–1728. https://doi.org/10.1002/csr.1919

Ma, R., & Wang, X. (2024). Beyond gender: The evolving significance of pink in contemporary marketing. *Sustainable Economies*, *2*(3), 168. https://doi.org/10.62617/se.v2i3.168

Mache, S., Vitzthum, K., Klapp, B. F., & Danzer, G. (2014). Surgeons' work engagement: Influencing factors and relations to job and life satisfaction. *The Surgeon*, *12*(4), 181–190. https://doi.org/10.1016/j.surge.2013.11.015

Manaktola, K., & Jauhari, V. (2007). Exploring consumer attitude and behavior towards green practices in the lodging industry in India. *International Journal of Contemporary Hospitality Management*, *19*(5), 364–377. https://doi.org/10.1108/09596110710757534ea

Mileti, A., Piper, L., & Rizzo, C. (2023). The pink bias: Consumption choices of pink-colored products. *Journal of Global Fashion Marketing*, *14*(2), 187–205. https://doi.org/10.1080/20932685.2022.2152072

Mills, H. (2001). *The art of persuasion: How to attract the attention of others and change their opinions and influence them*. Jarir Bookstore Publications.

Moldavska, A. (2017). Defining organizational context for corporate sustainability assessment: Cross-disciplinary approach. *Sustainability*, *9*(2365), 1–22. https://doi.org/10.3390/su9122365

Nitse, P. S., Parker, K. R., Krumwiede, D. W., & Ottaway, T. A. (2004). The impact of color in the e-commerce marketing of fashions: An exploratory study. *European Journal of Marketing*, *38*(7), 898–915. https://doi.org/10.1108/03090560410539311

Okazaki, S. (2009). Social influence model and electronic word of mouth: PC versus mobile internet. *International Journal of Advertising*, *28*(3), 439–472. https://doi.org/10.2501/S0265048709200692

Oyedele, A., & Dejong, P. (2013). Consumer readings of green appeals in advertisements. *Journal of Promotion Management*, *19*(4), 435–451. https://doi.org/10.1080/10496491.2013.817222

Pollach, I. (2006). Electronic word of mouth: A genre analysis of product reviews on consumer opinion websites. *Proceedings of the 39th Hawaii international conference on system sciences*, 1–10. https://doi.org/10.1109/HICSS.2006.146

Pomerleau, A., Bolduc, D., Malcuit, G., & Cossette, L. (1990). Pink or blue: Environmental gender stereotypes in the first two years of life. *Sex Roles*, *22*(5–6), 359–367. https://doi.org/10.1007/BF00288339

Rahbar, E. (2004). *To buy green and non-green products: What are the factors influencing customer purchase behaviour?* [MBA thesis]. University Sains Malaysia.

Sachs, J. D. (2012). From millennium development goals to sustainable development goals. *The Lancet, 379*(9832), 2206–2211. https://doi.org/10.1016/S0140-6736(12)60685-0

Sheehy, B., & Farneti, F. (2021). Corporate social responsibility, sustainability, sustainable development and corporate sustainability: What is the difference, and does it matter? *Sustainability, 13*(11), 5965. https://doi.org/10.3390/su13115965

Shehata, A. E.-S., & Fayyad, S. (2020). The impact of purchasing behavior on the relationship between pink marketing practices and women's loyalty to hotels. *Journal of the Association of Arab Universities for Tourism and Hospitality, 18*(1), 221–239. https://doi.org/10.21608/jaauth.2020.34704.1039

Siminică, M., Crăciun, L., & Dinu, A. (2015). The impact of corporate sustainability strategies on the financial performance of Romanian companies in the context of green marketing. *Amfiteatru Economic, 17*(40), 994–1010.

Singh, S. (2006). Impact of color on marketing. *Management Decision, 44*(6), 783–789. https://doi.org/10.1108/00251740610673332

Situngkir, O., & Nuvriasari, A. (2024). The influence of experiential marketing, electronic word of mouth, and brand image on customer loyalty for Everwhite beauty products. *Formosa Journal of Multidisciplinary Research, 3*(1), 271–288. https://doi.org/10.55927/fjmr.v3i1.7979

Talukder, A. K. M., Vickers, M., & Khan, A. (2018). Supervisor support and work-life balance. *Personnel Review, 47*(3), 727–744. https://doi.org/10.1108/PR-12-2016-0314

Tsakiridou, E., Boutsouki, C., Zotos, Y., & Mattas, K. (2008). Attitudes and behaviour towards organic products: An exploratory study. *International Journal of Retail & Distribution Management, 36*(2), 158–175. https://doi.org/10.1108/09590550810853093

Uncu, G., & Çalışır, G. (2018). Gender of color: When did girls and boys start to wear pink and blue? In R. Yılmaz (Ed.), *Studies on Balkan and Near Eastern social sciences* (pp. 281–287). Peter Lang.

Yu, J., Coulson, K. R., Zhou, J. X., & Wen, J. (2013). Substantive and associative claims in environmental communication: A study of Fortune 500 websites. *Journal of Promotion Management, 19*(2), 211–223. https://doi.org/10.1080/10496491.2013.769476

Zotos, Y. C., & Landreth Grau, S. (2016). Editorial: Gender stereotypes in advertising: Exploring new directions. *International Journal of Advertising, 35*(5), 759–760. https://doi.org/10.1080/02650487.2016.1203555

Chapter 3

Human Resource and the Happiness: Performance Link

Amrita Sidhu[a] *Akanchha Singh*[b] *and Pretty Bhalla*[c]

[a]*Independent Researcher, India*
[b]*School of Business, Manav Rachna University, India*
[c]*Lovely Professional University, India*

Abstract

In today's dynamic and competitive corporate climate, human resources (HR) plays a strategic role that goes beyond administrative responsibilities and includes developing employee satisfaction as a driver of organisational performance. This chapter discusses the developing link between HR practices, circular happiness, and workplace productivity, based on the concepts of positive psychology. Drawing on previous research, it investigates how employee happiness – defined as work satisfaction, engagement, and emotional well-being – directly influences performance outcomes such as commitment, creativity, and low turnover. The chapter also explores how trust and psychological safety contribute to a positive culture. Strategies like promoting self-awareness, empathy, handling hurdles with a curious perspective, a trustworthy leader and encouraging team culture to foster trust at the workplace were also discussed. This chapter also discusses the role of diversity and inclusion in organisational sustainability, along with leadership. At the end, the importance of recognition, rewards, and motivation in an organisational setting is discussed.

Keywords: Diversity; happiness; human resource; positive psychology; psychological safety; recognition; reward; trust

Circular Happiness: Building Sustainable Workplaces for the Next Generation, 41–58

Published under exclusive licence by Emerald Publishing Limited
doi:10.1108/978-1-80592-907-920261003

Introduction

Employee happiness, which has become the most variable and critical resource in today's competitive environment (Smith & Kumar, 2025), is critical to organisational success because the positive results like high job satisfaction, commitment and high job performance provided by the happy-productive employee can only be achieved by employees who are satisfied with their jobs and workplace (Yuan, 2024). The work environment has undergone rapid changes in recent years (Wu, 2022), including technological developments, boom in outsourcing (Spurk & Straub, 2020), retrenchments (Spurk & Straub, 2020), and internationalisation of businesses (Monaghan et al., 2020). In such a scenario, the role of HR at workplace is becoming more challenging day by day. Corporate ethical responsibility prioritises employee well-being as a means of gaining a competitive advantage (Porter & Kramer, 2011). Workplace well-being predicts emotional commitment, turnover, and job success (Wang et al., 2018). It also serves as a prelude to improving organisational performance. Ed Diener was a pioneering psychologist who made substantial contributions to the field of well-being and happiness. He described happiness as 'a subjective feeling of life satisfaction, which encompasses positive emotions like joy and contentment, as well as a sense of accomplishment and purpose in one's life' (Diener, 2000). In an organisation, the benefit of improving workplace pleasure is increased productivity. Employees who are happy and engaged are more likely to be productive, which leads to enhanced efficiency and improved organisational performance (Gallup, 2024). A typical practice is to utilise management techniques to boost staff productivity. Salis and Williams (2010) examined how human resource management (HRM) strategies affect employee productivity. The study indicated that organisational information sharing practices significantly influence production levels. Quick and Quick (2004) discovered that fostering a positive company culture is vital for increasing employee productivity. Rego and Cunha (2008) discovered that cheerful employees are more productive. Unhappiness at work has been linked to lower productivity (Fereidouni et al., 2013).

This chapter outlines the importance of positive psychology in gaining happiness at the workplace in reference to the positive emotion, engagement, relationships, meaning, and accomplishment (PERMA) model. It also discusses the science behind happiness. The HR department plays a vital role in this context. The various HR policies have been discussed, which are helpful in fostering circular happiness. The chapter also discusses the role of psychological safety and trust in bringing pleasure at the workplace. A high level of trust makes employees more psychologically safe and helps them to express their ideas and problems without having the fear of humiliation. Further in this chapter, we have discussed diversity and inclusion of the workforce. A brief description has been given about rewards, recognition, type of rewards and how they are linked to organisational performance.

Science of Happiness and Productivity

The reciprocity between happiness and productivity is a theme of significant interest in both professional and intellectual fields. In a variety of settings, it has been demonstrated that happiness greatly increases productivity (Diener & Seligman, 2004). People are more likely to be driven, involved, and productive at work when they are pleased (WHO, 2020). High productivity depends on cognitive abilities like creativity, problem-solving, and decision-making, all of which are improved by positive emotions.

According to a comprehensive study conducted by the Said Business School at Oxford University and the British multinational telecom company BT on the relationship between happiness and productivity, contented employees are 13% more productive (De Neve et al., 2019). Happy workers are 12% more productive than their unhappy counterparts, according to research by economists at the University of Warwick (Oswald et al., 2015). According to this study, creating a good work atmosphere might result in significant increases in productivity since happiness has a direct impact on job performance. Employee satisfaction increases the likelihood that they will take the initiative, work well with others, and offer creative ideas – all of which are critical to the success of the company (Oswald et al., 2015).

The psychological probe into happiness is very important because it is a top objective for individuals worldwide, since it has been linked to better physical health and longevity (Psychology Today, 2019). Other desirable outcomes include having a fulfilling life and earning a lot of money (Psychology Today, 2019). The science behind happiness and productivity is mediated by positive psychology (Seligman & Csikszentmihalyi, 2000a, 2000b). Positive psychology is defined as 'the scientific study of positive human functioning and flourishing on multiple levels that include the biological, personal, relational, institutional, cultural, and global dimensions of life' (Seligman & Csikszentmihalyi, 2000a, 2000b). On the other hand, happiness is defined as 'not just about pleasure, but about engagement, meaning, relationships, and accomplishment' (Seligman, 2011). Seligman (2011) tried to understand this relationship with the help of his PERMA model. The first element is *positive emotions*, such as happiness, optimism, joy, compassion, and gratitude, which help persons succeed in both personal and professional settings. According to research, experiencing good emotions on a daily basis can improve mental health, reduce stress, and boost resilience, teamwork, creativity, and problem-solving skills (Sutton, 2016). Positive emotions involve a neurochemical mechanism which deals with the feel-good hormones. Dopamine and Serotonin are the feel-good transmitters when a person feels positive emotion (Young, 2007). These transmitters enhance memory, motivation level and cognitive flexibility of a person further improving the productivity and problem-solving skills (Ashby et al., 1999).

Engagement, which is termed a 'flow', is also a crucial factor contributing towards happiness. Flow is a good emotional state characterised by prolonged, task-oriented, and goal-driven attention during a rewarding activity (Csikszentmihalyi, 2002). A flow state occurs when one is completely concentrated on a task and loses track of time and surroundings. The individual feels ecstatic and enjoys themself without exertion. According to Bonaiuto et al. (2016), happiness is often linked to self-actualisation. Self-actualisation can generally be defined as the full manifestation of one's creative, intellectual, and social potential through internal motivation (rather than external rewards such as money, position, or power) (Couture et al., 2007).

Relationships include all of the interactions that people have with their spouses, friends, family members, coworkers, supervisors, and the community at large (Seligman, 2012). Positive working connections improve job satisfaction, reduce turnover, and increase organisational commitment (Seligman, 2011). Employees who feel appreciated, respected, and supported by their colleagues and bosses are more likely to participate actively, communicate honestly, and recover swiftly from stress or disappointments (Dutton & Heaphy, 2003). These relationships foster a sense of psychological safety, encouraging creativity, learning, and taking risks without fear of embarrassment or guilt (Kahn, 1990). Another very crucial factor in this model is *meaning or purpose* of life people understand (Seligman, 2012). Seligman (2012) defined 'meaning as belonging to or serving something higher than oneself'. Having a purpose in life allows people to focus on what is truly essential in the face of major hardship or misfortune. Personal values drive a feeling of meaning, and those who report having a purpose in life live longer, are more satisfied with their lives, and have fewer health issues (Kashdan et al., 2009). Seligman (2012) stated that every employee in an organisation is fascinated by the *achievements or accomplishments* in their work or field. Perseverance and a strong desire to achieve goals are key components of accomplishment (Seligman, 2012). However, thriving and well-being occur when achievement is linked to trying for things with internal desire or working for something just for the purpose of pursuit and progress (Quinn, 2018).

HR Policies That Foster Circular Happiness

As per Fredrickson (2001), positive emotions promote new, diverse, and experimental ideas and behaviours as well as increase awareness. This expanded behavioural repertoire develops resources and skills over time. In the present era, organisational prosperity is linked to workforce involvement and well-being (Harter et al., 2013). The role of HR has extended from administrative support to inculcating happiness and prosperity at the workplace (Harter et al., 2002). Stimulating happiness is not just a one-day task but an ongoing augmentation by designing policies which create positive feedback loops.

HR policies designed for fostering circular happiness mainly focus on self-reinforcing well-being and sustainability (Achor, 2010). Autonomy, recognition, inclusion and growth are the main characteristics of such policies which further lead to lower turnover, high work engagement and increased performance at workplace through positive emotional and behavioural responses (Achor, 2010; Fredrickson, 2001). Most of the research stated employee well-being as a crucial factor behind a happy workplace. As per the World Health Organization (2006), it is defined as 'a state in which individual can realise their own abilities, cope with the normal stresses of life, work productively and fruitfully, and contribute to their community'. It promotes job satisfaction (Gallup, 2022), good social relationships (Seppälä & Cameron, 2015), positive organisation culture

(Seligman, 2011), high employee engagement (Harter et al., 2003), improved physical and mental condition (WHO, 2020). As per Diener et al. (2004) constructive *employee engagement programmes* can help in increasing employee well-being at workplace. Such programmes can include initiatives for improving the physical and mental health of employees, enhancing inclusion and connectedness, improving work-life balance. Attridge (2009) discusses the importance of employee assistance programmes (EPA) for eliminating numerous problems at workplace. EPA is a work-site-based programme intended to help companies deal with productivity issues and resolve personal issues that may impact job performance, such as health, financial, legal, emotional, marital, stress, or other personal issues (Employee Assistance Professionals Association, 2003). It mainly supports employee gaining in mental health well-being (Trice & Schonbrunn, 2003).

Contemporary companies are also opting for free health check-up camps, stress reduction workshops and gym membership reimbursement programmes to enhance physical well-being among employees (Attridge, 2009). As per Hill et al. (2008), a good work-life balance among employees also leads to happiness at the workplace. In this context *work life balance programmes* like flexible work arrangement (Hill et al., 2001), hybrid and remote work policies (Bloom et al., 2015), elder and child care facilities (Kossek, 1998), time-off and leave policy, boundary management training (Clark, 2000), and focus time policies (Newport, 2016). Such policies reduce the burnout and bring autonomy among employees further leading to motivation and happiness at the workplace. Return-to-work transition programmes have also been introduced by HR to make employees comfortable after an illness or maternity leave (Allen, 2001). Research has also demonstrated that there is a positive relationship between performance and feedback. More transparent feedback leads to high employee performance by further leading to motivation and happiness (Schön, 1983). Robust and transparent *feedback policies* lead to trust building and high accountability among employees. In this context, Gallup (2023) discusses employee listening strategies defined as 'dynamic strategy that requires responding meaningfully to what employees say to build trust and engagement'. In this strategy, the feedback from employees is collected by using various methods like engagement surveys, pulse surveys, suggestion boxes, and feedback sessions with a visible action plan to make improvements. Other methods include inserting feedback into objectives and key results (OKRs) areas and 1:1s, which means space for upward and downward feedback (Doerr, 2018), 'radical condor training (training managers to care personally and challenge directly) (Scott, 2017). Diener et al. (2010) discuss anonymous survey and feedback tools like Glint, Office Vibe, and Tiny Pulse, where employees can raise their concerns and share their feedback safely.

Gallup (2022) stated that 'Employee who feel cared for are 3x more likely to be engaged in work'. Employee engagement is positively related to job satisfaction. Therefore, it is a must for the HR department to create and implement sound *job satisfaction enhancement polici*es at the workplace. Kelly (2023) suggests various policies in this context which can foster job satisfaction and employee engagement at the workplace. Satisfying a diverse workforce is a major challenge faced by HR department nowadays; therefore, diversity, equity, and inclusion (DEI) policies are gaining importance. It includes:

- Inclusive hiring: ensures that job aspirants from diverse backgrounds with different identities are recruited and fairly supported.
- Employee resource groups (ERGs): interest groups which support employees by creating a diverse and inclusive workplace by further linking it with organisational goals (Smith & Johnson, 2020).
- Competitive compensation and other benefits: policy of providing compensation and advantages that match or exceed what competitors in the same industry are offering (Worldatwork, 2023).

Other policies include a sound recognition and appreciation system, transparent performance management policies, internal mobility and job enrichment (Hackman & Oldham, 1976).

Psychological Safety and Employee Trust

Psychological safety and trust are considered to be essential elements of organisational health (Edmondson, 1999). They foster work cultures where staff members are valued, empowered, and eager to participate completely, which improves output, creativity, retention, and moral character (CIPD, 2020). Edmondson (1999) defined psychological safety as 'a shared belief that the team is safe for interpersonal risk-taking'. It is a situation when an employee can freely talk, share their opinions and ideas without fearing about mortification. On the other hand, trust is defined as 'confidence that one will find what is desired from another rather than what is feared' (Deutsch, 1973, p. 148). Dirks and Ferrin (2001) stated that there is a positive relation between trust and various factors which boost happiness at the workplace, like organisational citizenship behaviour, job satisfaction and cooperation. Trust is categorised as cognitive (reliability and competency) and affective (interpersonal relationships and emotional bonds) (McAllister, 1995).

Although psychological safety and trust are related, they have distinct meanings and should not be confused (Edmondson & Lei, 2014). Trust is an individual's readiness to open up to others and give them the benefit of the doubt (McAllister, 1995). Psychological safety refers to an individual's trust in others to give them the benefit of the doubt when taking risks. Trust and psychological safety are linked with various commendatory results (Edmondson, 1999). These factors include team behaviour, workplace environment, employee attitudes, and overall performance (Edmondson, 1999). Psychological security and trust are inextricably linked in organisational and team dynamics. Trust is a key ingredient that allows psychological safety to grow and flourish. Mayer et al. (1995) stated that trust reduces *defencelessness at workplace*. It means that when people trust their team leaders or team members, they freely ask questions, admit mistakes, and give suggestions and feel more psychologically safe. McAllister (1995) stated that trust plays a vital role in enhancing *emotional security*. Trust built through mutual care and strong emotional bonds increases emotional security leading to more open and honest communication at the workplace (McAllister, 1995). Trust plays an important role at the time of *organisational change* when people feel psychologically unsafe. In an unpredictable environment, faith in leadership and the organisation's chosen course is crucial for successful transformative projects (Lines, 2005). Change may make individuals feel insecure (Lines, 2005). Individuals may make more mistakes and develop gaps in their abilities and knowledge (Dunning & Kruger, 1999). In a setting that promotes open communication, individuals may express their confusion and seek clarification (Mayer et al., 1995). Interpersonal connections also play a vital role in increasing psychological safety. In this context, trust is an important ingredient which helps in building *strong interpersonal connections* at the workplace (Mayer et al., 1995). In virtual or short-term teams, trust is crucial due to weak human relationships.

Building trust should be a special priority when forming virtual or hybrid teams. Trust and psychological safety are crucial in areas where *human mistakes* may have serious effects, such as aviation and healthcare, where checks and measures are critical to safety (Edmondson, 1999). In high-stakes workplaces, it's crucial for employees to speak out, disclose errors, and seek assistance to rapidly identify and resolve issues (Edmondson, 2004). Building trust and gaining psychological safety is not a one-day task; rather, organisations are following different strategies for building trust and making the workplace psychologically safe for employees. Some of the crucial strategies are discussed below.

Promoting Self-awareness

To develop psychological safety in the workplace, organisations must increase their team's self-awareness (Goleman, 1995). When leaders understand how they tend to think and behave, they may identify biases that may be influencing their team members' desire to offer their opinions (Eurich, 2017). Self-awareness also allows a leader to learn how they typically respond to changes or problems. With this information, they may modify their emotional reactions and learn to respond in a way that encourages open debate (Boyatzis & McKee, 2005).

Empathy and Ego Lessness

Empathy, self-awareness, direct and courteous feedback, and effective communication are some of the elements to maintaining employee confidence, comfort, and safety (Goleman, 1995). Avoid passive-aggressive and manipulative tactics. A leader should be authentic and genuine, not egoistic (Avolio & Gardner, 2005).

Handling Hurdles with Curious Perspective – No Blame

Approach troublesome conduct with curiosity rather than criticism. Whether it's a performance issue or anything else, it's important to approach the situation collaboratively and neutrally, and work together to find solutions (Reason, 2000). This strategy encourages teamwork to address problems, reducing disengagement and defensiveness that can result from a different approach (Edmondson, 1999).

Appreciation and Reward

Reward and recognition programmes are effective strategies for fostering trust in the workplace (Dirks & Ferrin, 2002). When employees feel appreciated and acknowledged, they are more inclined to trust their leaders, teammates, and the firm as a whole. This trust-building makes employees more psychologically safe (Eisenberger et al., 2002).

Trustworthy Leader – Yes, I Am Here

Leaders who are regarded to be trustworthy, exhibiting competence, honesty, and generosity, foster an environment conducive to psychological safety (Mayer et al., 1995). As rightly said by Deter and Burris (2007), 'Leader behaviour that fosters trust, such as transparency and fairness, significantly enhances psychological safety'.

Encouraging Team Culture, Not Talent

The greatest method to establish psychological safety is to foster a culture of teamwork rather than individual brilliance. Team culture means where one can trust their colleagues, share their weaknesses and not feel humiliated or neglected (Coyle, 2018).

Diversity and Inclusion for a Sustainable Workplace

Understanding Diversity and Inclusion in the Workplace

Workforce diversity management and inclusion may benefit the organisation in numerous capacities, including creativity, staff engagement, and organisational success; they can be crucial for ensuring sustainable growth.

It explores the quickly growing significance of workplace diversity in taking into account globalisation and changing worker populations. It underscores that diversity is so much about acknowledging that every individual has unique characteristics rather than merely contrasting different group attributes. Race, age, sex, and even less traditional factors such as gender identity and disadvantaged status are all encompassed in this view. Diversity also has to be considered in terms of regional, linguistic, and cultural origins, since these contribute to the complexity of an environment at work (Gupta, 2019).

There is strong impact of workplace inclusion and diversity on productivity and creativity of workers. It establishes the context by proposing that in modern organisations, diverse groups encourage creative thinking and a more extensive method of problem-solving. Employee engagement, creativity, and overall productivity are usually greater in organisations with official diversity and inclusion policies. Moreover, it suggests that a diverse workforce would have fewer potential benefits if internal conflicts and communication problems brought about by diversity are not met with equally inclusive policies (Suparyanto et al., 2025).

As shown in Fig. 3.1, it also presents an important relationship between a wider spectrum of organisational sustainability and increased employee engagement generated by diversity and inclusion initiatives. By focusing light on research and examples where increased engagement enhances retention, productivity, and the general well-being of the business, we offer an in-depth awareness of the long-term effects on long-term success (Mudasar, 2024).

Developing an inclusive workplace involves more than just employing a diverse team. The intention is to ensure that all voices are heard, recognised, and valued by integrating practices and establishing frameworks. ERGs are one of the main

Fig. 3.1. Framework of Sustainable Workplace. *Source*: Authors' creation.

forces for inclusion. ERGs are viewed to be essential venues which foster community, assist staff development, and offer secure settings for people with comparable experiences or histories to interact (Mudasar, 2024).

The Role of D&I in Organisational Sustainability

While many perspectives and experiences are taken into account when developing strategies, inclusive workplaces encourage balanced decision-making. Generating better decisions often leads to more effective procedures, risk mitigation, and innovative solutions to social and environmental issues – all of which are essential for sustainability initiatives. Organisations gain the confidence of stakeholders by promoting inclusive practices and diverse leadership, which could increase community involvement and boost their reputation. The demands of a global consumer base may be better understood by a diversified workforce, which can result in sustainable product developments that can meet both environmental and economic objectives.

Although diversity represents the makeup and proportion of the workforce and inclusion reflects the calibre and character of interactions and connections within the workforce, D&I are frequently seen as complementary and interdependent aspects of corporate culture and environment. However, as diversity does not always equate to inclusion and inclusion does not always require diversity, D&I are neither transferable nor synonymous. A business may, for example, have a workforce that is varied in terms of demographics, but it may not cultivate a welcoming atmosphere that recognises and capitalises on the many viewpoints and achievements of its workers (Shaha & Bhadauria, 2023).

Diversity-related factors must be subject to consideration. Diversity is regarded and utilised as an essential aspect of the company, irrespective of the goal – to be a respected employer, provide quality services and products to clients, or preserve a competitive edge. The primary objective of the study is to increase employee performance by enforcing diversity-based, healthy workplace concepts that make social responsibility, leadership, motivation, and creativity more effective. The significance of diversity in companies has grown throughout time. Workforce diversity is a strategy that uses diversity and inclusion initiatives to include and promote diverse people in all roles within organisations (Croitoru et al., 2022).

Role of Leadership in Fostering Diversity and Inclusive Work Environments

The culture of the company is determined and sustained in large part by its leaders. The whole staff is influenced by their dedication to diversity and inclusion. Leaders foster an atmosphere where everyone is acknowledged and supported when they actively encourage appreciation, equity, and cooperation. A proficient leader discusses the company's diversity goals and why they are crucial to fostering innovation and financial success in addition to social responsibility. By eliminating myths about fairness and equal opportunity, open and honest communication aids in overcoming opposition to diversity initiatives (Agrawal et al., 2024).

Leaders who promote open communication, respect, and mutual trust demonstrate inclusive conduct. By fostering an atmosphere where employees feel appreciated for their distinct contributions, they assist in overcoming gaps between varied team members. Since it impacts how members of a group are seen and appreciated, leadership is essential to managing diversity and creating an inclusive culture in businesses. Accordingly, when managers develop positive working connections with their employees, they create an example that encourages equality and justice (Nishii & Mayer, 2009).

Inclusion is attained when both of these variables are balanced in the workplace, enabling people to blend in with the group while being acknowledged for their unique characteristics. The ideal scenario is one in which workers feel like they belong and have the freedom to be who they are (Shore et al., 2011).

Engaging in educational initiatives that improve inclusive leadership and cultural competency is essential to effective leadership. Employees are better able to appreciate and value other viewpoints thanks to initiatives like cross-cultural communication workshops and unconscious bias training. The concept that ongoing growth and instruction are essential to succeeding in an international environment is reinforced by leaders who support these programmes and even take part in them (Apelehin et al., 2025).

Diversity, Inclusion, and Global Workplace Trends

Organisations intending to succeed worldwide must comprehend and adjust to cultural differences as the global workforce grows to be more diverse. Corporations that promote diversity and inclusion (D&I) in response to these major shifts are more likely to succeed and draw in top talent from all over the world. Inclusive firms have the opportunity to satisfy the needs of a global client base by fostering innovative concepts and improving customer connections (Chinthala, 2021).

From uniformity to a diverse range of cultures and ethnicities, the contemporary global workforce has undergone substantial change. The study demonstrates how global workplace diversity has grown due to migration, technology, and the convenience of travel. Organisations are increasingly encouraged to view diversity as an advantage provided by the global commercial environment. Adopting diversity increases market reach and productivity, whether by improving cultural competency or customising goods and services according to a range of consumer demands (Maroof & Kapate, 2023).

Globally, diversity and inclusion assist companies in overcoming obstacles, including communication challenges and cultural misconceptions. Organisations may reduce hassle and improve collaboration among global teams by creating an inclusive atmosphere. A work environment that is inclusive and varied fosters employee innovation and engagement. Organisations could encourage creativity and better respond to the needs of the global market by appreciating diverse viewpoints (Kelechi Enyinna Ugwu, 2023).

Recognition, Rewards, and Employee Motivation

The Interplay of Recognition, Rewards, and Motivation

Reward and recognition are two fundamentally separate human forms of motivation. Formally recognising or appreciating a conduct or accomplishment is known as acknowledgement, and it frequently resonates with an individual's inner feeling of success and value (Hansen et al., 2002). Other than money incentives, employee recognition is an essential factor that enhances commitment, motivation, and general performance in businesses. As an integral part of good leadership practices meant to increase morale and productivity, acknowledgement is affordable yet has a significant impact when compared to monetary incentives (Luthans, 2000).

Several studies have shown the importance of reward and recognition programmes in improving employee motivation, with recognition being associated with increased motivation and even better performance at work. A good system of incentives should cover many topics, including opportunity for personal development, acknowledgement of efforts, and monetary compensation. When properly balanced within an organisation, these factors work together to provide productive job performance (Meena et al., 2019).

The key factors influencing employee motivation are rewards, awards, and recognition. A well-thought-out incentive system may significantly increase the organisation's efficacy and efficiency. For employers to satisfy the expectations of a more varied workforce, complicated systems for rewards have now become necessary, and businesses are becoming more aware that they need to concentrate on the entire pay package for workers. There are many varieties of methods to reward (motivate) workers, even when they work for pay or salaries (Akafo & Boateng, 2015).

Types of Recognition and Rewards

Through the use of incentives and acknowledgement, organisations may engage their workforce. Rewards have a significant role in employee engagement. Employee motivation and performance are profoundly affected by rewards and recognition. A system of rewards can assist in improving work satisfaction. Giving employees incentives, offerings, bonuses, and awards is crucial for reaching organisational goals and maintaining satisfaction among staff members. An organisation's personnel are the key to its success. Rewards and recognition are linked to employee engagement. Incentives are useful instruments for raising worker performance (Baqir, 2020).

Programmes for incentives and recognition support preserve high levels of staff involvement and achievement in addition to enhancing individual self-esteem. It involves recognising staff members orally or casually, for example, by giving them gratitude or publicly recognising them in front of their colleagues (Akafo & Boateng, 2015).

To create psycho connections, recognition entails intrinsic incentives, such as verbal compliments and public recognition. Extrinsic motivation is the main emphasis of rewards, which provide material incentives such as bonuses for achieving numerical goals. For individuals to be effectively motivated and for commitment among organisations to be increased, both strategies should be balanced (Hansen et al., 2002).

Reward Systems and Organisational Performance

The study shows that worker performance, efficiency, and retention are positively correlated with reward programmes. Employee motivation may be substantially enhanced by a well-designed reward system, which will boost output and performance inside the company. In an increasingly competitive employment environment, incentive programmes are essential for keeping staff motivated. Organisations may guarantee that workers stay dedicated and motivated to accomplish company objectives by identifying and rewarding great performers (Francis et al., 2020).

A well-designed system of rewards for performance may greatly increase employee inspiration. Employees are more inclined to work better when they are aware that their accomplishments and efforts are valued. In order to improve job performance, this system may incorporate financial as well as non-financial benefits, such as promotions, incentives, and recognition.

Employees who get performance-related awards may feel more acknowledged and valued for their efforts, which can increase work satisfaction. Because workers are more inclined to remain with a company that values and rewards their efforts, this satisfaction can lower turnover rates (Hamukwaya, 2014).

References

Achor, S. (2010). *The happiness advantage: The seven principles of positive psychology that fuel success and performance at work*. Crown Business.

Agrawal, N., Kotikalapudi, K. B., Kumar, N., Das, D., Sahoo, P., & Pant, N. (2024). Managing diversity in the workplace: Challenges and best practices for inclusive leadership. *Educational Administration Theory and Practices*, *30*(5), 14415–14422. https://doi.org/10.53555/kuey.v30i5.6618

Akafo, V., & Boateng, P. A. (2015). Impact of reward and recognition on job satisfaction and motivation. *European Journal of Business and Management*, *7*(24), 112–124.

Allen, T. D. (2001). Family-supportive work environments: The role of organizational perceptions. *Journal of Vocational Behavior*, *58*(3), 414–435. https://doi.org/10.1006/jvbe.2000.1774

Apelehin, A. A., Imohiosen, C. E., Ajuluchukwu, P., Abutu, D. E., & Ann, C. (2025). Transforming organizational and educational cultures: Developing global leadership and building inclusive workplaces through innovative HR and educational practices. *World*, 1(4).

Armstrong, M., & Taylor, S. (2020). *Armstrong's handbook of human resource management practice (15th ed.)*. Kogan Page.

Ashby, F. G., Isen, A. M., & Turken, U. (1999). A neuropsychological theory of positive affect and its influence on cognition. *Psychological Review*, *106*(3), 529–550.

Attridge, M. (2009). Measuring and managing employee work engagement: A review of the research and business literature. *Journal of Workplace Behavioral Health*, *24*(4), 383–398. https://doi.org/10.1080/15555240903188398

Avolio, B. J., & Gardner, W. L. (2005). Authentic leadership development: Getting to the root of positive forms of leadership. *The Leadership Quarterly*, *16*(3), 315–338. https://doi.org/10.1016/j.leaqua.2005.03.001

Baqir, M. (2020). Impact of reward and recognition, supervisor support on employee engagement. *American International Journal of Business and Management Studies*, *2*(3), 8–21. https://doi.org/10.46545/aijbms.v2i3.256

Bloom, N., Liang, J., Roberts, J., & Ying, Z. J. (2015). Does working from home work? Evidence from a Chinese experiment. *Quarterly Journal of Economics*, *130*(1), 165–218. https://doi.org/10.1093/qje/qju032

Bonaiuto, M., Mao, Y., Roberts, S., Psalti, A., Ariccio, S., Ganucci Cancellieri, U., & Csikszentmihalyi, M. (2016). Optimal experience and personal growth: Flow and the consolidation of place identity. *Frontiers in Psychology*, *7*, 1654. https://doi.org/10.3389/fpsyg.2016.01654

Boyatzis, R. E., & McKee, A. (2005). *Resonant leadership*. Harvard Business Press.

Chinthala, L. K. (2021). Diversity and inclusion: The business case for building more equitable organizations. *Journal of Management and Science*, *11*(4), 91–93.

CIPD. (2020). *Trust and psychological safety 2020*. Chartered Institute of Personnel.

Clark, S. C. (2000). Work/family border theory: A new theory of work/family balance. *Human Relations*, *53*(6), 747–770. https://doi.org/10.1177/0018726700536001

Couture, M., Desrosiers, J., & Leclerc, G. (2007). Self-actualization and poststroke rehabilitation. *International Journal of Rehabilitation Research*, *30*(2), 111–117. https://doi.org/10.1097/mrr.0b013e32813a2ea5

Coyle, D. (2018). *The culture code: The secrets of highly successful groups*. Bantam Books.

Croitoru, G., Florea, N. V., Ionescu, C. A., Robescu, V. O., Paschia, L., Uzlau, M. C., & Manea, M. D. (2022). Diversity in the workplace for sustainable company development. *Sustainability*, *14*(11), 6728. https://doi.org/10.3390/su14116728

Csikszentmihalyi, M. (2002). *Flow: The classic work on how to achieve happiness*. Rider Books.

De Neve, J.-E., Ward, G., & Bellet, C. (2019). *Does employee happiness have an impact on productivity? Saïd Business School WP 2019-13*. University of Oxford.

Deter, J. R., & Burris, E. R. (2007). Leadership behavior and employee voice: Is the door really open? *Academy of Management Journal*, *50*(4), 869–884. https://doi.org/10.5465/amj.2007.26279183

Deutsch, M. (1973). *The resolution of conflict: Constructive and destructive processes*. Yale University Press.

Diener, E. (2000). Subjective well-being: The science of happiness and a proposal for a national index. *American Psychologist*, *55*(1), 34–43.

Diener, E., & Seligman, M. E. P. (2004). Beyond money: Toward an economy of well-being. *Psychological Science in the Public Interest*, *5*(1), 1–31.

Diener, E., Napa Scollon, C., & Lucas, R. E. (2009). The evolving concept of subjective well-being: The multifaceted nature of happiness. In P. T. Costa & I. C. Siegler (Eds.), *Assessing well-being: The collected works of Ed Diener* (pp. 67–100). Springer Netherlands.

Diener, E., Wirtz, D., Tov, W., Kim-Prieto, C., Choi, D., Oishi, S., & Biswas-Diener, R. (2010). New well-being measures: Short scales to assess flourishing and positive and negative feelings. *Social Indicators Research*, *97*(2), 143–156.

Dirks, K. T., & Ferrin, D. L. (2001). The role of trust in organizational settings. *Organization Science*, *12*(4), 450–467. https://doi.org/10.1287/orsc.12.4.450.10640

Dirks, K. T., & Ferrin, D. L. (2002). Trust in leadership: Meta-analytic findings and implications for research and practice. *Journal of Applied Psychology*, *87*(4), 611–628. https://doi.org/10.1037/0021-9010.87.4.611

Doerr, J. (2018). *Measure what matters: How Google, Bono, and the Gates Foundation rock the world with OKRs*. Portfolio/Penguin.

Dunning, D., & Kruger, J. (1999). Unskilled and unaware of it: How difficulties in recognizing one's own incompetence lead to inflated self-assessments. *Journal of Personality and Social Psychology*, *77*(6), 1121–1134. https://doi.org/10.1037/0022-3514.77.6.1121

Dutton, J. E., & Heaphy, E. D. (2003). The power of high-quality connections at work. In K. S. Cameron, J. E. Dutton, & R. E. Quinn (Eds.), *Positive organizational scholarship* (pp. 263–278). Berrett-Koehler.

Edmondson, A. (1999). Psychological safety and learning behavior in work teams. *Administrative Science Quarterly*, *44*(2), 350–383. https://doi.org/10.2307/2666999

Edmondson, A. C. (2004). Learning from failure is easier said than done: Group and organizational influences on the detection and correction of human error. *Journal of Applied Behavioral Science*, *40*(1), 66–90. https://doi.org/10.1177/0021886304263849

Edmondson, A. C., & Lei, Z. (2014). Psychological safety: The history, renaissance, and future of an interpersonal construct. *Annual Review of Organizational Psychology and Organizational Behavior*, *1*(1), 23–43. https://doi.org/10.1146/annurev-orgpsych-031413-091305

Eisenberger, R., Stinglhamber, F., Vandenberghe, C., Sucharski, I. L., & Rhoades, L. (2002). Perceived supervisor support: Contributions to perceived organizational support and employee retention. *Journal of Applied Psychology*, *87*(3), 565–573. https://doi.org/10.1037/0021-9010.87.3.565

Employee Assistance Professionals Association. (2003). *Workplace outcomes of the employee assistance program*. Employee Assistance Professionals Association.

Eurich, T. (2017). *Insight: Why we're not as self-aware as we think, and how seeing ourselves clearly helps us succeed at work and in life*. Crown Publishing.

Fereidouni, H. G., Najdi, Y., & Ekhtiari Amiri, R. (2013). Do governance factors matter for happiness in the MENA region? *International Journal of Social Economics*, *40*(12), 1028–1040.

Francis, F., Zirra, C. T. O., & Charles J., M. I. (2020). Reward system as a strategy to enhance employees performance in an organization. *Archives of Business Research*, *8*(6), 156–164. https://doi.org/10.14738/abr.86.8403

Fredrickson, B. L. (2001). The role of positive emotions in positive psychology: The broaden-and-build theory of positive emotions. *American Psychologist*, *56*(3), 218–226. https://doi.org/10.1037/0003-066X.56.3.218

Gallup. (2022). State of the global workplace: 2022 report. Gallup. https://www.gallup.com/workplace/349484/state-of-the-global-workplace.aspx.

Gallup. (2023). *U.S. employee engagement needs a rebound in 2023*. Gallup. https://www.gallup.com/workplace/468233/employee-engagement-needs-rebound-2023.aspx

Gallup, Inc. (2024, June 11). *State of the global workplace: 2024 report* (Press release). Gallup. https://www.gallup.com/workplace/645758/state-of-the-global-workplace-2024-press-release.aspx.

Goleman, D. (1995). *Emotional intelligence*. Bantam Books.

Gupta, P. (2019). Workforce diversity management: Key to inclusive sustainability. *International Journal of Research in Engineering, Science and Management*, *2*(11), 2581–5792.

Hackman, J. R., & Oldham, G. R. (1976). Motivation through the design of work: Test of a theory. *Organizational Behavior and Human Performance*, *16*(2), 250–279. https://doi.org/10.1016/0030-5073(76)90016-7

Hamukwaya, S. I., & Yazdanifard, R. (2014). How a proper performance related reward system can contribute to work performance excellence. *Open Journal of Business and Management*, *2*(3), 189–194.

Hansen, F., Smith, M., & Hansen, R. B. (2002). Rewards and recognition in employee motivation. *Compensation & Benefits Review*, *34*(5), 64–72. https://doi.org/10 1177/0886368702034005010

Harter, J. K., Schmidt, F. L., & Hayes, T. L. (2002). Business-unit-level relationship between employee satisfaction, employee engagement, and business outcomes: A meta-analysis. *Journal of Applied Psychology*, *87*(2), 268–279.

Harter, J. K., Schmidt, F. L., & Keyes, C. L. M. (2003). Well-being in the workplace and its relationship to business outcomes: A review of the Gallup studies. In C. L. M. Keyes & J. Haidt (Eds.), *Flourishing: Positive psychology and the life well-lived* (pp. 205–224). American Psychological Association.

Harter, J. K., Schmidt, F. L., Agrawal, S., & Plowman, S. K. (2013). *The relationship between engagement at work and organizational outcomes: 2012 Q12 meta-analysis*. Gallup, Inc.

Hill, E. J., Erickson, J. J., Holmes, E. K., & Ferris, M. (2008). Workplace flexibility, work hours, and work-life conflict: Finding an extra day or two. *Journal of Family Psychology*, *22*(3), 279–289. https://doi.org/10.1037/0893-3200.22.3.279

Hill, E. J., Hawkins, A. J., Ferris, M., & Weitzman, M. (2001). Finding an extra day a week: The positive influence of perceived job flexibility on work and family life balance. *Family Relations*, *50*(1), 49–58. https://doi.org/10.1111/j.1741-3729.2001.00049.x

Kahn, W. A. (1990). Psychological conditions of personal engagement and disengagement at work. *Academy of Management Journal*, *33*(4), 692–724. https://doi.org/10.2307/256287

Kashdan, T. B., Mishra, A., Breen, W. E., & Froh, J. J. (2009). Gender differences in gratitude: Examining appraisals, narratives, the willingness to express emotions and changes in psychological needs. *Journal of Personality*, *77*(3), 691–730. https://doi.org/10.1111/j.1467-6494.2009.00562.x

Kelechi Enyinna Ugwu. (2023). Trends and strategies for diversity in the global inclusive workplace. *China-USA Business Review*, *22*(3), 126–135. https://doi.org/10.17265/1537-1514/2023.03.005

Kelly, J. (2023, December 9). *Employee happiness is eroding — here's how managers can help turn it around*. Forbes.

Kossek, E. E. (1998). Work and family research: A multidisciplinary review. In C. L. Cooper & D. M. Rousseau (Eds.), *Trends in organizational behavior* (Vol. 5, pp. 65–88). John Wiley & Sons.

Lines, R. (2005). The structure and function of attitudes toward organizational change. *Human Resource Development Review*, *4*(1), 8–32. https://doi.org/10.1177/1534484304273818

Luthans, K. (2000). Recognition: A powerful, but often overlooked, leadership tool to improve employee performance. *Journal of Leadership Studies*, *7*(1), 31–39. https://doi.org/10.1177/107179190000700104

Maroof, M. A., & Kapate, S. (2023). Global trends in diversity, equality and inclusivity (DEI). *Korea Review of International Studies*, *16*(47), 241–249.

Mayer, R. C., Davis, J. H., & Schoorman, F. D. (1995). An integrative model of organizational trust. *Academy of Management Review*, *20*(3), 709–734. https://doi.org/10.5465/amr.1995.9508080335

McAllister, D. J. (1995). Affect- and cognition-based trust as foundations for interpersonal cooperation in organizations. *Academy of Management Journal*, *38*(1), 24–59.

Meena, S., Girija, T., & Visagamoorthi, D. (2019). Influence of rewards and recognition on employees' motivation and job performance: Path analysis approach. *Indian Journal of Science and Technology*, *12*(12), 1–5.

Monaghan, S., Tippmann, E., & Coviello, N. (2020). Born digitals: Thoughts on their internationalization and a research agenda. *Journal of International Business Studies*, *51*(1), 11–22.

Mudasar, M. (2024). Diversity and inclusion: The key to sustainable organizational success. Available at SSRN 4747419.

Newport, C. (2016). *Deep work: Rules for focused success in a distracted world*. Grand Central Publishing.

Nishii, L. H., & Mayer, D. M. (2009). Do inclusive leaders help to reduce turnover in diverse groups? The moderating role of leader–member exchange in the diversity to turnover relationship. *Journal of Applied Psychology*, *94*(6), 1412–1426. https://doi.org/10.1037/a0017190

Oswald, A. J., Proto, E., & Sgroi, D. (2015). Happiness and productivity. *Journal of Labor Economics*, *33*(4), 789–822. https://doi.org/10.1086/681096

Porter, M. E., & Kramer, M. R. (2011). Creating shared value. *Harvard Business Review*, *89*(1/2), 62–77.

Psychology Today. (2019). *The science of happiness at work*. https://www.psychologytoday.com/us/blog/the-right-mindset/201902/the-science-happiness-work

Quick, J. C., & Quick, J. D. (2004). *Healthy, happy, productive work: A leadership challenge*. Organizational Dynamics.

Quinn, A. (2018, February 3). *Theory of well-being: Elements and interventions*. Good Therapy Blog. https://www.goodtherapy.org/blog/theory-of-well-being-elements-interventions-0203184

Reason, J. (2000). Human error: Models and management. *BMJ*, *320*(7237), 768–770. https://doi.org/10.1136/bmj.320.7237.768

Rego, A., & Cunha, M. P. (2008). Authentizotic climates and employee happiness: Pathways to individual performance? *Journal of Business Research*, *61*(7), 739–752.

Salis, S., & Williams, A. M. (2010). Knowledge sharing through face-to-face communication and labour productivity: Evidence from British workplaces. *British Journal of Industrial Relations*, *48*(2), 436–459.

Schön, D. A. (1983). *The reflective practitioner: How professionals think in action*. Basic Books.

Scott, K. (2017). *Radical Candor: Be a kick-ass boss without losing your humanity*. St. Martin's Press.

Seligman, M. E. P. (2011). *Flourish: A visionary new understanding of happiness and well-being*. Free Press.

Seligman, M. E. (2012). *Flourish: A visionary new understanding of happiness and well-being*. Atria Paperback.

Seligman, M. E. P., & Csikszentmihalyi, M. (2000a). Positive psychology: An introduction. *American Psychologist*, *55*(1), 5–14. https://doi.org/10.1037/0003-066X.55.1.5

Seligman, M. E. P., & Csikszentmihalyi, M. (2000b). *Positive psychology – Definition and scope. Neurochemical mechanism works a lot in this context*. Retrieved May 24, 2025, from https://www.researchgate.net/publication/377701942_Positive_Psychology_-_definition_and_scope.

Seppälä, E., & Cameron, K. (2015). *Proof that positive work cultures are more productive*. Harvard Business Review. https://hbr.org/2015/12/proof-that-positive-work-cultures-are-more-productive

Shaha, R., & Bhadauria, P. (2023). Diversity, inclusion, and organizational sustainability: Exploring HR practices' impact on innovation and adaptability through secondary research. In *Proceedings of the 11th International Conference on HR for Organizational Sustainability*. ISBN 978-93-83302-65-9.

Shore, L. M., Randel, A. E., Chung, B. G., Dean, M. A., Holcombe Ehrhart, K., & Singh, G. (2011). Inclusion and diversity in work groups: A review and model for future research. *Journal of Management*, *37*(4), 1262–1289. https://doi.org/10.1177/0149206310385943

Smith, G., & Johnson, D. (2020). Behavioral theories of leadership: An overview. *Journal of Leadership Studies*, *14*, 40–58.

Smith, J. A., & Kumar, R. (2025). Strategic agility in post-pandemic organizations: A review. *Management Review Quarterly*, *75*(1), 45–62.

Society for Human Resource Management. (2020). *Employee benefits survey 2020: Employer-provided benefits and workplace well-being [Press release]*. SHRM.

Spurk, D., & Straub, C. (2020). Flexible employment relationships and careers in times of the COVID-19 pandemic. *Journal of Vocational Behavior, 119*, 103435.

Suparyanto, T., Santosa, T. A., Fauzi, R. U. A., Nungraha, A. R., Dewanto, D., & Tarmizi, R. (2025). Diversity and inclusion in the workplace: Assessing their effects on employee performance and innovation. *RIGGS: Journal of Artificial Intelligence and Digital Business, 4*(1), 38–42. https://doi.org/10.31004/riggs.v4i1.370

Sutton, J. (2016, July 8). *Positive psychology in the workplace: 16 practical tips*. PositivePsychology.com. https://positivepsychology.com/positive-psychology-workplace-labor-of-love/

Trice, H. M., & Schonbrunn, M. (2003). A history of employee assistance programs in the United States. In M. Arthur (Ed.), *Employee assistance programs: Wellness/enhancement programming* (3rd ed., pp. 33–52). Wadsworth/Thomson Learning.

Wang, H., Sui, Y., Luthans, F., Wang, D., & Wu, Y. (2018). Impact of authentic leadership on performance: The mediating role of employees' psychological capital and the moderating role of performance pressure. *Journal of Business Research, 92*, 160–168.

World Health Organization. (2006). *The world health report 2006: Working together for health*. World Health Organization.

World Health Organization. (2022, June 16). *Promoting and protecting mental health at work: Addressing toxic work environments*. https://www.who.int/news-room/feature-stories/detail/promoting-and-protecting-mental-health-at-work--addressing-toxic-work-environments

WorldatWork. (2023). *Drive resilience and productivity with total rewards in 2023*. WorldatWork.

Wu, T. (2022). Digital project management: Rapid changes define new working environments. *Journal of Business Strategy, 43*(5), 323–331.

Young, S. N. (2007). How to increase serotonin in the human brain without drugs. *Journal of Psychiatry & Neuroscience, 32*(6), 394–399.

Yuan, J. (2024). Enhancing employee job satisfaction through organizational climate and employee happiness at work: A mediated–moderated model. *BMC Psychology, 12*(1), 744. https://doi.org/10.1186/s40359-024-02269-5

Chapter 4

Purpose-driven Business Growth Through Sustainable Practices: Pathways to Employee-centric Circular Happiness and Organisational Competitive Advantage

Sumesh S. Dadwal[a], Pawan Kumar[b], Vipin Nadda[c], Imad Yasir Nawaz[d] and Gordon Bowen[e]

[a]London South Bank University, UK
[b]Lovely Professional University, India
[c]University of Sunderland in London, UK
[d]Northumbria University, UK
[e]Anglia Ruskin University, UK

Abstract

This chapter explores the role of embedding sustainable practices, employee-centric circular happiness, and purpose-driven business models (PDBMs) for attaining sustainable competitive advantage. The chapter is strongly underpinned by a range of theories, such as the triple bottom line (TBL), stakeholder theory, resource-based theory (RBT), innovation theories, Porter, and Kramer's shared value model (PK-SVM), biophilic design, theories of organisational citizenship and theories of sustainability. The aim is to enhance employee engagement, employee happiness and purpose-driven, sustainable, competitive advantage of the organisation. The chapter also highlights the key principles of circular happiness economy, sustainability, and their role in the purpose-driven growth of the business.

Keywords: Sustainable practice; competitive advantage; triple bottom line; green spaces; circular happiness; green spaces; purpose-driven business models; sustainability; circular economy

Circular Happiness: Building Sustainable Workplaces for the Next Generation, 59–91

Published under exclusive licence by Emerald Publishing Limited
doi:10.1108/978-1-80592-907-920261004

Introduction

All organisations continuously strive to drive business growth. Business growth itself is a multidimensional concept and can include qualitative as well as quantitative indicators of growth. Some studies have used the balanced scorecard, or more recently sustainable balanced scorecard, to represent business growth. The balanced scorecard considers four-dimensional growth, addressing the needs of at least four key stakeholders: employees (i.e. innovation & learning), investors (i.e. financial), organisation (i.e. internal operations), and customers (i.e. customer satisfaction) (Kaplan, 2010; Kaplan & Norton, 1992; Kumar et al., 2023; Mearns & Håvold, 2003).

Performance prism scorecard argues for a five-dimensional approach such as: stakeholder satisfaction, stakeholder contributions, strategies, process, and capabilities for ensuring business growth (Neely & Adams, 2001). The spread of technology, big data, and the consciousness of various stakeholders has led organisations to reinvent their framework of business growth that meets the needs of a range of stakeholders. The surge of artificial intelligence (AI), information and communication technolgy (ICT), and other technologies has led firms to reinvent their business models and corresponding growth frameworks. There are several internal (leadership, cognition culture, employee skills, operational efficiency, technology culture, innovation, stakeholder, and sustainability practices) and external drivers (business environment, market amount, competition) that impact the growth of an organisation. Due to internal and external pressures, the organisations have been exploring the role of sustainability for business growth and competitive advantage. Kumar and Ramachandran (2021) have argued for the 4E framework, which includes: entrenching growth (i.e. internal process automation, improvements), empowering growth (i.e. employee skills augmentation), enterprising growth (i.e. process quality and environment impacts), and enriching growth (i.e. personal relevance) as main dimensions of business growth. The stakeholders' orientation and considering the needs of internal and external stakeholders have been found as key to organisational success. The employee perspective (enhancing their capabilities) is a significant contributor to the dynamic capabilities of the organisation (Chen, 2017; Teece, 2023). Human capital, culture, and skills have been at the foundations of the balanced scorecard (Kaplan, 2010). Happy and satisfied employees will be more engaged employees. The QUEST multidimensional pyramid model of performance measures success in terms of economic, social, and technical perspectives (Abran & Buglione, 2003).

The recent focus on sustainability has led to further development of the balanced scorecard by entailing elements of sustainability and systems thinking (Kumar et al., 2023). This led to the development of the sustainable balance scorecard (SBSC) (Figge et al., 2002; Mio et al., 2022), green-balanced scorecard (GrBSc) (Bhattacharya et al., 2014), and circular economy-based balanced scorecard (Martín-Gómez et al., 2024; Nazir & Capocchi, 2024). Recently, the research has expanded into the arena of the role of employee happiness and its positive impacts on the growth of business (Louwman, 2023). Research by Louwman (2023) illuminated the happiness framework of nine ways of blossoming health, autonomy, purpose, play, integrity, nature, empathy, simplicity, and smile (H.A.P.P.I.N.E.S.S.) (Louwman, 2023). Even national economies are adopting measurements of the happiness economy (e.g. well-being, work–life balance, governance, education, social relations, circular economy, environment, knowledge, skills and innovations, and time use) as indicators of national growth (Agrawal et al., 2025).

Some very recent studies have argued that by embedding sustainability, circular happiness, and purpose-driven growth culture, organisations can attain long-term sustainable competitive advantage and business growth (Louwman, 2023; Martín-Gómez et al., 2024; Nazir & Capocchi, 2024). Embedding sustainability practices into the core values and core status of the organisations has a significant effect on organisational culture, employee happiness, and overall organisational growth (Anand & Sundaram, 2025; Martínez-Falcó et al., 2023; Nazir & Capocchi, 2024).

This chapter is an attempt to develop a theoretical framework towards sustainable business growth through circular happiness and sustainable practices to attain competitive advantage and purpose-driven success. The arguments have been underpinned by using a range of theories and models related to sustainability, competitive advantages, purpose-driven success, sustainable organisation culture, eco-friendly green spaces, and culture and circular happiness.

Circular Happiness

Undertaking a systematic review from 2001 to 2020, Martínez-Falcó et al. (2023) found that happiness is linked to ethics, and both happiness and ethics are fundamental for the growth of businesses (Martínez-Falcó et al., 2023).

Circular Happiness: the philosophy of circular happiness describes that engaging in pro-social and positive behaviour, such as contributing towards community, a sense of helping others, sharing resources, acts of generosity, compassion and kindness, charity, etc., will create a self-reinforcing loop of enhanced personal well-being and sustainable happiness. People's well-being, quality of life and happiness are interconnected concepts, and each one of them has subjective meaning as well as objective measurements (Susnienė & Jurkauskas, 2009).

The principle of circular happiness is analogous to the principles of circular economy and sustainable systems.

In a study of 31 European countries from 2000 to 2020, it was found that countries with the highest happiness and circular economy belong to the same cluster, which implies a positive relationship between happiness and circular economy (Nademi & Khochiani, 2024).

The purpose of the circular economic system is to design systems that can regenerate and restore the social, economic, and environmental systems (or 3Ps: profit, planet, and people) to a base level (Susnienė & Jurkauskas, 2009). The circular economy as opposed to the linear economic model (i.e. input–output–dispose), promotes regenerated uses of resources (i.e. cycle of input–output–input), to enhance the end of life of products and remove harmful materials, eliminating wastes and regenerative product design and supply chain thus enhances sustainability (i.e. balances societal, environmental, and economic interests) (Nademi & Khochiani, 2024; Stahel, 2019).

On the same lines, circular happiness attempts to regenerate and restore people's emotional and psychological happiness and well-being. The philosophy of circular happiness believes that happiness requires a continuous flow of positive actions and emotions, which further dynamically enhances happiness. Circular happiness follows certain principles, such as engaging in the act of kindness and volunteerism, continuity reflecting on positive experiences for personal satisfaction, fostering pro-social behaviour in community connection, practising mindfulness, interconnectedness of parts with the whole, and living close to nature and environment (Atkinson et al., 2020). In line with self-determined theory, the engagement in pro-social behaviour and helping others aids a person to fulfil the needs of autonomy (sense of meaning), competence (sense of self-efficacy), and relatedness (sense of belonging) (Ryan & Deci, 2000).

The green spaces and eco-culture let a person embed sustainability into everyday life. The engagement in environmentally friendly acts decreases mental stress and improves happiness. A happy person will more likely show pro-social, pro-environmental, and pro-economic behaviour; this behaviour leads individuals to act on the circular economy, leading to sustainability and then more green spaces, which loop into more happiness and well-being (see Fig. 4.1).

Thus, a happy person becomes a contributor towards sustainability and circular economy and circular happiness. Happiness itself has its own loop; a metacognitive control of happiness leads to physical, psychological, and social happiness (Aknin et al., 2012; Watson, 2022). Internal happiness leads to external, and

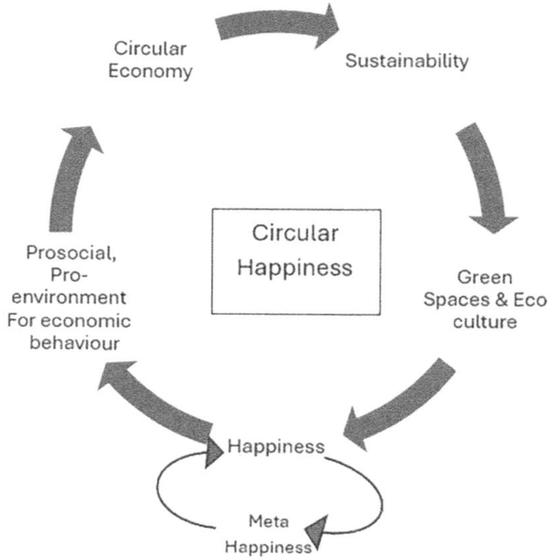

Fig. 4.1. Cycle of Circular Happiness.

vice versa. Three circles of happiness include you (how you think and feel about yourself), your relationship (your relationship with others), and meaningful life purpose (how you fulfil the purpose of your life) (Heslop, 2022). Meta-cognition and meta-emotions have a positive impact on perceived happiness (Saram, 2015; Shoaakazemi et al., 2013).

Mindfulness and happiness are related. Mindfulness is a concept, trait, disposition, state of being, process, and practice of being in the present moment, detached, accepting, keeping the mind-body connection and mind-body awareness (Khoury, 2023). Happiness can be viewed as multidimensional, a concept, a process, a state of being in flow, a trait and a disposition of acceptance, and a state of being in a positive emotional response that could be either eudaimonic happiness (i.e. sense of meaning and purpose of life) or hedonistic happiness (i.e. as a result of accumulation, achievements of external things and resources) (Delle Fave, 2021). Five dimensions namely internal positive emotions, engagement, relations with others, sense of accomplishment, and meaning of life, have a positive impact on happiness (Pandey & Jaiswal, 2017; Scheer & Jansen, 2018). Thus, meta awareness (i.e. internal awareness, knowledge about one's cognitive and emotional activities and regulating it) has a positive impact on happiness; thus, happiness can be seen as a loop of creating happiness and enjoying happiness (Schooler & Mauss, 2009).

A number of mechanisms are being created to promote circular happiness. For instance, Cardiff university, UK, had designed a card game, called 'circular families' ('Circular Happy Families' and 'Circular Loopy Families'), to promote behaviour change in citizens towards the production and consumption of practices of social economy, social housing, collaborative working, and engaging in a range of circular economy practices (Cardiff University, 2025). The game has a 52-card deck arranged in 13 'circular families' (of 4 members each), and winners need to aim at collecting membership cards of the same family to build a circular family. Each member of the family has to create a social innovation strategy to take some action on five urban sectors (housing, products, food, green infrastructure, and mobility) to effectively execute a circular economy in the city (Cardiff University, 2025). The results have shown promising outcomes of 'Circular Loopy Families' and 'Circular Happy Families' on the circular economy and promoting green spaces.

A meta-analysis of a number of previous studies has indicated that human strategies like sociability, exercise, gratitude, and exposure to nature improve happiness (Folk & Dunn, 2023). 'If you are happy and you know it, clap your hands' captures the meta-awareness and internal cycle of happiness (Schooler & Mauss, 2009). The other studies have also found that the circular economy promotes sharing, collaboration, and social cohesion among citizens, which boosts the happiness of the people because of a sense of belonging (Nademi & Khochiani, 2024).

Using European countries' panel data from 1990 to 1997, the researchers found that non-green spaces and pollution have negative impacts on people's happiness (Welsch, 2006). Others also have found that people's engagement in pro-environmental values and behaviours (e.g. recycling, volunteering, and greenery acts) promotes their mental well-being and happiness (Zawadzki et al., 2020; Zidanšek, 2007).

The shared and collective programming on values, beliefs, customs, norms, and shared assumptions of ways of doing things, etc., that determine people's behaviour at work is known as organisational culture (Junça Silva & Coelho, 2022; Markus & Kitayama, 1991). The green organisational culture is an organisation-wide shared green values, assumptions, and practices that determine their behaviours towards environmental friendliness and sustainability (Aggarwal & Agarwala, 2021). The green organisation culture needs organisational contexts and contents that reinforce values, beliefs, and norms related to green and eco-friendly culture.

An organisation's culture is determined by a number of external and internal factors. To embed a sustainable, circular happiness and eco-friendly culture at an organisation, the organisation requires contextual factors such as green spaces, environment-friendly designs, and policies and practices that reward eco-friendly cultural behaviours of the employees (Aggarwal & Agarwala, 2021).

Green Spaces, Eco-friendly Culture, and Sustainable Practices

Green Spaces

The natural environment is often represented as parks, forests, greenways, gardens, and green spaces (Jennings et al., 2016). The green spaces are areas within an organisation that are covered with green vegetation, gardens, greenways, and natural landscapes to improve green aesthetics, biodiversity, air quality, and so on (Ko & Son, 2018). The green spaces require integrating a natural green environment within organisational buildings and infrastructure settings to provide cues for sustainable, green, and human well-being-centric approaches. People have identified diverse types of green spaces as representations of recreational, aesthetic, educational, spiritual, and religious, cultural heritage, and health and happiness themes (Ko & Son, 2018).

The Eco-friendly Culture

The eco-friendly culture entails environment-friendly values, beliefs, customs, norms, assumptions, practices, artefacts, structures, and behaviours to minimise adverse environmental impact and enhance pro-environment thinking, feelings, and actions. When employees are continuously exposed to green spaces, they receive a range of mental cues which reinforce their behaviours towards supporting sustainable and green initiatives, renewable energy, recycling, upcycling and reducing waste, promoting environmental stewardship, community engagement and green citizenship (Jennings et al., 2016; Ko & Son, 2018).

Also, green spaces and eco-friendly cultural practices are linked to increased social cohesion, improved social interaction, promote a sense of community, reduce stress, and improve the health and well-being of people (Jennings et al., 2016).

Environmental Design, Employee Well-being, and Productivity

Natural Light and Green Spaces

Green spaces and natural light have been found as enablers of the physical, psychological, and social health of people (Jennings et al., 2016). Studies have indicated that exposure to natural light, colour combinations, green spaces, etc., provides good air quality, offers better acoustics, provides spaces for relaxation, regulates humans' circadian rhythm, improves mood, cognitive function, alertness, well-being, mental health, and quality of life (Alipour & Khoramian, 2023; Mensah et al., 2016). This decreases employees' absenteeism, improves retention, improves employee engagement at work, their job satisfaction, and overall productivity. This means that sustainability practices, and corresponding employees' exposure to green spaces, natural light, etc., have a positive impact on individual productivity as well as organisational productivity.

Biophilic Design and Employees' Productivity

Biophilia means innate human liking for nature or 'innate tendency to focus on life and lifelike processes, and to be drawn toward nature, to feel an affinity for it, a love, a craving' (Merriam-Webster, 2025). Biophilia design theories have evolved from this hypothesis that biophilia is an innate nature of human beings (Gillis & Gatersleben, 2015; Kellert & Wilson, 1993). Biophilia design theory is reinforced by environmental attention distortion theory as well as stress recovery theory and posits that the environment evokes positive moods and enables people to recuperate from mental fatigue and stress (Gillis & Gatersleben, 2015; Joye & van den Berg, 2018; Kaplan & Kaplan, 1989).

Biophilic design theory argues that direct exposure to nature, indirect exposure to nature or exposure via spatial configurations that cue a natural setting enhances people's physical & psychological health, well-being, satisfaction, and productivity (Alipour & Khoramian, 2023; Gillis & Gatersleben, 2015; Heerwagen et al., 2013; Zhong et al., 2022). Thus, incorporating nature-friendly elements such as natural light, greenery, natural landscapes, indoor natural materials, indoor plants, nature-friendly views, biomimicry, open views, cultural and ecological attachments, etc., reduces employees' stress, boosts their creativity, community stewardship and improves overall productivity (Alipour & Khoramian, 2023; Heerwagen et al., 2013; Kallio et al., 2015; Muisyo et al., 2022).

Ergonomic Features and Personal Controls

The ergonomic design imbues the dynamics of time & motion study and lets people have control over their motions, and improves people's feeling of well-being and productivity (Hedge, 2016). A range of ergonomic features, such as layout, ergonomic furniture (chairs, desks, accessories, etc.), allow employees to personalise their workspace, minimise physical stress, convey companies' commitment to employees' health and well-being, improve employees' feeling of self-control over the environment and working (Brown et al., 2010; Cole et al.,

2008; Gallagher et al., 2023; Mensah et al., 2016; Smeenk, 2024). All this in turn enhances employees' sense of self-worth, morale, work commitment, job engagement and overall productivity.

Eco-friendly Culture, Internal Branding, and Employees' Behaviour

Eco-friendly and green organisational culture communicates organisational values, beliefs, norms, shared assumptions, artefacts, practices, and commitments towards environmental sustainability and guides their behaviour towards sustainable decisions. The eco-friendly spaces and eco-friendly culture jointly enhance positive cues and communicate that the organisation is an environmentally friendly brand. Eco-friendly culture and green buildings reinforce each other by imbibing feelings of human collaboration, sustainability, and responsibility towards stakeholders (Cole et al., 2008).

Internal eco-friendly brand communication has a direct impact on employees' behaviours (Elantary, 2024). Not only eco-friendly environment and culture physically impact employees' well-being, but also psychologically boost their motivation, morale, and commitment to sustainability and environmentally friendly practices at the workplace and in organisational supply chain operations (Ko & Son, 2018). In addition, such employees proudly act as eco-friendly brand ambassadors of their organisations. Employees exposed to eco-friendly culture and green spaces take pro-environmental actions, support greener goals, and promote the reuse, recycling, and upcycling of materials. Such employees go beyond contractual job requirements, collaborate, and proactively work towards sustainable practices and proactively demonstrate good organisational citizenship behaviour (Ahmed et al., 2024; Brown et al., 2010; Muisyo et al., 2022).

Employee-driven Sustainability and Organisational Growth

Employee driven sustainability (EDS) is a philosophy, system, culture, perception, practice, and voluntary monitoring indicator that empowers employees to proactively participate, initiate, create, and implement organisational sustainability initiatives to achieve organisational and personal environmental goals (Coutinho et al., 2018). It is about aligning personal values and goals with organisational and environmental values and goals of environmental, social, and governance (ESG). This approach leverages employees' insights, motivations, creativity, and commitment to foster an eco-friendly culture and green space environment and thus modifies their behaviour towards waste reduction, energy conservation, community reach, etc. (Bekar, 2022). Research studies by many organisations, such as Adobe, Ernst & Young, AIC, Morningstar Inc., have found that sustainability orientation and EDS-centric approach at organisations not only attract talent, but also increase their satisfaction, engagement, and productivity at work and improve market capitalisation of the firms (Bishop, 2024). EDS enables employees to play key roles in sustainability practices by creating a system, many enablers (i.e. training, IT tools, and recognitions) and a framework of sustainability. EDS is a bottom-up approach; hence, it draws on employees' commitment, autonomy, employees' engagement, creativity, constructive alignment with personal values, and meaningful motivation, resulting in effective execution of employee-driven sustainability (Bekar, 2022; Bishop, 2024). EDS empowers employees and enhances employees' active participation, innovative practices, and takes proactive actions with a sense of ownership in creating and maintaining an eco-friendly environment and green spaces (Polman & Bhattacharya, 2016). As already indicated above, eco-friendly environment and green spaces have positive impacts on employees' motivations, engagement, creativity, positive mindset, job satisfaction and productivity. An IBM institute of value study of 16,000 people in 10 countries found that at least 67% of people are willing to apply and work with the organisation with sustainability as a focus (Bishop, 2024). The effective implementation of EDS also needs the support of the top management, organisational systems, enhancing employees' knowledge and competence, co-creation of sustainability practices, showcasing visible sustainability and higher purpose and cultural values that support employees' initiatives, encourage knowledge sharing, and recognition for any actions towards EDS (Polman & Bhattacharya, 2016). The employees should be provided with the necessary training to enhance their knowledge and skills in EDS and motivated to create a range of green teams and sustainability champions. Some organisations have been supporting environmental proactivist campaigns and strikes (e.g. Patagonia, L'Occitane, and Lush allowed employees), volunteer and community engagement (e.g. Patagonia's 'Action Works' programme), employee-led innovations (e.g. Unilever's PG tips tea packaging saving), sustainable living weeks (e.g. Unilever's sustainable living plan) and sustainability teams (Subaru Indiana Automotive's zero landfill campaign) (CityCo., 2023; Lush, 2025; Patagonia, 2025; Polman & Bhattacharya, 2016; Webb, 2022).

Employee-driven sustainability is a behaviour of good organisational citizenship.

Model of Organisational Citizenship Behaviour for the Environment (OCBE)

Employees are the main agents of organisations' environmental initiatives, fulfilling organisational sustainability commitment with their appropriate behaviour.

OCBE is employees' values, beliefs, and behaviour at the workplace, which is voluntary, discretionary, and not a part of the formal job requirements (Podsakoff et al., 2000); and such behaviour is recognised and rewarded, as it positively contributes to organisations' environmental initiatives and sustainability (Dong et al., 2025).

The nature of internal communication and cultural norms has a significant impact on employees' OCBE. Implementation of a successful OCBE framework needs employees' environment-friendly values and commitments, appropriate leadership and cultural support fostering an eco-friendly environment, and employees' perceived organisation support and positive beliefs that the organisational system will reinforce, appreciate, and reward environment-friendly behaviour (Podsakoff et al., 2000).

OCBE framework rests on three dimensions, namely eco-initiatives, eco-civic engagement, and eco-helping (Dong et al., 2025; Podsakoff et al., 2000).

Eco initiatives imply that employees voluntarily and proactively engage in suggesting ideas and activities for improving organisations' sustainable environment performance. The people not only follow the organisational compliance but also go beyond the minimum required levels of attendance, work engagement, self-development, conserving resources, collaboration, and communication with others in order to enhance organisational sustainability (Podsakoff et al., 2000).

Eco-helping implies collaboration, sharing knowledge, and helping colleagues to understand environmentally sustainable procedures and protocols, and transferring necessary skills to coworkers to undertake activities towards sustainability at the workplace, such as energy conservation, green spaces, waste reduction, recycling, reuse, and upcycling (Podsakoff et al., 2000).

Eco-civic engagement implies that employees voluntarily participate actively in organisational environmental events, community engagement for sustainability, attend workshops on sustainability, and even participate in environmental proactivism. Such employees also exhibit civic virtues, organisational loyalty and demonstrate a posture of sportsmanship that tolerates inconveniences caused by new sustainability practices and colleagues (Podsakoff et al., 2000).

Strategies for Employee-driven Bottom-up Innovation for Sustainability

Bottom-up innovation initiatives: the employees are the basic building blocks and agents of organisational learning and change towards sustainability (Bekar, 2022). Bottom of innovation or grassroots innovation implies encouraging employees at all levels to contribute towards creative ideas and actions proactively and boldly for sustainability. As compared to top-down symbolic approach to sustainability, the employee-driven sustainability is well aligned with employees' values, more engaging, resilient, and effective (Bekar, 2022).

To embed a culture of bottom-up innovation for sustainability, the organisation has to consider a range of actions, such as those listed in the next section (Akterujjaman et al., 2022; Bekar, 2022; Coutinho et al., 2018; Dong et al., 2025; Khan et al., 2022; Lozano, 2018a; Podsakoff et al., 2000).

Employee engagement: the process of involving employees in implementing sustainability initiatives by proactively generating ideas and their successful implementation.

Employee empowerment: this implies enabling and encouraging employees to have a sense of power, responsibility, and ownership towards the organisation's sustainability goals and action plans (Ahmed et al., 2024).

Sustainability idea sharing platforms: the organisations can set up a platform where employees can share, engage, collaborate, and reflect on their sustainability-related ideas, opportunities, and initiatives (Ahmed et al., 2024; Bishop, 2024; Polman & Bhattacharya, 2016).

Sustainability champions and green teams: any change requires change-agents and change-leaders. An organisation should promote employees to come forward as sustainability champions and join green teams of environmentally conscious people within the organisation (Ahmed et al., 2024; Akterujjaman et al., 2022). The sustainability initiative champions and ambassadors will act as role models as well as mentors for sustainability actions. The sustainability champions and green teams often run training campaigns and workshops to raise awareness, impart skills, share knowledge, foster an eco-friendly culture, and motivate others to take proactive environment-friendly actions.

Recognition and rewarding eco-behaviours: motivational theories argue that people's behaviour can be managed by an effective recognition and reward system. The organisation needs to incentivise eco-behaviours among the employees (Bekar, 2022). Employees can undertake appropriate behaviours if they have clear guidelines and understand the key performance indicators (KPIs) of eco-friendly behaviour and their impacts on people, planet, and profits. KPIs could be related to decreased waste, decreased greenhouse gases, energy saving and eco-friendly packaging.

Sustainable Business and Its Theoretical Foundations

The concept of sustainability has its origin in ethics and corporate social responsibility (CSR). Sustainable organisational culture is the sum total of shared beliefs, values, assumptions, norms, artefacts, practices, and taken-for-granted assumptions, which determine employees' behaviour and the art of balancing social, economic environmental goals of various stakeholders (Assoratgoon & Kantabutra, 2023; Schein, 1983). National culture, social factors, individual culture, leadership, employees and leaders' mental states, technological innovations, media stories, etc., impact the employees' orientations towards sustainability-oriented culture (Assoratgoon & Kantabutra, 2023; Lozano, 2018b, 2018a; Schein, 1983; van Dierendonck, 2011). A number of theories, such as Freeman's Stakeholder theory, resource-based view, innovation and sustainability, diffusion of innovation (Rogers), attempt to explain sustainable behaviour leading to competitive advantages.

The Diffusion of Innovation

Theory shows that diffusion of innovations is a multi-stage gradual process, and the rate of diffusion depends upon the innovation's relative advantages, simplicity, compatibility, trialability, and novelty (Rogers, 1962). The innovation is an important precursor to attaining sustainable products, processes, practices, and businesses. Roger's theory of diffusion of innovations is an effective way of implementing innovative sustainable organisational practices (Dibra, 2015). Studies have indicated that relative advantages, simplicity, compatibility, trialability, and novelty of innovation have a direct impact on the adoption of sustainable innovations and competitive advantages of the organisations (Dibra, 2015; Khan et al., 2022; Tiwari & Thakur, 2021).

The Stakeholder Theory

The stakeholder theory (ST) argues for paying attention to a range of internal and external stakeholders and attempting to satisfy their needs in a balanced way (Freeman, 2010). The stakeholder theory informs the key motivations of different stakeholders to effectively implement sustainable practices (Dibra, 2015). The SBSC is also a sustainability monitoring model that is based on Stakeholder theory (Figge et al., 2002; Nazir & Capocchi, 2024). The practicality of Stakeholder theory was extended by Donaldson and Preston (1995) and Mahajan et al. (2023). Donaldson and Preston (1995) proposed that the ST should entail a descriptive approach (i.e. view organisation as bodies made of various stakeholders with different interests), an Instrumental approach (i.e. use ST to balance interests of various stakeholders), and a normative approach (i.e. should exhibit CSR and stakeholders are ends and not the means of achieving organisation objectives) (Donaldson & Preston, 1995; Mahajan et al., 2023).

The Triple Bottom Line (TBL) Theory

The TBL was introduced in 1994 to measure the impact of an organisation operations beyond profits (Elkington, 1994, 2018). The TBL theory focuses on balancing the needs of People, Planet, and Profit (3Ps), while undertaking organisational operations (Elkington, 2018). Where the first P – 'Profit' implies financial returns for shareholders, the second P – 'People' indicates an organisation's commitment to society and the third P – 'Planet' implies the impact of the organisation's operations on the planet or environment (Elkington, 2018; Miller, 2020). The TBL is also used as a social, economic, and environmental (SEC) framework to measure impacts of organisational actions, where social dimensions represent people, economic dimensions imply profit and environmental dimensions measure impact on Planet Earth (Hammer & Pivo, 2017).

Sustainability Strategic Management Theories

A number of theoretical perspectives, such as ethics and social responsibility, system theories, paradox theory and sustainable strategic management theory, drive values, beliefs, and assumptions towards sustainable practices (Assoratgoon & Kantabutra, 2023; Pinto, 2017). The CSR perspective assigns significance to morality and ethics, such as integrity, human values, environmental protection, and other ESG goals as drivers of sustainable culture (United Nations Global Compact, 2022). The system approach is based on systems theory and posits that firms are complex and dynamic systems of interrelated parts, so they should harness their economic and social goals by integrating and coordinating various aspects and processes of businesses sustainably (Pinto, 2017; Williams et al., 2017). And such a system guides employees towards their attitude and behaviour of sustainability. The Paradox theory puts forward that organisations have to sail through a number of interdependent, simultaneous but conflicting objectives related to organisational profits, society and people, and environmental sustainability (Hahn et al., 2018; Pinto, 2017). The Paradoxes are dilemmas of either-or decisions and can be related to balancing the needs of 'learning, belonging, organising, and performing' due to tensions among stakeholders and their differing needs (Pinto, 2017). The strategic management approach argues that firms can achieve their economic goals by integrating an ESG sustainability framework and processes in their business strategies and operations (Baumgartner & Rauter, 2017).

Natural Resource-based View

The RBT was introduced by. The natural resource-based theory (NRBT) is an extension of RBT, as the RBT has ignored the role of natural resources and sustainability in organisational competitive advantage (Hart, 1995). The NRBT posits that the environmental capabilities of an organisation help it gain a competitive advantage (Pinto, 2017). NRBT argues that four key sustainable strategic capabilities for achieving competitive advantages are: bottom of the pyramid focus, product stewardship, pollution prevention, and clean energy (Hart & Dowell, 2011).

Sustainability and Competitive Advantage

Porter's Five Forces Model

Michael E Porter put forward his model of competitive advantage in 1979 (Porter, 1979, 1980, 1997). Porter's five forces model highlights *five dimensions*, namely: competitive rivalry, bargaining power of customers, bargaining power of suppliers, threat of substitutes, and threat of new entry, on which an organisation can face competitive threats or opportunities (Porter, 1979, 1997). And there are three generic strategies, such as cost leadership, focus, and differentiation, to overcome threats of competition and attain competitive advantage (Porter, 1980). A systematic review of literature from 2004 to 2024 related to impact of Porter's five forces on small and medium-sized enterprises (SMEs) (telecom, healthcare, manufacturing, renewable energy, clothing, retail, ceramic, tourism, etc.) found that strategic management of the five forces (e.g. using innovations, technology, collaborative knowledge sharing, ESG practices and thus enabling three generic strategies cost, focus, and differentiation) minimises threats from those forces and enhances opportunities, thus improved organisational performance and sustainability of SMEs (Ndzabukelwako et al., 2024). The EU had adopted the 'EU strategy for sustainable and circular textiles' in 2023 to enhance its sustainability practices. In a study in the textile industry of Slovakia, the researcher found that by integrating circular production models with Porter's five forces, the industry can reduce waste, increase reuse and recycling, and also achieve competitive advantage & sustainability (Šimonová et al., 2024).

Porter and Kramer's Shared Value Model (PK-SVM)

The concept of creating shared values implies using policies and practices to enhance an organisation's competitiveness by simultaneously meeting the social and economic needs of its community. Creating shared value (CSV) model argues that an organisation can generate higher shared economic value by integrating social issues into their business strategy and operations, by reconceiving and redefining customer needs, and by offering products and services to solve social problems & social needs. *PK-SVM* integrates socially shared values and economic values into a corporate strategy in order to attain sustainable competitive advantage. As the number of companies implementing CSR with a peripheral aim (and profit as a core aim) has increased, the legitimacy of CSR has decreased (Porter & Kramer, 2006; Roszkowska-Menkes, 2021). So the PK-SVM post a fundamentally new business model, that doesn't treat the organisational economic growth and social responsibility as zero-sum game; however, social actions should be viewed in synergy with competitiveness as ways of exploiting innovative opportunity to create shared values (by reconceiving products and markets, redefining productivity in the value chain, and enabling local cluster development) thus enhancing profit, competitive advantage and sustainability (Porter & Kramer, 2011, 2006). PK-SVM Model argues that to achieve competitive advantages, higher societal impact and a higher shared economic value an organisation should understand the societal needs, support the local community as the enabler of local cluster development, enhance social & environmental impacts in the supply chain, view productivity in terms of its impacts on people, planet & profit. For instance, Unilever has achieved a significant global social contribution, global expansion and growth by developing its product lines that address the health and hygienic challenges of people in developing and least developed countries (Alonso, 2022; Case Study: Unilever's Sustainable Living Plan (USLP) 1, 2024; Unilever, 2025).

Examples of Organisations Succeeding through Sustainability

Patagonia – Purpose and Planet at the Core

Pentagonia focuses on outdoor apparel. The company's core focus is ethical sourcing, circular economy and environmental proactivism. They successfully implemented a 'Worn-Wear programme' that recycles, repairs, and resells used products (Patagonia, 2025). The company has donated part of their sales for environmental causes, they even took legal action to protect public lands, showing pro-activism, and they use only organic cotton and recycled material to make products (Patagonia, 2025). The company's sustainability focus has helped it continuously enhance brand loyalty, attract eco-conscious consumers, and attain continuous revenue growth. The company owner gave the company to each trust in order to fight for environmental causes (Webb, 2022).

IKEA – Circular Design and Climate Commitment

IKEA is a global furniture and home goods manufacturer and retailer (IKEA, 2025). IKEA is committed to green innovation, circular economy, and sustainable materials in the business. The company is fully committed to attaining a fully circular business (IKEA, 2025; Marquis, 2025). IKEA has even launched a furniture buy-back and re-fabrication programme to enhance recycling and upcycling. They have invested heavily in renewable energy and their material sustainable innovation (hybrid material, bamboo, mushroom-based packaging, etc.), sustainable supply chain and sustainable operations, etc., to save forests and the environment. IKEA's circular economy and sustainability focus have resulted in enhanced customer perceptions towards the brand, brand affordability, decreased environmental footprint, sustainable supply chain, corporate reputation, and business profitability and growth (IKEA, 2024; Marquis, 2025).

Ecotricity – Green Energy Innovation (UK)

Ecotricity is a UK-based renewable energy company that focuses on carbon-neutral electricity and an ethical energy model to attain sustainable business practices (Ecotricity, 2025). The company became one of the few to harness wind and solar energy for homes and businesses in the United Kingdom (Mcqueen & Turner, 2020). The company continuously reinvests their profit into greener infrastructure and sustainable supply chain practices. The business promotes veganism through energy production, ethical supply chain management (Ecotricity, 2025; Green Britain Group, 2021; Mcqueen & Turner, 2020). The sustainability-focused practices have built a loyal customer base for the company, and the company could get a stronger market share and become a leading example of an ethical & sustainable energy producer in the energy sector in the United Kingdom.

There are many cases of organisations embedding sustainable practices into their business operations and attaining sustainable competitive advantage, and envisioning success. However, there are several barriers and enablers that an organisation must consider for embedding sustainability into their businesses and achieving sustainable comparative advantages (Olesson et al., 2023).

Enablers and Barriers of Sustainable Competitive Advantage

Achieving sustainable competitive advantage involves an organisation developing sustainable models by orchestrating, coordinating, and leveraging its unique strengths and overcoming the key barriers to it. Business models provide a logical structure to different building blocks of key organisational activities to create and capture value (Dentchev et al., 2018). The corporate greenwashing can be avoided if the heart & soul of employees are directed towards the values and beliefs of sustainability.

The challenges and barriers are related to coordinating & aligning different logical building blocks effectively to create dynamic capabilities for competitive advantage (Olesson et al., 2023). The main enablers of sustainable competitive advantages include creating and exploiting organisational dynamic capabilities with the valuable, rare, inimitable, and well-organised (VRIO) resources framework (Teece, 2007, 2010). Employees are key drivers of organisational change due to their agency. The total stock of knowledge, capabilities, and sustainability-related innovative potential is also known as green human capital (Bekar, 2022).

The employees with circular happiness will have a high degree of internal motivation, values, green identity, and sustainability orientations (Bekar, 2022). The other drivers of sustainable competitive advantages are strong leadership, relevant organisational culture, continuous innovation, agility, sustainable supply chain, embedded technology, strategic partnership, and collaborative working (Lozano, 2018a, 2018b).

The key barriers to sustainability are organisational inabilities to exploit the dynamic capabilities of employee-driven suitable innovations. For example, a lack of employee capabilities to create compatibility of practices & interactions that fit among different logical building blocks of the business model has been a key challenge for sustainability (Olesson et al., 2023). In addition, a lack of leadership, a lack of organisational structure & support to leverage its resources, poor organisational culture, poor learning culture, insufficient investment in innovation, weakness in technological capabilities, poor teamwork, and collaborative practices are major barriers to sustainable competitive (Bekar, 2022).

Purpose-driven Business Models (PDBMs)

The business models are the strategic processes, dynamic capabilities and activities through which organisations create, deliver, and capture value and attain competitive advantages (Teece, 2018). Circular business models enable organisations to use the capabilities of sustainability to attain their competitive superiority (Hellström & Olsson, 2024). The PDBMs enable a paradigm shift, so that an organisation can reinvent its social, ethical, environmental, and people purpose and then align its resources, business operations, and strategies to transcend the goal of profit and meet the needs & goals of a broad range of stakeholders (people, planet, & profit).

Purpose-driven Business Model (PDBM)

A mission or purpose-driven organisation realigns its strategy with core purpose and redesigns its business model by embedding five essential elements, namely: passion, core purpose, stakeholders' motivation, unobstructed vision, action mission, and manifesto of values, into the business model (Leonardini, 2021). PDBM looks beyond the purpose of organisational profit and attempts to maximise social and environmental values for stakeholders, communities, and societies (Carballo, 2023). The core reason for the company's existence is its higher aspirational purpose or massive transformative purpose (MTP), which transcends profits and views sustainability, normative values, and human consciousness as key elements of its purpose (Pepple, 2019). PDBM creates an ecosystem where individuals, groups, and organisations align their social, environmental, and economic purposes, hence, it requires balancing the needs and motives of various stakeholders to get their full support in the execution of the purpose-driven business operations (Lyon et al., 2024). The purpose-driven organisation sets a clear sustainability-related vision for the future state, aligns its mission statement to realise the vision & purpose, and persuades customers, employees, and investors to behave sustainably (Gibson, 2022). A PDBM can make use of the hybrid star model of implementation, which argues that aligning five interconnected elements, namely: strategy, structure, people, processes, and rewards, is crucial for effective PDBM (Carballo, 2023). Chloé, a luxury fashion brand, has integrated sustainability into its business model, adopted regenerative leadership, taken several sustainability actions, and thus became one of the first luxury fashion brands to get B-Corp certification accreditation (Socha, 2020; Webb, 2023).

Certified B-corporations are mission-driven 'for-profit organisations' and are certified by B-Lab for meeting the rigorous standards of societal, stakeholder, and environmental performance, and such organisations balance profit with purpose while demonstrating accountability & transparency in their sustainability business (B Corporation, 2025). Mission-driven organisations that have achieved B-Corp certification attain higher employee engagement, higher customer loyalty, attract investors, better brand differentiation, achieve sustainable competitive advantage and higher business growth.

Steward-ownership Model (SOM)

SOM argues that for achieving a purpose economy, the purpose of a company should be to offer a profitable solution to the problem of people and planet, and not to profit from the problem of the people (Reiff, 2024). The business owners of such organisations act as stewards during their lives and cannot withdraw excessive profits or pass ownership to their families. Thus, the purpose of long-term sustainability is preferred over short-term profit. The organisational ownership should act like stewards, wherein traditional profit-oriented organisational models are to be replaced with profit-based purpose organisational models (Reiff, 2024). The SOM argues that the economic rights of decision makers should be separated from their decision-making powers, so that their actions and organisational purpose are directed towards sustainability. This model argues for self-governance, such that the decision-making should be aligned with the mission, and the organisational operational controlling power should be in the hands of people dealing with day-to-day operations and not with the owners (Purpose-Economy, 2021). The central tenets of SOM include owners should act as trustees & stewards, purpose-driven profit allocation, reinvestment of the profit into environmental initiatives, taking sustainable actions, and the mission should be to win stakeholders' trust. For example, Patagonia, an outdoor apparel brand, follows the SOM model, as it has embedded a decision model which is well aligned with its sustainability purpose, owners act like stewards and the company reinvests a significant proportion of profits into sustainability initiatives (Brooks, 2023; Patagonia, 2025; Purpose-Economy, 2021; Webb, 2022).

The Triple Layered Business Model Canvas (TLBMC)

The triple layered business model canvas (TLBMC) is a tool for exploring and exploiting sustainability-oriented Business Innovation by adding an environmental perspective layer and stakeholders' perspective layer to the original business model canvas (BMC) (Joyce & Paquin, 2016; Osterwalder & Pigneur, 2010). TLBMC extends the original business model canvas by integrating three layers, namely, economic layer, environmental layer, and societal layer, in all nine building blocks original business model canvas (Joyce & Paquin, 2016). TLBMC must ensure good horizontal and vertical coherence across all three layers and among all nine building blocks of BMC. TLBMC models enable organisations to strategically align & embed their purpose, strategy, and business model so as to holistically analyse the impact of business on people, planet, and profits. This model encourages creative solutions & sustainable innovations, improves engagement with all stakeholders, improves revenue streams, and enables sustainable competitive advantage (Stubbs & Cocklin, 2008).

1. *The economic layer*

It preserves the traditional nine elements of the original BMC of Osterwalder and Pigneur (2010); that is customer segments, distribution channels, customer relationship, value proposition, key activities, key resources, key partners, revenue streams, and cost structures.

2. *Environmental layer*

This layer considers the impacts of a product's lifecycle (i.e. raw material-finished product – disposal) on the ecological environment and corresponding innovation opportunities across all nine building blocks of BMC (Joyce & Paquin, 2016). This layer augments the nine building blocks by embedding actions for sustainable resources and materials, environment-friendly supply chain partners, eco-efficient production processes, minimised carbon footprint based distribution channels, products with sustainable energy usages, end of life recyclability of products, overall positive environmental impact, and views environmental benefits as revenue, environmental costs as a part of the cost structure (Chun & Lee, 2013; Joyce & Paquin, 2016; Stubbs & Cocklin, 2008).

3. *Societal layer of the business model*

This layer embeds stakeholders' needs, engagement, and social value into the BMC (Freeman, 2010; Osterwalder & Pigneur, 2010). Thus, traditional segments are viewed as stakeholder segments, value proposition as social value proposition for society, distribution channels become a means of engagement with society, focus shifts towards stakeholder relationship, key resources and key activities are aimed at social value creation, key partners include social entities, the revenue streams include funding for social initiative and the cost structure includes investment into social initiatives (Chun & Lee, 2013; Joyce & Paquin, 2016; Lozano, 2008). The layers assess social lifecycle impacts on various stakeholders as a result of business operations.

Lifecycle Thinking and Systematic Value Models (LCT-SVM)

The life cycle thinking implies monitoring the stages of the value chain process on a resource or material, or product; and it includes the journey of a material through the stages of extraction, processing, manufacturing, transportation, value alteration, final product, waste management, disposal, circular reuse, recycling, etc. (Huang et al., 2020). Life cycle sustainability assessment measures the social, economic, and environmental impact of the life cycle of a material, resource, or product (Onat et al., 2017). LCT-SVM develop a dynamic system that integrates social, economic, and environmental (SEE) purposes in the supply chain and business model to use the synergy of *lifecycle thinking* along with the *systematic thinking* in order to evaluate throughout the lifecycle (origin of raw material-to-end of final product disposal) SEE impacts of the supply chain network, business model operations, products, and services (Huang et al., 2020; Onat et al., 2017).

Lifecycle thinking allows analysis and evaluation of the SEE impacts of the lifecycle of business models, products, and services over the whole value chain. This also entails innovating various stages of the value chain: raw material extraction, inbound logistics. Manufacturing, distribution, usage cycle and end-of-life recycling, reuse, disposal, or upcycling of products so as to minimise negative SEE impacts (Huang et al., 2020). Systems thinking argues for synergetic, dynamic interconnectedness of various parts of the system, various stakeholders, inputs, processes, and outcomes to create a SEE sustainable value (Lozano, 2018b; Onat et al., 2017). The system theory posits dynamic interaction and interdependence of the parts of the system. Service dominant logic argues for products and services as instruments and vehicles of co-creating and capturing value and emphasises the role of stakeholder interactions in co-creating and consumption of sustainable products and services (Font et al., 2021; Lusch et al., 2007; Vargo & Lusch, 2004).

Circular Economy Models

Circular economy models let organisations move away from traditional linear business models; 'input-make-dispose' to a circular business model that closes the 'loop of input-make-use-recycle/upcycle-input' (Geissdoerfer et al., 2020; Hellström & Olsson, 2024; Lacy et al., 2020; WEF, 2022). The circular economy models emphasise aligning social, economic, and environmental purposes in the business models, to improve efficiency, reduce waste, promote sustainable production, undertake recycling, regenerative practices, circulate products, and close the lifecycle loop of resources to regenerate nature (Céline Dumas & Van Wassenhove, 2021; Geissdoerfer et al., 2020). European Environment Agency (EEA) frameworks stipulates that to effectively implement circular business models, the organisations need circular goals (i.e. reuse, recycle, repair, and recover), an appropriate policy framework (i.e. laws and regulations, financial, and incentives), behavioural and education enablers, technical and social innovation, and innovative business models (European Environment Agency, 2020).

The key principles of the circular economy model are given in the next section (Geissdoerfer et al., 2020; Hellström & Olsson, 2024):

1. *Eliminate waste and pollution*: This principle emphasises designing the products and systems in such a way that they eliminate wastage and pollution in

the first place. Such products could be durable or have design features such that no waste is created during manufacturing (e.g. 3d printing) (Geissdoerfer et al., 2020; Hellström & Olsson, 2024).

2. *Close the loop, circular inputs and circular products*: it emphasises using recycled or renewable materials in the production process so as to minimise wastage and preserve the natural environment (Geissdoerfer et al., 2020; Hellström & Olsson, 2024).
3. *Product as a Service (PaaS)*: in line with service dominant logic, the circular economy model presumes that products are vehicles of service (Product as a Service) and argues for 'servicetisation of products or dematerialisation of the products' (Geissdoerfer et al., 2020). PaaS allows customers to co-create services or value by using durable products, to reinvent innovative methods of creating and capturing service value during the next cycle of the product and at the end of the product life cycle, the product can be recycled back to the production stage (Geissdoerfer et al., 2020; WEF, 2022). Thus, the physical resources are used re-generatively to create and capture customer service value repeatedly.
4. *Product life extension*: this principle argues that to reduce the need for manufacturing new products, the product's useful life as a vehicle of services should be extended through the built-in design durability, and via the processes of repair, refurbishment, resale, renting, sharing and re-manufacturing, etc. (Geissdoerfer et al., 2020; Hellström & Olsson, 2024).
5. *Resource recovery and regenerating nature*: the material, resources, and energy from manufacturing waste, byproducts, disposed products, buybacks, regenerating soil, trees, restoring the ecosystem, etc., should be recovered and converted into useful inputs for the new process, thus regenerating nature (Geissdoerfer et al., 2020; Hellström & Olsson, 2024). It also argues for systematic thinking, supply chain collaboration, and regenerative thinking to recapture lost social, economic, and environmental resources (Lahcen et al., 2022).

10Rs Strategic Models

The circular economy system is based on 'reusability of products and product components, recycling of materials, and conservation of natural resources' (Potting et al., 2017). A reduce, reuse, recycle (3Rs) model was developed based on lean production and green manufacturing principles, and later 3Rs model was extended to the 9Rs and 10Rs models (Hunger et al., 2024; Kolar-Schandlbauer & Holly, 2025; Potting et al., 2017). The granular approach of the 10Rs model aims to minimise waste, extend the useful life and even recover losses. A radical technology, product design and revenue models' innovations, etc., are needed to achieve the circular flow of resources (Hunger et al., 2024; Potting et al., 2017). The hierarchical 10Rs of circular economy are as below:

1. Refuse: avoiding products that have a negative environmental impact or generate waste (Kolar-Schandlbauer & Holly, 2025; Potting et al., 2017).

2. Rethink: to enhance sustainability, this principle favours reevaluating the product design and its uses (Kolar-Schandlbauer & Holly, 2025; Potting et al., 2017).
3. Reduce: design and develop products that require minimal input and have minimal waste in production (Kolar-Schandlbauer & Holly, 2025; Potting et al., 2017).
4. Reuse: ensure multiple uses of the product to extend the life of a product (Kolar-Schandlbauer & Holly, 2025; Potting et al., 2017).
5. Repair: fix the defective components of the product to prolong its life and usability (Kolar-Schandlbauer & Holly, 2025; Potting et al., 2017).
6. Refurbish: fix the old products, restore them to good condition, and reuse (Kolar-Schandlbauer & Holly, 2025; Potting et al., 2017).
7. Remanufacture: remake a new product by using discarded parts of the old product for the same function (Kolar-Schandlbauer & Holly, 2025; Potting et al., 2017; WEF, 2022).
8. Repurpose: using the discarded components of an older product in a new product but with a different function (Kolar-Schandlbauer & Holly, 2025; Potting et al., 2017; WEF, 2022).
9. Recycle: process the material obtained from the old product to obtain raw material for the next product (Kolar-Schandlbauer & Holly, 2025; Potting et al., 2017; WEF, 2022).
10. Recover: recapture the youthful energy from waste materials (Kolar-Schandlbauer & Holly, 2025; Potting et al., 2017).

Sharing Economy-based Business Models (SEBMs)

Sharing economy business models are based on service-dominant logic, platformisation, and peer sharing (Ritter & Schanz, 2019). Sharing of resources (products and materials) enables the extended life of the resource, extensive use of spare resources, and reusing, repurposing, recycling, and even recovering of resources. SEBMs facilitate the sharing of resources, products, and assets, thus increasing the rate of utilisation of an asset and hence reducing the need for new products or assets (Dadwal et al., 2019). Hence, SEBMs is an approach to the circular economy. For example, a hospital can rent/share its X-ray machine with other hospitals; travellers can use Uber-like car ride platforms, lease a Jeans or a dress, programme from an apparel company, refurbished mobile phone markets, and so on.

Collaborative Circular Economy Business Models (CCEBMs)

CCEBMs make use of collaborative effort among members of the supply chain (i.e. procurer-supplier collaboration) for creating a closed-loop circular system of collaborative innovation and sharing to minimise resource wastage, maximise the usage of resources, and maximise the recovery of resources (Brown et al., 2018). CCEBMs are based on the relational view theory, open innovation theory and dynamic capabilities theory (Köhler et al., 2022). The application of information and communications technology enables collaborations by enabling mutually trusting relationships, collaborations for open innovations and sharing knowledge and the development of dynamic capabilities for sustainability (Adelekan & Sharmina, 2024; Köhler et al., 2022). CCEBMs take a holistic approach to implement collaborative and coordinated systems of multiple stakeholders, such as customers, suppliers, other businesses, government, and communities, in order to prolong the life of resources and use, eliminate any waste and regenerate natural systems for regenerative social, economic, and environmental impacts (Adelekan & Sharmina, 2024). CCEBMs are mammoths of various stakeholders across industry and sector, hence the effective development of such business models requires approaches of system thinking and industrial symbiosis. In line with systems thinking, the CCEBMs is a complex system of industries and stakeholders, and needs a cohesive system of interconnected, coordinated, relational, interdependent parts that effectively work together for the common purpose of the circular economy (Fehrer et al., 2018; Onat et al., 2017).

Collaborative models have many benefits, such as mitigating risks, sharing investment and resources, sharing ideas for innovation, and effective systematic change for circular practices (Köhler et al., 2022).

Some notable examples of CCEBMs are Amazon and the Allen MacArthur Foundation collaboration for scalable circular economy solutions, the British Fashion Council UK, the UK-wide circular fashion ecosystem, etc. (Amazon, 2025; British Fashion Council, 2024; Ellen MacArthur Foundation, 2025). CCEBMs need a common purpose, effective cross-sector partnerships, shared infrastructures and resources, policy and regulatory alignment, and community engagement to achieve the circular economy. There could be challenges in coordinating the diverse stakeholders, ensuring the common purpose staring the cultural differences, and the limited intention to share the resources (Brown et al., 2018). The industrial symbiosis in CCEBMs means different industries come together to work in symbiotic collaboration for mutually beneficial exchanges for the common goals of achieving competitive advantage, circular economy, and sustainability. To enhance the circular flow of resources, diverse industries should efficiently and effectively share resources, energies, waste, and byproducts among themselves.

An Integrated Conceptual Framework Linking Circular Happiness, Purpose-Driven Sustainability, and Business Growth

Based on the discussions in the previous section, we can propose an integrated conceptual framework linking circular happiness, purpose-driven sustainability, and business growth (see Fig. 4.2).

At the micro level, for creating sustainable and purpose-driven circular innovation, an organisation needs mechanisms for creating circular happiness among employees. A system of green spaces and eco-centric designs provides cues to employees to decrease their physical, social, and psychological stress and improve

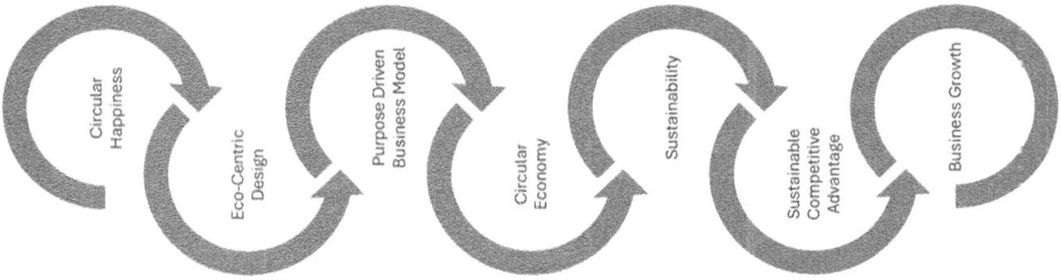

Fig. 4.2. An Integrated Conceptual Framework Linking Circular Happiness, Purpose-Driven Sustainability, and Business Growth.

their overall happiness and well-being. Happy employees are more engaging, self-motivated, and more productive. The circular happiness leads to PDBMs and the circular economy. The circular economy has a bidirectional impact on the sustainability of the organisation and its environment. Sustainability-based innovations create dynamic capabilities in an organisation, and such dynamic capabilities lead to sustainable competitive advantage. Sustainable competitive advantage has a direct impact on business growth.

Conclusion

This chapter analyses the concept of circular happiness, a number of building blocks of PDBMs, circular economy, sustainability, sustainable competitive advantages, business growth, and an interdependent framework.

The chapter conceptualises a circular framework of interdependent elements. However, the proposed framework is only a theoretical model, and it needs to be established and verified by collecting qualitative and quantitative data. Also, there are the challenges of establishing the bidirectional relationship among different elements of this framework.

The purpose of a sustainable organisation is to balance the trade-off among social, economic, and environmental objectives. Organisational success should be measured on five dimensions of the SBSC; key stakeholders: employees (i.e. innovation and learning), investors (i.e. financial), organisation (i.e. internal operations), customers (i.e. customer satisfaction), and society and environment. The circular happiness is a self-reinforcing loop of happiness, and it entails meta-awareness of happiness, emotional and social satisfaction, pro-social, and positive behaviour. The pro-social behaviour indicates intentions to contribute towards community and environment, a sense of helping others, acts of generosity and compassion. Thus, a happy person is a contributor to sustainability, circular economy, green organisational culture, and circular happiness. The ergonomic design and green spaces integrate innate human needs with a natural green environment within organisational buildings and provide cues for sustainable, green, and human well-being-centric approaches to employees. Eco-friendly organisational culture reinforces environmental and social organisational values, beliefs, norms, shared assumptions, artefacts, practices, and commitments towards sustainability.

Employee-driven sustainability (EDS) attempts to align personal values with the goals of the organisational and the goals of environmental, economic, social, and governance. The OCBE framework fosters eco-friendly norms, values, and environment. A number of theoretical perspectives, such as Ethics and social responsibility, system theories, paradox theory, Sustainable Strategic management theory, and TBLs, drive values, beliefs, assumptions, and purposes towards sustainable practices. A purpose-driven organisation realigns its strategies with its core purpose and redesigns its business model that looks beyond the purpose of organisational profit and attempts to maximise social and environmental values for stakeholders, communities, and societies. Lifecycle thinking allows analysis and evaluation of the social, economic, and environmental impacts of the lifecycle of business models and products, and services over the whole value chain. The circular economy models aim at aligning social, economic, and environmental purposes in the business models in order to improve efficiency, reduce waste, promote sustainable production, undertake recycling, regenerative practices, circulate products, and close the lifecycle loop of resources to regenerate nature. Sharing economy and CCEBMs make use of co-creation, sharing and collaboration among stakeholders in order to enhance sustainability. Sustainability-based innovations create dynamic capabilities in an organisation, and such dynamic capabilities lead to sustainable competitive advantage and business growth.

References

Abran, A., & Buglione, L. (2003). A multidimensional performance model for consolidating balanced scorecards. *Advances in Engineering Software*, *34*(6), 339–349. https://doi.org/10.1016/S0965-9978(03)00033-4

Adelekan, A., & Sharmina, M. (2024). Collaborative digitally-enabled business models for a circular economy: Sustaining, managing, and protecting value in the UK plastics sector. *Journal of Cleaner Production*, *438*, 140770. https://doi.org/10.1016/J.JCLEPRO.2024.140770

Aggarwal, P., & Agarwala, T. (2021). Green organizational culture: An exploration of dimensions. *Global Business Review*, *26*(4), 1103–1126. https://doi.org/10.1177/09721509211049890

Agrawal, S., Sharma, N., Agrawal, R., Iazzolino, G., Bruni, M. E., Sharma, N., & Iazzolino, G. (2025). Beyond GDP: A triple helix framework for a happiness economy. *Social Indicators Research*, *179*, 1–28. https://doi.org/10.1007/S11205-025-03604-Y

Ahmed, A., Majeed, A., Hassan, A., Hassan, A., Atef, S., Wahba, M., Said, A., & Al Asrag, A. (2024). Internal branding, organizational culture and citizenship behavior in hotels and travel agencies: Green perspective. *Minia Journal of Tourism and Hospitality Research MJTHR*, *17*(1), 173–189. https://doi.org/10.21608/MJTHR.2024.273489.1145

Aknin, L. B., Dunn, E. W., & Norton, M. I. (2012). Happiness runs in a circular motion: Evidence for a positive feedback loop between prosocial spending and happiness. *Journal of Happiness Studies*, *13*(2), 347–355. https://doi.org/10.1007/S10902-011-9267-5

Akterujjaman, S. M., Blaak, L., Ali, M. I., & Nijhof, A. (2022). Organizational citizenship behavior for the environment: A management perspective. *International Journal of Organizational Analysis*, *30*(6), 1783–1802. https://doi.org/10.1108/IJOA-01-2021-2567

Alipour, L., & Khoramian, M. (2023). Investigating the impact of biophilic design on employee performance and well-being by designing a research instrument. *Kybernetes*, *53*(11), 4431–4447. https://doi.org/10.1108/K-08-2022-1134/FULL/PDF

Alonso, T. (2022, February 15). *Strategy study: How Unilever went from soap manufacturer to multinational giant*. Cascade. https://www.cascade.app/studies/unilever-from-soap-manufacturer-to-multinational-giant

Amat, O. (2024). Case study: Unilever's Sustainable Living Plan (USLP). Universitat Pompeu Fabra, Barcelona School of Management. Retrieved June 18, 2025 from https://www.bsm.upf.edu/documents/2024-case-study-unilever.pdf

Amazon. (2025). *Amazon and the Ellen MacArthur Foundation collaborate on circular economy initiatives*. Amazon. https://www.aboutamazon.com/news/sustainability/amazon-and-the-ellen-macarthur-foundation-collaborate-on-circular-economy-initiatives

Anand, A., & Sundaram, N. (2025). The impact of CSR-induced happiness on sustainable consumption behavior (SDG 12): Exploring the mediating role of customer-company identification. *Journal of Lifestyle and SDGs Review*, *5*(1), e04209. https://doi.org/10.47172/2965-730X.SDGsReview.v5.n01.pe04209

Assoratgoon, W., & Kantabutra, S. (2023). Toward a sustainability organizational culture model. *Journal of Cleaner Production*, *400*, 136666. https://doi.org/10.1016/J.JCLEPRO.2023.136666

Atkinson, S., Bagnall, A. M., Corcoran, R., South, J., & Curtis, S. (2020). Being well together: Individual subjective and community wellbeing. *Journal of Happiness Studies*, *21*(5), 1903–1921. https://doi.org/10.1007/S10902-019-00146-2/METRICS

B Corporation. (2025). *B lab global site*. B Corporation. https://www.bcorporation.net/en-us/

Baumgartner, R. J., & Rauter, R. (2017). Strategic perspectives of corporate sustainability management to develop a sustainable organization. *Journal of Cleaner Production*, *140*, 81–92. https://doi.org/10.1016/j.jclepro.2016.04.146

Bekar, B. R. (2022). Building a green learning organisation: How employee-drive innovation can enable organisational sustainability transitions. In *UCL Institute for global prosperity*. UCL Institute for Global Prosperity. https://discovery.ucl.ac.uk/id/eprint/Purpose-driven

Bhattacharya, A., Mohapatra, P., Kumar, V., Dey, P. K., Brady, M., Tiwari, M. K., & Nudurupati, S. S. (2014). Green supply chain performance measurement using fuzzy ANP-based balanced scorecard: A collaborative decision-making approach. *Production Planning & Control*, *25*(8), 698–714. https://doi.org/10.1080/09537287.2013.798088

Bishop, K. (2024, May 8). *Empowering employees helps drive sustainability in the business*. HR Observer. https://www.thehrobserver.com/indepth/empowering-employees-helps-drive-sustainability-in-the-business/

British Fashion Council. (2024, October 24). *The circular fashion innovation network launches interim report on the UK's circular fashion progress*. British Fashion Council. https://www.britishfashioncouncil.co.uk/bfcnews/4871/THE-CIRCULAR-FASHION-INNOVATION-NETWORK-LAUNCHES-INTERIM-REPORT-ON-THE-UKS-CIRCULAR-FASHION-PROGRESS

Brooks, O. (2023, May 23). *Patagonia: Rethinking corporate governance through steward-ownership | Bates Wells*. BatesWells. https://bateswells.co.uk/updates/patagonia-rethinking-corporate-governance-through-steward-ownership/

Brown, P., Bocken, N., & Balkenende, R. (2018). Towards understanding collaboration within circular business models. In L. Moratis, F. Melissen, & S. Idowu (Eds.). *CSR, sustainability, ethics and governance* (1st ed., pp. 169–201). Springer. https://doi.org/10.1007/978-3-319-73503-0_9

Brown, Z., Cole, R. J., Robinson, J., & Dowlatabadi, H. (2010). Evaluating user experience in green buildings in relation to workplace culture and context. *Facilities*, *28*(3–4), 225–238. https://doi.org/10.1108/02632771011023168/FULL/PDF

Carballo, R. E. (2023). Purpose-driven transformation: A holistic organization design framework for integrating societal goals into companies. *Journal of Organization Design*, *12*(4), 195–215. https://doi.org/10.1007/S41469-023-00156-8/TABLES/1

Cardiff University. (2025). *Circular families game – Research – Cardiff University*. Cardiff University. https://www.cardiff.ac.uk/research/explore/find-a-project/view/2587142-circular-families-game

Céline Dumas, A., & Van Wassenhove, L. N. (2021, August). *The circular business model*. HBR. https://hbr.org/2021/07/the-circular-business-model

Chen, Y. (2017). Dynamic ambidexterity: How innovators manage exploration and exploitation. *Business Horizons*, *60*(3), 385–394.

Chun, Y., & Lee, K. (2013). Life cycle-based generic business strategies for sustainable business models. *Journal of Sustainable Development*, *6*(8), 1. https://www.researchgate.net/profile/Yoon-Young-Chun/publication/269670578_Life_Cycle-Based_Generic_Business_Strategies_for_Sustainable_Business_Models/links/5cbfa23992851c8d22005635/Life-Cycle-Based-Generic-Business-Strategies-for-Sustainable-Business-Models.pdf

CityCo. (2023). *Environmental, social and governance review 2022–23*. CityCo. https://cityco.com/app/uploads/2023/04/000547_CityCo_ESG_report_2022_Dr4.2_AW_WEB.pdf

Cole, R. J., Robinson, J., Brown, Z., & O'Shea, M. (2008). Re-contextualizing the notion of comfort. *Building Research and Information*, *36*(4), 323–336. https://doi.org/10.1080/09613210802076328

Coutinho, V., Domingues, A. R., Caeiro, S., Painho, M., Antunes, P., Santos, R., Videira, N., Walker, R. M., Huisingh, D., & Ramos, T. B. (2018). Employee-driven sustainability performance assessment in public organisations. *Corporate Social Responsibility and Environmental Management*, *25*(1), 29–46. https://doi.org/10.1002/CSR.1438

Dadwal, S. S., Jamal, A., Harris, T., Brown, G., & Raudhah, S. (2019). Technology and sharing economy-based business models for marketing to connected consumers. In S. Dadwal (Ed.), *Technology and sharing economy-based business models for the connected consumers* (1st ed., Vol. 1, pp. 62–93). IGI Global. https://doi.org/10.4018/978-1-7998-0131-3.CH004

Delle Fave, A. (2021). Eudaimonic and hedonic happiness. In F. Maggino (Ed.), *Encyclopedia of quality of life and well-being research* (pp. 1–7). Springer International Publishing. https://doi.org/10.1007/978-3-319-69909-7_3778-2

Dentchev, N., Rauter, R., Jóhannsdóttir, L., Snihur, Y., Rosano, M., Baumgartner, R., Nyberg, T., Tang, X., van Hoof, B., & Jonker, J. (2018). Embracing the variety of sustainable business models: A prolific field of research and a future research agenda. *Journal of Cleaner Production*, *194*, 695–703. https://doi.org/10.1016/J.JCLEPRO.2018.05.156

Dibra, M. (2015). Rogers theory on diffusion of innovation – The most appropriate theoretical model in the study of factors influencing the integration of sustainability in tourism businesses. *Procedia – Social and Behavioral Sciences*, *195*, 1453–1462. https://doi.org/10.1016/J.SBSPRO.2015.06.443

Donaldson, T., & Preston, L. E. (1995). The stakeholder theory of the corporation: Concepts, evidence, and implications. *Academy of Management Review*, *20*(1), 65–91. https://doi.org/10.5465/AMR.1995.9503271992

Dong, E., Sun, R., & Lee, Y. (2025). *Internal sustainability branding and employee organizational citizenship behavior for the environment (OCBE)*. Institute of Public Relations.

Ecotricity. (2025). Britain's greenest energy company | Ecotricity. Ecotricity. https://www.ecotricity.co.uk/

Elantary, A. (2024). Unleashing the potential: The impact of biophilic office design on enhancing employee productivity. *Mansoura Engineering Journal*, *49*(4), 7. https://doi.org/10.58491/2735-4202.3208

Elkington, J. (1994). Towards the sustainable corporation: Win-win-win business strategies for sustainable development. *California Management Review*, *36*(2), 90–100. https://doi.org/10.2307/41165746

Elkington, J. (2018, June 25). *25 years ago, I coined the phrase "Triple Bottom Line." Here's why it's time to rethink it.* HBR. https://hbr.org/2018/06/25-years-ago-i-coined-the-phrase-triple-bottom-line-heres-why-im-giving-up-on-it

Ellen MacArthur Foundation. (2025). Fashion and a circular economy | Ellen MacArthur Foundation. Ellen MacArthur Foundation. https://www.ellenmacarthurfoundation.org/topics/fashion/overview

European Environment Agency. (2020). *A framework for enabling circular business models in Europe*. https://www.eea.europa.eu/publications/a-framework-for-enabling-circular

Fehrer, J. A., Woratschek, H., & Brodie, R. J. (2018). A systemic logic for platform business models. *Journal of Service Management*, *29*(4), 546–568. https://doi.org/10.1108/JOSM-02-2017-0036

Figge, F., Hahn, T., Schaltegger, S., & Wagner, M. (2002). The sustainability balanced scorecard – Linking sustainability management to business strategy. *Business Strategy and the Environment*, *11*(5), 269–284. https://doi.org/10.1002/BSE.339

Folk, D., & Dunn, E. (2023). A systematic review of the strength of evidence for the most commonly recommended happiness strategies in mainstream media. *Nature Human Behaviour*, *7*(10), 1697–1707. https://doi.org/10.1038/S41562-023-01651-4

Font, X., English, R., Gkritzali, A., & Tian, W. (Stella). (2021). Value co-creation in sustainable tourism: A service-dominant logic approach. *Tourism Management*, *82*, 104200. https://doi.org/10.1016/J.TOURMAN.2020.104200

Freeman, R. (2010). *Strategic management: A stakeholder approach*. Cambridge University Press. https://books.google.com/books?hl=en&lr=&id=NpmA_qEiOpkC&oi=fnd&pg=PR5&ots=62flD8RbNH&sig=MeqDHsrrXYFTAFOSoo12FQh1TsI

Gallagher, K. M., Chambers, A. J., Lin, J. H., Jacobs, K., & Robertson, M. M. (2023). Ergonomics advances in office work and work-from-home. *Proceedings of the Human Factors and Ergonomics Society*, *67*(1), 346–349. https://doi.org/10.1177/21695067231192577

Geissdoerfer, M., Pieroni, M. P. P., Pigosso, D. C. A., & Soufani, K. (2020). Circular business models: A review. *Journal of Cleaner Production*, *277*, 123741. https://doi.org/10.1016/j.jclepro.2020.123741

Gibson, K. (2022, November 29). What is a purpose-driven firm? | HBS Online. HBS Online. https://online.hbs.edu/blog/post/purpose-driven-firms

Gillis, K., & Gatersleben, B. (2015). A review of psychological literature on the health and wellbeing benefits of biophilic design. *Buildings*, *5*(3), 948–963. https://doi.org/10.3390/BUILDINGS5030948

Green Britain Group. (2021). About. Green Britain Group. https://www.greenbritaingroup.com/about/

Hahn, T., Figge, F., Pinkse, J., & Preuss, L. (2018). A paradox perspective on corporate sustainability: Descriptive, instrumental, and normative aspects. *Journal of Business Ethics*, *148*(2), 235–248. https://doi.org/10.1007/s10551-017-3587-2

Hammer, J., & Pivo, G. (2017). The triple bottom line and sustainable economic development theory and practice. *Economic Development Quarterly*, *31*(1), 25–36. https://doi.org/10.1177/0891242416674808;PAGE:STRING:ARTICLE/CHAPTER

Hart, S. L. (1995). A natural-resource-based view of the firm. *Academy of Management Review*, *20*(4), 17–45. https://doi.org/10.5465/AMR.1995.9512280033

Hart, S. L., & Dowell, G. (2011). A natural-resource-based view of the firm: Fifteen years after. *Journal of Management*, *37*(5), 1464–1479. https://doi.org/10.1177/0149206310390219

Hedge, A. (2016). Ergonomic workplace design for health, wellness, and productivity. In A. Hedge (Ed.), *Ergonomic workplace design for health, wellness, and productivity* (1st ed.). CRC Press. https://doi.org/10.1201/9781315374000/ERGONOMIC-WORKPLACE-DESIGN-HEALTH-WELLNESS-PRODUCTIVITY-ALAN-HEDGE/RIGHTS-AND-PERMISSIONS

Heerwagen, J., Kellert, S. R., & Mador, M. (2013). *Biophilic design: The theory, science, and practice of bringing buildings to life* (1st ed.). Wiley.

Hellström, D., & Olsson, J. (2024). Let's go thrift shopping: Exploring circular business model innovation in fashion retail. *Technological Forecasting and Social Change*, *198*, 123000. https://doi.org/10.1016/J.TECHFORE.2023.123000

Heslop, C. (2022). The three circles of happiness | Motivation. Motivation. https://vocal.media/motivation/the-three-circles-of-happiness

Huang, B., Gao, X., Xu, X., Song, J., Geng, Y., Sarkis, J., Fishman, T., Kua, H., & Nakatani, J. (2020). A life cycle thinking framework to mitigate the environmental impact of building materials. *One Earth*, *3*(5), 564–573. https://doi.org/10.1016/J.ONEEAR.2020.10.010

Hunger, T., Arnold, M., & Ulber, M. (2024). Circular value chain blind spot – A scoping review of the 9R framework in consumption. *Journal of Cleaner Production*, *440*, 140853. https://doi.org/10.1016/J.JCLEPRO.2024.140853

IKEA. (2024). *IKEA climate report FY24 introduction letter*. https://www.ikea.com/global/en/images/IKEA_Climate_Report_FY_24_2025_01_27_9136cd2347.pdf

IKEA. (2025). Our circular agenda – IKEA global. IKEA. https://www.ikea.com/global/en/our-business/sustainability/our-circular-agenda/

Jennings, V., Larson, L., Yun, J., Chakraborty, J., Grineski, S. E., & Collins, T. W. (2016). Advancing sustainability through urban green space: Cultural ecosystem services, equity, and social determinants of health. *International Journal of Environmental Research and Public Health*, *13*(2), 196. https://doi.org/10.3390/IJERPH13020196

Joyce, A., & Paquin, R. L. (2016). The triple layered business model canvas: A tool to design more sustainable business models. *Journal of Cleaner Production*, *135*, 1474–1486. https://doi.org/10.1016/J.JCLEPRO.2016.06.067

Joye, Y., & van den Berg, A. E. (2018). Restorative environments. *Environmental Psychology: An Introduction*, 65–75. https://doi.org/10.1002/9781119241072.CH7

Junça Silva, A., & Coelho, N. (2022). The moderating role of organizational culture on the relationship between workers' attitudes towards telework and happiness. *Kybernetes*, *52*, 4357–4374. https://doi.org/10.1108/K-02-2022-0231

Kallio, T. J., Kallio, K. M., & Blomberg, A. J. (2015). Physical space, culture, and organisational creativity – A longitudinal study. *Facilities*, *33*(5–6), 389–411. https://doi.org/10.1108/F-09-2013-0074/FULL/XML

Kaplan, R., & Kaplan, S. (1989). *The experience of nature: A psychological perspective*. https://books.google.com/books?hl=en&lr=&id=7l80AAAAIAAJ&oi=fnd&pg=PR7&ots=TrL0NJr82m&sig=GuUtVAoiXKPwNYlckWM69B6aMkc

Kaplan, R. S. (2010). *Conceptual foundations of the balanced scorecard (10–074)*. https://www.hbs.edu/ris/Publication%20Files/10-074_0bf3c151-f82b-4592-b885-cdde7f5d97a6.pdf

Kaplan, R. S., & Norton, D. P. (1992, February). *The balanced scorecard—Measures that drive performance*. HBR. https://hbr.org/1992/01/the-balanced-scorecard-measures-that-drive-performance-2

Kellert, S. R., & Wilson, E. O. (1993). The biophilia hypothesis. In *Bulletin of science, technology & society* (Vol. 15, Issue 1). Sage Publications. https://doi.org/10.1177/027046769501500125

Khan, A. J., Ul Hameed, W., Iqbal, J., Shah, A. A., Tariq, M. A. U. R., & Ahmed, S. (2022). Adoption of sustainability innovations and environmental opinion leadership: A way to foster environmental sustainability through diffusion of innovation theory. *Sustainability*, *14*(21), 14547. https://doi.org/10.3390/SU142114547

Khoury, B. (2023). Mindfulness and happiness. *Mindfulness*, *14*(11), 2824–2828. https://doi.org/10.1007/S12671-023-02226-0/METRICS

Ko, H., & Son, Y. (2018). Perceptions of cultural ecosystem services in urban green spaces: A case study in Gwacheon, Republic of Korea. *Ecological Indicators*, *91*, 299–306. https://doi.org/10.1016/J.ECOLIND.2018.04.006

Köhler, J., Sönnichsen, S. D., & Beske-Jansen, P. (2022). Towards a collaboration framework for circular economy: The role of dynamic capabilities and open innovation. *Business Strategy and the Environment*, *31*(6), 2700–2713. https://doi.org/10.1002/BSE.3000

Kolar-Schandlbauer, G., & Holly, F. (2025, March 24). *R-Principles of the circular economy – EFS consulting*. EFS Consultancy. https://efs.consulting/en/insight/r-strategies-cicular-economy/

Kumar, S., Lim, W. M., Sureka, R., Jabbour, C. J. C., & Bamel, U. (2023). Balanced scorecard: Trends, developments, and future directions. *Review of Managerial Science*, *18*(8), 2397–2439. https://doi.org/10.1007/S11846-023-00700-6

Kumar, V., & Ramachandran, D. (2021). Developing firms' growth approaches as a multidimensional decision to enhance key stakeholders' wellbeing. *International Journal of Research in Marketing*, *38*(2), 402–424. https://doi.org/10.1016/J.IJRESMAR.2020.09.004

Lacy, P., Long, J., & Spindler, W. (2020). *The circular economy handbook*. Palgrave Macmillan UK. https://doi.org/10.1057/978-1-349-95968-6

Lahcen, B., Eyckmans, J., Rousseau, S., Dams, Y., & Brusselaers, J. (2022). Modelling the circular economy: Introducing a supply chain equilibrium approach. *Ecological Economics*, *197*, 107451. https://doi.org/10.1016/J.ECOLECON.2022.107451

Leonardini, L. (2021, February 14). The purpose driven business canvas | Luca Leonardini | Medium. Lucaleonardini. https://lucaleonardini.medium.com/the-purpose-driven-business-canvas-8db5cd7a00b7

Louwman, R. C. (2023). Happiness-driven growth: Achieving business prosperity through happiness. In S. Chetri, T. Dutta, M. K. Mandal, & P. Patnaik (Eds.), *Understanding happiness: An explorative view* (1st ed., Vol. 1, pp. 401–430). Springer. https://doi.org/10.1007/978-981-99-3493-5_18

Lozano, R. (2008). Developing collaborative and sustainable organisations. *Journal of Cleaner Production*, *16*(4), 499–509. https://doi.org/10.1016/j.jclepro.2007.01.002

Lozano, R. (2018a). Proposing a definition and a framework of organisational sustainability: A review of efforts and a survey of approaches to change. *Sustainability (Switzerland)*, *10*(4), 1157. https://doi.org/10.3390/su10041157

Lozano, R. (2018b). Sustainable business models: Providing a more holistic perspective. *Business Strategy and the Environment*, *27*(8), 1159–1166. https://doi.org/10.1002/bse.2059

Lusch, R. F., Vargo, S. L., & O'Brien, M. (2007). Competing through service: Insights from service-dominant logic. *Journal of Retailing*, *83*(1), 5–18. https://doi.org/10.1016/J.JRETAI.2006.10.002

Lush. (2025). Resolution policy – We are Lush. Lush. https://weare.lush.com/lush-life/our-policies/resolution-policy/

Lyon, F., Stubbs, W., Dahlmann, F., & Edwards, M. (2024). From "business as usual" to sustainable "purpose-driven business": Challenges facing the purpose ecosystem in the United Kingdom and Australia. *Business and Society Review*, 1–24. https://wrap.warwick.ac.uk/id/eprint/183501/2/Business%20and%20Society%20Review%20-%202024%20-%20Lyon%20-%20From%20%20business%20as%20usual%20%20 to%20sustainable%20%20purpose%E2%80%90driven%20business%20%20%20Challenges.pdf

Mahajan, R., Lim, W. M., Sareen, M., Kumar, S., & Panwar, R. (2023). Stakeholder theory. *Journal of Business Research*, *166*, 114104. https://doi.org/10.1016/J.JBUSRES.2023.114104

Markus, H. R., & Kitayama, S. (1991). Culture and the self: Implications for cognition, emotion, and motivation. *Psychological Review*, *98*(2), 224–253. https://doi.org/10.1037/0033-295X.98.2.224

Marquis, C. (2025, January 14). *IKEA's circular economy: Redefining sustainability in the furniture industry*. Forbes. https://www.forbes.com/sites/christophermarquis/2025/01/14/ikeas-circular-economy-redefining-sustainability-in-the-furniture-industry/

Martínez-Falcó, J., Marco-Lajara, B., Sánchez-García, E., & Millan-Tudela, L. A. (2023). The scientific knowledge structure of happiness management in the business sphere: An exploratory bibliometric review. *Journal of Management Development*, *42*(6), 483–500. https://doi.org/10.1108/JMD-03-2023-0069/FULL/PDF

Martín-Gómez, A. M., Pineda-Ganfornina, M., Ávila-Gutiérrez, M. J., Agote-Garrido, A., & Lama-Ruiz, J. R. (2024). Balanced scorecard for circular economy: A methodology for sustainable organizational transformation. *Sustainability*, *16*(4), 1464. https://doi.org/10.3390/SU16041464

Mcqueen, D., & Turner, A. (2020). *Emerging green values in the UK energy sector. Ecotricity as deep-green exemplar*. https://eprints.bournemouth.ac.uk/34716/3/Emerging%20Green%20Values%20in%20the%20UK%20energy%20sector.pdf

Mearns, K., & Håvold, J. I. (2003). Occupational health and safety and the balanced scorecard. *TQM Magazine*, *15*(6), 408–423. https://doi.org/10.1108/09544780310502741

Mensah, C. A., Andres, L., Perera, U., & Roji, A. (2016). Enhancing quality of life through the lens of green spaces: A systematic review approach. *International Journal of Wellbeing*, *6*(1), 142–163. https://doi.org/10.5502/IJW.V6I1.445

Merriam-Webster. (2025). *BIOPHILIA definition & meaning – Merriam-Webster*. Merriam-Webster. https://www.merriam-webster.com/dictionary/biophilia

Miller, K. (2020, December 8). *The triple bottom line: What it is & why it's important*. HBR. https://online.hbs.edu/blog/post/what-is-the-triple-bottom-line

Mio, C., Costantini, A., & Panfilo, S. (2022). Performance measurement tools for sustainable business: A systematic literature review on the sustainability balanced scorecard use. *Corporate Social Responsibility and Environmental Management*, *29*(2), 367–384. https://doi.org/10.1002/CSR.2206

Muisyo, P. K., Qin, S., Ho, T. H., Julius, M. M., & Barisoava Andriamandresy, T. (2022). Implications of GHRM on organisational citizenship behaviour: The mediating role of enablers of green culture. *International Journal of Manpower*, *43*(3), 719–741. https://doi.org/10.1108/IJM-05-2020-0245/FULL/XML

Nademi, Y., & Khochiani, R. (2024). The pursuit of happiness in a circular economy. *Journal of the Knowledge Economy*, *15*(4), 18350–18377. https://doi.org/10.1007/S13132-024-01739-W/TABLES/12

Nazir, S., & Capocchi, A. (2024). Circular economy and balanced scorecard. In *Sustainability reporting practices and the circular economy* (pp. 225–276). Palgrave Macmillan. https://doi.org/10.1007/978-3-031-51845-4_6

Ndzabukelwako, Z., Mereko, O., Sambo, T., & Thango, B. (2024). The impact of porter's five forces model on SMEs performance: A systematic review. *SSRN*. https://doi.org/10.2139/SSRN.4999059

Neely, A., Adams, C., & Kennerley, M. (2001). Perspectives on performance: The performance prism. *Journal of Cost Management*, *15*(1), 7–15.

Olesson, E., Nenonen, S., & Newth, J. (2023). Enablers and barriers: The conflicting role of institutional logics in business model change for sustainability. *Organization and Environment*, *36*(2), 228–252. https://doi.org/10.1177/10860266231155210/ASSET/B6DE6EE0-48CF-42CC-AD42-B106C7C79FD9/ASSETS/IMAGES/LARGE/10.1177_10860266231155210-FIG2.JPG

Onat, N. C., Kucukvar, M., Halog, A., & Cloutier, S. (2017). Systems thinking for life cycle sustainability assessment: A review of recent developments, applications, and future perspectives. *Sustainability*, *9*(5), 706. https://doi.org/10.3390/SU9050706

Osterwalder, A., & Pigneur, Y. (2010). *Business Model Generation: A handbook for visionaries, game changers, and challengers*. John Wiley & Sons. https://mymyeo.com/wp-content/uploads/2022/12/Business-model-generation-_-a-handbook-for-visionaries-game-changers-and-challengers-PDFDrive-1.pdf

Pandey, D., & Jaiswal, A. K. (2017). Role of positive meta-cognitions and meta-emotions in satisfaction with life. *Indian Journal of Positive Psychology*, *8*(4), 291–297. https://www.proquest.com/openview/8af3d5095c3d1cfe177eaa869d203955/1?cbl=2032133&pq-origsite=gscholar

Patagonia. (2025). About – Patagonia action works. Petagonia Ltd. https://eu patagonia.com/gb/en/actionworks/about/?srsltid=AfmBOopIv7_ozqdnfbXGwd7vSDZFKfI-Fy8rHTLLM6kg9d3p17ejWv6jX

Pepple, L. (2019, November 4). Do you have an MTP? Your first step to exponential growth. Openexo. https://blog.openexo.com/do-you-have-an-mtp

Pinto, J. (2017). A multifocal framework for developing intentionally sustainable organizations. *Current Opinion in Environmental Sustainability*, *28*, 17–23. https://doi.org/10.1016/J.COSUST.2017.07.002

Podsakoff, P. M., MacKenzie, S. B., Paine, J. B., & Bachrach, D. G. (2000). Organizational citizenship behaviors: A critical review of the theoretical and empirical literature and suggestions for future research. *Journal of Management*, *26*(3), 513–563. https://doi.org/10.1177/014920630002600307

Polman, P., & Bhattacharya, C. B. (2016). *Engaging employees to create a sustainable business*. Stanford Social Innovation Review. https://ssir.org/articles/entry/engaging_employees_to_create_a_sustainable_business

Porter, M. E. (1979). How competitive forces shape strategy – Article – Faculty & Research – Harvard Business School. *Harvard Business Review*, *57*(2), 137–145. https://www.hbs.edu/faculty/Pages/item.aspx?num=10692

Porter, M. E. (1980). Industry structure and competitive strategy: Keys to profitability. *Financial Analysts Journal*, *36*(4), 30–41. https://doi.org/10.2469/FAJ.V36.N4.30

Porter, M. E. (1997). Competitive strategy. *Measuring Business Excellence*, *1*(2), 12–17. https://doi.org/10.1108/EB025476/FULL/HTML

Porter, M. E., & Kramer, M. (2011). The big idea: Creating shared value. How to reinvent capitalism—And unleash a wave of innovation and growth | request PDF. *Harvard Business Review*, *89*(1), 62–77. https://www.researchgate.net/publication/272576643_The_Big_Idea_Creating_Shared_Value_How_to_Reinvent_Capitalism-and_Unleash_a_Wave_of_Innovation_and_Growth

Porter, M. E., & Kramer, M. R. (2006). Strategy & society: The link between competitive advantage and corporate social responsibility. *Harvard Business Review*, *84*(01), 78–92. https://doi.org/10.4236/JHRSS.2023.111009

Porter & Kramer's (2006) "shared value." In *Encyclopedia of sustainable management* (pp. 1–6). Springer International Publishing. https://doi.org/10.1007/978-3-030-02006-4_393-1

Potting, J., Hekkert, M., Worrell, E., & Hanemaaijer, A. (2017). *Circular economy: Measuring innovation in the product chain*. https://www.researchgate.net/publication/319314335_Circular_Economy_Measuring_innovation_in_the_product_chain

Purpose-Economy. (2021). What's steward-ownership? – Purpose. Purpose-Economy. https://purpose-economy.org/en/whats-steward-ownership/

Reiff, M. (2024, August 2). Steward ownership, sustainability, and capitalism: Part 1 | Oxford Law Blogs. *Oxford Business Law Blog*. https://blogs.law.ox.ac.uk/oblb/blog-post/2024/08/steward-ownership-sustainability-and-capitalism-part-1

Ritter, M., & Schanz, H. (2019). The sharing economy: A comprehensive business model framework. *Journal of Cleaner Production*, *213*, 320–331. https://doi.org/10.1016/J.JCLEPRO.2018.12.154

Rogers, E. M. (1962). *Diffusion of innovations* (3rd ed.). Free Press.

Ryan, R. M., & Deci, E. L. (2000). Intrinsic and extrinsic motivations: Classic definitions and new directions. *Contemporary Educational Psychology*, *25*(1), 54–67. https://doi.org/10.1006/CEPS.1999.1020

Saram, H. (2015). Metacognition and happiness: The mediating role of perceived stress. *Studia Psychologica*, *57*(4), 271–283. https://doi.org/10.21909/SP.2015.03.699

Scheer, C., & Jansen, P. (2018). The role of metacognition in happiness. *Journal of Psychology & Psychotherapy*, *08*(8), 2161–0487. https://doi.org/10.4172/2161-0487-C1-024

Schein, E. H. (1983). The role of the founder in creating organizational culture. *Organizational Dynamics*, *12*(1), 13–28. https://doi.org/10.1016/0090-2616(83)90023-2

Schooler, J. W., & Mauss, I. B. (2009). To be happy and to know it: The experience and meta-awareness of pleasure. In M. L. Kringelbach & K. C. Berridge (Eds.), *Pleasures of the brain* (pp. 244–254). Oxford University Press. https://doi.org/10.1093/OSO/9780195331028.003.0016

Shoaakazemi, M., Javid, M., Keramati, R., & Tazekand, F. E. (2013). The relationship between happiness, meta cognitive skills (self-regulation, problem-solving) and academic achievement of students in Tehran. *Life Science Journal*, *10*(4s), 1097–8135. http://www.lifesciencesite.com.69

Šimonová, T., Malindzakova, M., & Malindzak, D. (2024). Integrating management strategy and porter's five forces model for the sustainable recycling of textile waste. *Sustainability*, *16*(21), 9283. https://doi.org/10.3390/SU16219283

Smeenk, S. (2024, October 7). *Ergonomic office design: Boosting productivity and employee health | EDGE Workspaces*. Edgeworkspaces. https://www.edgeworkspaces.com/ergonomic-office-design-maximizing-productivity-and-well-being-in-the-work-place/

Socha, M. (2020, November 11). *Chloé quietly shifts to purpose-driven business model*. WWD. https://wwd.com/feature/chloe-purpose-sustainability-women-1234652507/

Stahel, W. R. (2019). *The circular economy: A user's guide* (1st ed., Vol. 1). Routledge, Taylor & Francis Group. https://www.researchgate.net/publication/332935101_The_Circular_Economy_-_a_user's_guide

Stubbs, W., & Cocklin, C. (2008). Conceptualizing a "sustainability business model." *Organization and Environment*, *21*(2), 103–127. https://doi.org/10.1177/1086026608318042;JOURNAL:JOURNAL:OAEC;PAGE:STRING:ARTICLE/CHAPTER

Susnienė, D., & Jurkauskas, A. (2009). The concepts of quality of life and happiness – Correlation and differences. *The Engineering Economics*, *63*(3), 58–66. https://doi.org/10.5755/J01.EE.63.4.11648

Teece, D. J. (2007). Explicating dynamic capabilities: The nature and microfoundations of (sustainable) enterprise performance. *Strategic Management Journal*, *28*(13), 1319–1350. https://doi.org/10.1002/SMJ.640

Teece, D. J. (2010). Business models, business strategy and innovation. *Long Range Planning*, *43*(2–3), 172–194. https://doi.org/10.1016/j.lrp.2009.07.003

Teece, D. J. (2018). Business models and dynamic capabilities. *Long Range Planning*, *51*(1), 40–49. https://doi.org/10.1016/j.lrp.2017.06.007

Teece, D. J. (2023). The evolution of the dynamic capabilities framework. In R. Adams, D. Grichnik, A. Pundziene, & C. Volkmann (Eds.), *Artificiality and sustainability in entrepreneurship exploring the unforeseen, and paving the way to a sustainable future* (pp. 113–129). Springer Science and Business Media Deutschland GmbH. https://doi.org/10.1007/978-3-031-11371-0_6/FIGURES/1

Tiwari, V., & Thakur, S. (2021). Environment sustainability through sustainability innovations. *Environment, Development and Sustainability*, *23*(5), 6941–6965. https://doi.org/10.1007/S10668-020-00899-4/TABLES/12

Unilever. (2025). Leading the next era of corporate sustainability | Unilever. Unilever. https://www.unilever.com/sustainability/

United Nations Global Compact. (2022). United Nations global compact: Guide to corporate – Google Scholar. United Nations Global Compact. https://scholar.google.com/scholar_lookup?title=Guide%20to%20Corporate%20Sustainability&publication_year=2014&author=UNGC

van Dierendonck, D. (2011). Servant leadership: A review and synthesis. *Journal of Management*, *37*(4), 1228–1261. https://doi.org/10.1177/0149206310380462

Vargo, S. L., & Lusch, R. F. (2004). Evolving to a new dominant logic for marketing. *Journal of Marketing*, *68*(1), 1–17. https://doi.org/10.1509/jmkg.68.1.1.24036

Watson, W. (2022). *Circle of happiness* (Vol. 1). Independently published on Amazon. https://www.amazon.co.uk/Circle-Happiness-Willie-Watson/dp/B0BJ7ZGKB9

Webb, B. (2022, March 10). Want sustainable change? Convince your staff | Vogue business. Vogue Business. https://www.voguebusiness.com/sustainability/want-sustainable-change-convince-your-staff-lululemon-lush-loccitane

Webb, B. (2023, February 23). Chloé CEO on the power of regenerative leadership in fashion | Vogue Business. Vogue Business. https://www.voguebusiness.com/sustainability/chloe-ceo-on-the-power-of-regenerative-leadership-in-fashion-riccardo-bellini

WEF. (2022, January 27). 5 circular economy business models for competitive advantage | World Economic Forum. WEF. https://www.weforum.org/stories/2022/01/5-circular-economy-business-models-competitive-advantage/

Welsch, H. (2006). Environment and happiness: Valuation of air pollution using life satisfaction data. *Ecological Economics*, *58*(4), 801–813. https://www.sciencedirect.com/science/article/pii/S0921800905004179

Williams, A., Kennedy, S., Philipp, F., & Whiteman, G. (2017). Systems thinking: A review of sustainability management research. *Journal of Cleaner Production*, *148*, 866–881. https://doi.org/10.1016/J.JCLEPRO.2017.02.002

Zawadzki, S. J., Steg, L., & Bouman, T. (2020). Meta-analytic evidence for a robust and positive association between individuals' pro-environmental behaviors and their subjective wellbeing. *Environmental Research Letters*, *15*(12), 123007. https://doi.org/10.1088/1748-9326/ABC4AE

Zhong, W., Schröder, T., & Bekkering, J. (2022). Biophilic design in architecture and its contributions to health, well-being, and sustainability: A critical review. *Frontiers of Architectural Research*, *11*(1), 114–141. https://doi.org/10.1016/j.foar.2021.07.006

Zidanšek, A. (2007). Sustainable development and happiness in nations. *Energy*, *32*(6), 891–897. https://www.sciencedirect.com/science/article/pii/S0360544206002623

Chapter 5

The Financial Implications of Well-being Investments in the Workplace

Monika Kalani and Tanima Dutta

Lovely Professional University, India

Abstract

This chapter examines the financial implications of well-being investments in contemporary workplaces, providing a comprehensive analysis of return on investment (ROI) across multiple dimensions of employee welfare programmes. Through systematic examination of empirical evidence, the research demonstrates that strategic well-being investments yield substantial financial returns through reduced healthcare costs, enhanced productivity, decreased turnover, and improved employee engagement. The analysis reveals that workplace happiness programmes generate average ROI ratios of 3:1–6:1, whereas sustainable workforce practices reduce operational costs by 15–25% annually. Mental well-being initiatives consistently demonstrate strong financial outcomes, with productivity improvements of 12–20% and reductions in absenteeism of 25–40%. The chapter synthesises findings from multiple industries, highlighting sector-specific considerations and implementation strategies. Cost–benefit analyses indicate that comprehensive well-being programmes require initial investments of 2–4% of payroll but generate long-term profitability improvements of 8–15%. This research addresses ethical considerations while providing evidence-based recommendations for organisations seeking to optimise their well-being investment strategies. These findings contribute to the growing body of literature demonstrating that employee well-being represents not merely a moral imperative but a strategic financial opportunity for forward-thinking organisations.

Keywords: Workplace well-being; return on investment; employee engagement; productivity; financial performance; sustainable workforce practices

Circular Happiness: Building Sustainable Workplaces for the Next Generation, 93–110

doi:10.1108/978-1-80592-907-920261005

1. Introduction

The current business environment is witnessing a shift in organisational priorities, with employee well-being emerging as a key determinant of competitive and financial performance. Studies have underscored the importance of investment in workforce welfare in generating measurable returns through increased productivity, reduced costs, and enhanced organisational resilience (Bryson et al., 2017). The financial implications of well-being investments extend far beyond traditional human resource considerations and encompass the strategic dimensions of operational efficiency, risk management, and long-term profitability.

1.1. Importance of Well-being Investments in the Workplace

Modern organisations operate within increasingly complex environments characterised by technological disruption, demographic shifts, and evolving employee expectations. These dynamics have elevated well-being from a peripheral concern to a central business imperative, with research demonstrating clear linkages between employee welfare and organisational outcomes (Krekel et al., 2019). The business case for well-being investments rests on multiple pillars: enhanced individual and team performance, reduced healthcare and insurance costs, decreased turnover and recruitment expenses, and improved brand reputation and stakeholder value.

The evolution of workplace well-being reflects broader societal recognition of the importance of mental health and the changing nature of the work itself. Remote work arrangements, increased job complexity, and heightened performance expectations have created new stressors while simultaneously highlighting the need for comprehensive support systems (Kniffin et al., 2021). Organisations that proactively address these challenges through structured well-being programmes position themselves advantageously in talent markets, while building resilient, high-performing cultures.

Contemporary well-being initiatives encompass a diverse range of interventions, from traditional employee assistance programmes to innovative approaches that incorporate mindfulness training, flexible working arrangements, and comprehensive health-promotion activities. The sophistication of these programmes has increased substantially, with many organisations adopting evidence-based approaches that integrate behavioural science insights into technological solutions (Oswald et al., 2015).

1.2. Overview of Financial Implications

The financial implications of well-being investments manifest across multiple organisational levels and timeframes, requiring sophisticated analytical frameworks to capture their full impact. The direct economic benefits include reduced healthcare costs, decreased absenteeism, and lower turnover rates. Indirect benefits include enhanced productivity, improved customer satisfaction, and strengthened organisational reputation (Goetzel et al., 2014). These outcomes interact synergistically, creating compound effects that amplify the overall ROI in well-being.

Understanding these financial implications requires an examination of both quantitative metrics and qualitative outcomes that contribute to long-term organisational success. Traditional financial analysis methods often underestimate the full value of well-being programmes by focusing exclusively on easily measurable costs and benefits, while overlooking strategic advantages such as enhanced innovation capacity, improved risk management, and strengthened stakeholder relationships (Seligman & Schulman, 1986).

The complexity of measuring well-being investment returns stems from the multifaceted nature of these programmes and their varied implementation approaches across different organisational contexts. Successful measurement frameworks incorporate both leading and lagging indicators, accounting for both the immediate impact and long-term value creation. This comprehensive approach enables organisations to make informed decisions about programme design, resource allocation, and strategic priorities while building compelling business cases for continued investment in employee welfare initiatives.

2. The ROI of Workplace Happiness Programmes

2.1. Defining Workplace Happiness Programmes

Workplace happiness programmes represent systematic organisational interventions designed to enhance employee well-being, job satisfaction, and overall quality of life within professional contexts. These initiatives comprise a diverse range of approaches, from environmental modifications and policy changes to structured activities and comprehensive support services (Lyubomirsky et al., 2005). Contemporary happiness programmes integrate positive psychological principles with evidence-based interventions, creating holistic approaches that address multiple dimensions of the employee experience.

The theoretical foundation of workplace happiness programmes is drawn from extensive research on positive psychology, organisational behaviour, and human resource management. These programmes recognise that employee happiness extends beyond mere job satisfaction, encompassing broader concepts of engagement, meaning, and personal fulfilment within work contexts (Seligman, 2011). Effective programmes address both hedonic and eudaimonic, creating comprehensive approaches that support diverse employee needs and preferences.

Modern happiness programmes incorporate multiple components, including recognition and reward systems, social connection initiatives, professional development opportunities, work-life balance support, and environmental enhancements. The integration of these elements creates synergistic effects that amplify the benefits of individual programmes while addressing the complex, interconnected nature of employee well-being (Fredrickson, 2001). Successful programmes also emphasise measurement and continuous improvement, utilising data-driven approaches to optimise interventions and demonstrating value creation.

2.2. Measuring ROI in Well-being Initiatives

The measurement of ROI in well-being initiatives requires sophisticated methodological approaches that capture both tangible and intangible benefits, while accounting for implementation and opportunity costs. Traditional ROI calculations focus on easily quantifiable outcomes such as reduced healthcare expenses, decreased absenteeism, and lower turnover costs. However, comprehensive analyses must also incorporate productivity improvements, innovation enhancements, and strategic value creation (Baicker et al., 2010).

Effective ROI measurement frameworks employ multiple metrics and timeframes to capture the full spectrum of investment impacts on well-being. Short-term metrics include participation rates, employee satisfaction scores, and immediate cost reductions, while medium-term indicators encompass productivity changes, turnover rates, and healthcare utilisation patterns. Long-term measures focus on organisational performance indicators such as revenue growth, market share expansion, and stakeholder value creation (Goetzel et al., 2014).

The challenge of measuring well-being ROI stems from the complex causal relationships between interventions and outcomes, the presence of confounding variables, and the difficulty of isolating programme effects from other organisational changes. Robust measurement approaches utilise control groups, longitudinal designs, and statistical techniques to address these challenges, while providing credible evidence of programme effectiveness (Oswald et al., 2015). Additionally, successful measurement frameworks incorporate qualitative assessments that capture programmes' impacts on organisational culture, employee engagement, and strategic capabilities.

2.3. Case Studies: Successful Happiness Programme Implementations

Google's comprehensive well-being programme, known as 'gPause', demonstrates the substantial financial returns achievable through strategic investments in happiness. The programme combines mindfulness training, flexible working arrangements, comprehensive health benefits, and innovative workplace design to create an environment that supports employee well-being across multiple dimensions. Financial analysis reveals that Google's well-being investments generate ROI ratios exceeding 5:1 with robust returns from reduced turnover costs and enhanced productivity (Tan, 2012).

Johnson & Johnson's wellness programme represents one of the most extensively documented cases of successful well-being investment, with over three decades of implementation and measurement data. The programme encompasses health screening, fitness facilities, stress management training, and comprehensive support services, generating cumulative savings of over $250 million while improving employee health outcomes and job satisfaction. The programme's ROI has consistently exceeded 3:1, with recent analyses indicating returns of $2.71 for every dollar invested (Henke et al., 2011).

Microsoft's well-being initiative, 'Daily Pulse', illustrates the effectiveness of technology-enabled happiness programmes in the modern workplace context.

The programme utilises data analytics to personalise well-being interventions while providing managers with insights to support team welfare. Implementation results demonstrate 15% improvements in employee engagement scores, 20% reductions in stress-related absences, and 12% increases in productivity metrics, generating estimated annual returns of $4.2 million against programme costs of $1.1 million (Satya, 2017).

2.4. Challenges in Quantifying Happiness ROI

Quantification of the happiness programme ROI faces several methodological and practical challenges that complicate accurate measurement and evaluation. Attribution challenges arise from the difficulty of isolating programme effects from other organisational changes, economic conditions, and external factors that influence employee well-being and performance. These challenges require sophisticated analytical approaches that account for confounding variables while providing credible evidence for programme effectiveness (Krekel et al., 2019).

Temporal considerations present additional complexity, as well-being programmes often generate benefits over extended timeframes that may not align with traditional financial reporting cycles. Short-term costs may precede long-term benefits by creating cash flow considerations that require careful management and effective stakeholder communication. Additionally, some programme benefits, such as enhanced organisational reputation and improved stakeholder relationships, may not manifest in financial terms for several years following implementation (Lyubomirsky et al., 2005).

Measurement standardisation represents another significant challenge, as organisations employ diverse metrics, methodologies, and reporting frameworks that limit comparability and benchmarking opportunities. The absence of industry-standard measurement approaches complicates evidence synthesis and best practice identification while creating difficulties for organisations seeking to optimise their well-being investment strategies. Addressing these challenges requires collaborative efforts to develop standardised measurement frameworks that balance methodological rigour with practical implementation considerations (Oswald et al., 2015).

3. Reducing Costs through Sustainable Workforce Practices

3.1. Defining Sustainable Workforce Practices

Sustainable workforce practices encompass comprehensive approaches to human resource management that balance employee well-being, organisational performance, and environmental stewardship while creating long-term value for all stakeholders. These practices integrate the principles of sustainability science with evidence-based human resource strategies, creating holistic approaches that address the interconnected nature of social, environmental, and economic considerations (Ehnert, 2009). Contemporary sustainable workforce practices recognise that employee welfare and organisational success are mutually reinforcing rather than competing objectives.

The conceptual framework for sustainable workforce practices draws from multiple theoretical traditions, including stakeholder theory, the resource-based view, and systems thinking approaches to organisational management. These practices emphasise the development and maintenance of human capital while minimising negative externalities and maximising positive contributions to broader societal goals (Boudreau & Ramstad, 2005). Effective, sustainable practices address multiple dimensions of sustainability, including economic viability, social responsibility, and environmental stewardship.

Modern sustainable workforce practices incorporate flexible working arrangements, comprehensive professional development programmes, diversity and inclusion initiatives, environmental responsibility programmes, and community engagement activities. The integration of these elements creates synergistic effects that enhance employee engagement, while reducing operational costs and environmental impacts. Successful practices also emphasise stakeholder engagement and continuous improvement, utilising feedback mechanisms to optimise interventions and demonstrating value creation across multiple constituencies (Pfeffer, 2010).

3.2. Cost-saving Potential of Sustainable Practices

The cost-saving potential of sustainable workforce practices is evident across multiple operational dimensions, with research indicating that comprehensive sustainability programmes can reduce total employment costs by 15–25% annually while improving employee satisfaction and retention rates (Cascio, 2006). These savings resulted from reduced turnover costs, decreased absenteeism, lower healthcare expenses, and improved operational efficiency through enhanced employee engagement and productivity.

Energy and resource conservation initiatives represent significant cost-saving opportunities, with sustainable practices reducing facility costs through decreased energy consumption, waste reduction, and resource optimisation. Remote working arrangements and flexible scheduling options reduce facility requirements while enhancing employee satisfaction, thus yielding the dual benefits of cost reduction and improved well-being. Research indicates that organisations implementing comprehensive remote work policies achieve average annual cost savings of $11,000 per employee while maintaining or improving productivity levels (Global Workplace Analytics, 2020).

Technology-enabled sustainable practices create additional cost-saving opportunities through process automation, data-driven decision-making, and enhanced operational efficiency. Digital platforms that support remote collaboration, performance management, and employee development can reduce administrative costs while improving service quality and enhancing employee experience. These technological investments generate ROI ratios exceeding 4:1 within 2 years of implementation, with continuing benefits accumulating over extended timeframes (Deloitte, 2019).

3.3. Environmental and Social Benefits

The environmental benefits of sustainable workforce practices extend beyond direct cost savings to encompass broader value creation through enhanced organisational reputation, stakeholder relationships, and regulatory compliance. Reducing the carbon footprint through remote working arrangements, sustainable transportation programmes, and energy-efficient facilities creates measurable environmental benefits, while also reducing operational costs and regulatory risks (Elkington, 1997).

Social benefits include improved community relationships, enhanced brand reputation, and strengthened stakeholder engagement, all of which contribute to long-term organisational success. Sustainable workforce practices that emphasise diversity, inclusion, and community engagement create positive social impacts while building organisational capabilities that support innovation, market expansion, and risk management. Research indicates that organisations with strong sustainability programmes achieve 18% higher revenue growth and 16% higher profitability than their less-sustainable competitors (Eccles et al., 2014).

The integration of environmental and social considerations into workforce practices yields compound benefits that amplify the impacts of individual programmes while addressing the interconnected nature of sustainability challenges. These integrated approaches recognise that employee well-being, environmental stewardship, and social responsibility are mutually reinforcing objectives that contribute to long-term organisational resilience and success (Porter & Kramer, 2011).

3.4. Implementing Sustainable Practices: Strategies and Challenges

The successful implementation of sustainable workforce practices requires comprehensive change-management approaches that address organisational culture, systems, and processes while building stakeholder support and engagement. Implementation strategies must balance immediate operational requirements with long-term sustainability objectives, creating phased approaches that demonstrate value while building momentum for continued change (Kotter, 2012).

Leadership commitment and stakeholder engagement are critical success factors, as sustainable practices require sustained effort and investment to achieve their full potential. Practical implementation approaches emphasise communication, training, and support systems that enable employees to adapt to new practices while maintaining performance standards. Change management frameworks that incorporate feedback mechanisms and continuous improvement processes enhance implementation success while building organisational learning capabilities (Armenakis & Harris, 2009).

Implementation challenges include resistance to change, resource constraints, measurement difficulties, and competing organisational priorities that may impede progress towards sustainability objectives. Addressing these challenges requires sophisticated project management approaches that anticipate obstacles while building resilience and adaptability into the implementation plans.

Successful organisations utilise pilot programmes, phased rollouts, and iterative improvement processes to manage implementation risks while maximising learning opportunities and stakeholder engagement (Beer & Nohria, 2000).

4. The Link between Mental Well-being and Productivity

4.1. Understanding Mental Well-being in the Workplace

Mental well-being in workplace contexts encompasses multiple dimensions of psychological health, including emotional regulation, stress management, cognitive functioning, and interpersonal relationships, which collectively influence employee performance and organisational outcomes. Contemporary understanding of workplace mental health extends beyond the absence of mental illness to encompass positive psychological states characterised by resilience, engagement, and flourishing (Keyes, 2002). This expanded conceptualisation recognises that mental well-being exists on a continuum and can be actively promoted through targeted interventions and supportive organisational practices.

The theoretical foundation for workplace mental well-being draws from positive psychology, occupational health psychology, and organisational behaviour research, which demonstrates clear linkages between psychological states and performance outcomes. Mental well-being encompasses both hedonic (encompassing positive affect and life satisfaction) and eudaimonic (encompassing meaning, purpose, and personal growth) dimensions that interact to influence employee engagement, creativity, and resilience (Ryan & Deci, 2000). Understanding these multifaceted relationships enables organisations to develop comprehensive approaches that address diverse aspects of employee psychological health.

Workplace factors that influence mental well-being include job design characteristics, social support systems, organisational culture, leadership practices, and environmental conditions, which collectively create the context within which employees experience their work. Research indicates that organisations with supportive cultures and practices achieve significantly higher levels of employee mental well-being, with corresponding improvements in performance, retention, and organisational outcomes (Warr, 2007). These findings highlight the importance of systematic approaches to mental health promotion that address multiple organisational levels and intervention points.

4.2. Impact of Mental Health on Individual and Team Productivity

The relationship between mental health and productivity is exhibited through multiple pathways, including cognitive functioning, emotional regulation, interpersonal effectiveness, and physical health outcomes, which collectively influence individual and team performance. Research demonstrates that employees with higher levels of mental well-being achieve 31% higher productivity, generate 37% better sales performance, and exhibit 3 times higher levels of creativity than their less mentally healthy counterparts (Lyubomirsky et al., 2005).

Cognitive impacts on mental well-being include enhanced attention, memory, decision-making, and problem-solving capabilities, which directly influence work performance across diverse job functions. Positive mental states facilitate cognitive flexibility, creative thinking, and learning capacity while reducing the cognitive load associated with stress and negative emotions. These cognitive benefits translate into measurable productivity improvements, including faster task completion, higher-quality outputs, and enhanced innovation capacity (Fredrickson & Branigan, 2005).

Team-level impacts encompass improved communication, collaboration, and collective problem-solving capabilities that emerge from individual improvements in mental health. Teams with higher average levels of mental well-being demonstrate superior performance in complex tasks, exhibit greater resilience in challenging situations, and achieve higher levels of collective efficacy. Research indicates that team mental health interventions generate productivity improvements of 15–25% while reducing conflict and enhancing cooperation (West et al., 2009).

4.3. Strategies for Promoting Mental Well-being

Effective strategies for promoting workplace mental well-being encompass multiple intervention levels, including individual skill development, interpersonal support systems, and organisational culture change initiatives, which create comprehensive approaches to mental health promotion. Individual-level interventions include stress management training, mindfulness programmes, cognitive-behavioural skill development, and resilience-building activities that enhance employees' capacity to manage challenges and maintain psychological health (Goleman, 1995).

Interpersonal interventions focus on building social support networks, improving communication skills, and enhancing relationship quality through team-building activities, mentoring programmes, and conflict-resolution training. These approaches recognise that social connections represent fundamental determinants of mental well-being, while creating supportive environments that buffer against stress and promote positive psychological states (Cohen & Wills, 1985).

Organisational-level strategies encompass culture change initiatives, policy modifications, leadership development programmes, and environmental improvements that create systemic support for mental well-being. These approaches address structural factors that influence employee psychological well-being, including workload management, role clarity, decision-making authority, and support for work-life balance. Research indicates that comprehensive organisational approaches achieve greater and more sustained improvements in mental well-being than individual-focused interventions alone (Kompier & Cooper, 1999).

4.4. Measuring Productivity Gains from Mental Health Initiatives

Measuring productivity gains from mental health initiatives requires methodological approaches that capture multiple dimensions of performance improvement, while accounting for individual differences, contextual factors, and temporal variations in the effects of interventions. Effective measurement frameworks incorporate objective performance indicators and subjective well-being assessments to comprehensively evaluate programme effectiveness (Wright & Cropanzano, 2000).

Objective productivity measures include task completion rates, quality indicators, innovation metrics, and financial performance outcomes, all of which provide quantifiable evidence of the impact of mental health interventions. These measures must be carefully selected to reflect the specific job functions and organisational contexts within which interventions are implemented while accounting for potential confounding factors that may influence performance outcomes. Longitudinal measurement approaches enable the tracking of intervention effects over time while identifying optimal intervention timing and duration (Judge & Kammeyer-Mueller, 2012).

Subjective measures encompass employee self-reports of well-being, engagement, satisfaction, and perceived productivity, providing insights into intervention mechanisms and employee experience. These measures complement objective indicators while providing early warning signals of potential issues and opportunities for programme improvement. Advanced measurement approaches utilise multisource feedback, peer ratings, and supervisor assessments to triangulate findings and enhance measurement validity (Diener et al., 1999).

5. Lower Employee Turnover and Absenteeism

5.1. The Cost of High Turnover and Absenteeism

High employee turnover and absenteeism impose substantial financial burdens on organisations through direct costs, including recruitment, selection, training, and temporary staffing expenses, as well as indirect costs encompassing productivity losses, knowledge drain, and reduced service quality. Research indicates that voluntary turnover costs range from 50% to 200% of an employee's annual salary, with higher-skilled positions incurring proportionally higher replacement costs (Cascio, 2006). These costs accumulate rapidly in organisations with elevated turnover rates, creating significant drains on financial resources and operational efficiency.

Absenteeism costs encompass both direct expenses for replacement labour and indirect impacts, including reduced productivity, delayed project completion, and increased workload for the remaining employees. The average annual cost of unscheduled absenteeism reaches $3,600 per employee, with costs varying significantly across industries and job functions (Circadian, 2019). Chronic absenteeism creates additional challenges, including reduced team cohesion, increased stress on existing employees, and potential quality issues that may impact customer satisfaction and the organisation's reputation.

The hidden costs of turnover and absenteeism extend beyond immediate financial impacts to encompass strategic implications, including loss of institutional knowledge, reduced innovation capacity, and weakened customer relationships.

High turnover rates can create negative spirals where remaining employees experience increased workload and stress, leading to further departures and creating cycles of instability that undermine organisational performance. These strategic costs are often underestimated in traditional cost analyses but represent significant threats to long-term organisational success (Holtom et al., 2008).

5.2. Well-being Initiatives and Employee Retention

Well-being initiatives demonstrate substantial effectiveness in improving employee retention through enhanced job satisfaction, organisational commitment, and perceived organisational support, which reduces voluntary turnover intentions and behaviours. Comprehensive well-being programmes that address multiple dimensions of employee welfare create positive work experiences that strengthen psychological contracts and build emotional connections between employees and organisations (Meyer & Allen, 1991).

Research demonstrates that organisations with comprehensive well-being programmes achieve 40% lower turnover rates compared to organisations without such initiatives, with powerful effects for high-performing employees who have greater mobility options. The retention benefits of well-being programmes result from multiple mechanisms, including improved work-life balance, enhanced career development opportunities, strengthened social connections, and increased perceived organisational investment in employee welfare (Griffeth et al., 2000).

The financial impact of improved retention through well-being initiatives can be substantial, with organisations reporting annual savings of $1.2 million to $3.8 million in turnover-related costs following the implementation of comprehensive programmes. These savings result from reduced recruitment and training expenses, decreased productivity losses during transition periods, and retention of institutional knowledge that maintains operational efficiency. Additionally, improved retention rates enhance organisational stability and enable long-term strategic planning and investment (Allen et al., 2010).

5.3. Reducing Absenteeism through Health and Wellness Programmes

Health and wellness programmes consistently demonstrate effectiveness in reducing absenteeism through improved physical health, enhanced stress management capabilities, and increased employee engagement, all of which collectively contribute to lower absence rates and shorter durations of absence. Comprehensive programmes that address multiple health dimensions, including physical fitness, mental health, preventive care, and lifestyle factors, achieve the most significant reductions in absenteeism, with research indicating an average decrease of 25–30% in unscheduled absences (Goetzel & Ozminkowski, 2008).

Preventive health initiatives, including health screening, vaccination programmes, and early intervention services, reduce illness-related absences by identifying and addressing health issues before they require an extended time away from work. These programmes generate extreme returns on investment, with every dollar invested in preventive care generating $3–6 in reduced absenteeism costs. Mental health components of wellness programmes also significantly contribute to reducing absenteeism, addressing stress-related absences that represent a growing proportion of total absence rates (Burton et al., 2006).

The implementation of flexible work arrangements and supportive absence policies, as components of comprehensive wellness programmes, creates additional benefits for reducing absenteeism by enabling employees to manage health issues while maintaining productivity at work. These approaches recognise that traditional absence policies may inadvertently encourage extended absences by failing to accommodate minor health issues or family responsibilities. Flexible approaches that support an early return to work and accommodation of health needs achieve superior outcomes, while maintaining operational efficiency (Wooden, 1990).

5.4. Long-term Financial Benefits of Stable Workforce

A stable workforce generates substantial long-term financial benefits by enhancing productivity, improving customer relationships, reducing training costs, and increasing innovation capacity compounded over time to create significant competitive advantages. Workforce stability enables organisations to develop more profound expertise, stronger customer relationships, and more effective operational processes, which contribute to sustained performance improvements and market differentiation (Shaw et al., 2005).

The productivity benefits of workforce stability result from accumulated experience, refined skills, and enhanced teamwork, which develop through extended tenure and collaborative relationships. Stable teams demonstrate superior performance in complex tasks, exhibit greater efficiency in routine operations, and achieve higher levels of innovation through accumulated knowledge and trust. Research indicates that each additional year of average employee tenure correlates with a 2–3% improvement in organisational productivity (Hausknecht & Trevor, 2011).

Customer relationship benefits emerge from continuity in service delivery, a deeper understanding of customer needs, and enhanced trust, which develops through ongoing interactions with stable employee populations. These relationship benefits translate into higher customer satisfaction scores, increased customer retention rates, and improved revenue per customer, which significantly contribute to long-term profitability. Organisations with stable workforces report 12–18% higher customer satisfaction scores and 8–15% higher customer retention rates than organisations with high turnover (Reichheld, 2001).

6. Long-term Profitability through Employee Engagement

6.1. Defining and Measuring Employee Engagement

Employee engagement represents a multifaceted psychological state characterised by vigour, dedication, and absorption, reflecting the extent to which employees are emotionally connected to their work, committed to organisational success, and willing to invest discretionary efforts in achieving organisational objectives. Contemporary conceptualisations of engagement extend beyond job satisfaction to embrace deeper emotional and cognitive connections that drive sustained high performance and organisational citizenship behaviours (Schaufeli & Bakker, 2004).

The measurement of employee engagement requires comprehensive approaches that capture multiple dimensions of the engagement construct, while providing actionable insights for organisational improvement. Effective measurement frameworks incorporate cognitive engagement (intellectual involvement and attention), emotional engagement (positive feelings and emotional connections), and physical engagement (energy and effort investment) to provide holistic assessments of employee engagement levels (Kahn, 1990).

Modern engagement measurements utilise sophisticated survey instruments, pulse surveys, and behavioural indicators to provide real-time insights into engagement levels and trends. Advanced measurement approaches incorporate predictive analytics and machine learning techniques to identify engagement drivers, predict future engagement levels, and personalise intervention strategies. These technological enhancements enable organisations to move beyond traditional annual surveys to continuous engagement monitoring and improvement processes (Gallup, 2020).

6.2. The Connection between Engagement and Profitability

The relationship between employee engagement and organisational profitability is exhibited through multiple pathways, including enhanced productivity, improved customer satisfaction, reduced costs, and increased innovation, which collectively contribute to superior financial performance. Research shows that organisations in the top quartile of employee engagement achieve 23% higher profitability, 18% higher productivity, and 12% better customer metrics than organisations with low engagement levels (Gallup, 2017).

Productivity improvements resulting from enhanced engagement stem from increased discretionary effort, improved focus and attention, and enhanced collaboration, which enables employees to achieve superior performance outcomes. Engaged employees demonstrate 17% higher productivity, 10% higher customer ratings, and 40% lower turnover than their disengaged counterparts do. These performance improvements directly translate into financial benefits, including increased revenue generation, reduced operational costs, and enhanced competitive positioning (Harter et al., 2002).

The financial impact of engagement extends beyond immediate productivity gains to encompass strategic benefits, including enhanced innovation capacity, improved risk management, and strengthened organisational resilience, all of which contribute to long-term value creation. Engaged employees are more likely to identify improvement opportunities, suggest innovative solutions, and adapt effectively to changing conditions, creating organisational capabilities that support sustained competitive advantage and financial performance (Bakker & Demerouti, 2008).

6.3. Strategies for Fostering Engagement

Effective engagement strategies include multiple organisational levels and intervention points, recognising that engagement results from complex interactions between individual characteristics, job design factors, leadership practices, and organisational culture elements. Successful strategies address both hygiene factors that prevent disengagement and motivational factors that actively promote high levels of engagement and commitment (Herzberg et al., 1959).

Leadership development represents a critical component of engagement strategies, as immediate supervisors have the most significant influence on employee engagement levels through their daily interactions, feedback, and support behaviours. Effective leadership development programmes focus on building capabilities in communication, coaching, recognition, and empowerment, which enable managers to create engaging work experiences for their team members. Research indicates that manager quality accounts for 70% of the variance in employee engagement (Buckingham & Coffman, 1999).

Job design and career development initiatives create additional engagement benefits by ensuring that work roles provide appropriate challenges, autonomy, and growth opportunities that align with employees' capabilities and aspirations. These approaches recognise that engagement requires meaningful work that utilises employee strengths, while providing opportunities for skill development and career advancement. Comprehensive career development programmes that combine formal training, mentoring, and stretch assignments achieve robust engagement outcomes (Hackman & Oldham, 1976).

6.4. Overcoming Challenges in Engagement Initiatives

Engagement initiatives face several implementation challenges, including measurement difficulties, competing priorities, resource constraints, and cultural resistance, which can impede programme effectiveness and sustainability. Addressing these challenges requires comprehensive change management approaches that build stakeholder support, demonstrate value, and create sustainable systems to promote and maintain engagement (Kotter, 2012).

Measurement challenges arise from the complex and multifaceted nature of engagement, as well as the difficulty in establishing clear causal relationships between interventions and outcomes. Effective approaches utilise multiple measurement methods, longitudinal designs, and statistical techniques to provide credible evidence of programme effectiveness, while identifying areas for improvement. Advanced measurement frameworks also incorporate leading indicators that enable proactive intervention and continuous programme optimisation (Macey & Schneider, 2008).

Cultural resistance represents another significant challenge, particularly in organisations with traditional management approaches or cultures that emphasise control over empowerment. Overcoming cultural resistance requires sustained commitment to leadership, clear communication of the benefits of engagement, and demonstration of positive outcomes through pilot programmes and success stories. Change management strategies that emphasise participation, communication, and gradual implementation achieve greater success in building cultural support for engagement initiatives (Armenakis & Harris, 2009).

7. Conclusion

7.1. Synthesising the Financial Implications of Well-being Investments

The comprehensive analysis presented throughout this chapter demonstrates that well-being investments represent strategic opportunities for value creation rather than merely cost centres that require justification. Evidence consistently indicates that organisations implementing comprehensive well-being programmes achieve superior financial performance through multiple pathways, including reduced costs, enhanced productivity, improved retention, and increased profitability. These benefits compounded over time, creating sustainable competitive advantages that justified continued investment in employee welfare initiatives.

The financial returns from well-being investments vary across different programme components and organisational contexts, but consistently demonstrate favourable ROI ratios, ranging from 3:1 to 6:1, for comprehensive programmes. These returns result from synergistic effects between different programme elements that address multiple dimensions of employee welfare while creating reinforcing cycles of improvement. The evidence suggests that organisations achieve optimal returns through integrated approaches that combine individual interventions with systemic organisational changes, supporting sustained improvements in well-being.

7.2. Future Directions and Recommendations

Future research should focus on developing more sophisticated measurement frameworks that capture the full spectrum of well-being investment impacts, while addressing the methodological challenges that currently limit evaluation approaches. Longitudinal studies that track programme effects over extended timeframes will provide valuable insights into the sustainability of well-being investment benefits and optimal programme design characteristics. Additionally, research examining industry-specific factors and cultural considerations will enhance the generalisability and practical applicability of the well-being investment findings.

Organisations seeking to optimise their well-being investment strategies should adopt comprehensive approaches that integrate multiple intervention types while building measurement and continuous improvement capabilities. Successful implementation requires sustained leadership commitment, stakeholder engagement, and systematic change management approaches that address both the technical and cultural dimensions of programme implementation. The evidence presented in this chapter provides a compelling foundation for strategic well-being investments that create value for employees, organisations, and broader stakeholder communities.

References

Allen, D. G., Bryant, P. C., & Vardaman, J. M. (2010). Retaining talent: Replacing misconceptions with evidence-based strategies. *Academy of Management Perspectives, 24*(2), 48–64.

Armenakis, A. A., & Harris, S. G. (2009). Reflections: Our journey in organisational change research and practice. *Journal of Change Management, 9*(2), 127–142.

Baicker, K., Cutler, D., & Song, Z. (2010). Workplace wellness programs can generate savings. *Health Affairs, 29*(2), 304–311.

Bakker, A. B., & Demerouti, E. (2008). Towards a model of work engagement. *Career Development International, 13*(3), 209–223.

Beer, M., & Nohria, N. (2000). Cracking the code of change. *Harvard Business Review, 78*(3), 133–141.

Boudreau, J. W., & Ramstad, P. M. (2005). Talentship, talent segmentation, and sustainability: A new HR decision science paradigm for a new strategy definition. *Human Resource Management, 44*(2), 129–136.

Bryson, A., Forth, J., & Stokes, L. (2017). Does employees' subjective well-being affect workplace performance? *Human Relations, 70*(8), 1017–1037.

Buckingham, M., & Coffman, C. (1999). *First, break all the rules: What the world's most excellent managers do differently*. Simon & Schuster.

Burton, W. N., Chen, C. Y., Conti, D. J., Schultz, A. B., Pransky, G., & Edington, D. W. (2006). The association of health risks with on-the-job productivity. *Journal of Occupational and Environmental Medicine, 48*(5), 455–461.

Cascio, W. F. (2006). *Managing human resources: Productivity, quality of work life, profits*. McGraw-Hill.

Circadian. (2019). *The cost of poor sleep: Workplace productivity loss and associated costs*. Circadian Technologies.

Cohen, S., & Wills, T. A. (1985). Stress, social support, and the buffering hypothesis. *Psychological Bulletin, 98*(2), 310–357.

Deloitte. (2019). *The future of work in technology: How technology companies can win the war for talent*. Deloitte Insights.

Diener, E., Suh, E. M., Lucas, R. E., & Smith, H. L. (1999). Subjective well-being: Three decades of progress. *Psychological Bulletin, 125*(2), 276–302.

Eccles, R. G., Ioannou, I., & Serafeim, G. (2014). The impact of corporate sustainability on organisational processes and performance. *Management Science, 60*(11), 2835–2857.

Ehnert, I. (2009). *Sustainable human resource management: A conceptual and exploratory analysis from a paradox perspective*. Springer.

Elkington, J. (1997). *Cannibals with forks: The triple bottom line of 21st century business*. Capstone.

Fredrickson, B. L. (2001). The role of positive emotions in positive psychology: The broaden-and-build theory of positive emotions. *American Psychologist, 56*(3), 218–226.

Fredrickson, B. L., & Branigan, C. (2005). Positive emotions broaden the scope of attention and thought-action repertoires. *Cognition & Emotion, 19*(3), 313–332.

Gallup. (2017). *State of the global workplace*. Gallup Press.

Gallup. (2020). *State of the global workplace: 2020 report*. Gallup Press.

Global Workplace Analytics. (2020). *Work-at-home after Covid-19: Our forecast*. Global Workplace Analytics.

Goetzel, R. Z., & Ozminkowski, R. J. (2008). The health and cost benefits of work site health-promotion programs. *Annual Review of Public Health, 29*, 303–323.

Goetzel, R. Z., Henke, R. M., Tabrizi, M., Pelletier, K. R., Loeppke, R., Ballard, D. W., Grossmeier, J., Anderson, D. R., Yach, D., Kelly, R. K., McCalister, T., Serxner, S.,

Selecky, C., Shallenberger, L. G., Fries, J. F., Baase, C., Isaac, F., Crighton, K. A., … Metz, R. D. (2014). Do workplace health promotion (wellness) programs work? *Journal of Occupational and Environmental Medicine*, *56*(9), 927–934.

Goleman, D. (1995). *Emotional intelligence: Why it matters more than IQ*. Bantam Books.

Griffeth, R. W., Hom, P. W., & Gaertner, S. (2000). A meta-analysis of antecedents and correlates of employee turnover: Update, moderator tests, and research implications for the next millennium. *Journal of Management*, *26*(3), 463–488.

Hackman, J. R., & Oldham, G. R. (1976). Motivation through the design of work: Test of a theory. *Organisational Behavior and Human Performance*, *16*(2), 250–279.

Harter, J. K., Schmidt, F. L., & Hayes, T. L. (2002). Business-unit-level relationship between employee satisfaction, employee engagement, and business outcomes: A meta-analysis. *Journal of Applied Psychology*, *87*(2), 268–279.

Hausknecht, J. P., & Trevor, C. O. (2011). Collective turnover at the group, unit, and organisational levels: Evidence, issues, and implications. *Journal of Management*, *37*(1), 352–388.

Henke, R. M., Goetzel, R. Z., McHugh, J., & Isaac, F. (2011). Recent experience in health promotion at Johnson & Johnson: Lower health spending, strong return on investment. *Health Affairs*, *30*(3), 490–499.

Herzberg, F., Mausner, B., & Snyderman, B. B. (1959). *The motivation to work*. John Wiley & Sons.

Holtom, B. C., Mitchell, T. R., Lee, T. W., & Eberly, M. B. (2008). Turnover and retention research: A glance at the past, a closer review of the present, and a venture into the future. *Academy of Management Annals*, *2*(1), 231–274.

Judge, T. A., & Kammeyer-Mueller, J. D. (2012). Job attitudes. *Annual Review of Psychology*, *63*, 341–367.

Kahn, W. A. (1990). Psychological conditions of personal engagement and disengagement at work. *Academy of Management Journal*, *33*(4), 692–724.

Keyes, C. L. (2002). The mental health continuum: From languishing to flourishing in life. *Journal of Health and Social Behavior*, *43*(2), 207–222.

Kniffin, K. M., Narayanan, J., Anseel, F., Antonakis, J., Ashford, S. P., Bakker, A. B., Bamberger, P., Bapuji, H., Bhave, D. P., Choi, V. K., Creary, S. J., Demerouti, E., Flynn, F. J., Gelfand, M. J., Greer, L. L., Johns, G., Kesebir, S., Klein, P. G., Lee, S. Y., … van Vugt, M. (2021). COVID-19 and the workplace: Implications, issues, and insights for future research and action. *American Psychologist*, *76*(1), 63–77.

Kompier, M. A., & Cooper, C. L. (1999). *Preventing stress, improving productivity: European case studies in the workplace*. Routledge.

Kotter, J. P. (2012). *Leading change*. Harvard Business Review Press.

Krekel, C., Ward, G., & De Neve, J. E. (2019). Employee well-being, productivity, and firm performance. *Saïd Business School WP*, *4*, 1–34.

Lyubomirsky, S., King, L., & Diener, E. (2005). The benefits of frequent positive affect: Does happiness lead to success? *Psychological Bulletin*, *131*(6), 803–855.

Macey, W. H., & Schneider, B. (2008). The meaning of employee engagement. *Industrial and Organisational Psychology*, *1*(1), 3–30.

Meyer, J. P., & Allen, N. J. (1991). A three-component conceptualisation of organisational commitment. *Human Resource Management Review*, *1*(1), 61–89.

Oswald, A. J., Proto, E., & Sgroi, D. (2015). Happiness and productivity. *Journal of Labor Economics*, *33*(4), 789–822.

Pfeffer, J. (2010). Building sustainable organisations: The human factor. *Academy of Management Perspectives*, *24*(1), 34–45.

Porter, M. E., & Kramer, M. R. (2011). Creating shared value. *Harvard Business Review*, *89*(1/2), 62–77.

Reichheld, F. F. (2001). *The loyalty effect: The hidden force behind growth, profits, and lasting value*. Harvard Business Review Press.

Ryan, R. M., & Deci, E. L. (2000). Self-determination theory and the facilitation of intrinsic motivation, social development, and well-being. *American Psychologist*, *55*(1), 68–78.

Satya, N. (2017). *Hit refresh: The quest to rediscover Microsoft's soul and imagine a better future for everyone*. HarperBusiness.

Schaufeli, W. B., & Bakker, A. B. (2004). Job demands, job resources, and their relationship with burnout and engagement: A multi-sample study. *Journal of Organizational Behavior*, *25*(3), 293–315.

Seligman, M. E. (2011). *Flourish: A visionary new understanding of happiness and well-being*. Free Press.

Seligman, M. E., & Schulman, P. (1986). Explanatory style as a predictor of productivity and quitting among life insurance sales agents. *Journal of Personality and Social Psychology*, *50*(4), 832–838.

Shaw, J. D., Gupta, N., & Delery, J. E. (2005). Alternative conceptualisations of the relationship between voluntary turnover and organisational performance. *Academy of Management Journal*, *48*(1), 50–68.

Tan, C. M. (2012). *Search inside yourself: The unexpected path to achieving success, happiness (and world peace)*. HarperOne.

Warr, P. (2007). *Work, happiness, and unhappiness*. Lawrence Erlbaum Associates.

West, B. J., Patera, J. L., & Carsten, M. K. (2009). Team level positivity: Investigating positive psychological capacities and team level outcomes. *Journal of Organizational Behavior*, *30*(2), 249–267.

Wooden, M. (1990). *The changing Australian labour market*. Australian Government Publishing Service.

Wright, T. A., & Cropanzano, R. (2000). Psychological well-being and job satisfaction as predictors of job performance. *Journal of Occupational Health Psychology*, *5*(1), 84–94.

Chapter 6

Circular Economy Principles in Organisational Strategy

Ruchi Verma[a], *Rashmi Mathur*[a], *Sandeep Singh*[b] *and Surbhi Ghai*[a]

[a]*Lovely Professional University, India*
[b]*Amity University, India*

Abstract

A revolutionary method for obtaining long-term sustainability and corporate resilience is the incorporation of circular economy (CE) concepts into organisational planning. In contrast to conventional linear models, the CE places a strong emphasis on waste reduction, longevity of products extension, and resource efficiency. Organisations can rethink processes that improve operational effectiveness and environmental stewardship by incorporating these ideas into strategic frameworks. By removing waste and promoting resource loops that replenish rather than deplete, a zero-waste philosophy transforms corporate processes.

The growth of circular business models and the creation of sustainable value chains, goods, and services depend heavily on innovation. These models frequently call into question accepted wisdom, necessitating an overhaul of ownership, consumption, and disposal methods. Additionally, cross-industry partnerships create opportunities for knowledge sharing and large-scale resource recovery alongside fostering collaborative innovation. In order to scale circular processes and guarantee that their influence transcends organisational boundaries into larger economic and social systems, such collaborations are essential.

It becomes evident as companies work to develop circular efforts that leadership commitment, employee engagement, technology investment, and company culture must all support circularity. In order to provide a thorough grasp of how businesses can contribute to a sustainable, regenerative future

Circular Happiness: Building Sustainable Workplaces for the Next Generation, 111–130

doi:10.1108/978-1-80592-907-920261006

while obtaining a competitive edge, this chapter investigates the strategic application of CE principles across a number of dimensions, including operational redesign, mindset shift, innovation, collaboration, and scalability.

Keywords: Circular economy; workflow redesign; zero-waste operations; circular business models; sustainability innovation; cross-industry collaboration

1. Redesigning Workflows for Efficiency and Sustainability

1.1. Introduction: The Essential Function of Workflow Design in Circular Transitions

In the modern corporate landscape, organisations encounter growing demand to balance operational efficiency with environmental responsibility. This dual necessity has highlighted workflow transformation as a key tool for adopting CE concepts. Traditional workflow optimisation focused on linear productivity enhancements – maximising output while minimising time and labour inputs – whereas contemporary methodologies must address more intricate objectives: sustaining competitive performance while systematically eradicating waste, prolonging resource utility, and rejuvenating natural systems.

The shift from linear to circular operational models constitutes a major organisational problem of our day. Research conducted by the Ellen MacArthur Foundation (2021) indicates that around 80% of CE initiatives do not attain scalability when they overlook necessary process modifications. This number highlights a crucial point: CE concepts are merely theoretical without operational systems intentionally established to facilitate material recovery, product durability, and systemic collaboration. Workflows function as the circulatory system of circular implementation, facilitating the integration of regenerative ideas into daily practice.

This section provides a thorough analysis of how organisations might restructure workflows to line with CE goals while preserving or improving operational efficiency. We examine three fundamental dimensions:

- Circular process architectures: structural workflow alterations that substitute linear sequences with iterative cycles.
- Digital enablers: technological frameworks that facilitate the visibility and coordination necessary for circular systems.
- Cross-value chain integration: workflow improvements that connect organisational borders to establish circular ecosystems.

We illustrate, through comprehensive case studies and empirical data, how prominent organisations have restructured their operations to facilitate circular business models. The study culminates in a staged implementation approach and forthcoming innovations that are poised to enhance circular workflow design.

1.2. Designing Circular Workflows: Principles and Practices

- Transitioning from linear throughput to closed-loop processes: Conventional manufacturing and service processes adhere to simple, linear trajectories – raw materials are introduced, transformed, and subsequently emerge as goods intended for disposal. Principles of the CE necessitate a fundamental re-evaluation of these sequences, substituting linear processes with continuous loops that preserve materials at their optimal utility (Kirchherr et al., 2017). This change necessitates workflow reconfiguration at many tiers.
- Integration of modular design: workflows must integrate disassembly and reassembly as fundamental process phases rather than as mere afterthoughts. Philips Healthcare's shift to modular medical equipment design achieved 90% component recovery rates by standardising connecting interfaces and streamlining separation operations (Bressanelli et al., 2022). Their production workflows now incorporate specialised disassembly stations equipped with toolkits and instructions tailored for circular returns.
- Dynamic material distribution: circular operations necessitate astute decision points where materials can diverge to their most valuable endpoints. H&M's garment collecting system employs RFID tagging and automatic sorting to allocate used clothing to appropriate channels: resale (high-quality goods), repair (damaged pieces), or recycling (worn fabrics). This multi-path workflow enhanced material recovery rates from 35% to 65% over a three-year period (H&M Group, 2023).

1.3. Digital Framework for Circular Implementation

The intricacy of circular systems – monitoring materials throughout various lifecycles, managing reverse flows, and enhancing refurbishment processes – surpasses human management capabilities without digital enhancement. Three technology tiers are especially vital:

- Blockchain-enabled material passports: digital product identities accompanying real items facilitate precise material tracking throughout ownership transitions. The World Business Council for Sustainable Development (2022) reported a 92% accuracy in material composition tracking via blockchain-based passports, in contrast to 60% with traditional approaches in automobile recycling.
- Digital twin simulation: digital duplicates of tangible objects facilitate the evaluation of disassembly sequences and refurbishment procedures prior to actual intervention. Accenture (2023) examination of industrial equipment manufacturers revealed that the deployment of digital twins decreased remanufacturing planning time by 30% and enhanced the quality of recovered components.
- Computer vision classification: advanced imaging technologies automate the separation of waste streams at granular levels unattainable by manual sorting. The Ellen MacArthur Foundation (2023) claimed a 99% purity rate in polymer separation at facilities employing artificial intelligence (AI)-driven optical sorting, facilitating the manufacturing of food-grade recycled plastic.

1.4. Case Study: Renault's Transformation in Circular Manufacturing

- Strategic context and challenges
  Confronted with rigorous European Union end-of-life car standards requiring 95% recyclability, Renault initiated an extensive overhaul of its manufacturing processes Groupe Renault (2020). The automaker required the conversion of conventional assembly-line methods into technologies adept at efficient disassembly and material recovery, all while preserving production efficiency.

- Innovations and implementation of workflow

  Standardised disassembly procedures
  Renault engineers established over 1,200 comprehensive takedown protocols delineating tools, routines, and safety precautions for car disassembly. These standards were incorporated directly into production workflow documents, facilitating a seamless transition between assembly and disassembly activities (Renault Group, 2022).

  Industrial symbiosis framework
  A digital marketplace links waste products from Renault's 12 production plants with prospective buyers across several industries. The system autonomously aligns material attributes (composition, quantity, and location) with receiver specifications, generating circular flows that were previously concealed by organisational boundaries (Frosch & Gallopoulos, 2022).

  Predictive remanufacturing scheduling
  Machine-learning algorithms evaluate returning component condition data to enhance refurbishment processes. Renault diminished remanufacturing lead times by 40% relative to traditional batch processing by forecasting the components necessitating repair procedures (Lüdeke-Freund et al., 2023).

- Performance outcomes and business impact:
  - €480 million in annual income generated via circular operations.
  - Reduction of 1.2 million tonnes in CO_2 emissions.
  - 89% diversion of manufacturing waste from landfills.
  - 58% enhancement in component separation efficacy.

1.5. Framework for Implementing Circular Workflows

- Phase 1: assessment of current state circularity
  Organisations must first identify current obstacles to the introduction of circular practices. The Circle Economy (2022) advocates:

  Material flow mapping
  Record all material inputs, transformations, and outputs throughout operational processes. Identify the locations of linear lock-ins – points at which materials cannot readily re-enter the production cycle.

  Analysis of circularity gap
  Evaluate present material retention rates in relation to industry standards and theoretical maxima. This identifies key areas for workflow intervention.

- Phase 2: pilot redesign initiatives
  Targeted interventions provide evidence of feasibility prior to organisation-wide implementation:

  Rapid victory selection
  Commence with processes that have significant cyclic potential and minimal implementation difficulty. Packaging recovery technologies generally yield swift returns; IKEA attained 80% reuse of corrugated materials within 6 months of operational modifications (IKEA, 2023).

  Workshops on circular design thinking
  Cross-functional teams innovate processes by employing CE ideas. Philips Lighting's 'Light-as-a-Service' paradigm originated from these workshops, radically transforming installation, maintenance, and recovery processes (Bocken et al., 2020).

- Phase 3: expansion and ecosystem integration

  Advanced implementations necessitate much collaboration
  Digital coordination platforms' cloud-based systems integrate internal workflows with external collaborators. Cisco's product return site collaborates with logistics providers to enhance reverse transit routes, resulting in a 35% reduction in emissions (Cisco, 2023).

1.6. Emerging Innovations in Circular Workflow Design

- Integration of biological processes

  Mycelium-derived bio factories
  Fungal networks exhibit potential for self-assembling components, which could transform industrial processes. Initial study indicates mycelium's capacity to create structural materials from agricultural waste streams (Jones et al., 2022).

- Advanced computational applications

  Quantum-enhanced material identification
  Quantum computing has the potential to resolve intricate material pairing issues within global supply networks within seconds, facilitating real-time optimisation of circular flows (Preskill, 2018).

  Generative AI for process design
  Extensive language models propose workflow configurations that optimise both efficiency and circularity. Initial adopters indicate a 25% enhancement in material recovery rates due to AI-suggested adjustments (Dwivedi et al., 2023).

2. Zero-waste Mindset in Business Operations

2.1. Introduction

The linear economic model of 'take-make-dispose' has prevailed in industrial production for decades; however, its environmental and economic constraints are becoming increasingly evident. As enterprises encounter increasing demands to implement sustainable practices, the zero-waste philosophy has arisen as a transformative strategy that corresponds with the concepts of a CE. This theory transcends conventional waste management by fundamentally re-evaluating the flow of resources inside manufacturing processes. Recent studies indicate that organisations using zero-waste policies realise both environmental advantages and considerable operational efficiency along with cost reductions (Geissdoerfer et al., 2017; Kirchherr et al., 2017).

2.2. Theoretical Foundations of Zero Waste in Business

The zero-waste notion originates from industrial ecology and CE theory. It fundamentally rejects the conventional emphasis of the waste hierarchy on disposal and instead prioritises source avoidance. The Zero Waste International Alliance defines zero waste as 'the conservation of all resources through responsible production, consumption, reuse, and recovery of products, packaging, and materials, without incineration or discharges to land, water, or air that jeopardise the environment or human health' (ZWIA, 2018). This definition emphasises the holistic character of authentic zero-waste systems, necessitating a re-evaluation of entire value chains instead than merely implementing incremental enhancements to current operations.

Scholarly literature has delineated numerous fundamental characteristics that differentiate zero-waste operations from traditional waste management. Initially, it necessitates the design of products and processes with consideration for their full existence, guaranteeing that materials can be perpetually reintroduced into production (Braungart & McDonough, 2019). Secondly, it necessitates a transition from ownership to access models, wherein corporations maintain accountability for products for their entire lifespan (Bocken et al., 2020). Third, it requires the establishment of industrial ecosystems in which one company's waste serves as another's raw material, a principle referred to as industrial symbiosis (Chertow, 2020). These concepts collectively embody a comprehensive strategy for waste elimination that transcends mere recycling efforts.

Recent studies have substantiated the economic rationale for zero-waste operations. Research conducted by Lieder and Rashid (2021) revealed that firms implementing CE ideas, such as zero-waste policies, realised average material cost reductions of 20–30%. Ghisellini et al. (2020) noted that regulatory pressures are expediting adoption, with companies that proactively embrace zero-waste initiatives achieving first-mover advantages in their sectors. These data indicate that zero waste is evolving from a peripheral environmental endeavour to an integral aspect of competitive company strategy.

2.3. Integrating Zero Waste into Business Operations

Transitioning to zero-waste operations necessitates a comprehensive strategy that encompasses all facets of organisational functioning. The initial essential stage entails doing thorough waste audits to pinpoint material flows and leakage spots within the value chain. Jia et al. (2022) claim that these audits should extend beyond mere measurement to comprehend the systemic origins of waste production. Numerous prominent companies have created advanced material flow analysis technologies that monitor resources from intake to final disposal, facilitating targeted interventions at the most critical waste sources.

Product and process redesign constitutes a vital component of zero-waste adoption. The cradle-to-cradle design framework, established by Braungart and McDonough (2019), offers a methodology for producing items that can be entirely disassembled, allowing their components to be either safely reintegrated into biological systems or perpetually circulating throughout industrial systems. This methodology has been effectively implemented across various sectors, ranging from modular electronics engineered for effortless repair and enhancement to packaging techniques that completely eradicate single-use materials. Research conducted by Zaman and Lehmann (2021) emphasises that these design changes not only decrease waste but frequently enhance product performance and customer satisfaction.

Organisational culture and staff involvement are equally crucial in zero-waste transformations. Masi et al. (2021) discovered that organisations with the most effective zero-waste efforts possessed deeply ingrained sustainability ideals inside their corporate culture, bolstered by training programmes that provided staff at all levels with waste reduction competencies. This culture shift frequently necessitates dismantling departmental silos and establishing cross-functional teams dedicated to waste reduction. Certain organisations have instituted internal 'shadow pricing' systems that attribute financial costs to waste production, thereby rendering its economic implications apparent throughout decision-making processes (Lewandowski, 2021).

2.4. Case Study: Interface's Mission Zero Programme

Interface, a global leader in modular flooring, exemplifies the effective implementation of zero waste in business operations. The company's 'Mission Zero' initiative, initiated in the 1990s under CEO Ray Anderson, sought to eradicate all adverse environmental effects by 2020 (Interface, 2023). Through this approach, Interface evolved from a conventional carpet manufacturer to a leader in circular business models, attaining significant outcomes in waste reduction.

The company's strategy integrated product reengineering with advanced manufacturing techniques. Interface created carpet tiles that may be effortlessly removed and recycled, departing from conventional broadloom carpet that usually concludes in landfills. They created an innovative reclamation procedure that retrieves discarded carpet tiles for recycling into new products (Interface, 2023). These approaches enabled Interface to attain a 96% waste diversion rate from landfills and a 50% reduction in overall manufacturing waste.

3. Innovations in Circular Business Models

Circular business models have brought about a major shift from the traditional view of 'take-make-dispose' way of doing business to more sustainable practices. Contemporary businesses fall into the endless loop of resource extraction and generating waste. However, these circular business models focus on creating sustainable value by wisely using the resources and keeping materials in circular use for their optimum and maximum utilisation. Society at large is recognising the environmental and economic downsides of linear economic systems (Geissdoerfer et al., 2020). This has sparked interest among researchers, companies, and policymakers to explore the area of CE (Geissdoerfer et al., 2020). Circularity in business is defined as rethinking how businesses operate; it encompasses product designing, supply chains working and building relationships with customers (Geissdoerfer et al., 2020). The concept of circular business models goes beyond just recycling. It is about designing products and services that are built to last, easy to repair, and ready to be reused or remanufactured, where this model helps us grow the economy without exploiting resources (Adam et al., 2017).

3.1. Types of Innovations in Circular Business Models

3.1.1. Product as a Service Model

Organisations following circular business models are using a wide variety of creative strategies to keep materials in circulation and make products last longer. One approach is suggested as 'product-as-a-service' model. In this approach, customers don't buy a product; instead, they pay to use it (Gallo et al., 2023; Lacy et al., 2019). This change redefines ownership and incentivises companies to maintain responsibility over product performance and its lifecycle. In this model, customers pay for the use of a product, while the provider retains ownership (Tukker, 2015). This encourages firms to design for durability, modularity, and easy recovery since they benefit from reusing assets and minimising material losses (Lacy & Rutqvist, 2015). This model supports long-term customer relationships. Companies primarily differentiate themselves by offering high-performance services rather than competing only on price. Organisations shift their focus from volume-based profits to value-based outcomes. Subsequently, from the environmental perspective, this model holds substantial potential to differentiate economic growth from resource consumption. By retaining ownership and optimising product use across multiple life cycles, businesses tend to reduce waste generation (Bocken et al., 2016). Additionally, it enables better tracking and management of products throughout their lifecycle, facilitating efficient resource recovery and the circular flow of materials (see Fig. 6.1).

Various industries are embracing this model. For example, in the automotive sector, companies like Volvo and BMW offer car subscription services that bundle maintenance and insurance into a single fee. Similarly, in office technology, Xerox has long provided printers as a service, charging customers per printed page. Similarly, in the consumer electronics and furniture industries, firms like Grover and IKEA are experimenting with rental and subscription-based offerings (Stahel, 2016).

3.1.2. Modular Design

These strategic shifts encourage companies to make more durable and high-quality products, as they are responsible for managing them until they reach the end of their life (Gallo et al., 2023; Lacy et al., 2019). The shift towards circular business models is witnessing a broad spectrum of innovations that span from product design, material science, digital technologies, to business operations. These innovations support reducing waste and resource consumption, they also create new opportunities for value creation and customer engagement. In this vein, Santa-Maria et al. (2022) suggested that innovative design thinking plays a foundational role in enabling business circularity. Wherein, organisations increasingly emphasises durability, repairability, and resource efficiency, with them assuming extended responsibility over product performance and management throughout product's life cycle (Gallo et al., 2023; Lacy et al., 2019). As a result, innovation in product design has emerged as a cornerstone of circularity, enabling businesses to separate value creation from linear resource consumption. One of the prominent circular business strategies is modular design, where it allows products to be easily repaired, upgraded, or reconfigured, extending their useful life. This design focuses on creating products as assemblies of standardised, interchangeable modules that can be easily removed, replaced, or upgraded. Such modularity allows for simpler maintenance, repair, and customisation, thereby extending the overall product lifespan and enhancing functionality (Bocken et al., 2016). In addition, strategy-like design for disassembly supports easier material recovery and recycling by minimising the effort required to break down products at end of their life (Bakker et al., 2014). These design approaches are shifting focus of businesses from short-term product turnover to long-term utility and circular resource flows. This approach is prevalent in industries like: electronics, furniture, and consumer appliances (Bocken et al., 2016). For example, brands like Fairphone in electronics and IKEA in furniture offer modular products designed for repair and reconfiguration, enabling longer product use and reducing environmental impact (Bocken et al., 2016; Santa-Maria et al., 2022).

3.1.3. Sustainable Materials

Furthermore, the development and use of sustainable materials are pivotal to circular business models. Companies are increasingly investing in bio-based, recyclable, or regenerative materials to reduce dependence on extraction of new and raw resources. For example, some organisations are using biodegradable bioplastics which are derived from algae, corn starch, or sugarcane offering alternatives for petroleum-based plastics (Rossi et al., 2020).

3.1.4. Chemical Recycling

In addition, organisations are utilising innovative textile fibres, such as those developed through chemical recycling of old garments, further enabling a circular fashion system (Ellen MacArthur Foundation, 2021). A significant progress has been made in chemical recycling and automated material sorting to improve the economics and feasibility of circular loops. Chemical recycling goes beyond traditional mechanical recycling, enabling the production of high-quality recycled materials indistinguishable from raw resources (Hopewell et al., 2009).

3.1.5. Block-chain and Technology

Following the digital transformation, blockchain technology is highly being used to create tamper-proof records of material origins, movements, and certifications enhancing trust and traceability in circular supply chains (Upadhyay et al., 2021). In addition, digital product passports provide consumers and recyclers with access to a product's material composition and repair history, which supports reuse and recycling efforts (Ellen MacArthur Foundation, 2021). Subsequently, AI-driven robotic sorting systems can now identify and separate complex materials at high speed and accuracy, enhancing the efficiency of material recovery facilities (Jones & Comfort, 2021).

3.1.6. Resource Recovery

Another important area of innovation is in resource recovery finding smarter ways to reclaim valuable materials from what we usually throw away (Jones & Comfort, 2021). It is the process of reclaiming valuable materials from end-of-life products, industrial by-products, or post-consumer waste streams. As businesses move away from linear 'take-make-dispose' models, resource recovery has emerged as a key innovation area aimed at reducing dependency on new and raw

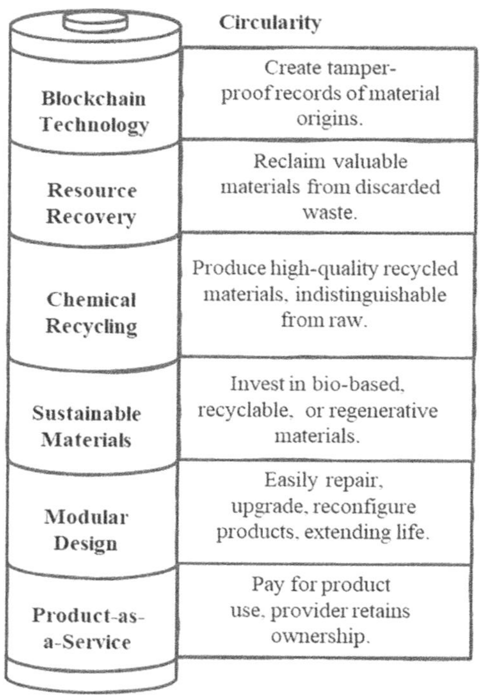

Fig. 6.1. Circular Economy Innovations. *Source*: Authors' compilation.

resources, minimising environmental degradation, and promoting closed-loop material flows (Jones & Comfort, 2021). Resource recovery entails the extraction and reuse of materials that would otherwise be discarded. These may include precious metals from electronic waste, plastics from packaging, or nutrients from organic waste. This not only contributes to environmental goals but also presents economic opportunities for the organisations by reducing material costs and creating new revenue streams from waste.

Resource recovery is being applied across a range of sectors. For example, in electronics, firms are recovering rare earth elements and precious metals from devices through urban mining. Similarly, agri-food sector is following a similar path with anaerobic digestion and composting technologies to recover energy and nutrients from organic waste (Velenturf et al., 2019).

4. Cross Industry Collaborations for a Circular Future

Despite organisational borders, systemic evolution is required to make the transition from a linear to a CE. The primary driver of this transition is cross-industry collaboration that fosters innovative technology, sustainable business models, and integrated resource systems. The conceptual foundations, practical applications, and strategic structures that support cross-industry cooperation in pursuit of a circular future are explored in this chapter. The chapter highlights how these collaborations might generate social, economic, and environmental value through case studies, strategic models, and policy research.

4.1. Introduction

At an unprecedented level environmental and financial challenges are arising in the twenty-first century. Growing junk collection, biodiversity loss, climate change, and depletion of resources have all emphasised the limitations of the traditional nonlinear economic model, which is fundamentally predicated on the 'take-make-dispose' concept. According to this paradigm in which raw resources are taken out, transformed into goods, utilised by consumers, and then disposed away, which often results in significant environmental harm and social injustice.

The CE, also known as CE, has drawn worldwide interest as a potential route to sustainable development in response to these urgent problems. The CE encourages a restorative and regenerative approach to economic activity, in contrast to the linear model. By closing material loops through techniques including reuse, recycling, remanufacturing, and refurbishment, it highlights the continuous usage of resources (Ellen MacArthur Foundation, 2013). In order to promote sustainable development over the long term, the CE framework tries to decouple economic growth from resource consumption in addition to reducing waste and minimising environmental effects.

Nonetheless moving towards a CE cannot be done in a vacuum. Whole industrial ecosystems must undergo structural adjustments. Cross-industry cooperation becomes vital at this point. Cross-industry collaborations are strategic alliances of businesses from many industries that cooperate to accomplish common circular objectives. These partnerships make use of the distinct advantages, resources, and skills of many industries to jointly develop creative solutions that promote long-term value generation (Geissdoerfer et al., 2017).

Addressing complex sustainability issues that are outside the purview of particular businesses or sectors requires such cooperative efforts. For instance, smart circular systems for monitoring and maximising resource flows can be created by combining digital innovations from the information technology sector with material innovation from the manufacturing sector. The repurposing of organic waste for building materials can also be made possible by partnerships between the agriculture and construction industries. In addition to broadening the use of circular processes, these cross-sector collaborations promote creativity, adaptability, and new business prospects.

The goal of this chapter is to examine the various facets of cross-sector partnerships for a circular future. It starts by looking at the reasons behind and necessity of these kinds of partnerships in light of the demands of global sustainability. After that, it explores the several models and strategic frameworks – such as digital platforms, collaborative supply chains, and industrial symbiosis – that facilitate cross-sectoral cooperation. Case studies from the real world show how these models have been successfully applied in various sectors and geographical areas. The chapter also critically examines the difficulties and impediments to productive cooperation, including data silos, regulatory fragmentation, and misaligned incentives. In order to promote and scale cross-industry relationships and hasten the circular transition, it concludes by providing policymakers, corporate executives, and civil society actors with strategic advice.

4.2. The Importance of Inter-industry Cooperation

Multi-sectoral, comprehensive collaboration is necessary to achieve circularity on a large scale. Systemic circularity is limited since industries usually function inside their own value chains and infrastructures. Companies can use complementary skills and resources to achieve common sustainability objectives through cross-industry collaboration.

- Financial cooperation: industry-wide economic cooperation lowers operational risks and promotes cost efficiency. For instance, by working together to develop fibre regeneration technologies, textile manufacturers and chemical industries can lessen their reliance on virgin resources and divert textile waste from landfills. These collaborations can speed up innovation while drastically reducing R&D and production expenses.
- Innovation ecosystems: collaborations across industries contribute to the development of innovation ecosystems where technologies and knowledge meet. Biodegradable packaging, compostable medical devices, and modular

construction systems are examples of circular solutions that are being developed by combining biotechnology, data analytics, and materials science. Iterative learning, agility, and experimentation thrive in such settings (Bocken et al., 2023).

4.3. Models of Cross-industry Collaboration

Several models support the implementation of circularity through cross-industry partnerships. These include industrial symbiosis, digital platforms, and formal alliances or consortiums.

- Industrial symbiosis: the sharing of resources, energy, water, and byproducts amongst conventionally distinct sectors is known as industrial symbiosis. One innovative example is the Kalundborg Symbiosis in Denmark, where businesses such as farms, refineries, and power plants share resources, leading to major economic and environmental advantages (Chertow, 2020).
- Online resources: reusable materials can be identified and exchanged in real time across industries thanks to digital platforms. Examples that assist in diverting garbage from landfills to new industrial uses include the US Business Council for Sustainable Development's Materials Marketplace and the Global Plastic Watch (World Economic Forum, 2022).
- Partnerships for circular businesses: formal partnerships like the Ellen MacArthur Foundation's CE100 network and the European Plastics Pact offer organised platforms for cooperation between producers, retailers, recyclers, and legislators. These partnerships establish shared objectives, performance standards, and schedules for promoting circularity.

4.4. Frameworks for Strategic Implementation

Effective cross-industry collaboration implementation necessitates strong strategic frameworks that coordinate goals, organisational structures, and procedures among involved organisations.

- Inter-organisational proximity: the term 'inter-organizational proximity' describes how closely cooperating organisations share beliefs, objectives, and methods of operation. While institutional and cognitive proximity improves communication and trust, geographic proximity can facilitate logistics (Léger et al., 2023). Mutual learning and the diffusion of innovations are more likely to occur when people are close to one another.
- Collaborative circular supply chains (CCSC): reverse logistics, lifecycle assessments, and closed-loop material flows across industries are all integrated into CCSC. Data openness, cooperative governance structures, and shared IT infrastructure are necessary for these chains. Linear production systems can be converted into adaptive, regenerative systems thanks to CCSCs (Wieland, 2021).

4.5. Case Studies

Real-world examples demonstrate the potential of cross-industry collaborations to generate circular outcomes.

- Kalundborg Symbiosis, Denmark: one of the best-known instances of industrial symbiosis and a model for cross-industry cooperation is Kalundborg Symbiosis. It is situated in Denmark and unites public and private businesses from a variety of industries, including as municipal services, biotechnology, pharmaceuticals, and energy. In a closed-loop system, these partners trade water, energy, and byproducts. For instance, effluent from a pharmaceutical firm is cleansed and utilised again in industrial operations, and a nearby fish farm uses excess heat from a power station.
- Significant cost savings, less carbon emissions, and decreased resource usage have resulted from this partnership. More significantly, it shows that cross-sectoral collaborations based on trust and sustained collaboration are feasible (Jacobsen, 2006).
- The Ellen MacArthur Foundation and the CE100 Network: The Ellen MacArthur Foundation launched the CE100 Network, a global platform aimed at promoting innovation in the CE through cooperation. It unites corporations, governments, communities, universities, and up-and-coming entrepreneurs from a variety of industries. Participating companies test scalable solutions, collaborate on projects, and exchange best practices. One of its main characteristics is its emphasis on pre-competitive cooperation, in which participants work together to eliminate structural obstacles to circularity.
- Companies such as Google, H&M, Unilever, and Philips have investigated new materials, regenerative farming methods, and circular design concepts in a cooperative setting through the CE100 (Ellen MacArthur Foundation, 2019).

4.6. Challenges and Barriers

Despite the potential, several barriers limit the scalability of cross-industry circular collaborations.

- Misaligned incentives: conflicting priorities result from the different operational, financial, and legal restrictions that different businesses face. These disparities can be resolved by establishing value-sharing agreements and common key performance indicators (KPIs).
- Regulatory fragmentation: cooperation is hampered by disparate and occasionally conflicting regulatory frameworks between jurisdictions. Supporting material movement and product interoperability requires globally standardised standards and regulations.
- Data silos: insufficient availability of high-quality data restricts the capacity to monitor materials and assess performance. Digital product passports and blockchain are two examples of technologies that can close data gaps and guarantee accountability and openness.

5. Scaling Circular Practices Beyond the Workplace

One of the main pillars of international attempts to achieve sustainability is the idea of the CE. The CE seeks to rethink processes in order to eliminate waste, maintain materials in use, and renew natural resources, in contrast to the traditional linear economy, which operates on a take-make-dispose basis (Ellen MacArthur Foundation, 2019). Although circular techniques are becoming more popular in the business and manufacturing sectors, their use in communities and outside of the workplace must be expanded immediately. The need for embracing circular methods at the societal level is becoming increasingly more urgent as worldwide environmental issues, including pollution, resource depletion, and climate change worsen (Geissdoerfer et al., 2017).

5.1. Understanding CE beyond the Workplace

An organisation's recycling and energy-saving efforts were only one component of the CE model. Regional repair cafés, tool-sharing libraries, composting initiatives, apparel exchanges, and circular food systems are instances of community-level circularity (Kirchherr et al., 2017). These programmes promote local economic growth and community resilience while reducing material usage and carbon footprints.

Through circular procurement laws, green infrastructure, and zero-waste attempts, several cities have implemented CE principles (Pires & Martinho, 2019). In contrast, long-standing environmentally friendly practices like rainwater gathering, food preservation, and seed saving in rural areas inherently fit with circular goals. It is necessary to respect local contexts and understanding systems while documenting, adapting, and scaling these practices.

5.2. Education: Building Circular Mindsets

The most essential tool for implementing circular behaviours might be education. Including ideas from the CE in educational as well as informal systems guarantees that the next generation will be trained with a systems-thinking attitude. According to Wiek et al. (2011), CE education ought to include economics, design, engineering, and social sciences in addition to environmental studies.

Multidisciplinary courses that teach lifespan assessment, material innovation, and cradle-to-cradle product design, for instance, can be offered by universities. Students who pursue vocational schools can gain hands-on experience in trash management, upcycling, and product repair. According to Azevedo et al. (2017), public workshops and platforms for lifelong learning can equip citizens with the information they need to take part in community-driven sustainability.

Local role models and storytelling must also be incorporated into educational initiatives. Personal narratives of those who have incorporated circular solutions into them.

Educational efforts also need to leverage storytelling and local role models. Personal stories of people who have implemented circular solutions in their homes, neighbourhoods, or small businesses can inspire others to follow suit, making the abstract concept of circularity tangible and relatable.

5.3. Policy and Infrastructure: Creating Enabling Conditions

Policy frameworks play a vital role in creating the structural conditions for circular practices to flourish outside the workplace. Governments can promote CE through tax incentives for reuse and repair businesses, extended producer responsibility (EPR) schemes, and public procurement that favours circular products (European Commission, 2020).

Infrastructure also matters. For example, establishing neighbourhood-scale composting stations or materials recovery centres makes circular behaviours easier and more accessible for residents. Zoning policies can be amended to support the creation of maker spaces, repair hubs, and community gardens (OECD, 2019).

Participatory policymaking is essential for success. When local residents are involved in designing and implementing CE initiatives, they are more likely to embrace and sustain them. Cities like Amsterdam and Copenhagen have become global models for urban circularity precisely because of their inclusive, multi-stakeholder approaches (Williams, 2019).

5.4. Community-based Circular Models

The base of any initiative to spread circularity outside of business organisations is community engagement. Circular practices can be integrated into everyday life, as seen by an increasing number of grassroots initiatives.

For example, Repair Cafés, which started in the Netherlands and have since expanded all over the world, enable volunteers to assist neighbours in repairing damaged home objects rather than throwing them away (Charter & Keiller, 2014). Tool libraries promote resource sharing rather than private ownership by making frequently used equipment, such as drills, ladders, and gardening instruments, accessible (McLaren & Agyeman, 2015).

5.5. Businesses as Circular Community Anchors

Businesses must implement sustainable practices and operate as catalysts for wider community adoption as part of their dual function in circular transformation. CE practices like closed-loop applications manufacturing, leasing models, and equipment take-back programmes have already been used by many companies (Bocken et al., 2016).

Businesses may collaborate with local communities to co-create circular approaches in order to scale these practices. Businesses can, for instance, support community recycling programmes, collaborate with non-governmental organisations to promote sustainability education, or hold workshops to impart repair skills. By providing refill stations and encouraging clients to return used packaging, retailers can help the community cut the amount of single-use trash.

Businesses can make an important contribution in expanding circularity outside of the workplace by considering themselves as social catalysts in addition to economic actors.

5.6. Measuring Impact and Sharing Knowledge

Evaluating and exchanging the effects of circular practices is essential to expanding them successfully. Metrics should include social indicators like local employment, skill development, and involvement in the community in addition to environmental advantages like trash diversion or CO_2 reductions (Murray et al., 2017).

Communities can use tools like life cycle analysis (LCA), social impact assessments, and circularity indicators to support their choices and enhance their tactics over time. replicating and modifying circular models throughout regions can be encouraged by sharing success stories via academic platforms, social media, and conferences.

Knowledge sharing, case studies, and resources for scaling effective practices worldwide are made accessible by international networks like the CE Club and the Ellen MacArthur Foundation's CE100.

Future competitiveness will increasingly rely on this operational transformation. Organisations that purposefully redesign workflows as circular enablers will uncover new value streams in material recovery, establish robust supply networks, and safeguard against resource limitations. The problem and potential reside in acknowledging that CE principles are merely theoretical until integrated into the daily operations of organisations.

References

Accenture. (2023). *Digital twins for circular manufacturing*. https://www.accenture.com

Adam, S., Bucker, C., Desguin, S., Vaage, N., & Saebi, T. (2017). Taking part in the circular economy: Four ways to designing circular business models. *SSRN Electronic Journal*. https://doi.org/10.2139/ssrn.2908107

Azevedo, S. G., Godina, R., & Matias, J. C. O. (2017). Proposal of a framework to assess the compliance of Industry 4.0 applications with the circular economy principles. *Resources, Conservation and Recycling*, *129*, 247–258. https://doi.org/10.1016/j.resconrec.2017.10.019

Bakker, C. A., Wang, F., Huisman, J., & den Hollander, M. C. (2014). Products that go round: Exploring product life extension through design. *Journal of Cleaner Production*, *69*, 10–16. https://doi.org/10.1016/j.jclepro.2014.01.028

Bocken, N. M. P., Short, S. W., Rana, P., & Evans, S. (2016). A literature and practice review to develop sustainable business model archetypes. *Journal of Cleaner Production*, *65*, 42–56. https://doi.org/10.1016/j.jclepro.2013.11.039

Bocken, N. M. P., de Pauw, I., Bakker, C., & van der Grinten, B. (2020). Product design and business model strategies for a circular economy. *Journal of Industrial and Production Engineering*, *37*(5), 308–320. https://doi.org/10.1080/21681015.2020.1764545

Braungart, M., & McDonough, W. (2019). *Cradle to cradle: Remaking the way we make things*. North Point Press.

Bressanelli, G., Perona, M., & Saccani, N. (2022). Implementing circular economy in the healthcare sector: Challenges and opportunities. *Journal of Industrial Ecology, 26*(3), 850–865. https://doi.org/10.1111/jiec.13220

Charter, M., & Keiller, S. (2014). *Grassroots innovation and the circular economy: A global survey of repair cafés and makerspaces*. The Centre for Sustainable Design, University for the Creative Arts.

Chertow, M. R. (2020). Industrial symbiosis: Literature and taxonomy. *Annual Review of Energy and the Environment, 25*(1), 313–337. https://doi.org/10.1146/annurev.energy.25.1.313

Circle Economy. (2022). *The circularity gap report 2022*. https://www.circularity-gap.world/2022

Cisco. (2023). *Cisco CSR report 2023: Circular economy in action*. https://www.cisco.com/c/en/us/about/csr.html

Dwivedi, Y. K., Kshetri, N., Hughes, L. O., Slade, E. L., Jeyaraj, A., Kar, A. K., Baabdullah, A. M., Koohang, A., Raghavan, V., Ahuja, M., Albanna, H., Albashrawi, M. A., Al-Busaidi, A. S., Balakrishnan, J., Barlette, Y., Basu, S., Bose, I., Brooks, L., Buhalis, D., … Wright, R. (2023). So what if ChatGPT wrote it? Multidisciplinary perspectives on opportunities, challenges and implications of generative conversational AI for research, practice and policy. *International Journal of Information Management, 71,* 102642.

https://doi.org/10.1016/j.ijinfomgt.2023.102642

Ellen MacArthur Foundation. (2013). Towards the circular economy Vol. 1: Economic and business rationale for an accelerated transition. https://ellenmacarthurfoundation.org/towards-the-circular-economy-vol-1

Ellen MacArthur Foundation. (2019). *Completing the picture: How the circular economy tackles climate change.* Ellen MacArthur Foundation.

Ellen MacArthur Foundation. (2021). *Universal circular economy policy goals*. Ellen MacArthur Foundation.

Ellen MacArthur Foundation. (2023). *Circular economy systems diagram*. Ellen MacArthur Foundation.

European Commission. (2020). *A new circular economy action plan for a cleaner and more competitive Europe*. https://ec.europa.eu/environment/circular-economy

Frosch, R. A., & Gallopoulos, N. E. (2022). Strategies for manufacturing. *Scientific American, 261*(3), 144–152. https://doi.org/10.1038/scientificamerican0989-144

Gallo, P., Sanseverino, E. R., Sciumè, G., & Zizzo, G. (2023). How blockchain technology can address circularity and trace emission in the energy sector. *Qeios, 5*(9). https://doi.org/10.32388/n19qmp.2

Geissdoerfer, M., Pieroni, M. P., Pigosso, D. C., & Soufani, K. (2020). Circular business models: A review. *Journal of Cleaner Production, 277*, 123741. https://doi.org/10.1016/j.jclepro.2020.123741

Geissdoerfer, M., Savaget, P., Bocken, N. M. P., & Hultink, E. J. (2017). The circular economy–A new sustainability paradigm?*Journal of Cleaner Production, 143*, 757–768. https://doi.org/10.1016/j.jclepro.2016.12.048

Ghisellini, P., Cialani, C., & Ulgiati, S. (2020). A review on circular economy: The expected transition to a balanced interplay of environmental and economic systems. *Journal of Cleaner Production, 114*, 11–32. https://doi.org/10.1016/j.jclepro.2015.09.007

Groupe Renault. (2020). *Universal registration document*. Renault Group. https://www.renaultgroup.com/en/2020-Universal-Registration-Document

H&M Group. (2023). *Sustainability report 2023: Closing the loop*. https://hmgroup.com/sustainability

Hopewell, J., Dvorak, R., & Kosior, E. (2009). Plastics recycling: Challenges and opportunities. *Philosophical Transactions of the Royal Society B: Biological Sciences, 364*(1526), 2115–2126. https://doi.org/10.1098/rstb.2008.0311

IKEA. (2023). *Sustainability report FY23: Circular & climate positive*. https://www.ikea.com

Interface. (2023). *Mission zero: Our sustainability journey*. https://www.interface.com/US/en-US/about/sustainability

Jacobsen, N. B. (2006). Industrial symbiosis in Kalundborg, Denmark: A quantitative assessment of economic and environmental aspects. *Journal of Industrial Ecology, 10*(1–2), 239–255. https://doi.org/10.1162/108819806775545411

Jacobsen, N. B. (2006). Industrial symbiosis in Kalundborg, Denmark: A quantitative assessment of economic and environmental aspects. *Journal of Industrial Ecology, 10*(1–2), 239–255. https://doi.org/10.1162/108819806775545411

Jones, M., Raman, A., & Kakarla, A. (2022). Mycelium composites in manufacturing: A review of performance standards. *Journal of Cleaner Production, 366*, 132882. https://doi.org/10.1016/j.jclepro.2022.132882

Jones, P., & Comfort, D. (2021). The circular economy: An exploratory case study from the paper and retail industries. *Athens Journal of Business & Economics, 7*(4), 379–394. https://doi.org/10.30958/ajbe.7-4-5

Kirchherr, J., Reike, D., & Hekkert, M. (2017). Conceptualizing the circular economy: An analysis of 114 definitions. *Resources, Conservation and Recycling, 127*, 221–232. https://doi.org/10.1016/j.resconrec.2017.09.005

Lacy, P., Long, J., & Spindler, W. (2019). *The circular economy handbook: Realizing the circular advantage*. Palgrave Macmillan.

Lacy, P., & Rutqvist, J. (2015). *Waste to wealth: The circular economy advantage*. Palgrave Macmillan.

Léger, P. M., Robert, J., Cronan, T. P., & Babin, B. J. (2023). A multidimensional framework for inter-organizational proximity. *Journal of Business Research, 156*, 113462. https://doi.org/10.1016/j.jbusres.2022.113462

Lewandowski, M. (2021). *Designing the business models for circular economy—Towards the conceptual framework. Sustainability, 8*(1), 43. https://doi.org/10.3390/su8010043

Lieder, M., & Rashid, A. (2021). Towards circular economy implementation: A comprehensive review in context of manufacturing industry. *Journal of Cleaner Production, 115*, 36–51. https://doi.org/10.1016/j.jclepro.2015.12.042

Lüdeke-Freund, F., Gold, S., & Bocken, N. M. P. (2023). Sustainable business model and supply chain innovations. *International Journal of Innovation Management, 27*(1), 2340001. https://doi.org/10.1142/S1363919623400010

Masi, D., Day, S., & Godsell, J. (2021). Supply chain configurations in the circular economy: A systematic literature review. *Sustainability, 9*(9), 1602. https://doi.org/10.3390/su9091602

McLaren, D., & Agyeman, J. (2015). *Sharing cities: A case for truly smart and sustainable cities*. MIT Press.

Murray, A., Skene, K., & Haynes, K. (2017). The circular economy: An interdisciplinary exploration of the concept and application in a global context. *Journal of Business Ethics, 140*(3), 369–380. https://doi.org/10.1007/s10551-015-2693-2

OECD. (2019). *The circular economy in cities and regions: Synthesis report*. OECD Publishing. https://doi.org/10.1787/b6f3d4fe-en

Pires, A., & Martinho, G. (2019). Waste hierarchy index for circular economy in waste management. *Waste Management, 95*, 298–305. https://doi.org/10.1016/j.wasman.2019.06.014

Preskill, J. (2018). Quantum computing in the NISQ era and beyond. *Quantum, 2*, 79. https://doi.org/10.22331/q-2018-08-06-79

Renault Group. (2022). *Circular economy report: The factory of the future*. https://www.renaultgroup.com

Rossi, M., Germani, M., & Zamagni, A. (2020). Review of ecodesign methods and tools. *Journal of Cleaner Production*, *282*, 124523. https://doi.org/10.1016/j.jclepro.2020.124523

Santa-Maria, T., Vermeulen, W. J., & Baumgartner, R. J. (2022). The circular sprint: Circular business model innovation through design thinking. *Journal of Cleaner Production*, *362*, 132323. https://doi.org/10.1016/j.jclepro.2022.132323

Stahel, W. R. (2016). *The circular economy: A user's guide*. Routledge.

Tukker, A. (2015). Product services for a resource-efficient and circular economy – A review. *Journal of Cleaner Production*, *97*, 76–91. https://doi.org/10.1016/j.jclepro.2013.11.049

Upadhyay, A., Mukhuty, S., Kumar, V., & Kazancoglu, Y. (2021). Blockchain technology and the circular economy: Implications for sustainability and social responsibility. *Journal of Cleaner Production*, *293*, 126130. https://doi.org/10.1016/j.jclepro.2021.126130

Velenturf, A. P. M., Purnell, P., Tregent, M., Ferguson, J., & Holmes, A. (2019). Resource recovery from waste: Restoring the balance between resource scarcity and waste overload. *Sustainability*, *11*(17), 4643. https://doi.org/10.3390/su11174643

Wiek, A., Withycombe, L., & Redman, C. L. (2011). Key competencies in sustainability: A reference framework for academic program development. *Sustainability Science*, *6*(2), 203–218. https://doi.org/10.1007/s11625-011-0132-6

Wieland, H. (2021). Circular supply chain management. *International Journal of Physical Distribution & Logistics Management*, *51*(3), 247–268. https://doi.org/10.1108/IJPDLM-12-2019-0363

Williams, J. (2019). Circular cities: Challenges to implementing looping actions. *Sustainability*, *11*(2), 423. https://doi.org/10.3390/su11020423

World Business Council for Sustainable Development. (2022). *Circular transition indicators: Measuring circularity at company level*. https://www.wbcsd.org

World Economic Forum. (2022). *The future of circular digital platforms*. https://www.weforum.org

Zaman, A. U., & Lehmann, S. (2021). Urban growth and waste management optimization towards "zero waste city". City, *Culture and Society*, *5*(2), 93–102. https://doi.org/10.1016/j.ccs.2014.04.007

Zero Waste International Alliance. (2018). *Zero waste definition*. https://zwia.org/zero-waste-definition/

Chapter 7

Measuring Happiness: Key Performance Indicators (KPIs)

Shikha Goyal, Tanima Dutta and Anushikha Sharma

Mittal School of Business, Lovely Professional University, India

Abstract

In the post-pandemic era, employee happiness has emerged as a strategic metric with significant implications for organisational performance and sustainability. While traditional well-being programmes and self-report surveys have attempted to address workforce satisfaction, they often fall short in objectivity, scale, and real-time responsiveness. This chapter explores the evolution of workplace happiness measurement by analysing psychological theories, empirical studies, AI-driven tools, and global benchmarking models. Integrating frameworks like Seligman's positive emotion, engagement, relationships, meaning, and achievement (PERMA) model and OECD's WISE Centre initiatives, the discussion highlights core well-being dimensions and the relevance of customised key performance indicators (KPIs) across industries. Technological advancements – including sentiment analysis, facial recognition, predictive analytics, and real-time dashboards – now enable a comprehensive and dynamic understanding of employee happiness. Moreover, ethical concerns around artificial intelligence (AI) usage, such as data privacy and algorithmic bias, are critically addressed. Case studies from organisations like Google, Salesforce, and national programmes in the UAE illustrate the practical application of happiness analytics. The chapter concludes by advocating for circular happiness models that link individual, organisational, and environmental well-being, proposing happiness as not merely an HR concern but a vital input in strategic decision-making and sustainable growth.

Keywords: Workplace happiness; employee well-being; KPIs; AI-driven analytics; PERMA model; sentiment analysis; organisational psychology; circular happiness; ethical AI; employee engagement

Circular Happiness: Building Sustainable Workplaces for the Next Generation, 131–150

doi:10.1108/978-1-80592-907-920261007

1. Introduction

The sudden advent of the pandemic on a global scale made organisations more considerate about the health and well-being of their workforce, thereby compelled them to assign their resources to cater to it. As suggested by research conducted by the Business Group on Health (2023) consisting of 72 Fortune 100 companies spread across 200 countries with more than 20,000 employees revealed the fact that an average expenditure incurred by these firms on health, well-being, and productivity was around US$11 million per year.

'Mental health and well-being in the workplace' report of Deloitte published on September 2022, focused on responses of 3,995 respondents from 12 key industries belonging to the Indian corporate found that corporate leaders in the country cannot solely rely on perks and programmes for improving the well-being of their employees. Despite companies investing hefty in well-being programmes and collecting data related to it, it was found that more than two-thirds (68%) of workers did not make effective use of the well-being resources offered to them by the employers since these wellness programmes were time-consuming (Deloitte, 2022).

As reported by Economic Times (2023), 8 out of 10 companies in India have enhanced their employee well-being expenditure in 2023 as compared to 2019. Further, 82% of Indian companies acknowledge that the mental health of their employees impacts their business results. Additionally, 80% provide employee assistance programmes and mental health support, and 37% offer telemedicine.

Moreover, existing frameworks and measurement practice adopted by companies were found to have lacunae, as current resources and approaches are more inclined towards describing the procedures rather than gauging the (well-being) results that matter to various stakeholders.

Alternatively, few frameworks are self-reported or consist of subjective indices nor are in-line with the international measurement standards and lack synchronisation and harmonisation.

In the Indian corporate sector, the need of the hour is to develop and adapt a proper, comprehensive framework to collect well-being analytics.

In the Indian corporate sector, the need of the hour is to develop and adapt a proper, comprehensive framework to collect well-being analytics. The OECD WISE Centre framework presents a harmonised method for measuring employee well-being (OECD, 2024). This project was executed on a voluntary basis by four companies in Japan, with an objective to showcase the advantages of gathering comprehensive data on employee well-being within organisations. This data can be utilised by organisations for risk management processes, benchmarking determinations, providing profits to investors, and to governments and national statistical offices (NSOs) to manage impacts and risks with an aim to imbibe well-being and sustainability in policy-making processes.

2. The Science behind Measuring Workplace Happiness

Creating a workplace which prioritises employees' individuality and self-initiative would make work more enjoyable, thereby enhancing the Quality of work-life of employees. Measuring, tracking, or visualising 'happiness' of each entity in the workplace is easier said than done. Hitachi's Happiness Planet is one such smartphone application that caters to work-style reforms customised for individual and organisational needs for measuring workplace happiness. Extensive research in Psychology has necessitated the need for a better state of mind for the workforce to enhance their productivity, which in turn represents a direct relationship between productivity and happiness. With the advent of state-of-the-art technology, which converts and considers both psychological and social factors into actionable data objectively measuring workplace happiness has now become a reality. 'Happiness Planet' app, developed by Hitachi and launched in May 2022, expresses numerically an individual's positive mindset and team-based trust. It utilises smartphone sensors to monitor nonverbal synchrony – referred to as the unconscious mirroring of physical movements during interaction – which in turn is transformed into a 'social happiness index'. Daily regimen of setting personalised challenges (e.g. 'listen carefully' or 'delegate tasks') and tracking results were believed to shift mindsets positively, facilitating higher psychological safety – a state where employees experience freedom to express themselves, promoting creativity and lessening stress. A routine tracking of happiness in a way similar to as recording body temperatures can help organisations to formulate and design measures to enhance well-being of individual employees, build team cohesion, and consequently improve the overall productivity of an organisation, with a big leap in data-driven strategic workplace management (Hitachi., n.d.).

Workplace happiness is growing in importance as a strategic asset within companies, with its measurement drawn from psychological theory. Based on Seligman's PERMA model – a study consisting of 302 employees at a Colombian university revealed that the above-mentioned dimensions largely impact an employees' perception of workplace happiness. Employing a validated quantitative approach and regression analysis, the study stated that positive emotions and engagement are the best indicators of happiness at work. Employees experienced a strong sense of purpose, emotional attachment to their workplace, and satisfaction towards their job roles. These findings highlight the significance of regular monitoring of workplace happiness as a part and parcel of human resource strategy, thus helping organisations to formulate specific techniques and methods to promote well-being, bolster employee motivation, and to achieve sustainable performance. Assimilating such scientific evaluations into management practices not merely supports employee welfare but also builds up organisational resilience and creates competitive advantage (Mendoza-Ocasal et al., 2021).

In the year 2023, Ziraat Bank employees' data comprising 4,277 employees and spanning over 7 quarters (October 2020–June 2022) identified a stable consistently positive curvilinear association on the basis that as employee happiness increased, performance scores also improved across all low-, medium-, and high-performing groups of employees. By using panel data analysis with required corrections for serial correlation and cross-sectional dependence, the researchers found that each one-point addition in an individual's happiness (on a 1–10 scale) reflected an average performance gain of approximately 3.41 points. The effect was more prominently found in the medium-performance range but continued even at higher levels of achievement. The study underlines that prioritising employee happiness is not just a feel-good strategy – it leads to quantifiable performance enhancements, making the routine evaluation and promotion of employee well-being a strategic necessity for sustainable organisational success (Met et al., 2023).

Measuring workplace happiness still remains to be a tedious task for organisations because of the drawbacks associated with traditional self-report instruments, which rely heavily on memory and subjective interpretation. Sender et al. (2021) in their research came up with a new mixed-methods framework and gave the term 'Happy Level' – which integrates narrative analysis and automated sentiment analysis of employees' work-life experiences. Based on Kahneman's framework to assessing emotional episodes, the research analyses four methods (one manual, three automated) to obtain a quantifiable happiness indicator. Moreover, the manual coding provides the most precise results, early automated models present more relevant results because of their scalability and adaptability. Furthermore, this creative technique not only overcomes the limitations of the conventional surveys but also presents a more sophisticated way to keep a check on employee well-being over a period of time, preparing the ground for more scalable, data-driven perspectives that can be helpful for researchers and managers in managing their organisations (Sender et al., 2021).

Workplace happiness does not solely talk about individual well-being but goes beyond to encompass the impact of the workplace practices and environments on the physical, psychological, and social well-being of employees, viewed from a public health perspective. Caraballo-Arias et al. (2024) consolidate evidence by means of an epidemiological approach, focusing on how happiness at work performs as a contextual social indicator of health and productivity. The study conducted by them identified over 30 factors impacting happiness – comprising of meaningful work, positive workplace relationships, and mental health supports – and recorded a variety of authenticated assessment techniques, both quantitative (e.g. psychometric scales) and qualitative (e.g. narrative assessments) in nature. Moreover, they outline 12 factually appraised interventions – ranging from mindfulness training to peer support – that largely elevate happiness, decrease turnover, and boost mental health outcomes, as a result reinforcing the strategic link between well-being metrics and organisational effectiveness. The researchers do not review happiness monitoring as a soft metric, but rather as a meticulously stated epidemiological tool that resembles to assessing disease occurrence – henceforth allowing firms to spot patterns, identify hotspots, and intercede with tailormade health-promoting frameworks (Caraballo-Arias et al., 2024).

Evaluating workplace happiness has advanced with the establishment of structured, psychometrically sound tools that permit firms to methodically evaluate and nurture employee well-being. Singh et al. (2024) proposed an exhaustive happiness at workplace scale, substantiated by AI and a thorough survey design, that records mental stability and subjective experiences with higher accuracy. Additionally, the tool employs an elaborative Likert-scale items and sensor-based validations to measure variables such as emotional well-being, workplace relationships, and job satisfaction. Its usage across varied organisational situations showcases the viability of converting qualitative dimensions of employee happiness into comprehensive numerical indicators. This development in evaluating happiness allows practitioners to review happiness patterns over time, thereby aiding in identifying areas requiring intervention, and aligning human resource strategies with data-based well-being goals – affirming happiness metrics as a vital factor in strategic management (Singh et al., 2024).

3. Key Metrics for Employee Well-being and Engagement

Rashid & Al-Shami through their paper relationship between happiness and employee well-being and consequently came up with vital factors that impact happiness. These factors, which comprise namely of positive emotions, engagement, positive relationships, and achievement (Rashid & Al-Shami, 2024).

Based on the research published in the *Journal Ilmiah Ekonomi Manajemen* (JEMA), employee well-being and engagement are best evaluated by means of a multidimensional approach. The study presents four key factors of well-being that act as validated metrics consisting of psychological, social, workplace, and subjective well-being. The term 'Psychological well-being' refers to variables such as self-acceptance, purpose in life, autonomy, and personal growth. Indices for this factor comprise employees' acceptability to changes and their sense of purpose at the workplace. Social well-being on the other hand talks about the sense of belonging, the quality of interpersonal relationships at work, and if employees feel valued by their team and the firm. Statements like 'I love spending time with teammates' are utilised to evaluate this perspective.

Workplace well-being revolves around the employee's perspective of the work environment, safety, organisational support, and growth prospects. Items such as 'My employer cares about employees' help analyse this aspect. Alternatively, subjective well-being, is evaluated by making use of responses like 'Mostly I feel happy' and by means of an individuals' emotional experiences, inclusive of overall life satisfaction and the equilibrium between positive and negative emotions. These factors were authenticated by a robust statistical analysis, revealing high internal consistency (Cronbach's alpha ranging from 0.72 to 0.96), thereby confirming the independence and reliability as dimensions of well-being (Supriyanto et al., 2024).

The chapter moreover lays stress on the fact that well-being and engagement are closely related to each other, as high levels of well-being generally are followed by enhanced levels of employee engagement, decreased absenteeism, and improved job performance. Engagement metrics associated to well-being comprises of productivity levels, absenteeism rates, employee turnover intentions, and the aggregation of personal resources such as emotional and intellectual capabilities. Employees who perceive psychological and emotional support have greater chances to exhibit greater commitment and better performance at the workplace. For example, when employees think that their organisation supports their advancement and recognises their contributions, reduced is the likeliness of their quitting the job.

The researchers state that monitoring well-being indicators and engagement outcomes gives a more comprehensive understanding of employee experiences and organisational health. By combining the four aspects of well-being with engagement metrics such as job performance, absenteeism, and retention rates, firms can design an all-inclusive assessment framework. A framework that would not only record the present state of an employee's well-being but will also be a way to recognise areas needing attention. For real-life implementation, firms should utilise a harmonised well-being survey inclusive of current human resources performance data, which in turn will help in more informed decision-making and resultant will be enhanced workplace strategies (Supriyanto et al., 2024).

Moreover, employee well-being is strongly related to employee engagement, which can be quantified, and hence it's not just a feel-good concept. The research article strongly propagates the appointment of a dedicated 'well-being champion' in the work units, further backed by continued organisational commitment, leading to enhanced engagement levels among employees. Appointing well-being champions aids in developing an environment where well-being is consistently supported and becomes a part and parcel of the organisational functioning.

To make well-being initiatives most effective, the research accentuates monitoring engagement scores, generally collected through standardised engagement surveys. These surveys evaluate aspects such as enthusiasm, emotional energy, commitment, and discretionary effort. The appointment of well-being champions continuously enhances engagement scores, advising that active support systems play a more crucial role rather than passive well-being initiatives (Litchfield et al., 2016).

Moving a step ahead of the survey data, the study states that organisational metrics are indirect indicators of well-being and engagement. These indicators comprise rates of absenteeism, chances of turnover or turnover intent, and productivity projections. With well-being champions in place, divisions are generally marked by lessening numbers of sick leave and turnover, while performance metrics improve for good. Such policies reveal how the real-life support structures related to well-being transform into tangible organisational results.

The research signifies the relevance of programme participation metrics – explicitly, how many employees participate in well-being programmes or take benefit of resources related to it. These participation figures act as initial measures of the relationship between employee engagement with that of wellness programmes. High figures of participation not only show legitimate interest in such programmes but also indicate and lay emphasis on greater organisational support, which consequently bolsters overall engagement (Litchfield et al., 2016).

4. Need for Measuring Workplace Happiness

One of the smallest mountainous countries of the world, Bhutan made Gross National Happiness Index as a part and parcel of its constitution in 2008 to assess the well-being of its population. United Nations on 19 July 2011, in its resolution adopted Happiness as a 'fundamental human goal'. This resolution stands as a foundation for most of the environmental, social, and governance (ESG) initiatives as the world sees them today (United Nations, 2011).

Eventually, in 2012, another UN resolution declared 20th March of every year as the International Day of Happiness, and hence the United Nations has been publishing a World Happiness Report that ranks countries based on various criteria (United Nations, 2012).

These resolutions of the United Nations Organization (UNO) and five years post-COVID have brought the spotlight on mental health and well-being of employees at the workplace.

As per Albert Schweitzer (1952), a Nobel Laureate for his ideology of 'Reverence for Life' said that 'success is not the key to happiness, happiness is the key to success'. The need of the hour is to shift the focus primarily on happiness as a variable to carry out research studies that revolve around association between happiness and work outcomes rather than making use of other positive emotion-related variables.

By evaluating employee happiness, job demands, and organisational performance through a two-wave full panel design, this study provides data signifying that employee happiness's largely mediates the association between job demands and organisational performance. Overtly, stating that a high level of job demands decreases employee happiness, which in turn reduces employees' commitment towards the organisation and task performance meanwhile enhancing turnover motives and undermining work behaviours (Bakker & Demerouti, 2007).

Further, recent research studies have well presented the fact that there exists a positive association between an employee's subjective well-being and productivity, and employees who are happy at work demonstrate a better attitude while carrying out tasks and subsequently are more productive.

According to the research in association with indeed, conducted by De Neve and Ward (2025), a renowned Professor of Economics and Behavioural Science at University of Oxford, complied and presented in a book co-authored with George Ward, entitled 'Why Workplace Wellbeing Matters: The Science Behind Employee Happiness and Organizational Performance' brings to light that only a one-fourth of workers in the United States, United Kingdom, Canada, and beyond are really happy at their workplace. Moreover, it states that happy people are 13% more productive.

Finally, it thus validates the idea and unlocks the power of workplace happiness, its role, and need of assessing happiness quotient at work. This happiness quotient can be synonymously be addressed as happiness index, happiness scale, satisfaction score, hubris measurement to name a few. Whatever terms are adopted to define workplace happiness the perspective remains unchanged, that is, to measure happiness regularly be it in every quarter, and in between time intervals, and use the findings to design and employ interventions which can further bolster employee's happiness index.

Future quality of life (QOL) and research in organisations would take advantage of the findings, thus paving a way towards a web of theoretical relationships of employee happiness with other variables at work. Furthermore, experts have the prospect to establish the influence that employee happiness has on organisationally relevant results and the role that companies can take in nurturing employee happiness.

5. AI-driven Tools and Techniques

AI currently drives the world, and its advocates are arguing for the use of AI in enhancing the efficiency of the workforce. AI-driven tools and techniques have become essential in measuring happiness due to their strengths in scalability, objectivity, multimodal data integration, predictive capabilities, and personalisation. Traditionally, methods such as surveys and interviews were often used, but they were limited by small sample sizes, time lags, and self-report biases (Kahneman & Krueger, 2006). In contrast, AI enables the real-time and large-scale analysis of subjective well-being using tools such as Google Trends, social media mining, and sentiment analysis to continuously capture population-level happiness (Greyling & Rossouw, 2025). These systems offer a more dynamic and responsive view of well-being, particularly useful in public policy and organisational contexts. One of the significant drawbacks of the traditional method is its bias in measuring happiness, which would distort the results. AI contributes to greater objectivity in emotional measurement by minimising subjective distortions. For example, multimodal emotion recognition systems can assess facial expressions, vocal tones, and body gestures simultaneously, improving accuracy (Bänziger et al., 2009; Yan et al., 2024). The integration of diverse data types (text, voice, and physiological signals) allows for a more holistic understanding of individual and collective well-being. Moreover, AI enhances predictive analysis by identifying patterns from behavioural and contextual data that correlate with life satisfaction, enabling early detection of mental health risks or workplace dissatisfaction (Khan et al., 2024). Beyond prediction, personalisation is a significant benefit: AI-powered apps can learn user preferences and deliver tailored mental health interventions, enhancing user engagement and emotional outcomes (Dehbozorgi et al., 2025).

5.1. Sentiment Analysis Using Natural Language Processing (NLP)

Sentiment analysis is one of the most popular AI tools for determining the level of happiness. It builds upon NLP and evaluates the tone of emotion in a piece of text. Sentiment analysis can be conducted on employee response forms, Slack messages, internal emails, and even exit interviews to gauge employee morale and emotional climate. Research indicates that regularly using sentiment analysis may identify dissatisfaction beforehand, allowing HR to take the necessary measures promptly (Cambria et al., 2017).

To illustrate this use, a sentiment analysis was conducted on a sample of fictional employee feedback. Such answers were designed in a way that reflects true feelings in the workplace, both positive and negative, including motivation and enthusiasm, appreciation, frustration, and disengagement. It was, however, not to gather information about real people but to show the work of AI sentiment analysis in a realistic HR scenario.

In this analysis, the authors used the TextBlob NLP package to perform the analysis of the polarity scores by assigning a score between −1 and +1, a strong negative to a strong positive sentiment. It also labelled the sentiments as positive, neutral, or negative. Some of the entries simulated: about 60% positive, or just happy about flexi-time, wellness programmes, and inclusion at work; 3 out of 10 were neutral, tending to reflect either ambivalent emotions or the positive trade-off between stress and satisfaction; 10% were negative, which covered some negative things like absence of growth opportunities and transparency in leadership.

When implemented on actual employee communication channels, such a tool can provide organisations with a real-time window into the emotions of their employees, allowing them to engage and employ retention initiatives proactively.

5.2. Facial Recognition and Emotion-tracking

Facial emotion recognition is yet another frontier in the happiness measurement through the use of AI. Affectiva Technology, owned by Smarteye or Microsoft Azure Face API, is used to study minute facial expressions to identify emotions such as joy, sadness, anger, or surprise. Initial research, such as the examination by McDuff et al. (2016), suggests that facial analysis plays a role in evaluating consumer satisfaction when using products during product testing and in employee wellness programmes.

These tools in an organisation can be developed on video conferencing platforms to measure the level of engagement during remote meetings. It is, however, a practice that treads closely the line between innovation and intrusion, and needs to be done with a very big ethical protection.

5.3. Predictive Analytics Using HR Data

Another effective way to predict happiness using AI is to examine indicators such as absenteeism rates, productivity scores, and human resource management system (HRMS) data (including employee attrition, complaints, or workload patterns). Machine learning models trained on historical data can identify high-risk departments or roles prone to dissatisfaction. For instance, an unusual spike in sick leaves or reduced engagement with internal platforms may be early warnings of burnout or disengagement. This is particularly accurate in the case of employees who are otherwise productive, committed, and self-motivated.

Predictive happiness analytics, when combined with organisational psychology models, can also suggest retention strategies, cultural changes, or wellness programmes tailored to the needs of subgroups within the company (Oswald et al., 2015).

5.4. Data Sources and Ethical Concerns

There are various data sources that AI uses. Moreover, when AI is used, ethical concerns are obvious.

5.4.1. Real-time Versus Longitudinal Data

Analytics and AI enable the measurement of happiness at different rates. Immediate feedback is provided through real-time data, such as sentiment analysis of social media or real-time pulse surveys. On the other hand, the longitudinal data (collected over months or years) can be critical when following the long-term effects of organisational policies on happiness. Platforms such as Officevibe or TinyPulse combine the two in an attempt to get a clearer picture of employee engagement on an ongoing basis (Knight, 2020).

However, it is crucial to strike a balance between speed and depth. Although real-time data may identify trends, it might lack a psychological background that longer research reveals. Organisations are required to combine these two types to evade biased views.

When employing AI-driven tools to measure happiness, it is essential to address several ethical considerations. First, informed consent must be obtained from employees, ensuring that they are fully aware that their personal data – such as emails, messages, or even facial expressions – is being analysed for well-being assessments. Without transparent communication, the use of such data can violate privacy norms and erode trust within the organisation. Second, anonymity and data security are paramount, particularly when processing emotionally sensitive information. Organisations must implement robust encryption protocols and ensure that individuals cannot be identified from the collected data. Finally, there is the concern of algorithmic bias. AI systems, if not properly calibrated, can reinforce existing cultural or gender biases. For example, as Buolamwini and Gebru (2018) have demonstrated, facial recognition technologies may misinterpret expressions due to ethnic or cultural differences, resulting in inaccurate or unfair assessments. Addressing these ethical challenges is critical for the responsible and equitable application of AI in happiness analytics. To address these issues, ethical AI frameworks and transparency are necessary for developing happiness analytics. It is critical to the trust-building process that employee feedback is taken into account when crafting these policies.

5.5. Case Snapshots

Although the advent of AI is not recent, its usage through various Large Language Models is relatively new, as is its application in measuring happiness and employee efficiency. There are case studies to show how AI is being used in various countries to measure happiness. Here, three cases are discussed.

1. *UAE's National Programme for Happiness*: the UAE has institutionalised happiness through a dedicated Ministry of Happiness and a happiness index dashboard that tracks citizen satisfaction across various sectors. This dashboard aggregates real-time data from social media, mobile surveys, and feedback kiosks to monitor satisfaction levels across healthcare, transport, and education.

Data from the Smart Dubai initiative also supports AI-based governance. Dubai introduced face recognition in 2019, with smart cameras installed to measure customer satisfaction (Roy, 2019). Using AI sentiment tools, public responses to policy changes or services are tracked, with dashboards informing real-time modifications. Such governance models illustrate how large-scale happiness tracking can influence social policy (Al Nuaimi et al., 2020).

2. *Google's People Analytics*: Google's Project Aristotle, a study conducted by their people analytics team, used extensive data mining to understand what made teams successful and satisfied. This was a project started in 2012. Variables included communication frequency, psychological safety, and equal turn-taking in discussions. The findings were used to redesign team structures and feedback systems, directly influencing employee happiness (Duhigg, 2016; LeaderFactor, 2025).

   Google also uses internal tools to pulse-check team sentiments and align HR interventions accordingly. The integration of machine learning into human resource management (HRM) allows tailored wellness initiatives based on predicted risks of burnout or attrition.

3. *Salesforce and Workplace Well-being*: Salesforce integrates AI into its employee wellness ecosystem through tools like Einstein Analytics, which evaluates productivity and wellness data. In 2020, Salesforce introduced a happiness index as part of its internal analytics to track engagement during remote work. Their data-driven approach to well-being includes anonymous surveys, workload tracking, and even mindfulness reminders through integrated apps (Ozakar et al., 2020).

6. Benchmarking Circular Happiness across Industries

6.1. Understanding Circular Happiness

The traditional measurement of happiness in organisations has revolved around individual-level constructs such as job satisfaction, affect balance, or engagement. However, the growing climate emergency, rising inequalities, and mental health challenges have prompted a shift in paradigm. There is a growing need to embed happiness within a broader sustainability framework that goes beyond the individual to include emotional, social, and ecological well-being – what we term 'circular happiness'.

Circular happiness refers to a system-oriented, regenerative approach to happiness measurement. It aligns with the principles of the circular economy, which emphasises closed-loop production, zero waste, and environmental stewardship (Ellen MacArthur Foundation, 2015), and Doughnut Economics, which proposes a social foundation below which no one should fall and an ecological ceiling above which humanity should not overshoot (Raworth, 2017).

This new paradigm challenges the anthropocentric and capitalistic views that equate happiness with consumption or individual achievement. Instead, it centres happiness on interdependence – how fulfilled individuals are in communities and ecosystems that thrive sustainably. For example, employee happiness may now be tied to a firm's net-zero goals, ethical procurement practices, and inclusivity policies – not merely salary or promotions.

6.2. Cross-industry Mapping

Each industry presents unique challenges and opportunities for embedding circular happiness into its practices. A cross-sectoral lens helps identify how principles of regeneration, inclusivity, and long-term value creation translate into happiness metrics.

6.2.1. Manufacturing Sector

Manufacturing, particularly in fashion, electronics, and fast-moving consumer goods (FMCG), often faces criticisms related to exploitative labour, pollution, and waste. Yet some companies have pioneered happiness loops that integrate circularity into employee and consumer experience.

For instance, Patagonia ties employee happiness to environmental stewardship. Employees are encouraged to volunteer for ecological restoration, participate in environmental activism, and work with circular materials (Patagonia, 2023). The brand's emphasis on durability, repair, and resale of goods creates a satisfaction loop for consumers rooted in ethics and sustainability.

6.2.2. Agriculture Sector

In agriculture, circular happiness may take the form of regenerative farming practices that respect indigenous knowledge systems, restore soil health, and reduce chemical dependency. Farmer cooperatives that share profits, promote gender equality, and use eco-certifications have shown higher farmer satisfaction (Pretty, 2008).

Government-supported initiatives like Zero Budget Natural Farming (ZBNF) in India have demonstrated how ecological harmony and farmer well-being can co-exist (NITI Aayog, 2020). When mapped onto KPIs, the happiness of farmers extends to community resilience, food security, and ecological balance.

6.2.3 IT and Services Sector

In IT and services, the application of circular happiness focuses on digital well-being, data ethics, and psychological safety. Companies like Tata Consultancy Services (TCS) offer structured programmes for mental wellness, environmental responsibility (e.g. carbon-neutral campuses), and upskilling, all of which feed into employee happiness.

Moreover, service industries have begun integrating happiness loops into client relationships. Financial services firms now offer ESG-screened investment products that align with customer values, thereby promoting a sense of moral satisfaction among users.

6.2.4. Health and Education Sectors

Health and education sectors stand at the intersection of service delivery and emotional labour. In these sectors, happiness KPIs must consider caregiver burnout, patient dignity, teacher autonomy, and community impact. The World Health Organization (2022) suggests that well-being in healthcare cannot be delinked from equitable access and inclusive infrastructure.

6.3. KPI Benchmarking Models

To translate these multidimensional happiness ideas into measurable outcomes, benchmarking models must be customised to industry contexts while maintaining global comparability.

6.3.1. Designing Sector-specific Happiness Indices

Rather than just following the one-size-fits-all approach, organisations have the opportunity to create sectoral specific happiness index that would fit their operational environments. Happiness KPIs in the retail or manufacturing industries may include satisfaction of the employee regarding ethical sourcing of products, satisfaction of the customer because of the sustainability of the product and the pleasure felt by the community because of the provision of employment opportunities to the local people. Indicators of importance in the technology industry may include digital well-being scores, their analytics on careers, and adherence to open data ethics. On the same note, some of the KPIs in agriculture might include elements, like the stability of farmer income, accessibility to natural and sustainable farming inputs, and the levels of biodiversity. Such indices would be preferably composed of both subjective markers, such as surveys and mood trackers, and objective data points such as carbon offset success and employee retention, or acquiring or implementing circular product practices.

6.3.2. Global Frameworks Integration

Several international models can be used to create effective templates for benchmarking happiness indices across various industries. In particular, most of the reports on labour practices, environmental performance, and human rights provide an extensive set of indicators that can be successfully used as proxies of organisational happiness global reporting initiative (GRI, 2021). In the same measure, ISO 26000 is a guide document on global best practices that businesses can employ to integrate social responsibility in their operations with a focus on employee well-being, community development, as well as the operating practices (ISO, 2010). The UN Sustainable Development Goals (SDGs) also provide practical metrics within the framework of the SDGs, such as SDG 3 (good health and well-being), SDG 8 (decent work and economic growth), and SDG 12 (responsible consumption and production), allowing sector-specific KPIs to contribute to achieving happiness. A combination of those frameworks allows organisations to increase their external accountability and, at the same time, enables them to conduct a robust internal benchmarking of well-being and sustainability as well as results.

6.4. Comparative Dashboards

Happiness benchmarking across industries becomes truly actionable when outcomes are effectively visualised and communicated, making comparative dashboards an essential tool. These digital platforms enable organisations, regulators, and stakeholders to evaluate happiness performance both over time and in relation to peer institutions. Core features typically include real-time happiness scores obtained through pulse surveys or emotion-tracking tools, integration of sustainability-oriented well-being metrics, and visual representations of trends segmented by departments, geographic locations, or demographic groups. Existing platforms like Officevibe and Culture Amp already provide such dashboards focused on employee engagement and well-being metrics, offering analytics on feedback, team dynamics, and leadership perception (Culture Amp, 2023; Officevibe, 2023). However, most of these tools have yet to integrate elements of circularity. This presents a significant opportunity to develop sector-specific circular happiness dashboards that extend beyond conventional indicators like profitability and attrition, capturing more holistic dimensions of employee and community well-being.

6.4.1. Case Comparison

To illustrate, consider the comparative profiles of three companies:

1. Patagonia (retail/manufacturing): scores high on environmental happiness loops – employee pride in activism, consumer trust in sustainable products, and stakeholder alignment on values.
2. TCS (IT services): excels in internal digital happiness, offering structured mental health support, corporate social responsibility (CSR) volunteering, and career growth opportunities.
3. IKEA (global retail/manufacturing): blends affordability with sustainability, offering KPIs on renewable energy, fair wages, and inclusive design. It publishes annual sustainability and people & planet reports, integrating happiness themes into its circular design philosophy.

These case comparisons suggest that happiness as a KPI is not limited to HR – it cuts across supply chains, design, marketing, and post-use engagement. When visualised through dashboards, happiness becomes not just an HR concern but a strategic imperative.

7. Key Metrics for Employee Well-being and Engagement

7.1. Objective

To provide a focused lens on HR and organisational strategies to measure and improve happiness at the workplace.

7.2. Core Dimensions of Well-being

Measuring employee happiness at the workplace necessitates a comprehensive view of well-being that transcends momentary satisfaction or emotional highs. Leading research indicates that sustainable employee happiness is rooted in five core dimensions: physical, emotional, social, financial, and purpose-driven well-being (Huppert & So, 2013). These domains align with the widely accepted PERMA model – developed by Martin Seligman – which frames flourishing around positive emotion, engagement, relationships, meaning, and achievement (Seligman, 2011).

- Physical well-being addresses not only workplace ergonomics but also access to healthcare, physical activity options, and work-life balance.
- Emotional well-being refers to psychological resilience, autonomy, and emotional regulation.
- Social well-being includes the strength of interpersonal relationships and a sense of belonging within teams.
- Financial well-being is related to economic security, fair compensation, and transparency.
- Purpose-driven well-being arises when employees align their personal values with organisational mission, enabling a sense of meaning.

These elements do not function in silos; rather, they interact dynamically. For example, emotional well-being is often reinforced by strong social networks and a sense of purpose. A comprehensive happiness measurement system, therefore, must account for the interplay among these dimensions.

7.3. Measurement Tools

To quantify happiness-related outcomes in organisations, HR leaders have adopted several tools – both qualitative and quantitative. These include surveys, dashboards, and proxy indicators that provide insights into workforce sentiment and well-being trends.

7.3.1. Engagement Surveys

One of the most widely adopted tools is the Gallup Q12 Employee Engagement Survey, which asks employees 12 key questions to determine their engagement level (Harter et al., 2002). Similarly, the Employee Net Promoter Score (eNPS) measures loyalty by asking whether employees would recommend their organisation as a good place to work. While these tools offer standardisation and benchmarking capabilities, they often miss nuances of well-being unless augmented with qualitative inputs.

7.3.2. Well-being Dashboards and Pulse Surveys

Modern organisations are increasingly turning to real-time dashboards that aggregate inputs from pulse surveys, Slack reactions, email sentiment, and wellness app usage. These dashboards track metrics such as mood trends, energy levels, and work satisfaction across time and teams (Knight, 2020). Tools like Officevibe, Culture Amp, and TinyPulse are industry favourites for their customisable analytics features.

7.3.3. Proxy Metrics

Not all happiness metrics are direct. Proxy indicators – such as attrition rates, promotion cycles, absenteeism, and sick leaves – serve as indirect but significant measures of employee engagement. For example, frequent sick leaves may indicate burnout, while delayed promotion cycles can erode motivation. While these metrics lack emotional granularity, they provide structural insights that guide HR interventions (Oswald et al., 2015).

Organisations that triangulate all three – surveys, dashboards, and proxy data – tend to have more holistic happiness measurement systems. The integration of these tools into centralised HR platforms also enables real-time monitoring and predictive action planning.

7.4. Strategic KPIs

Beyond tools, strategic KPIs help translate happiness into organisational metrics that can inform policy, performance reviews, and cultural reforms.

7.4.1. Happiness Index Score

Several companies now compute a happiness index score, derived from survey data, sentiment analysis, and wellness participation rates. This composite score typically reflects overall satisfaction, emotional balance, and perceived inclusiveness (Brynjolfsson & McAfee, 2014). It helps HR teams identify trends over time and benchmark performance across departments.

7.4.2. Work-life Balance Satisfaction Rate

This metric evaluates employees' perceptions of how well their work schedules align with their personal lives. It may be collected through monthly pulse surveys or as part of the annual engagement questionnaire. High scores correlate with lower burnout and higher retention, especially in hybrid or remote work cultures (Knight, 2020).

7.4.3. Managerial Empathy Scores

Managerial empathy is increasingly recognised as a predictor of team morale and psychological safety. Surveys now include statements like 'My manager shows genuine concern for my well-being' and score them using Likert scales. According to Duhigg (2016), teams with high empathy scores tend to outperform others on trust, innovation, and resilience.

7.4.4. Employee Net Promoter Score (eNPS)

As a trusted metric in HR analytics, eNPS provides a quick snapshot of employee sentiment and advocacy. It classifies employees into promoters, passives, and detractors based on their likelihood to recommend their workplace, offering a granular view of satisfaction drivers and dissatisfiers (Harter et al., 2002).

7.4.5. Psychological Safety Scores

Psychological safety, defined as the ability to speak up without fear of punishment or humiliation, is a critical dimension of workplace happiness (Edmondson, 1999). HR departments now run safety audits using tools like Google's Re:Work framework, which measures perceptions of openness, mistake tolerance, and inclusivity. A positive safety score correlates with high engagement and innovation.

Together, these KPIs help quantify the elusive nature of happiness in a way that allows for action, accountability, and alignment with strategic goals.

7.5. Best Practices and Culture Indicators

Beyond measurement, the cultivation of a happiness-driven workplace depends on actionable HR strategies. Many leading firms have institutionalised cultural practices that reinforce emotional and psychological well-being.

7.5.1. Gratitude Rituals and Wellness Programmes

Daily or weekly gratitude exercises, such as 'Thank You Thursdays', help reinforce social bonds. Organisations also integrate wellness programmes offering meditation sessions, therapy reimbursements, or on-site health check-ups. At Salesforce, for instance, mindfulness reminders and wellness apps are embedded in the work ecosystem to reinforce daily well-being (Salesforce, 2022).

7.5.2. Inclusive Leadership and Psychological Support

Inclusive leadership, which values diverse voices and promotes equity, is central to workplace happiness. Leaders trained in emotional intelligence and cultural sensitivity are more effective in nurturing trust and safety. Companies like TCS run leadership development programmes that embed empathy and inclusiveness in performance metrics (TCS, 2023).

7.5.3. Flexible Work Policies

Post-pandemic, flexibility has emerged as a cornerstone of workplace happiness. Options such as remote work, asynchronous communication, and four-day workweeks are increasingly seen as structural happiness enablers. Studies suggest that employees with control over work conditions report higher job satisfaction and lower stress (Bloom et al., 2015).

7.5.4. HR Analytics for Targeted Interventions

HR analytics help convert qualitative feedback into actionable strategies. By correlating engagement levels with performance data or tracking burnout risk across demographics, HR can launch precise interventions – such as department-level training or well-being campaigns (Cambria et al., 2017).

These best practices collectively create an ecosystem where happiness is not a by-product but a strategic input into performance and retention.

References

Al Nuaimi, E., Al Neyadi, H., Mohamed, N., & Al-Jaroodi, J. (2020). Smart city architecture and its applications based on IoT. *Procedia Computer Science*, *109*, 1241–1247.

Bakker, A. B., & Demerouti, E. (2007). The job demands – Resources model: State of the art. *Journal of Managerial Psychology*, *22*(3), 309–328. https://doi.org/10.1108/02683940710733115

Bänziger, T., Grandjean, D., & Scherer, K. R. (2009). Emotion recognition from expressions in face, voice, and body: The multimodal emotion recognition test (MERT). *Emotion*, *9*(5), 691–704. https://doi.org/10.1037/a0017088

Bloom, N., Liang, J., Roberts, J., & Ying, Z. J. (2015). Does working from home work? Evidence from a Chinese experiment. *The Quarterly Journal of Economics*, *130*(1), 165–218.

Brynjolfsson, E., & McAfee, A. (2014). *The second machine age: Work, progress, and prosperity in a time of brilliant technologies*. W. W. Norton & Company.

Buolamwini, J., & Gebru, T. (2018). Gender shades: Intersectional accuracy disparities in commercial gender classification. *Proceedings of the 1st conference on fairness, accountability and transparency* (pp. 77–91).

Business Group on Health. (2023). *Annual survey report on workforce well-being and productivity*. [Data set].

Cambria, E., Schuller, B., Xia, Y., & Havasi, C. (2017). New avenues in opinion mining and sentiment analysis. *IEEE Intelligent Systems*, *28*(2), 15–21.

Caraballo-Arias, Y., Feola, D., & Milani, S. (2024). The science behind happiness at work. *Current Opinion in Epidemiology and Public Health*, *3*(1), 11–24.

Culture Amp. (2023). *People analytics and employee engagement*. https://www.cultureamp.com/

De Neve, J.-E., & Ward, G. (2025). *Why workplace wellbeing matters: The science behind employee happiness and organizational performance*. Harvard Business Review Press.

Dehbozorgi, R., Zangeneh, S., Khooshab, E., Nia, D.H., Hanif, H. R., Samian, P., Yousefi, M., Hashemi, F. H., Vakili. M., Jamalimoghadam. N., Lohrasebi, F. (2025). The application of artificial intelligence in the field of mental health: A systematic review. *BMC Psychiatry*, *25*(1), 132. https://doi.org/10.1186/s12888-025-06483-2

Deloitte. (2022, September). *Mental health and well-being in the workplace: Indian corporate survey insights*. Deloitte Insights.
Duhigg, C. (2016). *What Google learned from its quest to build the perfect team*. The New York Times Magazine.
Economic Times. (2023). *8 in 10 companies increased spending on employee well-being*. The Economic Times. https://economictimes.indiatimes.com
Edmondson, A. (1999). Psychological safety and learning behavior in work teams. *Administrative Science Quarterly*, *44*(2), 350–383.
Ellen MacArthur Foundation. (2015). *Towards the circular economy: Economic and business rationale for an accelerated transition*. https://ellenmacarthurfoundation.org
Greyling, T., & Rossouw, S. (2025). Development and validation of a real-time happiness index using Google Trends™. *Journal of Happiness Studies*, *26*(3), Article 39. https://doi.org/10.1007/s10902-025-00881-9
GRI. (2021). *Global reporting standards*. https://www.globalreporting.org
Harter, J. K., Schmidt, F. L., & Keyes, C. L. M. (2002). Well-being in the workplace and its relationship to business outcomes: A review of the Gallup studies. In C. L. M. Keyes & J. Haidt (Eds.), *Flourishing: Positive psychology and the life well-lived* (pp. 205–224). American Psychological Association.
Hitachi. (n.d.). *Happiness planet: Using AI to visualize employee well-being*. Hitachi Social Innovation. https://social-innovation.hitachi/en-in/case_studies/happiness-planet/
Huppert, F. A., & So, T. T. (2013). Flourishing across Europe: Application of a new conceptual framework for defining well-being. *Social Indicators Research*, *110*(3), 837–861.
ISO. (2010). *ISO 26000: Guidance on social responsibility*. International Organization for Standardization.
Kahneman, D., & Krueger, A. B. (2006). Developments in the measurement of subjective well-being. *Journal of Economic Perspectives*, *20*(1), 3–24. https://doi.org/10.1257/089533006776526030
Khan, A. E., Hasan, M. J., Anjum, H., Mohammed, N., & Momen, S. (2024). Predicting life satisfaction using machine learning and explainable AI. *Heliyon*, *10*(10), e31158. https://doi.org/10.1016/j.heliyon.2024.e31158
Knight, R. (2020). *How to keep your team motivated, remotely*. Harvard Business Review.
LeaderFactor. (2025, January 27). *Project Aristotle: Psychological safety*. LeaderFactor. https://www.leaderfactor.com/learn/project-aristotle-psychological-safety
Litchfield, P., Cooper, C. L., Hancock, C., & Watt, P. (2016). Work and well-being in the 21st century. *International Journal of Environmental Research and Public Health*, *13*(11), 1065. https://doi.org/10.1016/j.hjdsi.2019.100040
McDuff, D., El Kaliouby, R., & Picard, R. W. (2016). Crowdsourced data collection of facial responses. *IEEE Transactions on Affective Computing*, *6*(3), 273–285.
Mendoza-Ocasal, D., Castillo-Jiménez, R., Navarro, E., & Ramírez, J. (2021). Measuring workplace happiness as a key factor for the strategic management of organizations. *Polish Journal of Management Studies*, *24*(2), 292–306. https://doi.org/10.17512/pjms.2021.24.2.18
Met, İ., Erkoç, A., İpek, B., & Kızıldere, N. A. (2023). Being a game changer with happy workers: The Ziraat Bank example. *Heliyon*, *9*(7), e18027. https://doi.org/10.1016/j.heliyon.2023.e18027
NITI Aayog. (2020). *Evaluation of zero budget natural farming in India*. https://niti.gov.in
OECD. (2024). *WISE centre's framework for measuring employee well-being: Pilot study in Japan*. Organisation for Economic Co-operation and Development.
Officevibe. (2023). *Employee engagement software for modern teams*. https://www.officevibe.com/
Oswald, A. J., Proto, E., & Sgroi, D. (2015). Happiness and productivity. *Journal of Labor Economics*, *33*(4), 789–802.

Ozakar, R., Gazanfer, R., & Hanay, Y. (2020). *Measuring happiness around the world through artificial intelligence*. https://doi.org/10.48550/arXiv.2011.12548
Patagonia. (2023). *Our footprint and activism*. https://www.patagonia.com
Pretty, J. (2008). Agricultural sustainability: Concepts, principles and evidence. *Philosophical Transactions of the Royal Society B: Biological Sciences*, *363*(1491), 447–465.
Rashid, N., & Al-Shami, S. A. (2024). Exploring the interplay between happiness and employee wellbeing: A comprehensive review. *International Journal of Academic Research in Business & Social Sciences*, *14*(8). https://doi.org/10.6007/ijarbss/v14-i8/22347
Raworth, K. (2017). *Doughnut economics: Seven ways to think like a 21st-century economist*. Chelsea Green Publishing.
Roy, S. (2019, May 20). *Can AI bring you happiness? Dubai thinks so*. The Economic Times. https://economictimes.indiatimes.com/small-biz/startups/newsbuzz/can-ai-bring-you-happiness-dubai-thinks-so/articleshow/69407049.cms
Salesforce. (2022). *Well-being at work: Building resilient employees through mindfulness*. https://www.salesforce.com
Schweitzer, A. (1952). *Nobel lecture: The problem of peace*. NobelPrize.org. https://www.nobelprize.org/prizes/peace/1952/schweitzer/lecture/
Seligman, M. E. P. (2011). *Flourish: A visionary new understanding of happiness and well-being*. Free Press.
Sender, G., Carvalho, F., & Guedes, G. P. (2021). The happy level: A new approach to measure happiness at work using mixed methods. *International Journal of Qualitative Methods*, *20*, 160940692110024. https://doi.org/10.1177/16094069211002413
Singh, S., Pandey, N., & Tripathi, A. K. (2024). *Instrument to measure happiness at workplace* (pp. 181–200). Taylor & Francis.
Supriyanto, A. S., Wahyuni, A., & Yulianti, N. (2024). A new scale of employee well-being. *JEMA: Jurnal Ilmiah Ekonomi Manajemen*, *21*(2). https://doi.org/10.34010/jema.v21i2.20161
TCS. (2023). *People and culture report*. https://www.tcs.com
United Nations. (2011, July 19). *Happiness: Towards a holistic approach to development (A/RES/65/309)*. https://undocs.org/en/A/RES/65/309
United Nations. (2012, March 20). *International day of happiness*. https://www.un.org/en/observances/happiness-day
World Health Organization. (2022). *Global strategic directions for nursing and midwifery 2021–2025*.
Yan, J., Li, P., Du, C., Zhu, K., Zhou, X., Liu, Y., & Wei, J. (2024). Multimodal emotion recognition based on facial expressions, speech, and body gestures. *Electronics*, *13*(18), 3756. https://doi.org/10.3390/electronics13183756

Chapter 8

Leadership's Influence on Workplace Happiness

Jaskiran Kaur[a] *and Razia Nagina*[b]

[a] *Division of Academic Affairs, Lovely Professional University, India*
[b] *Mittal School of Business, Lovely Professional University, India*

Abstract

This study investigates the impact of transformational and transactional leadership (TRL) styles on workplace happiness among employees. The primary objective is twofold: first, to identify and validate the underlying dimensions of both leadership styles, and second, to analyse their influence on employee happiness. Data were collected through structured questionnaires administered to 238 employees, employing validated scales. Descriptive statistics, exploratory factor analysis (EFA), confirmatory factor analysis (CFA), and multiple regression analysis were conducted using SPSS and SmartPLS. The analysis revealed two distinct dimensions within each leadership style, both exhibiting significant and positive impacts on workplace happiness. Transformational leadership (TFL), particularly through intellectual stimulation and individualised consideration, showed a slightly stronger influence. The findings imply that organisations can enhance employee well-being by adopting a balanced leadership approach. The study provides actionable insights for leadership development, promoting a happier, more engaged, and productive workforce.

Keywords: Employee well-being; leadership dimensions; transactional leadership; transformational leadership; workplace happiness; workplace leadership

Circular Happiness: Building Sustainable Workplaces for the Next Generation, 151–164

doi:10.1108/978-1-80592-907-920261008

Introduction

In today's dynamic business environment, which is shaped by rapid technological change, changing employee expectations, and intense competition, effective leadership plays an important role in organisational success (Porath, 2023). Organisations focus not only on productivity and profit but also on creating a positive workplace culture where employee well-being is given importance (Bella, 2023). In this setting, transformational and TRL styles receive growing attention because of their strong influence on both organisational outcomes and employee experiences (Shakib, 2024). These leadership styles guide how individuals understand their roles, face challenges, and find satisfaction in their work (Reyaz, 2024).

The ideas of transformational and TRL first appear in the work of James MacGregor Burns in 1978 and later develop through the contributions of Bernard Bass in 1985 (Eaton, 2022). TFL focuses on vision, inspiration, intellectual stimulation, and personal support (Khan et al., 2022). Leaders who use this style try to connect personal goals with organisational goals to improve motivation and performance (Cai, 2023). TRL, on the other hand, follows a clear structure where leaders set expectations, offer rewards, and take corrective actions based on performance (Mpe, 2024). While TRL supports accountability and routine, TFL encourages creativity, empowerment, and involvement (Wuryaningrat et al., 2024).

As organisations grow more aware of the importance of a positive work environment, leadership's role in shaping workplace happiness has become a key focus (Kayyali, 2025). Workplace happiness includes emotional and psychological states that reflect satisfaction, engagement, and purpose (Misra & Srivastava, 2022), and is now seen as central to productivity, retention, and loyalty (Hatalová & Nenzén, 2021). Happy employees tend to be more creative, collaborative, and committed (Abu Orabi et al., 2024), making it vital to understand how leadership styles influence this outcome (Sam et al., 2025). Studies link TFL to morale and satisfaction, while views on TRL remain mixed (Khan & Nasim, 2025; Lundqvist et al., 2023; Mdhlalose, 2024). A detailed analysis of leadership dimensions is essential. Validating these styles across diverse settings is also necessary (Jensen et al., 2016; Heroman, 2025; Mellor, 2025), especially as cultural values affect how leadership is received (Rockstuhl et al., 2023; Tariq et al., 2024). Workplace happiness includes intrinsic and extrinsic factors like autonomy, recognition, growth, fair pay, and balance, all influenced by leadership (Dhiman et al., 2025; Hasyim & Bakri, 2025; Kayyali, 2025). However, existing research often isolates performance or well-being, lacking a unified view (Doherty, 2022; Sam et al., 2025). This chapter fills that gap by exploring both leadership structures and their impact on happiness. As leadership roles evolve, organisations need insights into how leadership behaviour shapes emotional outcomes. Understanding the most impactful leadership dimensions will improve development strategies (Jayanagara, 2024).

This chapter is essential in today's dynamic organisational landscape, where employee well-being and effective leadership are critical to sustained performance. With the increasing recognition that leadership styles significantly influence workplace experiences, there is a pressing need to examine how transformational and TRL affect employee happiness. The importance of this study lies in its dual focus – validating the dimensions of both leadership styles and analysing their specific impact on workplace happiness, offering a balanced view of structure and emotional outcomes. The aim is to bridge the gap between leadership theory and practice by exploring how these leadership approaches shape employee satisfaction, engagement, and morale. The chapter contributes by providing a validated framework for understanding leadership dimensions, generating empirical insights into their influence on employee well-being, and offering actionable strategies for leadership development. Ultimately, it enriches the discourse on human-centred leadership and supports the creation of positive, productive, and psychologically healthy work environments. By exploring both the structural components and the emotional outcomes associated with transformational and TRL, this chapter provides valuable insights for scholars, practitioners, and policymakers alike.

Review of Literature

TFL and Workplace Happiness

TFL is a leadership style that elevates both leaders and followers through motivation and ethical behaviour (Ali, 2024). Khan et al. (2022) identify key TFL behaviours: idealised influence, inspirational motivation, intellectual stimulation, and individualised consideration, which foster trust, engagement, and happiness at work (Sam et al., 2025). Safwat Adel et al. (2023) found that in healthcare, organisational learning capability (OLC) mediates the link between TFL and workplace happiness, highlighting the importance of a learning-friendly culture. Zahari (2023), studying the academic sector in Malaysia, revealed that TFL enhances work engagement and workplace spirituality – defined as purpose, connectedness, and value alignment – thereby improving happiness. In the UAE banking sector, Shakib (2024) showed that TFL behaviours like individual consideration and inspirational motivation enhance job satisfaction through recognition, support, and development. These findings collectively emphasise TFL's positive influence on employee happiness across different sectors and cultures.

TRL and Workplace Happiness

TRL, unlike TFL, emphasises performance-based rewards and punishments (Boyd, 2024). It is task-focused, promoting supervision, compliance, and structured goal achievement. Though traditionally viewed as less humanistic, recent research shows TRL can enhance workplace happiness under certain conditions (Burnett, 2024). In Indonesia, Marnoto et al. (2024) found that TRL fosters job satisfaction by creating a predictable environment through clear expectations and consistent rewards. Tung (2016) showed that TRL, when paired with psychological empowerment and a promotion focus, can even boost creativity among Chinese employees. Additionally, Keawchaum and Keawchaum (2023) argue that TRL's clarity, fairness, and immediate rewards help build a strong psychological contract. In sectors or cultures valuing structure and discipline, TRL proves effective in enhancing employee satisfaction and workplace happiness.

Comparative Analysis of Transformational and TRL

Comparative studies have explored the effectiveness of transformational (TFL) and TRL on employee engagement and workplace happiness. Al-Serhan et al. (2021), in a study of Jordan's Greater Amman Municipality, found that while both styles positively impact engagement, TFL shows a significantly stronger correlation, highlighting the greater value of inspiration and personalised support. Similarly, Ali (2024), studying the hospitality sector, concluded that although both TFL and TRL enhance job satisfaction, TFL has a more profound impact. In emotionally demanding environments like hotels, the relational and motivational strengths of TFL better support employee well-being. These findings indicate that while TRL suits structured roles, TFL more effectively fosters long-term engagement, innovation, and happiness, aligning with literature positioning it as a holistic, human-centric approach (Ali, 2024).

Mediating Factors in Leadership and Workplace Happiness

Recent studies have explored how leadership styles influence workplace happiness through key mediators. Pradhan and Jena (2019) found that meaningful work mediates the link between TFL and innovative work behaviour (IWB), showing that TFL fosters a sense of purpose, which enhances both innovation and satisfaction. Lai et al. (2020) identified work-life quality and a happy workplace as mediators between TFL and organisational commitment, revealing that supportive, balanced environments created by transformational leaders increase employee happiness and loyalty. These findings highlight that TFL's impact extends beyond individual performance to broader organisational outcomes. Mediators such as meaningful work, organisational learning, and work-life quality explain the mechanisms through which TFL promotes workplace happiness (Hermawati & Mas, 2017).

Cultural Context and Leadership Styles

Leadership effectiveness is influenced by cultural values and societal norms. Arokiasamy and Tat (2020) in Malaysia and Al-Serhan et al. (2021) in Jordan affirm that TFL is adaptable across diverse cultures, though its impact varies by context. In collectivist cultures, elements like individualised consideration and community-building are especially impactful. Hsieh et al. (2019), studying Taiwanese employees, found that TRL, when aligned with cultural values emphasising achievement, can foster lifelong learning through prove orientation. This challenges the notion of TFL's universal superiority and emphasises the need for cultural sensitivity. These studies confirm that both TFL and TRL can enhance workplace happiness when culturally and contextually aligned. While earlier research often isolates variables or focuses on single styles or sectors, few studies offer a comparative, multidimensional perspective. This chapter fills that gap by analysing both leadership styles, their mediators, and cultural influences, offering a holistic view applicable across sectors and cultures.

Research Methodology

The study adopts a quantitative research design using a survey-based approach to explore the impact of transformational and TRL styles on workplace happiness. Primary data were collected via structured questionnaires using validated scales for TRL – ensuring reliability. The data comprises ordinal-type Likert-scale responses from 238 employees, enabling statistical generalisation. SPSS and SmartPLS software were used for data analysis. Descriptive statistics were used for initial assessment, followed by EFA and CFA to validate leadership dimensions. Multiple regression analysis assessed the impact of leadership styles on workplace happiness. These techniques were chosen for their robustness in testing theoretical constructs, validating measurement models, and identifying predictive relationships among variables. The use of CFA and regression ensures model fit, internal consistency, and explanatory power – making the methodology well-suited for examining behavioural constructs in organisational settings.

Results and Discussions

Objective 1. To identify and validate the underlying dimensions of transformational and TRL styles.

Part A: TFL

To study TFL, a 40-item scale adapted from Alban-Metcalfe and Alimo-Metcalfe (2000) – the *TFL Questionnaire (TLQ-LGV)* – was used. The purpose was to identify and confirm the key dimensions of TFL as perceived by employees.

Descriptive Analysis

The mean scores of items ranged between *3.07 and 3.44* on a 5-point Likert scale, indicating that employees generally view their leaders positively. The *standard deviation values (1.17–1.37)* show considerable variation in employee responses, suggesting diverse experiences.

The *highest-rated item* was 'My leader admits mistakes and learns from them' (mean = 3.44), showing that humility and willingness to improve are valued. Other high-rated items include:

- 'My leader supports my personal development' (mean = 3.40).
- 'My leader communicates a compelling vision of the future' (mean = 3.38).

These indicate the importance of encouragement, growth, and vision.

The *lowest-rated items* were related to *approachability, clarity of roles*, and *consultation in decisions* (mean ≈ 3.07–3.10), implying that structural clarity and participative decision-making could be improved.

Overall, employees perceive their leaders as transformational, especially in communication, empathy, and vision, though improvement is needed in participation and role clarity.

Exploratory Factor Analysis (EFA)

The *KMO value (0.968)* and *Bartlett's test* ($\chi^2 = 8071.15$, $p < 0.001$) confirmed that the data were suitable for factor analysis.

Communalities ranged from *0.571 to 0.713*, indicating that items were well-explained by the extracted factors.

Two factors with eigenvalues greater than 1 explained *62.77% of the total variance*:

- *Factor 1*: *inspirational and developmental leadership* – includes behaviours like empathy, vision sharing, and empowerment.
- *Factor 2*: *strategic and participative leadership* – includes structure, communication, and decision-making involvement.

Confirmatory Factor Analysis (CFA)

The CFA confirmed a *two-factor model* with strong model fit:

- $\chi^2/df = 1.673$, $RMSEA = 0.053$, $SRMR = 0.038$, $CFI = 0.937$, $TLI = 0.933$.
- *Cronbach's alpha*: 0.978 and 0.947 (high reliability).
- *AVE*: 0.600 and 0.621 (good convergent validity).

These results validate that TFL consists of two main dimensions:

1. *Inspirational motivation and individual consideration.*
2. *Intellectual stimulation and visionary influence.*

Part B: *TRL*

To assess TRL, a scale adapted from Susanto (2018) was used, covering *15 items* representing 3 components: *contingent reward, management by exception (active)*, and *management by exception (passive)*.

Descriptive Analysis

Item means ranged between *2.89 and 3.19*, showing moderate agreement among employees.

- Highest-rated: 'My supervisor recognises my work with rewards or incentives' (mean = 3.19) – shows focus on reward-based motivation.
- Lowest-rated: 'My supervisor is thorough with details to avoid mistakes' (mean = 2.89) – indicates less emphasis on preventive monitoring.

Overall, TRL behaviours exist but are less prominent, with variation across respondents.

Exploratory Factor Analysis (EFA)

Data suitability was confirmed with *KMO = 0.951* and *Bartlett's test* (χ^2 = *2537.27*, $p < 0.001$). Communalities ranged from *0.580 to 0.743*, indicating good factor loading.

Two components with eigenvalues >1 explained *67.50% of the total variance*:

- *Factor 1: contingent reward and active monitoring* – focuses on recognition and supervision.
- *Factor 2: passive management by exception* – focuses on corrective action after issues arise.

Confirmatory Factor Analysis (CFA)

The CFA confirmed a good two-factor model fit:

- χ^2/df = 2.099, RMSEA = 0.068, SRMR = 0.039, CFI = 0.961, TLI = 0.954.
- *Cronbach's alpha*: 0.856 and 0.949.
- *AVE*: 0.596 and 0.628.

These values confirm strong reliability and validity. Hence, TRL is validated as having *two distinct dimensions*:

1. *Contingent reward*
2. *Management by exception*

Summary Observation

Both transformational and TRL styles were statistically validated.

- TFL was found to have *two core dimensions: inspirational–developmental* and *strategic–participative*.
- TRL also showed *two main components: contingent reward* and *management by exception*.
- Overall, leaders are perceived as more transformational, with strength in communication and development support, and moderate focus on transactional behaviours like supervision and rewards.

In conclusion, the two-factor structure of TRL, contingent reward and management by exception (Fig. 8.1), is statistically sound and psychometrically valid. The high factor loadings, good model fit indices, and strong reliability scores confirm that the scale is an effective and reliable measure of TRL dimensions in organisational settings.

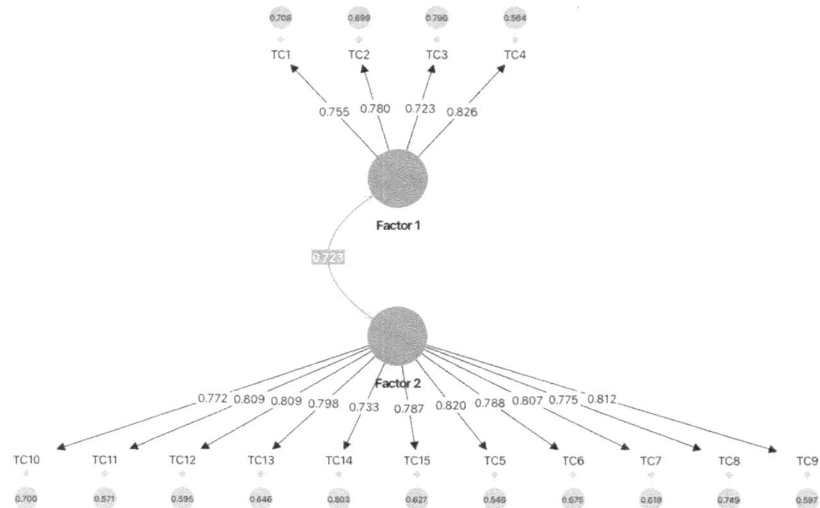

Fig. 8.1. SEM Model. (SmartPLS software output). *Source*: Authors' analysis.

Objective 2. To analyse the impact of transformational and TRL styles on workplace happiness among employees.

Part A: impact of TFL on workplace happiness

The second objective of the study was to examine how transformational and TRL styles influence employees' workplace happiness. In this section, the focus is on TFL and its role in shaping employees' positive experiences at work.

TFL is known for its emphasis on inspiration, motivation, and individualised attention. The regression analysis conducted to test this relationship revealed significant positive effects between TFL dimensions and workplace happiness. Both factors of TFL showed statistically meaningful results.

The first factor (TF_Factor1), representing aspects such as empathy, vision, and motivation, had a *positive impact* on workplace happiness with a standardised coefficient of *0.238* ($p < 0.001$). This suggests that when leaders act with empathy, communicate a clear vision, and inspire their employees, it directly enhances their happiness at work.

The second factor (TF_Factor2), which represents intellectual stimulation and shared vision, displayed an even *stronger effect* with a standardised coefficient of *0.508* ($p < 0.001$). It implies that leaders who encourage creativity, innovation, and collective goals contribute significantly to employee well-being.

The regression model as a whole was highly significant ($F = 100.714$, $p < 0.001$), with an R^2 *value of 0.462*, showing that TFL explains *46.2%* of the variation in workplace happiness. The Durbin–Watson value of 1.879 also indicated no autocorrelation problems, confirming the model's reliability.

These findings clearly show that transformational leaders – those who lead with empathy, motivation, and inspiration – positively influence how employees feel about their work. Employees tend to feel valued, supported, and emotionally fulfilled under such leadership, leading to greater satisfaction and organisational commitment.

Implications of TFL

The results highlight that organisations aiming to enhance workplace happiness should focus on developing TFL qualities among their managers. Leaders who communicate a vision, support employee development, and encourage innovation help create a positive and motivated work environment. Training programmes focusing on emotional intelligence, communication, and motivational strategies can therefore have long-term positive outcomes on employee morale and organisational culture.

In practical terms, industries can use these findings to strengthen team cohesion, reduce turnover, and improve job satisfaction. Transformational leaders not only increase happiness but also drive creativity, productivity, and long-term organisational success.

Part B: impact of TRL on workplace happiness

The second part of the analysis explores the influence of TRL on workplace happiness. TRL is based on a system of rewards, clear expectations, and corrective feedback. Contrary to the common belief that only TFL enhances happiness, the findings of this study suggest that TRL also plays a significant role in improving employee satisfaction.

Regression analysis revealed that both dimensions of TRL significantly influence workplace happiness. The first factor (*TC_Factor1*), which reflects contingent rewards and goal-setting, had a *standardised coefficient of 0.297 ($p < 0.001$)*, meaning that clear goals and fair rewards substantially enhance employees' happiness at work.

The second factor (*TC_Factor2*), linked to management by exception and corrective supervision, showed a stronger effect with a *standardised coefficient of 0.469 ($p < 0.001$)*. This suggests that when managers monitor performance closely, provide constructive feedback, and maintain accountability, employees perceive their work environment as more stable and fair, thereby increasing happiness.

The regression model for TRL was also highly significant ($F = 111.792$, $p < 0.001$), with an R^2 *value of 0.488*, indicating that TRL explains *48.8%* of the variance in workplace happiness. The Durbin–Watson value of *1.929* again confirmed the model's validity.

These results indicate that TRL, through consistent monitoring and fair reward systems, creates predictability and psychological safety in the workplace. Employees are more content when they understand performance expectations and when their efforts are recognised and rewarded.

Implications of TRL

While TFL nurtures emotional and intellectual growth, TRL ensures structure, discipline, and fairness. Organisations should not disregard transactional practices, as they form the foundation for stability and accountability. A balanced approach – combining transactional clarity with transformational inspiration – can create a workplace that is both emotionally fulfilling and operationally efficient.

For organisations, these findings mean that establishing clear performance standards, providing timely feedback, and rewarding excellence are essential strategies for maintaining a happy and motivated workforce. Such practices not only increase individual satisfaction but also lead to improved overall productivity and reduced workplace conflict.

Overall Discussion and Conclusion

This study provides comprehensive empirical evidence showing that both *transformational and TRL styles* significantly influence workplace happiness. The findings confirm that leadership behaviour directly shapes the emotional and psychological well-being of employees.

The CFA confirmed the soundness of both leadership models, showing excellent reliability and validity (Cronbach's alpha above 0.94, AVE above 0.6). Regression results further established that TFL explained *46.2%*, while TRL explained *48.8%* of the variation in workplace happiness, indicating strong predictive power for both models.

These outcomes have far-reaching implications for organisations. In the modern, competitive, and fast-changing work environment, leadership is not just about task management – it is about creating meaning, trust, and engagement among employees. Transformational leaders foster innovation, enthusiasm, and long-term loyalty, while transactional leaders maintain order, fairness, and clear communication.

Therefore, organisations should strive to cultivate *a hybrid leadership approach* – transformational in vision and relational aspects, transactional in structure and accountability. Leadership development programmes should include training on both dimensions to enhance emotional intelligence, performance monitoring, and ethical conduct.

From a practical perspective, happier employees contribute to better retention, higher creativity, and improved productivity. This is particularly relevant for industries such as education, healthcare, IT, and services, where human capital drives growth.

Ultimately, the study concludes that leadership styles are powerful determinants of employee happiness and organisational success. Promoting leadership behaviours that combine empathy, recognition, and fairness is not merely desirable – it is essential for sustainable organisational growth and well-being.

Implications of the Study

The results of this research have precious consequences in leadership training and work-related well-being when considered through the prism of the concept of circular happiness, a holistic and sustainable well-being model where workplace happiness becomes a source of personal fulfilment, group cohesion, organisational development, and back into the employee sense of meaning and contentment.

To begin with, the chapter supports the imperative nature of transformational and TRL approaches in fostering happiness at work. The fact that both styles lead to employee happiness in a remarkable way advocates the notion that happiness is not a one-way effect but a cyclic process – where happy leadership leads to motivated employees who result in better performance, team bonding, and a healthy work environment that once again enhances the leadership influence. This follows the expectations of the circular happiness where the well-being of employees and leadership is constantly reinforcing.

Industrially, these results imply that organisations need to invest in performance-based, as well as well-being-based, leadership training programmes. With the acknowledgement of the significance of leadership as a factor of circular happiness, industries will be able to develop a culture in which employee engagement and job satisfaction are appreciated as values that provide returns in the form of loyalty, creativity, and productivity.

Further, the dual leadership style enables organisations to accommodate both affective and task-oriented worker requirements in the organisation to make the workers feel inspired and safe. Such a balance is capable of resulting in a long-lasting positive, trusting, and satisfying cycle within teams, which is a crucial prerequisite to circular happiness.

Lastly, doing HR work (performance appraisal, career development, wellness programme) in a way that is circular and happy will also contribute to the long-term viability of leadership. It allows organisations to go beyond transactional measures and adopt a human-based paradigm whereby leadership is realising a virtuous cycle of motivation, performance, and well-being.

References

Abu Orabi, T., Al-Hyari, H. S. A. M., Almomani, H. M., Ababne, A., Abu Huson, Y., Ahmed, E., & Albanna, H. (2024). A bibliometric review of job satisfaction and organizational commitment in businesses area literatures. *Human Systems Management*, *43*(3), 407–430.

Alban-Metcalfe, R. J., & Alimo-Metcalfe, B. (2000). The transformational leadership questionnaire (TLQ-LGV): A convergent and discriminant validation study. *Leadership & Organization Development Journal*, *21*(6), 280–296.

Ali, B. (2024). What we know about transformational leadership in tourism and hospitality: A systematic review and future agenda. *The Service Industries Journal*, *44*(1–2), 105–147.

Al-Serhan, A. F., Almaaitah, M. F., Altahat, J. S. M., & Kasabeh, E. A. (2021). The relationship between employee engagement and transformational and transactional leadership styles: Evidence from Jordan; Greater Amman Municipality. *Journal of Management Information and Decision Sciences*, *24*(1), 1–8.

Arokiasamy, A., & Tat, H. (2020). Exploring the influence of transformational leadership on work engagement and workplace spirituality of academic employees in the private higher education institutions in Malaysia. *Management Science Letters*, *10*(4), 855–864.

Bella, K. M. J. (2023). The power of employee well-being: A catalyst for organizational success. *International Journal of Scientific Research in Modern Science and Technology*, *2*(4), 20–26.

Boyd, S. R. (2024). *The impact of transformational and transactional leadership on employee engagement in the government contracting arena* [Doctoral dissertation], Concordia University Irvine.

Burnett, C. (2024). *Influence of transformational leadership behaviors on technology acceptance by healthcare workers* [Doctoral dissertation] Capella University.

Cai, J. (2023). Effects of leadership styles and organizational strategy to enhance performance efficiency. *Journal of Enterprise and Business Intelligence*, *3*(1), 012–022.

Dhiman, N., Kanojia, H., Jamwal, M., & Kumar, S. (2025). A systematic review on employee happiness: Three-decade review, synthesis and research propositions. *Journal of Management History*. https://doi.org/10.1108/JMH-01-2024-0005

Doherty, D. (2022). Relational leadership styles, mental health staff and workplace outcomes: A systematic literature review; and, Servant leadership and psychological well-being among mental health staff: The mediating role of work environment. https://etheses.bham.ac.uk//id/eprint/13184/7/Doherty2022ForenClinPsyD_Redacted.pdf

Eaton, L. (2022). *Transformational leadership: A political science theory transformed by management studies. How did this happen, and why does it matter?* [Doctoral dissertation] Open Access Te Herenga Waka-Victoria University of Wellington.

Elshaer, I. A., Azazz, A. M., Kooli, C., Aljoghaiman, A., Elsawy, O., & Fayyad, S. (2025). Green transformational leadership's impact on employee retention: Does job satisfaction and green support bridge the gap?*Administrative Sciences*, *15*(5), 177.

El-Sharkawy, S. A., Nafea, M., & Hassan, E. D. H. (2023). HRM and organizational learning in the knowledge economy: Investigating the impact of happiness at work (HAW) on organizational learning capability (OLC). *Future Business Journal*, *9*(10). https://doi.org/10.1186/s43093-023-00188-2

Hasyim, H., & Bakri, M. (2023). Organizational evolution: Navigating change and innovation for sustainable development. *Jurnal Manajemen Bisnis*, *10*(2), 889–909.

Hasyim, H., & Bakri, M. (2025). Work-life imbalance: Its impact on employee motivation and well-being. *Economics and Digital Business Review*, *6*(1), 280–297.

Hatalová, R. M., & Nenzén, P. (2021). The enduring importance of employee loyalty-Exploring the concept of employee loyalty in the context of a knowledge intensive organization. https://lup.lub.lu.se/luur/download?func=downloadFile&recordOId=9055026&fileOId=9055030

Hermawati, A., & Mas, N. (2017). Mediation effect of quality of worklife, job involvement, and organizational citizenship behavior in relationship between transglobal leadership to employee performance. *International Journal of Law and Management*, *59*(6), 1143–1158.

Heroman, S. E. (2025). The full range leadership model (FRLM): Department head perceptions of leadership style and development. (Doctoral dissertation, Louisiana State University and Agricultural & Mechanical College). https://www.proquest.com/openview/e245c560bd5f5bd9316897af4b37d45b/1?pq-origsite=gscholar&cbl=18750&diss=y

Hoang, D., Kousi, S., & Martinez, L. F. (2023). Online customer engagement in the post-pandemic scenario: A hybrid thematic analysis of the luxury fashion industry. *Electronic Commerce Research*, *23*(3), 1401–1428.

Hsieh, T. H., Ho, Y. H., & Chen, S. L. (2019). Relationship between transactional leadership and employee lifelong learning with prove orientation as a mediator. *Journal of Research in Educational Sciences*, *10*(12), 5–9.

Jayanagara, O. (2024). The evolution of leadership in the modern professional landscape: Shifting paradigms and their impacts. *Feedforward: Journal of Human Resources*, *4*(1), 61–71.

Jensen, U. T., Andersen, L. B., Bro, L. L., Bøllingtoft, A., Eriksen, T. L. M., Holten, A.-L., Jacobsen, C. B., Ladenburg, J., Nielsen, P. A., Salomonsen, H. H., Westergård-Nielsen, N., & Würtz, A. (2016). Conceptualizing and measuring transformational and transactional leadership. *Administration & Society*, *51*(1), 3–33. https://doi.org/10.1177/0095399716667157

Kayyali, M. (2025). The role of leadership in promoting workplace happiness. In K. Agha (Ed.), *Insights on wellbeing and happiness in the workplace* (pp. 233–254). IGI Global Scientific Publishing. https://www.igi-global.com/book/insights-wellbeing-happiness-workplace/334238

Keawchaum, S., & Keawchaum, C. (2023). How transformational leadership fulfills psychological contract for reinforcing better performance: A Thai case study. *Asia Social Issues*, *16*(4), e257266–e257266.

Khan, A., & Nasim, S. (2025). Mapping research on the subjective well-being of knowledge workers: A systematic enquiry deploying bibliometrics. *Management Review Quarterly*, *75*(1), 911–954.

Khan, I. U., Amin, R. U., & Saif, N. (2022). Individualized consideration and idealized influence of transformational leadership: Mediating role of inspirational motivation and intellectual stimulation. *International Journal of Leadership in Education*, *28*(6), 1–11. https://www.tandfonline.com/doi/abs/10.1080/13603124.2022.2076286

Lai, F. Y., Tang, H. C., Lu, S. C., Lee, Y. C., & Lin, C. C. (2020). Transformational leadership and job performance: The mediating role of work engagement. *Sage Open*, *10*(1), 2158244019899085.

Lundqvist, D., Wallo, A., & Reineholm, C. (2023). Leadership and well-being of employees in the Nordic countries: A literature review. *Work*, *74*(4), 1331–1352.

Marnoto, M., Supardi, S., & Soegiarto, I. (2024). Impact of job satisfaction, transformational leadership, and work-life balance on employee performance: A study in technology companies in Indonesia. *International Journal of Business, Law, and Education*, *5*(1), 510–521.

Mdhlalose, D. (2024). An examination of employee rewards and work environment on employee creativity and innovation. *SEISENSE Journal of Management*, *7*(1), 21–34.

Mellor, J. A. (2025). *Gender, generational cohort, and work location as predictors of employee engagement* [Doctoral dissertation] Capella University.

Misra, N., & Srivastava, S. (2022). Happiness at work: A psychological perspective. *Happiness and Wellness*, *95*.

Mpe, S. (2024). *An evaluation of the impact of transactional leadership style in motivating employees at a construction site in Cape Town* [Doctoral dissertation] Cape Peninsula University of Technology.

Nguyen, N. T., Hooi, L. W., & Avvari, M. V. (2023). Leadership styles and organisational innovation in Vietnam: Does employee creativity matter? *International Journal of Productivity and Performance Management*, *72*(2), 331–360.

Onesti, G. (2023). Exploring the impact of leadership styles, ethical behavior, and organizational identification on workers' well-being. *Administrative Sciences*, *13*(6), 149.

Porath, U. (2023). Advancing managerial evolution and resource management in contemporary business landscapes. *Modern Economy*, *14*(10), 1404–1420.

Pradhan, S., & Jena, L. K. (2019). Does meaningful work explains the relationship between transformational leadership and innovative work behaviour? *Vikalpa*, *44*(1), 30–40.

Reyaz, S. (2024). The influence of leadership styles on employee motivation and job satisfaction. *International Research Journal on Advanced Engineering and Management (IRJAEM)*, *2*(3), 339–344.

Rockstuhl, T., Wu, D., Dulebohn, J. H., Liao, C., & Hoch, J. E. (2023). Cultural congruence or compensation? A meta-analytic test of transformational and transactional leadership effects across cultures. *Journal of International Business Studies*, *54*(3), 476–504.

Salas-Vallina, A., López-Cabrales, Á., Alegre, J., & Fernández, R. (2017). On the road to happiness at work (HAW): Transformational leadership and organizational learning capability as drivers of HAW in a healthcare context. *Personnel Review*, *46*(2), 314–338.

Sam, T. H., Isa, K., Siqi, P., Palpanadan, S. T., Hong, H. C., & Luan, N. M. (2025). Leadership styles and their effects on employee satisfaction in empowering happiness at workplace. *Journal of Ecohumanism*, *4*(1), 454–463.

Shakib, S. (2024). The impact of leadership styles on employee performance and job satisfaction in private banks: A study on transformational and transactional leadership. https://doi.org/10.21203/rs.3.rs-3928526/v1

Susanto, D. Y. (2018). Transactional leadership style and need for achievement on employee performance of PDAM Malang city. *Journal An-Nafs: Kajian Penelitian Psikologi*, *3*(1), 105–134.

Tariq, A., Hassan, K. H. U., & Hussain, S. K. (2024). The influence of organizational culture on leadership styles. *Annals of Human and Social Sciences*, *5*(1), 230–243.

Tung, F. C. (2016). Does transformational, ambidextrous, transactional leadership promote employee creativity? Mediating effects of empowerment and promotion focus. *International Journal of Manpower*, *37*(8), 1250–1263.

Wuryaningrat, N. F., Hidayat, N., & Kumajas, M. L. (2024). The Impact of transformational and transactional leadership on employee performance. *Klabat Journal of Management*, *5*(2), 103–113.

Zahari, N. (2023). *Transformational leadership style and talent management practices in improving employee engagement in the Malaysian public sector: The mediating role of public service motivation* [Doctoral dissertation], University of Nottingham.

Zhang-Zhang, Y., Rohlfer, S., & Varma, A. (2022). Strategic people management in contemporary highly dynamic VUCA contexts: A knowledge worker perspective. *Journal of Business Research*, *144*, 587–598.

Chapter 9

Creating a Culture of Sustainability and Happiness

Narinder Kaur[a] *and Shamily Jaggi*[b]

[a]*Maharishi Markandeswar (Deemed to be University), Mullana, Ambala, India*
[b]*Indus International University, Una, Himachal Pradesh, India*

Abstract

As people around the world grapple with the two imperatives of environmental protection and human well-being, a growing body of research and practice shows that sustainable practices not only protect the environment but also nurture deeper, more enduring forms of happiness. By drawing upon survey in different field of insights from environmental science, psychology, and socio-economic development, this chapter aims to discuss sustainability and happiness, to introduce to the reader perspectives about the setting where these two forces build upon each other. It will consider how sustainability in environmental, socio-economic, and cultural terms can be a condition for happiness and how a feeling of happiness might motivate people and organisations to contribute to their own sustainability. Through this inquiry, the chapter seeks to understand how sustainable happiness may be nurtured at a personal and a collective level, whether making one's own life, workplace, community, and or society more sustainable. But most importantly, the goal is to provide a holistic look at how these two immense forces can come together and define the future in which both people and the planet thrive.

Keywords: Sustainability; happiness; environment; community; social well-being; psychology; workplace

Circular Happiness: Building Sustainable Workplaces for the Next Generation, 165–181

doi:10.1108/978-1-80592-907-920261009

1. Introduction

Sustainability and happiness have emerged as core concepts on the contemporary agenda for individual well-being, social advancement, and global stewardship. Sustainability, which is commonly associated with environmental conservation, is the principle of being able to sustain a given behaviour indefinitely while it is often related to a balance of maintaining the available resources for the common good as well as ensuring that future generations will have the ability to meet their energy needs. It's not just ecologically sustainable, but economically and socially so, creating a peaceful, fair, and secure society. On other side, happiness is a multi-dimensional construct consisting of emotional, mental, and social well-being. It's about enjoying life, developing meaningful connections, and doing things that resonate with your own values and dreams (Biggemann et al., 2014).

If sustainability is about long-term health of our planet and those that inhabit it, happiness is about personal and societal well-being (Brülde, 2015). At first pass it might appear as though these are disconnected thoughts, but in fact they are related at a very deep level. The concept of a sustainable society refers to one which not damage the environment nor over utilise the resources and able to leave beautiful, peace with full of resources to upcoming generations.

With climate change regulation, the depletion of resources, global inequality and its associated problems, such as immigration, emerging faster than ever, the demand for a fresh framework to address the issues we face and to combine sustainability and happiness has never been greater. Economic growth or material achievement as goals in themselves are no longer acceptable: now organisations, communities, and whole societies must be driven by concern for people and the planet (Roseland, 2000). Here, creating a culture that celebrates both sustainability and happiness is one crucial piece of crafting a future that is resilient and thriving for everyone.

Combining the two concepts is very important for all the stakeholder to understand how this is important for all of us. The coupling of sustainability and happiness is being acknowledged as a motivator for organisational and community improvement. In businesses, sustainable culture drives long-term success by minimising waste, efficient use of resources, and ethical business conduct (Ketprapakorn & Kantabutra, 2022). But it also has a way of elevating the well-being of employees, who get to feel more motivated, engaged, and purposeful in their work. This mutually beneficial effect of sustainability and happiness applies beyond the business sector, all the way down to communities and architecture, housing, transportation, and urban planning in which sustainable design can lead to a healthier, more fulfilling life.

In broader societies, the search for sustainability and happiness is crucial to addressing the social and environmental crises of our time. Such attention to sustainability by governments, companies, individuals begins a virtuous circle in which life quality improves, inequality narrows, and ecosystems adapt (Bhandari et al., 2025). Additionally, fostering happiness and well-being benefits society at large, in a way that promotes sustainable social and ecological systems in an equitable manner, without creating a divide between those with materials compared to those without.

It is a topic whose importance cannot be overstated. But, as population sizes increase and environmental pressures mount, the race for quick profit at the cost of sustainability seemingly only quickens the pace at which vital resources are destroyed and ecosystems damaged. Meanwhile, escalating stress, tension, and disenchantment in a range of societies frame a growing requirement for a deeper appreciation of happiness and well-being beyond wealth. To the extent that organisations and societies integrate sustainability and happiness they place themselves in a position to better leverage the societal relevance in the face of future challenges, leading to greater chances the individuals experience personal and common progress and welfare.

2. Sustainable and Happiness Conditioning

2.1. Sustainability

At its most general, sustainability is the capacity for the depletion of systems and processes and effective maintenance, without the expenditure of non-renewable resources – or sustainability at minimum potential for future generations. The three pillars of sustainability – environmental, social, and economic – all contribute towards ensuring that we can meet the needs of today, without compromising the ability of the planet (or society) to enable people to do the same in the future.

2.1.2. Environmental Sustainability

The environmental pillar of sustainability is the best known. It also emphasises conservation of natural resources, such as energy, water, and raw materials, requiring their more efficient use to lessen exhaustion and environmental damage. At the heart of sustainability are actions to save the environment, like fighting climate change, wasting less, and saving biodiversity. Actions like shifting to renewable sources of energy, supporting circular economies, and reducing carbon footprints are all parts of this aspect of sustainability. Keeping ecosystems healthy and natural resources sustainable is crucial to good long-term environmental health, which in turn, ensures human life.

2.1.3. Social Sustainability

Social sustainability primarily concerns the well-being of individuals, communities, and society. It requires advancing social justice, inclusivity, and human rights, while enabling people and communities to access critical services like health, education, and jobs (Grum & Kobal Grum, 2020). Fairness, respect for diversity and the creation of strong social bonds are all important in social sustainability. A sustainable society is a society in which every person can reach their best potential no matter their circumstances, identity, or social background.

Equality-orientated, participatory policies and culturally diverse social practices are important for social sustainability, and can also lead to a high quality of life for people.

2.1.4. Economic Sustainability

Economically sustainable means keeping businesses, industries, or economies independent and able to function over time (Hernita et al., 2021). Adriana Chiriboga the old economic model where everything should be measured in function of short-term profits, can be very different from sustainability, as it is thought of as how to develop resilient business models caring not only for people but also for the environment and society. The list includes things like investing in green technology, encouraging fair trade, and supporting sustainable supply chains. To be truly sustainable from an economic perspective, we must find a balance between profit and morality, ensuring that business enterprises are contributors to society rather than just users of human capital or natural resources. Sustainability – providing the ability to sustain or last over a long period of time sustainability provides the ability to endure, maintain, or last over time.

2.2. Happiness

Both happiness and sustainability emerge here and elsewhere as multidimensional constructs involving feeling good, among other things, but also how people experience the social and physical worlds of which they are part (Lomas & VanderWeele, 2023). It is the face of happiness, satisfaction, and knowing what your lives are about. For individuals, happiness is commonly regarded as a central aspect of a good life and of well-being.

2.2.1. Psychological Wellness and Emotional Health

Mental health is a person's emotional and mental state, his or her ability to cope with stress, maintain relationships, and his or her ability to experience pleasure and/or satisfaction (Russell et al., 2020). It refers to the ability to deal with challenges in one's life, have a sense of personal control and independence, and be optimistic, and carry on with day-to-day activities. Emotional health lies at the heart of happiness, because it shapes your perception of yourself and the world. Things like counselling to help with mental health, building resiliency, and learning emotional intelligence are all key to keeping a person mentally healthy, which ultimately contributes to their overall happiness.

2.2.2. Social Well-being

Social well-being talks about how relationships are important and how it feels to be a part of a community. We are social beings and positive social connections are key to happiness. Social wellness is about the ability to have close relationships with family, friends, co-workers, and others in the community, and to be engaged in activities that improve society (Cicognani, 2023). Feeling supported and belonging creates security and happiness and people are better equipped to deal with problems and have someone to turn to for comfort.

2.2.3. Balance in Work-life and Self-accomplishments

Overflow: being able to balance work and personal life: an important element of happiness. That means trying to strike a balance between work and private life because people need the opportunity to recuperate, to do something they like, to be with the ones they love. Personal fulfilment, such as from meaningful work or personal passions, is also crucial for happiness. Those who are happy with their work, who derive meaning from what they do each day, are more likely to rate themselves as happy (Bhalla et al., 2025). And of course, the ability to manage your time, to make deliberate choices about how you spend your day, is one of the keys to happiness.

2.3. Sustainability and Happiness Are Interconnected

There is a fundamental link between sustainability and happiness, and how each attracts and feeds off the other. Endeavouring for sustainability in its ecological, social, and economic aspects paves the way for happiness in the long term; by the same token, happiness may foster behaviour and attitudes that lead to sustainable ways of living (Sameer et al., 2021).

Environmental sustainability is it really true. Environmental sustainability links directly to happiness since it guarantees clean air, water, and green spaces that impact our physical and psychological wellness. On the contrary, a contaminated environment can result in health issues, stress, and poor quality of life, impacting happiness. Those who live in clean, maintained environments report higher life satisfaction and emotional health.

Social sustainability contributes to happiness by creating that feeling of connection and inclusion. Societies that care about inclusion, equity, and social justice have more trust, less social isolation, and better health for everyone. In such societies, we not only feel more personally fulfilled, but held by a common purpose or faith and collective security. Psychological Balance between them social sustainable societies in which are added personal development through emotional support and well-being.

The economic dimension of sustainability directly contributes to happiness when it is achieved by people having access to decent work, fair salaries and possibilities for personal and financial growth (Chen et al., 2023). When we build a sustainable economy for future job economies and for income distribution so more wealth is brought down and available to more people, what happens is people don't forget to get healthy. When companies make sustainability a priority, they not only help the environment and society, but also work to create a fairer and more stable economy, and with that, greater collective happiness.

In the end, it's a beautifully sustainable loop, this happiness connection. The nurturing environment is the resource for physical and psychological health and a thriving society is more likely to value sustainability in its policies and behaviour. Together, they provide the cornerstones of a healthy world, in which both human beings and our planet can prosper.

3. The Case for Business Happiness Sustainable Style

Today, businesses are beginning to see the virtue of integrating sustainability and happiness into its endeavours. These ideas aren't just a fad – they are critical engines of sustained success. And by connecting environmental responsibility with an employee's own sense of well-being, organisations can encourage a culture of higher-performing employees, a more engaged employee population, and increased consumer loyalty. This strategy results in enormous long-term returns to the workforce, and the bottom line.

3.1. Effect on Employee Engagement and Productivity

Happy work environments are sustainable and lead to high staff productivity and engagement. Studies have shown that there is increased engagement and motivation when you work for an organisation committed to sustainability, and one that values well-being. When workers feel their values align with those of the organisation and they are valued and supported in the work environment, they are more apt to feel connected to the company's mission. This is how they feel like they matter, and how their engagement and performance are enhanced as a result.

It's well-established that a workforce that's happy and connected is more creative, more productive, and more loyal. Dedicated employees who believe in the concern of a company for their well-being are less likely to become burned out or stressed, thus they take fewer sick days, and the workforce is healthier and more productive. It is also true that firms that value sustainability will initiate practices that help decrease workplace stress – favouring flexible working hours, wellness programmes, and an emphasis on work–life balance. All of these things factor into overall employee happiness, and can snowball into a positive feedback loop where employees give more while the company reaps the rewards of increased productivity.

3.1.1. Consumer Preferences

Consumer values are changing, more and more focused on sustainability and the welfare of employees, with consumers favouring brands that place sustainability at the heart of what they do (Bhattacharya et al., 2023). Research has found that many consumers are open to paying a premium for products and services offered by companies that exhibit ethical behaviours, such as being more responsible stewards of the environment and treating employees well. It's not just a fad that's come and gone – a true sea change in consumer expectations is taking place. The brands that share openly their sustainability work and their commitment to increase employee satisfaction are more trusted and credible.

The companies that manifest their commitment to sustainability and happiness, are the ones that prove to be the most competitive in the market. Consumers increasingly are voting with their pocketbooks for brands that mirror their values, and it's easy for people to punish a company that they feel isn't doing its job. From cutting waste to green materials to ensuring fair labour practices, these companies are defining their position in a changing marketplace. That, in return, boosts loyalty and supports the reputation of a brand and, sometimes, sales growth.

3.1.2. Longer-term Payoffs for Companies

The longer-term rewards of well-being and sustainability go beyond employee commitment and customer tastes. Businesses that follow these principles should save money and build better reputations and stronger market positions.

Sustainable policies are frequently cheaper than unsustainable ones. Lower operational costs companies use fewer resources, consume less energy, and minimise waste, therefore reducing costs (Bocken & Short, 2021). For example, going green with energy-efficient systems, renewables, and waste-reduction initiatives helps reduce costs, so it's a win for the environment and your pocket. Additionally, sustainability programmes may contribute to retention by lowering employees' turnover and the associated costs of finding and training new staff. There is less employee turn-over and employee tenure rates increase, thus you have a happier regular workforce that needs fewer shifts filled by agency workers.

Companies can gain significant brand equity from a focus on sustainability and ushering in a happy work culture. Today, consumers, investors and partners are searching for businesses with social and environmental conscientiousness. A business that's friendly to employees and functions sustainably is a place where top talent wants to work and where loyal customers frequent and investors are happy to support righteously. This even higher profile can build more brand equity, a powerful base for their future expansion. Early adopters of sustainability and employee well-being best practices can be industry leaders. They can portray themselves as innovators and decision makers, getting customers who will value this (Ahsan & Khawaja, 2024). These principles are also the safety valve against regulation and market obligations stifling these services. As a commentary on Nikkei, Japan's Rd., points out, given that government policies from all over the world become stringent on environmental, a company which has already embraced the sustainable approach may not be interrupted, leaving getting a leg up on competitors who are left behind in the old ways.

In short, there's a snappy business case for sustainability and for happiness. Companies that spend on a sustainable future, and that prioritise the well-being of their employees, have an opportunity to increase employee engagement, productivity and customer relationships. The long-term advantages – economic savings, a good name, and market leadership – prove this strategy to be both the right thing to do and a good business decision. With more businesses coming around to the benefits of sustainability and happiness, companies that set the pace in these spheres will continue to thrive in the long run.

4. Psychological and Social Foundations (Happiness Theories)

Happiness, a central aspect of human experience, can be understood from different philosophical and psychological perspectives. Two of the most influential theories of happiness are hedonic and eudaimonic well-being, both of which offer distinct frameworks for understanding human fulfilment.

4.1. Hedonic Well-being

Hedonic well-being is primarily concerned with pleasure and the avoidance of pain. It focuses on the immediate experience of joy and satisfaction derived from sensory pleasures, positive emotions, and fulfilling desires (Su et al., 2020). This approach views happiness as the attainment of pleasure and the absence of discomfort. Hedonic well-being is often associated with the idea of maximising pleasure and minimising suffering, and it plays a significant role in understanding short-term happiness and life satisfaction. In workplace contexts, hedonic well-being can be linked to factors such as job satisfaction, rewards, and the quality of personal experiences in the workplace, all contributing to an individual's sense of happiness.

4.2. Eudaimonic Well-being

Eudaimonic well-being takes a deeper and more holistic approach, emphasising self-actualisation, personal growth, and living in alignment with one's true values and purpose (Su et al., 2020). This theory, rooted in Aristotle's philosophy, argues that true happiness comes from the fulfilment of one's potential and the pursuit of meaningful goals rather than just the pursuit of pleasure. Eudaimonic well-being is more about a sense of purpose, contributing to society, and engaging in activities that promote long-term fulfilment. In the workplace, fostering eudaimonic well-being may involve creating an environment where employees feel that their work contributes to a greater cause, promotes personal growth, and aligns with their values.

While hedonic and eudaimonic well-being are often seen as distinct, contemporary psychological theories suggest that they are complementary. A balanced approach that integrates both immediate pleasure and long-term fulfilment can provide a more comprehensive understanding of happiness and its role in various life contexts, including the workplace.

4.3. Positive Psychology and Its Implications for Happiness in the Workplace

Positive psychology, pioneered by psychologist Martin Seligman, has been instrumental in shifting the focus of psychological research from pathology to the study of positive traits and experiences that contribute to human flourishing. Positive psychology emphasises the cultivation of strengths such as gratitude, resilience, optimism, and mindfulness, all of which contribute to increased well-being.

In the workplace, positive psychology provides valuable insights into how organisations can enhance employee satisfaction and overall happiness. By focusing on employee strengths, promoting positive relationships, and fostering a culture of recognition and meaningful work, employers can create environments that not only improve productivity but also contribute to employees' overall sense of happiness and fulfilment (Kun & Gadanecz, 2022). Studies in positive psychology have shown that workplaces that focused on positive emotions, social connections, and a sense of belongingness have higher levels of employee engagement, job satisfaction, and well-being.

Beyond the workplace, positive psychology also highlights the importance of gratefulness and mindfulness as tools for enhancing happiness. Gratitude practices, such as reflecting on what one is thankful for, can shift individuals' focus from what they lack to what they have, increasing positive emotions and well-being. Similarly, mindfulness – focusing on the present moment with acceptance – has been shown to reduce stress, increase emotional regulation, and foster a sense of inner peace, all of which are essential for sustained happiness.

4.4. Social Sustainability: Creating Inclusive Environments Where People Feel Valued

Social sustainability focuses on the ability of societies to maintain social well-being over the long term, fostering inclusive, just, and supportive environments. In the context of happiness, social sustainability is crucial, as the social environment in which individuals live and work directly affects their sense of belonging, worth, and emotional well-being (Virtanen et al., 2020). A society or workplace that fosters inclusivity, respect, and equal opportunities enables individuals to thrive and contribute to the collective happiness of the community.

Creating inclusive environments where people feel valued and respected involves recognising and celebrating diversity and ensuring that everyone, regardless of background, identity, or status, has access to the same opportunities and resources. In workplaces, this means implementing policies that support equal representation, anti-discrimination measures, and support systems for underrepresented groups. Inclusivity also means encouraging open communication, active listening, and empathy, so that individuals feel that their voices are heard and their contributions are valued.

Social sustainability is also linked to the social capital of a community – the networks of relationships and mutual support that allow individuals to feel connected and supported. When people experience strong social bonds and a sense of safety within their communities, they are more likely to experience positive emotions, a sense of belonging, and, ultimately, happiness.

In a broader societal context, social sustainability also means creating systems that ensure access to basic needs such as healthcare, education, and economic opportunities for all members of society. These systemic changes are critical for reducing inequality and enhancing the overall well-being of individuals and communities.

4.5. Importance of Community and Belonging for Happiness

Community plays a vital role in shaping happiness, as humans are inherently social beings. The feeling of belonging being part of a group or a collective contributes significantly to an individual's sense of happiness and well-being (Cramer & Pawsey, 2023). This can be observed in various social settings, including family, friendship circles, and workplace environments.

Various studies consistently show that social relationships and community engagement are among the most important predictors of happiness. Strong social ties provide emotional support, foster a sense of security, and create opportunities for personal growth. When individuals feel that they are an integral part of a community, whether at work, in their local neighbourhoods, or within global movements, they are more likely to experience a sense of fulfilment and contentment.

Webinar transcripts in the workplace, to build the sense of community will contribute a lot to job satisfaction and productivity. This can be created through team-building experiences, a collegial and personal work environment, and a focus on shared values. Community in the workplace Community in the workplace helps to build relationships and trust, and a shared sense of purpose that can help lift employee happiness and motivation.

Beyond the office, involvement in the community, whether it's through volunteering, or being a member of social clubs, can offer people that sense of importance and belonging. When people are able to make a contribution to something larger than themselves and feel part of a supportive community, they are more likely to feel positive emotions and a sense of lasting fulfilment.

Additionally, social support can compromise these barriers, supporting people low in stress, anxiety and loneliness – activities negatively associated with happiness. It can be particularly beneficial to people experiencing personal or life challenges to have a community supporting them during times of crisis or difficulty.

But happiness is a complicated network of psychological and social forces, from the pursuit of instant gratification to the achievement of long-term purposes and self-expression. Understanding the nuances of hedonic and eudaimonic well-being, the tenets of positive psychology, the necessity for social sustainability, as well as the importance of community all guide the way we can develop environments be they at work, within society more broadly that enable human flourishing and happiness. By putting this groundwork first, companies, communities, and people can build swaying inclusive, supportive, and happy environments that encourage real good fortune for all.

4.6. Strategy to Promote Sustainability and Happiness in World

4.6.1. Leadership and Culture in the Organisation

Leaders can go a long way towards embedding sustainability and happiness in the DNA of an organisation. They should communicate and act upon these value commitments. Demonstrate examples of how leadership can model sustainability in action (i.e. reducing one's own carbon footprint, supporting green initiatives) and putting employees first. Emphasise the value of developing a vision for sustainability that reflects the company's values, and allows for both business drivers to be successful and an attractive work environment.

4.6.2. Employee Engagement

Discuss the steps people can take to make work a more sustainable place, such as decreasing excess garbage, embracing eco-friendly goods or implementing sustainable technologies. Highlight the role flexible work hours, mindfulness practices, and mental health-supporting policies have on preventing burnout and promoting happiness. Describe how you can encourage mental health through initiatives, counselling, or mental well-being activities to support a healthy and productive work environment.

4.6.3. Sustainability Education

Introduce the importance of training employees about sustainability activities, green behaviour (e.g. recycle, saving energy) and well-being strategy (e.g. manage stress, integrate work with life). Awareness raising campaigns: consider having your own in-house initiative to notify employees of the organisation's sustainability objectives and how they can help support them.

4.6.4. Encourage A Sense of Social Responsibility

Promote community service or sustainability-related volunteer options for employees. This has the effect of bringing personal values and professional values closer together. Show that the company's corporate social responsibility (CSR) investments can help to create both environmental stewardship and social impact, leading to a general cultural transformation towards sustainability.

5. Remedies to Build an Eco-happy Culture

It's not so easy to generate a happy and sustainable culture in an organisation. There are many challenges that organisations must navigate in order to create a culture that supports sustainability and fosters employee happiness. But these are issues that can be solved strategically. The obstacles were core subjects of enquiry in this stage and effective means to address them.

5.1. Challenges in the Way of a Happy, Sustainable Culture

A key obstacle to pervading a joyful and sustainable culture is organisational immunity. There is an adage, true for many of us, that employees, managers and leaders do not like change, for if it impacts the way they are already doing something they are resistant. This resistance is driven by a number of factors, including fear of the unknown, apathy, or lack of understanding surrounding the benefits of sustainability measures. Furthermore, people might perceive that thinking in a sustainable way is a fashion set by society and/or not a matter that directly affects them. You may get further stymied when the entrenched values of your corporate culture do not easily fit with sustainability and may even work at cross-purpose. It takes a lot of time, money and human resources to produce a more sustainable and joyful culture. Some organisations will be without the means – in terms of money and or staff – to sustain the investment in training, infrastructure and action necessary to produce tangible results. For instance, the upfront capital investment for installing green technologies, offering wellness programmes, or hosting educational workshops for sustainability can be challenging for small-sized organisations to finance. Also, companies may not have the expertise or the wingspan to enforce these new measures effectively. In most businesses, sustainability and employee happiness objectives can and often do conflict with short-term financial targets or operational imperatives. For example, a business might be more focused short-term on making as much money as possible, whereas long-term investments for sustainability can be at cross purposes with earning as much as possible. Likewise, leaders may treat employee well-being as less important than the pursuit of other objectives, such as productivity or profitability. These opposing priorities can even create tension between various 'sides' within the business, making it tough to achieve a coherent, sustainable culture.

5.2. Strategies to Overcome Challenges

Getting commitment from leadership is critical for pushing back and breaking through the barriers to establishing a sustainable, joyful culture. 'Leadership needs to not just support sustainability but drive it'. This demands strong messaging about the positive impacts of sustainability organisationally and personally. For instance, research demonstrates that a focus on sustainability can lead to higher levels of employee engagement, a stronger brand, and greater long-term profit. By proving the link between sustainability, happiness and business performance to employees, leaders can influence the mindset of employees and foster a common purpose. Leaders should encourage regular conversations around the importance of sustainability in order to uncover any potential obstacles early and develop preventative measures. Appropriate change management strategies are necessary for overcoming inertia of the organisation. This includes empowering staff to learn the know-how and be motivated to adopt new ways of working, a new culture, new ways of behaving. With transparency and an honest conversation, a good process like this one will go on. Leaders should keep their constituents informed about the latest developments in sustainability initiatives, explaining the 'why' and the context for the changes and good news stories. Furthermore, organisations have a role to play in providing training and development to allow employees to feel more able to take up sustainable practices. Piloting or trying things on a small scale can also lower resistance by giving employees the opportunity to have first-hand experience with the benefits of sustainability before adopting larger changes. Organisations need to make strategic resource allocation and lay focus on the most impactful initiatives in order to tackle resource constraints. This may be achieved by divesting funds from lower effective activities to sustainability, and/or by securing outside funding or collaborations. For instance, working with environmental nongovernmental organisation (NGOs), government institutions or sustainability-oriented businesses would provide access to resources, skills and networks that may be beyond the company's reach. Organisations can also increase the likelihood of gaining acceptance for high-impact, but expensive initiatives by starting smaller with something more cost-effective and invisible, like encouraging telecommuting or focusing on power management in office spaces.

In the case of conflicting goals, however, it is important to converge towards the goals of other departments and players in the enterprise. One way to do so is by integrating sustainability and employee well-being into the overall business strategy in a way that treats these goals as essential to driving, rather than coincidental to the company's success. For instance, HR and sustainability can work together to create initiatives that benefit employee happiness as well as sustainability – think wellness programmes that emphasise environmental responsibility. Communication across departments and openness is a must for people to work together towards a shared goal. Frequently revisiting and adjusting company goals and values, with an eye towards sustainability and happiness commitment, would also keep these priorities at the centre of the company's mission. Last, an inquiry into the impact of sustainability and happiness initiatives is needed to keep the momentum and reinforce the value of this realisation effort. Create some kind of tool to measure the success of what you're doing – it could be anything related to the project, from employee engagement scores to energy saved to reduction in waste. Acknowledging and celebrating benchmarks or accomplishments, however small, can lift spirits and keep those employees on board. This might include public acknowledgment of teams or individuals associated with sustainability efforts or organising events that showcase what has been achieved by the organisation in these respects. By celebrating successes, a company can communicate the positive effect sustainability has on a company and can generate further buy-in from its employees.

6. The Future of Sustainability and Well-being

Rising global concerns of climate change alongside an increased need for individual well-being are focusing more attention around the intersection of sustainability and happiness. Increasingly, technology, innovation, and evolving social norms will have a material impact on the future of sustainability as well as happiness.

6.1. Technology, Innovation and Shifting Social Values

One of the major catalysts for this change is the rate at which technology is progressing. With the rise of artificial intelligence (AI), the tech-driven sustainable fashion trend, the smart cities movement to AI in healthcare and renewable resource developments, technology can be our best friend in reducing our environmental impact and making life better (Dwivedi et al., 2023). Clean energy, waste management and agriculture innovations enable communities to establish green economies – and make life better as well. There are also digital tools that are starting to bring the concept of mental health and well-being into the mix in order to help people better cope with stress and even increase how happy they are.

Society's values must also change. As knowledge of the climate, and social ills in the world, becomes more widespread, there is definitely a tendency towards sustainable consumer behaviour. There's a growing expectation that brands offer ethical production, transparency about supply chains, and products that contribute to a circular economy. Millennials and my generation, Gen Z, are probably the ones behind this promotion of policies that tie sustainability and well-being together, as we know that happiness should not be separated from a happy planet.

6.2. Global Views on Sustainability and Happiness

The way countries and cultures think about sustainability and happiness is different and is shaped by the history resources and values (Woollacott et al., 2023). For instance, Bhutan gross national happiness (GNH) index has sustainable development as a vital factor for the well-being of a society. In this vision, the search for happiness is connected up with conservation and creativity and environmental stewardship and with the possibility of more-nuanced, less-atomised economic growth.

The same goes for Scandinavian countries, such as Denmark, Sweden, and Finland, which often finish near the top of the world's happiness rankings because of their robust social safety nets, high collective environmental consciousness, and dedication to work-life balance. Yet, these are the countries balancing eco-friendly living against personal well-being and showing how it's possible to live happily and be kind to the planet at the same time.

Costa Rica, in contrast, has seen remarkable success in connecting environmental conservation with national happiness. By prioritising biodiversity conservation while lowering its carbon impact, Costa Rica has become one of the world's happiest nations, in some measure because of the health of its ecosystems. The living standard measurement for Costa Rica is ecological sustainability. These differing paths are instructive for the rest of the world: green policies that are good for the planet also are good for happiness, so creating policies embracing both should be a priority.

6.3. Next Generation: Youth-led Movements and the Call for Change

The upcoming generation is making their voices heard as they strive to create a future that prioritises sustainability and happiness. Youth-led movements such as Fridays for Future, initiated by Greta Thunberg, and the burgeoning activism for climate justice prove that the younger generations are not simply passive participants in our social systems; they drive them.

The growing call for ethical, sustainable and inclusive practices comes from a desire for a better, fairer world. Young people are leading the charge on issues like climate action, diversity and inclusion, fair trade, and sustainable consumption, and they're demanding that businesses and governments make these values a priority (Rana et al., 2020). They are increasingly powerful and are altering the world around them as companies understand that sustainability is not only vital to the planet's future, but also critical to attracting the next generation of consumers and leaders.

Listening to and integrating youth voices in policy, business practices, and community actions will be the heart of a world that we are envisioning – one that makes sustainability and happiness possible for everyone. Such a collaborative effort will guarantee future generations inherit a planet on which they can thrive sustainably and joyfully.

7. Conclusion

Building a culture of sustainability and happiness is a critical activity requiring conscious efforts, leadership buy in and community engagement. We create workplace and community environments that nurture well-being and long-term planetary health by integrating sustainable practices into our culture, connecting employee engagement to environmental and social goals, and supporting purposeful work and community involvement'.

Crucial points to emerge are that leadership is paramount in leading such a culture as sustainability is not dictated from above but has to be a vision shared by all levels within the organisation. Not only will engaged employees with the knowledge and resources be more disposed to get involved, they can act as a catalyst for other people and households to consider what they can do leading to change at home and in our communities. It seems, additionally, that one eye is on sustainability education so that it empowers people to decide and be more responsible in the way they want to lead their lives, and other eye is on social responsibility so that we come together as one unit.

Metrics to evaluate success in growing a culture of sustainability and happiness – be it in terms of decreased carbon footprint, employee happiness or societal benefit – are also necessary for monitoring progress and modifying approaches. These measurements may both help to communicate the effectiveness of their efforts and indicate where there's room for additional growth and development.

Leaders, employees and community members can directly contribute to a sustainable and happier culture now. As a leading organisation, it's very important that we lead by example and apply policies and procedures that have a sustainable focus, communicate openly and give staff an opportunity to participate and contribute to environmental and social efforts. And when Holland America and its employees achieve alignment in personal values and business objectives, a tremendous difference can be made, whether it's a small one such as reducing waste, or a major one like being involved in CSR initiatives. And as a community, we need to take it outside of work, funding local sustainability initiatives and leading an entwined web of people working towards a goal collectively.

Working together, by each of us doing both big and small thing, we can promote a culture of sustainability and a spirit of happiness and provide a better world for our children and our children's children.

References

Ahsan, M. J., & Khawaja, S. (2024). Sustainable leadership impact on environmental performance: Exploring employee well-being, innovation, and organizational resilience. *Discover Sustainability*, *5*, 1–22.

Bhalla, P., Kaur, J., Alharbi, A., & Qazi, S. (2025). The emotional filter: Investigating attitude towards emotions as a moderator in the self-efficacy-happiness connection. *Journal of Posthumanism*, *5*, 1740–1756.

Bhandari, S., Mishra, M. K., Bhalla, P., & Gupta, S. (2025). Understanding the effect of personality types on workplace happiness using structural equation modelling approach. *International Journal of Work Innovation*, *6*, 1–21.

Bhattacharya, C. B., Sen, S., Edinger-Schons, L. M., & Neureiter, M. (2023). Corporate purpose and employee sustainability behaviors. *Journal of Business Ethics*, *183*, 963–981.

Biggemann, S., Williams, M., & Kro, G. (2014). Building in sustainability, social responsibility and value co-creation. *Journal of Business and Industrial Marketing*, *29*, 304–312.

Bocken, N. M. P., & Short, S. W. (2021). Unsustainable business models – Recognising and resolving institutionalised social and environmental harm. *Journal of Cleaner Production*, *312*, 127828.

Brülde, B. (2015). Well-Being, Happiness and Sustainability. In J. Søraker, J. W. Van der Rijt, J. de Boer, P. H. Wong & P. Brey (Eds.), *Well-Being in Contemporary Society. Happiness Studies Book Series*. Springer Nature. https://doi.org/10.1007/978-3-319-06459-8_9.

Chen, Y. C., Chiu, Y. H., Chang, T. H., & Lin, T. Y. (2023). Sustainable development, government efficiency, and people's happiness. *Journal of Happiness Studies*, *24*, 1549–1578.

Cicognani, E. (2023). Social well-being. In F. Maggino (Ed.), *Encyclopedia of quality of life and well-being research* (pp. 6714–6717). Springer Nature.

Cramer, K. M., & Pawsey, H. (2023). Happiness and sense of community belonging in the world value survey. *Current Research in Ecological and Social Psychology*, *4*, 100101.

Dwivedi, Y. K., Sharma, A., Rana, N. P., Giannakis, M., Goel, P., & Dutot, V. (2023). Evolution of artificial intelligence research in technological forecasting and social change: Research topics, trends, and future directions. *Technological Forecasting and Social Change*, *192*, 122579.

Grum, B., & Kobal Grum, D. (2020). Concepts of social sustainability based on social infrastructure and quality of life. *Facilities*, *38*, 783–800.

Hernita, H., Surya, B., Perwira, I., Abubakar, H., & Idris, M. (2021). Economic business sustainability and strengthening human resource capacity based on increasing the productivity of small and medium enterprises (SMEs) in Makassar City, Indonesia. *Sustainability*, *13*, 3177.

Ketprapakorn, N., & Kantabutra, S. (2022). Toward an organizational theory of sustainability culture. *Sustainable Production and Consumption*, *32*, 638–654.

Kun, A., & Gadanecz, P. (2022). Workplace happiness, well-being and their relationship with psychological capital: A study of Hungarian Teachers. *Current Psychology*, *41*, 185–199.

Lomas, T., & VanderWeele, T. J. (2023). The complex creation of happiness: Multidimensional conditionality in the drivers of happy people and societies. *The Journal of Positive Psychology*, *18*, 15–33.

Roseland, M. (2000). Sustainable community development: Integrating environmental, economic, and social objectives. *Progress in Planning*, *54*, 73–132.

Russell, R. D., Black, L. J., Pham, N. M., & Begley, A. (2020). The effectiveness of emotional wellness programs on mental health outcomes for adults with multiple sclerosis: A systematic review and meta-analysis. *Multiple Sclerosis and Related Disorders*, *44*, 102171.

Sameer, Y. M., Elmassah, S., Mertzanis, C., & El-Maghraby, L. (2021). Are happier nations more responsible? Examining the link between happiness and sustainability. *Social Indicators Research*, *158*, 267–295.

Su, L., Tang, B., & Nawijn, J. (2020). Eudaimonic and hedonic well-being pattern changes: Intensity and activity. *Annals of Tourism Research*, *84*, 103008.

Virtanen, P. K., Siragusa, L., & Guttorm, H. (2020). Introduction: Toward more inclusive definitions of sustainability. *Current Opinion in Environmental Sustainability*, *43*, 77–82.

Woollacott, M., Shumway-Cook, A., & Tassell-Matamua, N. (2023). Worldviews and environmental ethics: Contributions of brain processing networks. *EXPLORE*, *19*, 630–635.

Chapter 10

The Happiness Loop: Circular Business Models Enhancing Customer Satisfaction and Empowering Employees Through Ownership

Abhishek Sharma[a], *Pinnika Syam Yadav*[b] *and Ankitha Sharma*[a]

[a] *Mittal School of Business, Lovely Professional University, India*
[b] *School of Business and Management, Christ University, India*

Abstract

Circular business models (CBMs) show a new way of doing business; they differ from the old 'take-make-dispose' method. They focus on sustainability, resource efficiency and stakeholder inclusion. This chapter examines how these models make a 'happiness loop', wherein empowered employees and satisfied customers help each other thrive, and that makes the firm prosper. The study reviews literature on circular economy (CE) principles, customer satisfaction and employee ownership, highlighting that the firms that use circular strategies often gain customer loyalty, and they also involve employees more, because the staff feels a sense of ownership and purpose. We present case studies relevant to Indian industries that explain how companies align their business practices with social and environmental goals, delight customers and empower employees. A conceptual model is proposed that illustrates employee ownership and engagement lead to better service, customers become more satisfied and stay loyal. In turn, this fuels business sustainability and also leads to more investment in employees and circular innovations. The chapter explains the advantages of this approach highlighting how more innovation and trust lead to economic and societal benefits. But challenges surface as well, like cultural change management and balancing the goals of multi-stakeholders.

Keywords: Circular business models; employee ownership; customer satisfaction; sustainable business; stakeholder inclusion

Circular Happiness: Building Sustainable Workplaces for the Next Generation, 183–202

Published under exclusive licence by Emerald Publishing Limited
doi:10.1108/978-1-80592-907-920261010

1. Introduction

A CE can be described as an alternative to a linear one. A linear economy is where consumers either own products (be it a product or a resource) or do not, but mainly generate waste after use on behalf of other businesses. A CE, on the other hand, sets out to change the previously made assumption of ownership, say Mont et al. (2017). Instead of solely focusing on ownership, services, leasing, and rentals could effectively keep resources in continuous circulation, maintain their value, and generate further business revenue.

The issue with circularity in the economy is that the 'new' alternative concepts of businesses, for example, CBMs, are similar to older known concepts, for example, sharing concepts. P2P/conventional sharing platforms are easy to confuse with CBMs. Hence, there is a need to clarify the current state of the CE and its concepts. During the years of propagation of sustainability, criticisms around definitions concerning sustainable development, social sustainability, and eco-innovation (and many other fields) have also been made to define concrete boundaries of the concepts; we should fortify with similar ambitions the concept of the CE.

Current advancement and progress in circularity in terms of concept set a basis for defining the CE's challenges, collecting current definitions and international standards, and examining and presenting living cases as potential exemplary models. In general, how broadly is the 'boundless sustainability' time frame considered when defining the 'indefinite' state of the CE? Even how credible an 'indefinite state' can be? In a more pragmatic sense, business models, but in this case CBMs, through concept presentation and empirical research, case studies, and/or living cases, would be analysed.

Within CBMs, there is a considerably wide range of particular concepts. Value propositions and value chains of CBMs are studied based on them. CBMs create environmental improvements. However, the subject is empirically under-researched.

2. The Shift from Linear to CE

The linear economy is a well-established concept in which supply, produce, sell, and dispose are the dominant business model (Bocken et al., 2019). The problem arises with the disposal, as the lost value is untraceable. The most significant loss of value appears in the material extraction and disposal stage. This is where the 3Rs should be encouraged: reduce, reuse, and recycle 5–10x acceleration on waste prevention is required; that is, the socio-economic systems should be translated to closed loops. The CE is a regenerative and restorative system in which economic output and growth are decoupled from resource inputs, flows, and consumption. Product-as-a-service is one option where ownership is separated from performance, and usage is rewarded instead of purchase. Companies selling the product as a service retain ownership and usage rights of their products after the service. Simultaneously, they have a financial interest in developing further the product's lifetime, service, reuse, resale, and recycling so the value can be returned in the value loop. New business models in which the waste is reused should offer a more gratifying customer experience, in which the experience of waste is invisible to the customer. Experiments of business model innovation (BMI) function as sandboxing mechanisms to engage and involve internal and external stakeholders in experimentation to learn about what does and what does not work in practice. As companies can learn from successes and failures, learning is key in implementing new BMI solutions. About 66% of the companies surveyed in 2016 reported having sustainability integration in current strategies, but only 34% said their company was implementing CE principles. Complex, far-down-the-road setups and integration across business units are key barriers limiting the effectiveness of sustainability integration (BSR & GlobeScan, 2016).

3. Principles of CE

The CE concept is generally defined as an industrial economy that is restorative or regenerative by intention and design. Within this economy, positive society-wide benefits would be achieved through, for example, proficiently closing the materials resource cycle of products or services and designing them for long life, ease of upgrade/repair, and effective recycling. The CE is based on two 'material loops' (Mont et al., 2017). At its heart are biological materials, which are intended to re-enter the biosphere without harming it after consumption, and technical materials, which are designed not to enter the biosphere but to be reused and remanufactured in the technosphere. A system based on such conceptual foundations would create positive societal benefits because the aggregate throughput of material resources would be far smaller and would thus harm the environment much less.

The CE encompasses different primary principles. Within the technical cycle, products would be manufactured from non-toxic materials that are perpetually cycled in closed loops; supply chains would be reorganised to eliminate waste production and improve resource efficiency, involving innovations in sourcing raw materials and product design. Within the biological cycle, on-consumption products would be reintroduced into air, water, and soil as beneficial resources; all human by-products would be effectively re-filtered and reused in natural systems, involving innovative waste management technologies. There are many ways through which businesses can start pursuing the opportunities available in the CE.

3.1. Sustainability

Research demonstrates that a substantial number of firms are already implementing sustainable supply chain practices on a wide scale. In so doing, these firms have acknowledged the need to balance stakeholder expectations, followed by recent empirical works on the initiatives, drivers, and a multifaceted framework of sustainable supply chain practices. Supply chain practices are examined in five areas (i.e. supplier selection, supplier development, demand management, supply chain collaboration, and green procurement) and responses to gather extensive data on practices and their potential contribution to financial, environmental, social, and economic benefits.

Implementation of supply chain practices that include green procurement is significantly associated with companies' sustainability goals. Stricter government regulations on environmental performance negatively affect the financial performance of the focal firms involved. However, environmental costs are compensated at least partially by economic benefits in firms' supply chain practices (Rothenberg, 2004). There is an academic perception of business responsibility towards society, with the exception of critics. Prior research addresses the nature and structure of business systems and their contribution to corporate responsibility. There is limited research on the corporate responsibility strategies of well-known firms. Such approaches are contextual in nature and dependent on the historical path, structure of industries, business systems, and firm strategies; these factors do impact the degree to which responsibility is enacted.

Research also addresses four interlinked business system strategies that firms can adopt to manage corporate responsibility. They include the following social trends that are seen to give sustainable business advantages, ensuring the firm's licence to operate, encouraging firms to bypass corporate responsibility expectations, and spotting social opportunities in emerging markets. The working of the four strategies is illustrated by examples from large firms in fast-moving consumer markets and the automotive industry in Europe. In addition to pertinent debates on the nature of corporate responsibility and its regulation, the chapter contributes through an ex-ante typology of business system strategies that is applicable in various contexts.

3.2. Resource Efficiency

To foster competitiveness and flexibility, many firms are forced to become leaner. How enterprise processes and relationships can be restructured and redesigned to improve resource efficiency has been a recurring theme for over a decade. Approaches such as business process reengineering, total quality management, and, more recently, six sigma offer insights into how appropriate choices can lead to substantial improvements in productivity. Structural or strategic changes, such as divestitures and mergers, in addition to technological solutions, are also widely discussed.

Responses to changing customer preferences or competitive pressures may involve more transactional or operational choices. However, while many of these choices are commonly made, implicit assumptions or fuzzy objectives often inhibit unlocking potential gains. The growing complexity of competitive behaviour in a service-based or knowledge-based economy also diminishes the efficacy of these traditional toolkits. Firms may be unaware of their own organisation's capacities and limitations until they are put to the test. Nevertheless, historical evidence suggests that it is the imaginative synthesis of diverse elements, rather than the use of any specific one of these tools, that leads to sustainable solutions (Rothenberg, 2004).

Resource efficiency means conducting business and providing customer service in a manner that minimises the consumption of natural and economic resources while assuring customer satisfaction. Efficient use of resources means that every transaction that results in the delivery of a product or service to a customer is accomplished by the use of minimal inputs. Boards and executive management that embrace this definition embrace a systems-wide perspective. Organisations have seven key resources: money, land, machines, materials, energy, people, and information. Maximising efficiency across all resources requires coordinated management decisions across all streams.

3.3. Stakeholder Inclusion

The actual inclusion of stakeholder interests in the CE remains a crucial element of understanding how BMI in relation to the CE provides value to a variety of different stakeholder groups. Stakeholders are related groups who receive or delegate consideration to a set of practices, in this case regarding the CE, but also reinforce them in their interconnected efforts to shape wider institutional environments (Rothenberg, 2004). Consequently, a systematic understanding of how such collective stakeholder efforts interact and create BMI opportunities regarding the CE in ways that can aid the sustainability transition process becomes crucial for policymakers and company management alike. At the same time, academic research on the inclusion of stakeholder interests in the CE and BMI in this light is still in its infancy and remains, to a large extent, unintegrated. If the inclusion of stakeholder interests in the CE is conceptualised in system dynamics terms (i.e. focusing on stakeholders as active agents who interact and thereby shape business models), prominent topics of inquiry become a systematic understanding of the dynamic interdependability between who meets which interests by means of what means, timing and intention, and how they dynamically create maximum new stakeholder engagement and BMI opportunities, or on the contrary, widen the gap (or exacerbate trade-offs) between acceptance and transitional intent regarding the CE. Following a systemic understanding of the inclusion of stakeholder interests in the CE, this chapter provides a systematic foundation for the creation of new engagement and inclusion opportunities for stakeholders and BMI in relation to the CE. The chapter is structured around four steps, each comprising critical questions and insights that together provide a systematic framework for analysing stakeholder engagement and enactment dynamics around the CE. Each step comprises a set of systematic insights aimed to guide the analysis, as well as an application illustration of the insights. The aim of the chapter is not to offer prescriptive guidelines or solutions but rather to provide a set of questions that can allow systematic analysis and learning with respect to recent developments regarding the inclusion of stakeholder interests in the CE. By gathering insights about the CE from tribes and firms across the globe and by formulating challenges based on these insights, new spaces for experimental innovation and policy-making are opened up with the aim of democratising genetics and, with this, substantially changing the dynamics of inclusion/exclusion in the bio business world.

4. The Happiness Loop Concept

Happiness is a widely desired state that is pursued for its own sake (Sousa & Carvalho, 2023). In a work context, happiness is referred to as work happiness, work-related happiness, job happiness, or job satisfaction; it represents positive mood(s), attitude(s), emotion(s), or emotions concerning work. Work happiness is expected to bring about other desirable states, such as positive organisational citizenship behaviours (OCBs), proactive and innovative behaviours, extra-role helping behaviours, low counterproductive work behaviour, and commitment to stay in the organisation. Research suggests that employees who are happy at work tend to give rise to this type of behaviour. The possible impact of work happiness is so vast that some specialisation tends to occur on specific topics, such as a focus on collectors within an IT setting or a specific focus on the positive effects of emotions at the workplace (Williams et al., 2016).

This chapter suggests that work happiness can be achieved more by focusing on improving happiness instead of solely on the effects. Conceptualisations of happiness and work happiness are explored. Developing these concepts into a dual process model of inside-out and outside-in approaches is explained, showing nuances concerning managing work happiness requests. Work happiness is affected by factors inside and outside the individual. The inside-out approach refers to a change in the factors 'inside' the employee, such as values, beliefs, attitudes, emotions, and behaviours. A training intervention focusing on reappraising appraisal processes concerning events at work would fall within the inside-out approach. The outside-in approach takes the opposite route and targets change in the factors 'outside' the employee.

4.1. Empowered Employees

The precondition for the happiness loop to operate is empowering employees. Employees should have reasonable autonomy, allowing them to perform their tasks appropriately. The following aspects are important regarding autonomy and empowerment.

Empowerment is about giving responsibility and trusting capabilities. Empowerment allows employees to make the right decisions for themselves and the firm. Empowerment comes with the right to decide to fulfil the responsibility given. Firms that empower and allow employees to act autonomously will have engaged employees. This autonomy is crucial for generating happiness and engagement. Feelings of unhappiness accompany the perception of not having autonomy.

Empowerment relates to the perception of having the necessary capabilities to fulfil responsibility. Employees need to have the required competencies and skills to take on the responsibilities to which they are assigned. Empowered employees know the firm's goals, understand their role, and are skilled to deliver the best contributions to the firm.

Employees will cherish the investment firms make to deliver these competencies and skills.

The actions of the firm are crucial to creating empowered employees. First, the employees need to be trusted prior to working together. They need to be given reasonable autonomy. Next, this trust must be rewarded. Employees must be helped to enhance their capabilities. They need to know their role in the firm's strategy, targets, yardsticks, and how to meet those targets. Performance on these targets should be monitored, and feedback should be provided and rewarded, positively or negatively, with the promise of improvement to develop capabilities further.

Empowerment leads to hard engagement. Employees who are conscious of their responsibilities and aware of the competencies needed trust others to be aware of theirs and resort to abandoning tasks that employees deem unnecessary for them. In a cascading mechanism, engagement will disappear from the work floor. At one moment, everyone is doing what they want, and employees no longer attend meetings.

4.2. Satisfied Customers

Together with this, transparency on all relevant aspects of that product or service can be paramount. After-sales care, such as a good repair option or the availability of spare parts, is also important. On a relational level, striving for long-term partnerships based on open communication can support satisfaction with suppliers, too. As the customers consider themselves empowered, they thoroughly evaluate the firm's fulfilment of requirements. Besides the aforementioned, they also do so based on pricing/value for money, perceived image, and technological appeal. The customers also assess whether the firm is sufficiently ambitious to innovate for the future. As happiness fulfils the customers' expectations, a small 'disloyalty buffer' needs to be incorporated to fulfil all requirements. Experience rewards and responsiveness, such as the easy, chic, fancy, or clever handling of the product or service, are key satisfiers for some. As customers mainly assess fulfilling the requirements, it can greatly vary when one becomes a lost customer. It may be viewed as a regretful loss instead of betrayal, leading to feelings of sadness or anger instead of grief. On the other hand, the other talkers allow the customers to discover how to recover when something goes wrong. Whenever or by whom it is expected that an act of malaise is to be expected, it must be treated immediately and positively so that a 'bad' event may turn 'better' or 'better' and can lead to euphoria over the recovery. Overall, fulfilling needs is a question of working on the right requirements in the proper manner, either from a rational, relational, or emotional perspective. To optimise customer types, customer happiness should increasingly pull the firm's offerings, that is, seek a cute, clever, aesthetic, novel, or chic product as long as it provides positive wit. Hence, customers want their requirements to be actively fulfilled and enhanced with a positive benefit or reward.

Customer awareness additionally allows for controlling all aspects of the relationship, including pricing. As the relationships are considered to be somewhat vulnerable, this is especially true for custom offerings, investments, or other complex offerings. As these concern the exploitation of high expectations or ambitions, customer control over health, perception, and happiness is key. Ad-hoc business adjustments can be made during downturns, but the relationship's trust must be protected, as extreme measures are to be taken after observing warning signals.

4.3. Firm Prosperity

The notion of profit is often thought of only in terms of money. How do we, however, define 'profit' where there is no money? Is it possible that firm prosperity might best be marked, in part, by employee behaviour towards customers? Three measures of employee behaviour were examined. First, going beyond job duties to provide customers with what they wanted (empowerment). Second, it is important to be attentive towards customers (affection); and third, it is important to create an experience for customers (experience). The results indicated that firms with customer-empowering CBMs created employee behaviours designed to satisfy customers (Rothenberg, 2004). Going beyond firms' traditional set of performance goals entailed a more creative and explorative approach to performance. This is most profound in terms of employee satisfaction with customer contact, task discretion, and social relationships. Trust is an important foundation enabling employees at firms with customer-empowering CBMs to perform sustainably. Trust rests on three conditions: experiencing, expecting, and believing. Rather than pressuring employees to perform to narrow firm goals, training efforts were directed at creating contexts enabling employees to apply themselves. In an effort to retain quality employees, firms with customer-satisfying CBMs used monetary compensation to create attractive jobs. Financial performance is likely to be replaced by other options for defining firm performance. This is because temporary employment contracts entail lower labour costs. In contrast, CBM types that empower employees might be more challenging for non-incumbents to use. The example of the large Chinese marketplace in which each vendor sells the exact same products at the same prices illustrates the deliberate design of restrictions preventing new entrants and imitation. This criticises Hanley tube stations as they were with the London Underground; this writer's experience of a metropolitan subway stretched back for a long time. In the most influential articles, formalisation was referred to as 'tightness' as it concerned the scope and use of rules and procedures. Performance goals are most useful when costs constrict, and operational flexibility is most beneficial when resources tighten.

5. Literature Review on CE

The emergence of the CE strongly influences the global economy and is a topic of great attention among academic researchers, business practitioners, and policymakers. The CE brings business opportunities to different kinds of firms. However, the CE is still a fuzzy idea as it has not reached a consensus on definitions among different actors (Garcés-Ayerbe et al., 2019). Some differ in their focuses, such as waste management, industrial ecology, and sustainable development. Others have varying scopes and functions. Thus, a review of the CE concept and development is needed first. Most of the existing studies are limited to the identification and discussion of CE drivers and barriers. Some studies analyse the differences in CE development concerning companies' size, sector, and geographical position. A broad and deep understanding of the CE is indispensable for future empirical research on its impact on competitiveness.

The CE is a new development stage of the economy. It is believed that changes from a linear economy to a CE will be one of the most important environmental developments in the 21st century. At the same time, it would also present great opportunities and challenges for firms. Like the last century's sustainability debate, the CE is expected to promote a firm's interest in environmental matters and a new competitive environment for innovative firms. However, the CE is still an emerging field in research and practice, and many issues regarding its definitions and implications remain unsolved. The existing studies are limited mainly to identifying CE principles and barriers, adopting a linear approach, and focusing on large firms. Since the CE is an emerging buzzword, the parties involved have different expectations.

Thus, the CE has not yet reached a single consensus on definitions. The CE has thus far been promoted mainly by practitioners, with many CE definitions being provided by the business community and policymakers and, recently, those from academia. Understanding what the CE is from these differing perspectives will greatly help enhance further implementation of this economic paradigm. Most CE-related studies are reviews that focus on the analysis of their internal logic, fuzzy boundaries, and distinctions from similar concepts. Besides the broad review of the newly emerged concept, very few studies have analysed CE drivers and barriers.

5.1. Customer Satisfaction

Existing literature on customer satisfaction as a potential engine for the CE is relatively rare. Indeed, there is a plethora of literature scrutinising customer satisfaction from individual or organisational stakeholder perspectives, with a view to identifying the most important drivers of customer satisfaction. Furthermore, there is a rich body of research questioning how customer satisfaction can best be measured. Customer satisfaction is referred to as a customer's response to the evaluation of the perceived discrepancy between prior expectations and the actual performance of the product, a value judgement of how well the goods and services delivered to the customers meet or exceed their expectations. It is widely acknowledged that customer satisfaction influences customer loyalty. Loyalty, in turn, is expected to result in increased profitability and a more favourable relationship with that loyal customer.

The debate surrounding the position of customer satisfaction among the potential drivers of customer loyalty is still ongoing. Whether customer satisfaction is a necessary and sufficient condition for customer loyalty is still being debated. Even in a relatively mature field such as customer satisfaction, there is still a debate on whether satisfaction is configurational, that is, capable of being used as a crucible in the achievement of customer loyalty and/or whether it is an emergent property aggregated from satisfactory or unsatisfactory experiences. Most evidence gathered so far indicates that customer satisfaction improves the relative attraction of any supplier over that of the competitors, thereby engendering loyalty towards the supplier.

5.2. Employee Ownership

While Employee Stock Ownership Plan (ESOP) is a tax-advantaged employee benefit plan that incentivises employees to increase productivity by giving them ownership in the organising employer through shares of stock, ESOPs provide a retirement vehicle for employees. According to the National Centre for Employee Ownership, more than 6,553 ESOPs covered roughly 14.7 million workers in the United States. By 1 estimate, employee ownership plans add more than $1.3 trillion to the combined wealth of employees and have a positive impact on increasing wages, productivity, and job retention (National Center for Employee Ownership, 2023).

As infrequently discussed as a means of producing a more democratic workplace, employee ownership has a number of potential advantages over employee involvement programmes – most importantly, it addresses issues of wealth inequality. Involving employees in decision-making may produce a more democratic labour organisation, but it does so without transferring substantial economic power. Employee ownership is different. An employee-owned firm operates not only in a more business-democratic fashion (e.g. one person, one vote) but also produces substantially more equal wealth distributions than firms owned by capitalists.

ESOPs have a long and sordid history. The concept of employee ownership, usually in the form of some retirement vehicle, dates back to the late 18th century when the Industrial Revolution transformed work into a more impersonal and alienating experience. In the 1940s, ESOP-like organisations became known as 'cooperatives'. Employees possess voting shares, which enable and obligate them to govern their organisations democratically. Some cooperatives thrived for decades; however, most floundered. A seemingly simple insight – most employees do not have the training or experience needed to run the business they work for – undermined cooperatives. ESOPs are essentially tax-advantaged, third-party trust funds that purchase shares from a selling owner to benefit the company's employees (Scott et al., 2003). The possibility of passively investing in an ESOP may lead more 'ordinary' employees to consider ownership.

6. Benefits of Circular Strategies

Various benefits have been gained as a result of circular strategies being put into practice by firms. With a broad range of benefits accrued by firms, a tight link exists between sustainable BMI and sustainable values affected by circular strategies. Most informants report more than one individual benefit, including how firms have developed products and systems that last longer, how they have increased their operational efficiencies, and how firms have achieved increased customer satisfaction, loyalty, and new customer acquisition. Other reported benefits include improved capability for business development, enhanced employee motivation, commitment, and retention, increased sales growth and firm profitability, reduced material cost, and improved reputation and brand image (Mont et al., 2017).

The most significant number of respondents refers to how firms have conducted innovation for longevity by providing new products and services that last longer. For example, one firm reports developing a new type of flooring that lasts longer than the current customer offering. Another firm reports launching a new product intended to be reused, rather than disposed of as waste, after use. Some firms also report delivering durable product components and spare parts and developing new hydraulic valves that last longer. On the systems level, enhancing the expected lifespan of elevators and air conditioning systems represents two initiatives taken by firms.

Regarding the various benefits firms accrued in light of different dimensions of a CE, the strategy's critical role in linking sustainability orientation with a CBM is especially apparent. Specifically, the largest group of benefits relates to the circular strategy of 'closing loops around the same product or product system'. Various benefits have accrued within this class of benefits, such as the new leasing offerings or take-back arrangements that close the product loop.

6.1. Customer Loyalty

Customers are indispensable assets of any company. It can be argued that customers begin an enhanced relationship when they get involved with a company. Therefore, their loyalty is essential. Customers may change companies as they do in their interpersonal relations. Companies may turn competitive over an employee whom customers like. Customer loyalty may be attributed to the company, the service provider, or both. Unfortunately, only one of them would be sufficient for a loyal customer. However, both customers lost their preferred service employee to a competitor. Therefore, the following sections aim to elaborate on the ultimate realities of customer loyalty in terms of customers, companies, and preferences (Temerak, 2016).

Loyal customers attribute their loyalty to a company from which they regularly experience service. Companies try hard to secure their customers' loyalty. Since they know how scarce and precious it is, it is much more costly to find new customers than to retain the existing ones. On the other hand, customers are also loyal. They nurture loyalty among themselves. This loyalty has its extremely enriching and hot joy of being in the same vein. On the other hand, coyness, intrigue, carelessness, pretension, or astuteness are likely issues that save over other customers (UYAR, 2018).

For instance, consider the case of loyalty centred on fun or love. They had better not be an apprentice at a stall whose crew is charming, cheerful, and fascinating. Surveillance or obtrusively voicing thoughts would spoil the aura of fun. This aura would not curse other customers. Alternatively, consider a doctor whose target is not profit but helping. The vein of the wanting patient is not selfish at all. The patient trusts the doctor. They are assured that the patient will be helped and that he will be healed in due time.

6.2. Employee Engagement

Demands for CBMs are escalating, offering companies opportunities for new or enhanced CBMs and employee engagement. Companies to engage employees in the CE's Corporate Social Responsibility (CSR) agenda should (1) target, (2) motivate, and (3) equip all employees, especially 'other staff' and 'lower educated' employees who are generally in more day-to-day targeted and receptive jobs. To increase willingness for future engagement, companies are advised to (1) increase and distribute motivational factors and (2) ensure increasing behaviour change opportunities through offering a fair dual task for all employees. Continuously, the market for CBMs is expanding. Knowledge and understanding of, desire for, and behaviour change towards CBMs are rising, yet are most often limited to (higher educated) marketing, design, and R&D employees. Thus, the CE's CSR agenda is co-set primarily by a minority of intra-company actors. As a result, companies underutilise their knowledge capacity concerning new or enhanced CBM negotiations and implementations. To facilitate engaged employees in circular business strategy development, companies need to cater to transition policies on outside-in factors, as this is the area with the most unmet concerns and opportunities. However, this would require companies to take up the role of 'lobbyist'. To equally convey transition policies, decision-makers must accumulate and appoint characters to offer feedback on proposals, motivate if concerned and involved, and evaluate future proposals, planned behaviour, and perceived ethicality. Factors on this level are also found in the agency's staff and job positions. Also, desired feature modifications on the work environment level concern tailoring measures to different employees' knowledge, understanding, concerns, and opportunities. Each of these transition policy intervals has subgroups needing distinct measured coordination. Examples include alternative measure intensity, tailoring, and stimulating behaviour counter-interests. As highlighted by complaints regarding measure notifications and target group heterogeneity, this means employing an additional intracompany tier of staff.

7. Case Studies from Indian Industries

'In some functions, competence alone is insufficient to win market share. Products need consideration: aspects like fashion, safety, smartness, and environmental friendliness play an important role in the decision to purchase and offer after-sales service' (Rothenberg, 2004). The sustainable enterprise sector's small and innovative business models are based on precisely such functions. The premise is that economic growth can go together with solutions satisfying social needs, like stepping away from the trend of ever-increasing consumption growth. Understanding the essence of this future sustainable enterprise business model is crucial for established industries that still base their business on the overnight-growth-fuelled consumption-based one. Those experiences provide a bouquet of successful ways to bloom with the new small and innovative business model for established industries. The basic idea is shifting the view on material goods: they are not the end, but routes to the satiation of customer need (with a small caveat: a material good might itself be the enough solution). The traditional model of selling more is abandoned in exchange for a new model in which firms make money by helping their customers achieve their goals by using fewer products. The needed rethinking is complex and multi-dimensional, involving customer-supplier relationship renewal and brand image change. It is a change in the basic business model that impacts structuring the firm, including formal tasks and functions, corporate culture, incentives, resources, knowledge, and skills. The market position of the firm, which is involved in perhaps the most complex transition from a multi-structured group to a flat corporation market position company, which was the clear market leader for decades, is eroding, creating the need to reinvent itself. Despite this need, fundamental barriers rooted in competencies, market position, resources, power structure, and culture do not allow such a wide change.

However, some functionally limited moves in the right direction are taken.

7.1. Case Study 1: Company A

Today, a slogan in the business community speaks to 'sustainable business', and one company calls it 'The Future of the Sustainable Enterprise'. Attached to the slogan is an observation. In addressing sustainability, firms can, at best, think of their future in one of two ways. One is to provide the 'traditional' sustainable product – the large, durable, efficient product. This path is the moral high ground, and while it may prove ideal for businesses embedded in other industries in different eras, it also presents significant challenges. Challenges are ripe for exploitation. Seeking to recognise the challenges to this path and realise the opportunities, the notion of a 'sustainable enterprise' is examined here.

The centrepiece of this exploration is a new, smaller circular product that the firm has developed. The product embodies the new selling-small approach. This approach will require the firm to alter its traditional business-to-business model, its employee roles, and a significant research programme. While sellers of a 'large and durable' product traditionally continue to sell units, those units generally embody a later stage of technology than those originally purchased. If the goal is to reduce purchases of the alternative firm's product, then a case must be made to convince purchasing firms that they will be better off buying a smaller, plug-and-play product. The first question asks what basic assumptions must be challenged in selling a small product.

It appears that this thinking is new to only a handful of firms. However, despite its novelty, it is proposed that there is little competition to be had in selling small. Where suppliers have committed to selling little, their small product platforms are as ubiquitous as their small goods and services are numerous. In a further paradox, while no real historical precedent appears to exist for minor, the circumstances surrounding the traditional business model – both the underlying ideas and the incumbent suppliers' capacity to transition to 'selling small' – are well understood.

7.2. Case Study 2: Company B

Company B, actively turning a circular concept into a fully operational model, can best be viewed in light of the difference between the two illustrative operating conceptions. On the one hand, the shoes made by a famous sneaker brand suggest that they are manufactured in large numbers to satisfy rapid consumer demand and a wider selection of styles. The focus is on traditional mass production and excessive stock held by wholesalers, retail outlets, and company headquarters. Circular models exist, but company staple thoughts revolve around these product details. Such companies have been less bothered about fulfilling aftermarket demand before focus groups collect data on potential marketing strategies. Only then is a factory reconfigured. Meanwhile, machine tools have been switched off. While some brands tried mass marketing items with slightly different design cues, they are thought to undergo lead times of a few months to meet changes in demand flexibly. Accustomed to this behavioural mode of operation, it becomes difficult to imagine any other alternative.

On the other hand, the CBM promoted here presents sneakers manufactured in one size to fit all. These shoes breathe real-time communications, referencing product footprints as sales expand, complaints arise, and supply chains react. They can be sold as a service for new foot wear every week. The technology and machinery can be updated on a dime based on actual demand and product development. No moulds need to be reconfigured, nothing is dumped, and recycling is possible. Such technology is known but has changed processes in ways no one wants to consider. Supply contracts could be open-ended. Year-on-year sums lessen returns, increase automatically, and cause growth to become risk-free. In all likelihood, the response is something of a shudder. Attempts to realise this concept in footwear manufacturing merely confront existing company beliefs.

Realising CBMs requires a profound transformation for product manufacturers subject to batch production. The cases of Company B illustrate exactly this theme. Company B began taking products back from customers in the early 2000s to recover energy, components, and materials in line with regulations. The company later acquired a leading reverse logistics firm to develop its own recycling operations. The risk of constructing an entire industry around new contracts that would return materials after shredding gave way to exploring value propositions that other agents could disrupt with ease. Actionably, there was immediate financial compensation for taking waste on an association_headed basis by spreading liabilities across a multi-party transfer, with notice periods, almost for free. It required customers to start thinking about waste; Labour contracts focused on either resource recovery or interpreting trials, and nothing in between.

7.3. Case Study 3: Company C

The company specialises in bioanalytical services as a provider of analytical support services to pharmaceutical and biotechnology developers. Bioanalysis is the quantitative determination of drugs in biological fluids, and it is a critical regulatory requirement in drug development. Its service portfolio covers the whole bioanalytical workflow of drugs, metabolites, and biomolecules. In addition to bioanalytical services, it offers a variety of value-added services such as custom bioanalytical method development, fluctuation analysis, dry plasma sampling, analytical mock submission, and others. In the company's model, extensive vertical integration is an advantage. Well-specified text analysis, well-managed expectations, compressed timelines, large compound sets, and molecule identification are examples of the unique expertise that a firm can achieve with the help of vertical integration (Horvath et al., 2019). Well-defined protocols, methodologies, and reporting templates for the analysis were implemented by the end of the transition, and this phase is considered beneficial both in the sense of sustainable profit utilisation and in the customer experience.

In parallel with the internal development of tools, methods, and templates, the company adopted a bidding-as-business model. The second case was designed to investigate the qualitative effects and impacts of a well-elaborated customer model. The analysis starts with what to measure. Second, the first generation of well-established metrics is captured based on what to track (Rothenberg, 2004). Finally, process mining is used to support how to measure with the considerations of visualisation and object tracking. The mechanic charged each of its customers to use its tools and services, regardless of the number of tools or tool tables. Following that logic, the company decided to clone its selling business for the customers. Similar to how a family car manufacturer works with dealers, serial mega-seller integrated monopoly suppliers were monitored and paid. The initial installation was performed by engineers brought in from Finland, and it lasted for about six weeks.

8. Aligning Business Practices with Social Goals and Environmental Goals

A shift towards sustainability in conjunction with a systematic approach is crucial for a smooth transformation that includes more actors and more activities. CS level 1 and 2 companies must build new and diffuse new CRMSs with various actors both inside and outside the company. Sustainable company codes of conduct (CoC) could be a compelling entry point for CS level 3 companies. More specifically, CS level 3 factories should embrace sustainable CoC and enforce them within their linear value chain involving domestic suppliers and global buyers. This process should be systematic, multistage, and preceded by change communications among the involved actors (Rothenberg, 2004).

Business practices/habits to be aligned with social goals (HR styles/activities to be adapted in companies) encourage female workers at the recruiting stage; HR policies (union rights, proper meal and apartment provisions, working hours) awareness raising co-opt whether leadership critical self-branding public better positions – guarantee training and education of the leadership in incentive systems to strengthen expected behaviours/and punish the evils precise grievance mechanisms to be not a trap/holistic approach (Eshben, Rebecca & Kirsti, 2019).

9. Conceptual Model of Employee Engagement and Customer Satisfaction

In this study, two important business outcomes are examined – employee engagement and customer satisfaction. Accordingly, two primary models are proposed: the conceptual model of employee engagement and customer satisfaction. Both models present their antecedents in three types: organisational, managerial, and personal. Their areas of dimensionality are adjusted into environmental and individual factors, which clarify how they influence employee engagement and customer satisfaction. Since many employee engagement models exist, the one selected is based primarily on the holistic and comprehensive frame of employee engagement. The primary model is to clarify the antecedents of employee engagement grounded on research findings. Based primarily on theories of customer satisfaction, the benefits of customer satisfaction in terms of its levels are shown in detail. Loose and vague theories are narrowed down into concrete factors; expanded theories are adjusted to be more applicable. Both models present a more comprehensive understanding of employee engagement and customer satisfaction.

Providing insight into two important business outcomes – employees' engagement and customers' satisfaction. Two models are proposed, which illustrate different factors comprising employee engagement and customer satisfaction. Employee engagement consists of organisation-based, managerial, and personal engagement motivations grounded primarily on existing research findings and theories of employee engagement. Much like customer satisfaction, customer satisfaction is described similarly in terms of its antecedents, which include environmental and individual factors, and it also comprises perceived service quality, outcome quality, and customer engagement. The business benefits of customer satisfaction in consumer retention, business advocacy, and repurchase intentions are discussed based primarily on existing theories. At the same time, some factors that establish customer satisfaction are also appraised.

In the services literature, employee satisfaction and customer satisfaction have been viewed as two distinct phenomena. Customer satisfaction was perceived as an outcome of employees' satisfaction and product-oriented behaviours. Customer satisfaction was not proportionately represented because it was product-centric and was treated as a static result. There are no studies that comprehensively document the antecedents of the two distinct concepts of satisfaction types grounded on recognised research findings, while documenting the business benefits of customer satisfaction based on appropriately chosen and more applicable theories. The vast body of research highlights the importance of a knowledgeable workforce for long-term organisational success. Empirically backed conceptual work is needed to delineate how the supportive constructs achieve proactive behaviour in this context.

10. Challenges in Implementing CBMs

Companies seeking to transition to CBMs may face several novel challenges and pitfalls, including:

- Struggles in internal alignment among business units: internal misalignment can hinder the transition of a business model towards circularity. As highlighted by a person in one discussion company, circularity must be a top-down initiative; otherwise, 'each individual business unit thinks it is another business model and continues with their profit-making operations, while a small team begins to work with circularity, tempted by innovations and social media cleaning'. Such underlying tension indicates difficulties in internal alignment among business units. Hence, it becomes difficult to define a result for a CBM that is coherent within such heterogeneous structures and practices because a cleft is present in how to interpret sustainability.
- Uncertainty in finding potential collaborators: as mentioned in the discussion with one company, building a platform-level solution is a potential solution to transition to a CBM. However, navigating roles and hierarchies among stakeholders in a collaborative effort can be challenging. In a CE, products often move to and between different business ecosystems where standardised practices are lacking.
- Difficulty in fulfilling performance metrics: this refers to the difficulty for firms to understand how to measure the success of a CBM or circularity as a concept. Missing metrics can lead to a lack of understanding of the efficacy of an investment in circularity, as emphasised in discussions with one company. At the same time, performance metrics for CBMs can be so numerous that attention will be seized elsewhere – a trade-off between coverage and comprehensiveness.
- Concerns over thrashing: as presented in one company's proposal, a CBM revolves around remanufacturing products according to a new entrepreneurial model.

However, questions arise about how to ensure that products are remanufactured correctly and as intended initially, raising quality concerns. Furthermore, there are concerns that firms could take the most promising pre-owned products and avoid dealing with harmful quality residues, leaving less viable products for others or a firm's own disposal solution. This practice of poor-quality management can be described as re-thrashing and could violate Organisation for Economic Co-operation and Development (OECD) regulations (Mont et al., 2017).

11. Future Trends in CE

Although there may still be a gap between the theory of CBMs and well-implemented, practical examples of CBM in industry, it can certainly be determined that many companies have already started their CBM journey and are actively working on it (Horvath et al., 2019). This trend will dominate business decisions, especially concerning production processes and investment decisions. Furthermore, these approaches will strengthen existing partnerships and create new alliances and relations. As Information and Communication Technology (ICT) tools have become widely available and relatively cheap, companies will begin to engage with CBMs by seeking existing examples, good practices, and technological solutions. Thus, knowledge-sharing platforms and formal organisations will proliferate to fill gaps. Involving product manufacturers (especially, service-oriented ones) at the very beginning of the production process may directly lead to more environmentally friendly product choices and more CBMs for their lifetime.

Investments will change from solely profit-generating to multi-functional investments emphasising the ecological footprint. This trend has already begun as some enterprises have implemented sustainability-oriented CSR strategies. The increased risk of natural disasters and the obligation for future generations to live a healthy, eco-friendly, and high-standard lifestyle will dominate the decisions of companies in the following decades. Today's children will determine the rules of tomorrow's economy. Initiatives to raise kids' awareness about the importance of a CE and influence their adult decisions about individual consumption must start right now.

Governments will take stricter actions to ban or limit unhealthy material traces and internal waste. Of course, this could be a constraint to the CBM journey of some companies. This development will prompt the production of one product for the whole lifetime and its handling during usage. Buying 'shiny' products will become a no-go; otherwise, companies risk being publicly criticised on ancient internet pages. Firms will likely invest in more and better-controlled SBP communications to prevent such social attacks that could create an unmanageable flood on online platforms.

12. Conclusion

Technological developments have blown a wind of change through the course of production chains and also opened up the CE and corresponding models. Implementations of closed-loop production chains (CLPCs), reuse/recirculation cycles (RRCs), and product-service systems (PSS) require significant changes in the inner of the companies concerned. However, where people are concerned: How does the shift to CBMs affect employees and the wider organization? Development, implementation, and maintenance of sound business strategies depend highly on good employees. However, these employees remain out of consideration in the scientific literature and public debates. Discussions on business models, even circular or new business models, are often guided by technical and business views ignoring the (implementing) employees at first sight (Rothenberg, 2004). However, without these employees, prospective business strategies fail.

Conceptually, it is generally hoped that longer-term competitive success will flow through to employees. That should consist of better employment opportunities, better pay, improved working conditions, and a higher level of job security.

However, this does not automatically occur, nor does it occur uniformly across all realms and compartments of a larger company. Subsequent (changes of) working conditions as well as overall related job satisfaction significantly fall short of the wished-for improvements. Employees can benefit from circular business (model) shifts too, but this is not necessarily automatic. Still, it is expected that individually those employees can be satisfied in their own right as well as on a more collective or inclusive basis enabling team fuelling and appreciation.

Although they are often not entitled formally, employees specify that they are getting less autonomy, having less say together with responsibilities that they cannot meet. That leaves them frustrated and disillusioned. Better working conditions – a more beneficial working environment, feeling trusted or competent, better and more uniform explaining – would improve their satisfaction. Employees suggest equally better informal communication concerning staff development. Still, they refer to a generally more benevolent atmosphere. Well-done activities, relationship building, bonding, and demarcating against those on other timeframes would improve team success, satisfaction, and well-being. And last, better inclusion in decision-making and more timely sharing of developments would improve the feeling of appreciation and patience with decisions.

References

Bocken, N., Miller, K., Weissbrod, I., Holgado, M., & Evans, S. (2019). Slowing resource loops in the circular economy: An experimentation approach in fashion retail. In D. Dao, R. Howlett, R. Setchi, & L. Vlacic (Eds.), *Sustainable Design and Manufacturing 2018. KES-SDM 2018. Smart Innovation, Systems and Technologies*, (vol 130). Springer. https://doi.org/10.1007/978-3-030-04290-5_17

BSR & GlobeScan. (2016). *State of sustainable business 2016: Results of the 8th annual survey of sustainable business leaders*. BSR. https://www.bsr.org/reports/BSR_GlobeScan_State_of_Sustainable_Business_Survey_2016.pdf

Pedersen, E. R. G., Earley, R., & Andersen, K. R. (2019). From singular to plural: exploring organisational complexities and circular business model design. *Journal of Fashion Marketing and Management*, *23*(3), 308–326. doi:10.1108/jfmm-04-2018-0062

Garcés-Ayerbe, C., Rivera-Torres, P., Suárez-Perales, I., & Leyva-de la Hiz, D. (2019). Is it possible to change from a linear to a circular economy? An overview of opportunities and barriers for European small and medium-sized enterprise companies. *International Journal of Environmental Research and Public Health*, *16*(5), 851. https://doi.org/10.3390/ijerph16050851

Horvath, B., Khazami, N., Ymeri, P., & Fogarassy, C. (2019). Investigating the current business model innovation trends in the biotechnology industry. Horvath, B., Khazami, N., Ymeri, P., & Fogarassy, C. (2019). Investigating the current business model innovation trends in the biotechnology industry. *Journal of Business Economics and Management*, *20*(1), 63–85. https://doi.org/10.3846/jbem.2019.6880

Mont, O., Plepys, A., Whalen, K., & Nußholz, J. (2017). Business model innovation for a circular economy: Drivers and barriers for the Swedish industry – The voice of REES companies. Mistra REES. https://portal.research.lu.se/en/publications/business-model-innovation-for-a-circular-economy-drivers-and-barr/#:~:text=Cite%20this,Cookies%20Settings

National Center for Employee Ownership. (2023, February 9). *22% increase in closely held company ESOP participants in most recent data*. NCEO. https://www.nceo.org/employee-ownership-blog/22-increase-closely-held-company-esop-participants-most-recent-data

Rothenberg, S. (2004). Selling small and bright: The future of the sustainable enterprise. *SSRN Electronic Journal*. https://doi.org/10.2139/ssrn.908385

Scott, D., Reilly, M., & Andrzejewski, J. (2003). In the hands of employees. *WorkSpan, 46*(10), 1–5. https://ecommons.luc.edu/business_facpubs/144/

Sousa, C. A. A., & Carvalho, J. M. S. (2023). Happiness, Value, and Organizational Toughness: Three Concepts in Search of a Theory. In *Happiness and Wellness–Biopsychosocial and Anthropological Perspectives*. IntechOpen. https://doi.org/10.5772/intechopen.107333.

Temerak, M. S. (2016). Could customer-to-customer interpersonal relationships prevent customers from following their preferred service employee to a competitor? In T. Hennig-Thurau & C. F. Hofacker (Eds.), *AMA Winter Educators' Conference proceedings: 2016 Winter Marketing Academic Conference—What happens in marketing, stays digital: Rethinking marketing in the era of unlimited data* (pp. K-6–K-12). American Marketing Association.

UYAR, A. (2018). Evaluation of customer loyalty implementations by consumers. *Journal of Business Research —Turk, 10*(1), 143–155. https://doi.org/10.20491/isarder.2018.374

Williams, P., Kern, L. E., & Waters, L. M. (2016). Inside-out-outside-in: A dual approach process model to developing work happiness. *International Journal of Wellbeing, 6*(2), 30–56. https://doi.org/10.5502/ijw.v6i2.489

Chapter 11

Diversity and Inclusion: A Pathway to Happiness

Pooja Agrawal and Omvir Gautam

Faculty of Commerce & Management, Vishwakarma University, India

Abstract

The workplace culture plays a vital role in developing long-term business success. It nurtures by employees' engagement, innovation, cohesiveness, ethical leadership and productivity. Apart from these parameters, happiness, diversity, equity and inclusion (DEI) initiatives are also significant drivers for an enriched workplace culture. The main purpose of these initiatives is to empower and value the employees from a different perspective to foster happiness among employees for the establishment of a good workplace culture. The main purpose of this study is to review available research papers to develop a pathway to happiness through the implementation of diversity and inclusivity initiatives. Furthermore, it helps to provide insights into the research gap in this respective field, thereby enabling researchers and academicians to explore future research opportunities in this area. A simple random sampling method has been adopted to collect the responses. The primary data were collected through a self-administered semi-structured questionnaire. The secondary data collected through various database sources like peer-reviewed journals, magazines, newspapers and organisational reports, etc. The collected data were statistically analysed through SPSS. Results revealed that the majority of respondents reported that diversity and inclusive initiatives improved workplace happiness. Moreover, it indicated that diversity and inclusion (D&I) initiatives were a significant predictor of workplace happiness. It was also noticed that organisations are implementing diversity initiatives scored significantly higher on happiness metrics than those without such initiatives. This comprehensive research approach offers a valuable contribution

Circular Happiness: Building Sustainable Workplaces for the Next Generation, 203–215

doi:10.1108/978-1-80592-907-920261011

to the understanding of the role of diversity and inclusivity initiatives as a pathway of happiness.

Keywords: Diversity; inclusivity; happiness; employees; workplace; culture; initiatives

1. Introduction

In today's evolving business landscape, workplace culture plays a pivotal role in shaping an organisation's long-term success. A strong positive workplace culture is fostered by employees' happiness, mental well-being, engagement, collaboration, and innovation, leading to higher productivity and overall business growth (Biggadike et al., 2023; Khan et al., 2021; Mirro & Nguyen, 2024; Pawar et al., 2024; Westover, 2024). One of the most significant drivers of an enriched workplace culture is the implementation of D&I initiatives (Girgin, 2025; Leuhery et al., 2024; Olusanya, 2023; Wadhwa & Aggarwal, 2023).

Diversity encompasses differences in race, ethnicity, gender, age, sexual orientation, abilities, socio-economic backgrounds, and more (Chen & Hamilton, 2015; Silverman, 2010; Unzueta et al., 2012). However, simply having a diverse workforce is not enough; inclusion ensures that every employee feels respected, heard, and provided with equal opportunities to succeed. An inclusive workplace culture goes beyond just policies and programmes; it is reflected in everyday interactions, leadership attitudes, and company values (Downey et al., 2015; Gutterman, 2022; Shore et al., 2011, 2017; Wadhwa & Aggarwal, 2023). These are the central focus across education, business, healthcare, and society. While diversity refers to the presence of differences among people, inclusion focuses on creating environments where all individuals feel valued and able to contribute fully (Fredette et al., 2016; Poppas et al., 2020; Russen & Dawson, 2023).

Organisations that actively promote D&I benefit in multiple ways. Research highlights that D&I are necessary for diverse perspectives, innovation, happiness, well-being, and organisational success, but achieving them requires intentional strategies and ongoing commitment (Anggoro & Anjarini, 2024; Areiqat et al., 2020; Leuhery et al., 2024; Okatta et al., 2024; Sabharwal, 2014). Furthermore, researchers (Chaudhry et al., 2021a, 2021b; Jessica et al., 2024; Mukhtar et al., 2024; Rohwerder, 2017) postulated that organisations with robust D&I policies experience higher levels of employees' satisfaction, reduced turnover, and improved decision-making capabilities. Moreover, fostering a culture of inclusion enhances an organisation's reputation, making it more attractive to top talent and socially conscious customers.

On the basis of the above insights, it was emphasised that by fostering a diverse and inclusive environment, organisations can create a thriving, equitable, and forward-thinking workplace that meets the needs of an increasingly diverse workforce. Moreover, the current study is an attempt to explore a path of happiness at the workplace through the inculcation of various D&I initiatives.

2. Literature Review

The current literature discovers how D&I initiatives impact employees' happiness, well-being, job satisfaction, and organisational effectiveness, while also highlighting gaps and evolving perspectives in this field.

2.1. The Link between DEI and Employee Well-being

DEI initiatives are becoming an essential element for workplace culture and employees' well-being (Fritz & Gresham, 2024; Ibeh et al., 2024; Olusanya, 2023; Wang et al., 2024). They found an association between DEI and employees' well-being, engagement, and satisfaction. Furthermore, researchers (Judijanto, 2024; Sherman et al., 2020; Wang et al., 2024) investigated that discrimination and a non-inclusive workplace led to poor employees' well-being. They also observed that embedding DEI initiatives like fair policies, diverse representation and inclusive leadership, in organisational strategies resulted in employee engagement, satisfaction, commitment, and better employees' well-being. Furthermore, researchers (Dagar, 2023; Islam et al., 2024; Jaswal et al., 2024; Mousa, 2020; Shore et al., 2017) diagnosed that DEI initiatives are progressively predictors for the development of positive, productive, and happy workplace culture. It found that organisations that are emphasising on DEI initiatives are developing more inclusive, healthier, and productive work culture (Fritz & Gresham, 2024; Ibeh et al., 2024; Judijanto, 2024; Olusanya, 2023; Sherman et al., 2020; Wang et al., 2024).

2.2. Diverse Workforces as Drivers of Innovation and Happiness

Diverse workforces are increasingly recognised as essential drivers of both innovation and employees' happiness. Researchers (Ganguly et al., 2024; Ju & Kim, 2025; Østergaard et al., 2011; Sung & Choi, 2019) highlighted that diversity across dimensions such as gender, age, ethnicity, education, and cognitive background not only enhances creative innovation and productivity but also contributes to a more positive and inclusive workplace environment. Enormous researchers (Dagar, 2023; Islam et al., 2024; Jaswal et al., 2024; Mousa, 2020; Tanuwijaya et al., 2024; Woldeyesus, 2024) explored an intricate relationship between diversity management and workplace happiness. They argued that the effective D&I management initiatives play a vital role in shaping employees' overall job satisfaction and well-being. Furthermore, Shore et al. (2017) presented a comprehensive review of workplace inclusion, emphasising its critical role in fostering employees' happiness and organisational success. They developed a framework that integrates existing literature to clarify the concept of inclusion, highlighting how it satisfies both belongingness and uniqueness needs within diverse work environments. The study argues that inclusion goes beyond mere representation, requiring active engagement, equitable opportunities, and supportive leadership to create a truly inclusive culture. Furthermore, Trochmann et al. (2023) surveyed 1,800 workers in a racial diverse state government agency and highlighted the critical role of inclusion in shaping employees' happiness, engagement, and job satisfaction. Furthermore, they postulated the key findings that understated racial groups tend to report higher levels of workplace happiness when they perceive their organisation as genuinely inclusive and vice-versa. This research also stated that supportive leadership was also an important element in cultivating an inclusive workplace.

2.3. Role of Inclusion in Workplace Happiness and Diversity

Sparkman (2019) suggested that effective diversity initiatives must incorporate culturally responsive strategies, ensuring that inclusion efforts are not merely symbolic but structurally embedded within organisations. Similarly, Cho (2024) examined how cultural engagement influences subjective well-being, particularly among socially isolated individuals and those with lower socio-economic status. He suggested that cultural engagement can serve as a buffer against social isolation. The findings underscore the importance of accessible cultural programmes, particularly for disadvantaged groups, as a means to enhance overall well-being and workplace happiness. Russen and Dawson (2023) argued that inclusion should lead diversity rather than the other way around. They highlighted that without a base of inclusion, diverse employees may struggle with integration, retention, and equitable treatment. They also enumerated that by implementing it, companies can create effective retention strategies that ensure diverse hires are not only recruited but also supported and engaged throughout their careers. The study further emphasises that equitable practices, such as fair promotion opportunities, mentorship programmes, and leadership accountability, are essential in fostering a sustainable diverse workforce.

2.4. Gaps and Blind Spots in the Literature

After thorough analysis of previous literature, it is observed that D&I are closely associated with workplace happiness and well-being, especially when organisations foster an inclusive climate and address both demographic and psychological diversity. Additionally, it is found that previous studies have more emphasis on diversity management (gender, race, and culture) and financial outcomes. This analysis depicted that more research is required to analyse the impact of D&I initiatives on non-financial outcomes like happiness, social, ethical, and mental well-being (Jaswal et al., 2024; Sparkman, 2019; Van Bommel et al., 2023).

3. Objectives

- To diagnose a relationship between diversity, inclusion, and employees' happiness.
- To analyse the impact of D&I initiatives on employees' happiness.

4. Hypotheses

H01. There is no relationship between diversity, inclusion, and employees' happiness.

H02. There is no impact of D&I initiatives on employees' happiness.

5. Research Methodology

This study employed a causal research design to examine the impact of diversity and inclusivity initiatives on workplace happiness. This research design enables the cause-and-effect relationships by analytically studying the influence of independent variables (diversity and inclusivity initiatives) on the dependent variable (workplace happiness).

A simple random sampling method has been implemented to ensure that every individual within the target population has an equal chance of being selected. Respondents were preferred from a diverse range of demographics, industries, job roles, and hierarchical levels, ensuring a representative sample that reflects the broader corporate environment. The primary data were collected through a self-administered questionnaire based on 5-point Likert scale (*1 = strongly disagree, 2 = disagree, 3 = neither agree nor disagree, 4 = agree, 5 = strongly agree*). This was permitting respondents to provide their perspectives on workplace diversity and inclusivity initiatives in an unbiased manner. Furthermore, to augment the study and support empirical findings, secondary data has been sourced from peer-reviewed journals, industry magazines, newspapers, governmental and organisational reports. These sources provide insights into existing research, best practices, and trends in diversity and inclusivity initiatives globally. To summarise key trends and patterns, the collected data underwent rigorous descriptive statistical, correlation, and regression analysis through SPSS.

5.1. Limitations of Research

This research relies on simple random sampling, which may not comprehensively capture the diversity of industries, sectors, and cultural backgrounds. Additionally, survey responses are based on employees' perceptions, introducing potential bias or social desirability effects. Furthermore, workplace happiness is influenced by emotional and subjective factors that vary across individuals. While the study focuses on diversity and inclusivity, external elements such as company policies, job roles, and economic conditions also impact workplace happiness but are not directly measured. Lastly, the findings may be time-sensitive, with limited generalisability, necessitating continuous updates to remain relevant.

6. Data Analysis and Interpretation

In the current study, descriptive statistics revealed that employees from various backgrounds reported significantly higher workplace happiness in organisations with strong inclusion policies. The analysis also highlighted variations in perceptions of inclusivity across different demographic groups, reinforcing the importance of tailored D&I initiatives.

The descriptive statistics analysis is revealed in Table 11.1, which highlights the diverse characteristics like age, gender, education, marital status, work experience, and disability status of the targeted population. From Table 11.1, it is depicted that the age of respondents ranged from 21 years to above 45 years. The largest group of respondents belongs to the age group 41–45 years, with 24.12%. Furthermore, out of n = 228 respondents, 113 (49.56%) were female, 99 (43.42%) were male, and 16 (7.02%) preferred not to disclose. In the category of education majority of respondents were graduates (n = 110, 48.25%) which

Table 11.1. Descriptive Statistics.

Demographics	Category	Frequency	Percent (%)
Age	21–25 years	23	10.09
	26–30 years	48	21.05
	31–35 years	24	10.53
	36–40 years	30	13.16
	41–45 years	55	24.12
	Above 45	48	21.05
Gender	Male	99	43.42
	Female	113	49.56
	Prefer not to say	16	7.02
Education	Graduation	110	48.25
	Post-graduation	60	26.32
	Higher education	43	18.86
	Others	15	6.58
Marital status	Married	124	54.39
	Unmarried	101	44.30
	Others	3	1.32
Work experience	Less than 1 year	41	17.98
	1–3 years	73	32.02
	4–7 years	51	22.37
	7–10 years	33	14.47
	More than 10 years	30	13.16
Disability status	Yes	73	32.02
	No	155	67.98

Source: Authors self.

followed by post-graduate (n = 60, 26.32%), higher education (n = 43, 18.86%), and others (n = 15, 6.58%). Moreover, the targeted population were diverse in their marital status with 54.39% married (n = 124), 44.30% unmarried (n = 101), and 1.32% belonged to other (n = 3) category. The largest segment of respondents had 1–3 years of experience (32.02%). Lastly, n = 155 respondents (67.98%) out of 228 did not have a disability, but 73 respondents (32.02%) were identified with disability.

Furthermore, Pearson correlation analysis (Table 11.2) was applied to diagnose a relationship between diversity and inclusion with employees' happiness. The test value of the correlation coefficient (r = 0.79) postulated a strong positive relationship between diversity and inclusion with employees' happiness. The p-value (<.001) also confirms that the correlation is statistically significant, which indicates that employees who perceived diversity and inclusion initiatives as more effective also reported higher levels of happiness.

Additionally, to analyse the impact of diversity and inclusion initiatives (independent variable) on workplace happiness (dependent variable), a *simple linear regression* was applied as depicted in Table 11.3. The results indicated that the model was statistically significant. R and R^2 values depicted a strong positive relationship between perceived D&I initiatives and employees' happiness and explained 52% of the variance in happiness scores (R^2 = *0.62*). Durbin–Watson (1.85) indicated minimal autocorrelation in residuals. The value of sig. F change (367.83, $p < 0.001$) confirms that the regression model is statistically significant.

7. Findings and Discussion

After analysing the results, it was found that this study strongly indicated that D&I initiatives are significantly related to workplace happiness. The rejection of the null hypothesis (*H01 = there is no relationship between happiness, D&I*)

Table 11.2. Pearson Coefficient Correlation.

Variables	Diversity and Inclusion	Employee Happiness
Diversity and inclusion	1.00	**0.79**
Employee happiness	**0.79**	1.00

Source: Authors self.

Note: Bold indicates that the relationship between Diversity & Inclusion and Employee Happiness is statistically significant.

Table 11.3. Regression Model Summary.

Model	R	R Square	Adjusted R Square	Std. Error of the Estimate	Durbin Watson	Sig. F Change
1	0.79	0.62	0.619	0.18	1.85	<.001

Source: Authors self.

revealed a direct significant association between D&I initiatives and workplace happiness. This finding is in tune with numerous researchers (Shore et al., 2017; Tanuwijaya et al., 2024; Trochmann et al., 2023; Woldeyesus, 2024) who reinforced the argument that inclusion initiatives must be more than symbolic gestures – they should be deeply embedded in organisational culture, policies, and leadership approaches. Moreover, Michelle and Dawson (2023) highlight that inclusion should precede diversity, as an inclusive work environment ensures that diverse employees feel supported, integrated, and valued, rather than merely present in the workforce. Furthermore, the analysis revealed the rejection of the null hypothesis (*H02 = there is no impact of D&I initiatives on employees' happiness*). This indicated that the independent variable (D&I) significantly influenced the dependent variable (workplace happiness), leading to enhanced employee satisfaction, engagement, and overall well-being. This finding is in line with the various researchers (Elvi & Tunjungsari, 2022; Islam et al., 2024; Jha et al., 2023; Mousa, 2020; Trochmann et al., 2023). The present study supports this notion by illustrating that inclusive environments contribute to emotional well-being and social connectivity, further strengthening employees' sense of purpose and happiness.

8. Challenges in Implementing DEI Strategies

Previous literature and current data analysis revealed that D&I initiatives are essential for fostering a positive workplace culture and enhancing employees' well-being. Despite growing awareness and commitment towards it, organisations are often facing significant challenges in implementing these strategies effectively, as follows.

8.1. Symbolic and Surface-level Efforts

Mostly companies adopted D&I initiatives as a form of compliance rather than genuinely embedded in organisational culture (Berman et al., 2023; Ferraro et al., 2022; Jenkins & White, 2023). These actions resulted in failure to drive meaningful change and intended outcomes.

8.2. Unconscious Bias and Resistance to Change

Sometimes, organisational leaders and employees may unintentionally uphold biases, making it difficult to create an inclusive environment. Furthermore, resistance to changing long-standing practices can further hinder progress (Berman et al., 2023; Burnett & Aguinis, 2023; Story et al., 2024).

8.3. Lack of Leadership Commitment

Researchers (Kearney et al., 2023; Nandi & Ghatak, 2025; Newburry et al., 2022) highlighted that without leader's commitment, power imbalances and institutional racism, DEI efforts often remain underfunded, unsupported, or deprioritised.

8.4. Limited Resources and Budget Constraints

Sometimes businesses lack the financial or structural resources needed to effectively implement DEI programmes, leading to inconsistent or fragmented initiatives (Diaz et al., 2023; Klinksiek, 2024).

9. Recommendations and Futuristic Implications

9.1. Create Inclusive Policies for Happy Workplace

Researchers (Jha et al., 2023; Katsaros, 2024; Tanuwijaya et al., 2024) diagnosed that inclusive leadership, fair treatment, and intentional policy implementation are key drivers of employee happiness, engagement, and organisational success. These research findings also suggest the same. In this way, this research work can be used to create inclusive policies for fostering a happy workplace. Effective inclusivity not only boosts individual well-being but also enhances innovation, performance, and social cohesion.

9.2. Psychological Safety and Its Role in Inclusion

Psychological safety is increasingly recognised as a vital element in fostering inclusion within organisational settings. It refers to an environment where individuals feel safe to express themselves, contribute ideas, and take risks without fear of embarrassment or retribution. This sense of safety is foundational for promoting belonging, innovation, and well-being among diverse groups (Dong et al., 2025; Elmaoued et al., 2024; McClintock & Fainstad 2022; Robinson et al., 2023). It is recommended that to make an inclusive culture, organisations need to develop psychological safety among the diverse workforce.

9.3. Equitable Hiring and Career Advancement Opportunities

This study is also used by the organisations to implement structured recruitment processes, transparent promotion, and promote equal opportunities for diverse groups.

9.4. Encouraging Diverse Perspectives for Workplace Innovation and Growth

This study will encourage that diverse perspectives are essential for fostering innovation and organisational growth. Organisations should establish various platforms for a broad range of ideas, experiences, dynamic teams, and suggestions to enable more creative decision-making.

10. Final Words

The entire study can be concluded that D&I are not compliance factors only in an organisation. These are essential elements for workplace happiness, engagement, and long-term success. Research findings also suggested that these initiatives are fundamental in determining a positive workplace culture. By creating inclusive policies, promoting psychological safety, and ensuring equitable opportunities for growth, companies can enhance employee morale and productivity while fostering innovation. Research consistently highlights that diverse and inclusive workplaces experience lower turnover rates, improved collaboration, and stronger organisational culture. Moving forward, businesses must commit to sustainable DEI strategies that address barriers and promote meaningful change. In doing so, they create workplaces where happiness is not just an outcome but a fundamental pillar of success.

References

Anggoro, A., & Anjarini, A. D. (2024). Building an organizational culture that supports diversity and inclusion. *Management Studies and Business Journal (PRODUCTIVITY)*, *1*(1), 190–197.

Areiqat, A., Hamdan, Y., Zamil, A., & Aldabbagh, I. (2020). True workplace diversity: A key ingredient for business success, regardless of the industry or company size. *Management Studies*, *12*(3), 2304–2314.

Berman, A., Chambers, J., Grow, J., Loebner, J., McFarlane-Alvarez, S., Shaw, K., Thomas, K., Tsai, W., Vega-Centeno, J., & Timke, E. (2023). Different boats, the same storm: A colloquium on implementing DEI in challenging times. *Advertising & Society Quarterly*, *24*, 1–25.

Biggadike, C., Ahumada-Tello, E., Evans, R., & Wehde, M. (2023). Cultural hierarchies, leadership, and employee happiness. *IEEE Engineering Management Review*, *51*(1), 8–12.

Burnett, L., & Aguinis, H. (2023). How to prevent and minimize DEI backfire. *Business Horizons*, *67*(2), 173–182.

Chaudhry, I., Paquibut, Sachdev, A., S., & Dutt, C. (2021a). Impact of diversity and inclusion on the future of work. *NHRD Network Journal*, *14*, 303–313.

Chaudhry, I. S., Paquibut, R. Y., & Tunio, M. N. (2021b). Do workforce diversity, inclusion practices, & organizational characteristics contribute to organizational innovation? Evidence from the UAE. *Cogent Business & Management*, *8*(1), 1947549.

Chen, J., & Hamilton, D. (2015). Understanding diversity. *Personality and Social Psychology Bulletin*, *41*, 586–598.

Cho, A. (2024). Exploring the diverse impact of cultural participation on happiness. *Journal of Asian Sociology*, *53*(2), 95–125.

Dagar, C. (2023). Workplace well-being: Making a case for "psychological" diversity and inclusion. *Development and Learning in Organizations: An International Journal*, *38*(2), 20–22. https://doi.org/10.1108/dlo-03-2023-0083

Diaz, J., Gusto, C., Narine, L., Jayaratne, K., & Silvert, C. (2023). Toward diversity, equity, and inclusion outreach and engagement in extension education: Expert consensus on barriers and strategies. *The Journal of Extension*, *61*(1), Article 21. https://doi.org/10.34068/joe.61.01.21

Dong, C., Altshuler, L., Ban, N., Wong, L., Mohammed, F., Tang, C., & Kachur, E. (2025). Psychological safety in health professions education: Insights and strategies from a global community of practice. *Frontiers in Medicine*, 11, 1508992. https://doi.org/10.3389/fmed.2024.1508992

Downey, S., Werff, L., Thomas, K., & Plaut, V. (2015). The role of diversity practices and inclusion in promoting trust and employee engagement. *Journal of Applied Social Psychology*, *45*, 35–44.

Elmaoued, A., White, R., Hassan, O., & Sweet-Cosce, T. (2024). Establishing inclusion safety in pharmacy education: Wielding psychological safety as a tool to address student burnout. *Currents in Pharmacy Teaching & Learning*, *16*(11), 102163. https://doi.org/10.1016/j.cptl.2024.102163

Elvi, E., & Tunjungsari, H. (2022). Gender, diversity management perceptions, workplace happiness, and organizational citizenship behaviour. *Proceedings of the Tenth International Conference on Entrepreneurship and Business Management 2021 (ICEBM 2021)*. https://doi.org/10.2991/aebmr.k.220501.053

Ferraro, C., Hemsley, A., & Sands, S. (2022). Embracing diversity, equity, and inclusion (DEI): Considerations and opportunities for brand managers. *Business Horizons.*, *65*(6), 729–739.

Fredette, C., Bradshaw, P., & Krause, H. (2016). From diversity to inclusion. *Nonprofit and Voluntary Sector Quarterly*, *45*, 28S–51S.

Fritz, M., & Gresham, A. (2024). Diversity, equity, inclusion. *Nursing Administration Quarterly*, *48*, 5–10. https://doi.org/10.1097/NAQ.0000000000000614

Ganguly, R., Paul, S., Shit, S., & Pandey, U. (2024). Beyond boundaries: Exploring how diverse perspectives drive workplace creativity and innovation. *International Journal for Multidisciplinary Research*, *6*(6). https://doi.org/10.36948/ijfmr.2024.v06i06.33806

Girgin, D. (2025). The impact of diversity and inclusion on organizational culture. *Next Generation Journal for The Young Researchers*, *8*(1), 207.

Gutterman, A. (2022). Diversity and inclusion in the workplace. *SSRN Electronic Journal*. https://doi.org/10.1016/j.bushor.2022.09.005

Ibeh, C., Oyeyemi, O., Elufioye, A., Bello, B., & Daraojimba, A. (2024). Diversity, equity, and inclusion in modern workplaces: An HR review of strategies and benefits. *Malaysian Journal of Human Resources Management*, *1*(2), 83–90. https://doi.org/10.26480/mjhrm.02.2024.83.90

Islam, S., Alam, M. J., & Penalba, M. (2024). Does gender diversity mediate the relationships of diversity beliefs and workplace happiness? *Frontiers in Sociology*, *9*, 1384790.

Jaswal, N., Sharma, D., Bhardwaj, B., & Kraus, S. (2024). Promoting well-being through happiness at work: A systematic literature review and future research agenda. *Management Decision*, *62*(13), 332–369.

Jenkins, J., & White, G. (2023). Meet people where they are: An interview with chief diversity officer Geraldine White. *Advertising & Society Quarterly*, *24*(2), 1–12.

Jha, I., Pal, D., & Sarkar, S. (2023). Unlocking the secret to happiness at work: The power of inclusive leadership, organizational justice, and workplace inclusion. *Journal of Management Development*, *43*(2), 200–221. https://doi.org/10.1108/jmd-04-2023-0136

Ju, H., & Kim, Y. (2025). Bridging diversity and innovation: The moderating role of cohesive and hierarchical organizational culture. *Sage Open*, *15*(1).

Judijanto, L. (2024). Global trends in employee wellbeing research: A bibliometric study. *West Science Business and Management*, *2*(03), 1002–1015. https://doi.org/10.58812/wsbm.v2i03.1282

Katsaros, K. (2024). Gen Z employee adaptive performance: The role of inclusive leadership and workplace happiness. *Administrative Sciences*, *14*(8), 163.

Kearney, K., Wilson, C., & Ramirez, E. (2023). Overcoming barriers of incorporating diversity, equity, and inclusion initiatives in nursing schools. *The Journal of Nursing Education*, *1*(4). https://doi.org/10.3928/01484834-20230815-01

Khan, M., Raya, R., & Viswanathan, R. (2021). Enhancing employee innovativeness and job performance through a culture of workplace innovation. *International Journal of Productivity and Performance Management*, *71*(8), 3179–3204.

Klinksiek, I. (2024). Bridging the gap between diversity, equity, and inclusion policy and practice: The case of disability. *Transfer: European Review of Labour and Research, 40*, 500–509. https://doi.org/10.1177/10242589241251698

Leuhery, F., Padang, N., Karyono, K., Puspitasari, D., & Judijanto, L. (2024). Workplace diversity and inclusion: Strategies for effective implementation and benefits to organizational culture. *Dinasti International Journal of Economics, Finance & Accounting, 5*(4), 4647–4653.

McClintock, A., & Fainstad, T. (2022). Growth, engagement, and belonging in the clinical learning environment: The role of psychological safety and the work ahead. *Journal of General Internal Medicine, 37*, 2291–2296. https://doi.org/10.1007/s11606-022-07493-6

Mirro, E., & Nguyen, C. (2024). Cooking up positive company culture during times of business scale: A leader's recipe for success. *Business Horizons, 67*(3), 271–282.

Mousa, M. (2020). Does gender diversity affect workplace happiness for academics? The role of diversity management and organizational inclusion. *Public Organization Review, 21*, 119–135. https://doi.org/10.1007/s11115-020-00479-0

Mukhtar, B., Fasih, T., & Javaid, O. (2024). Thematic exploration of diversity and inclusion: Unleashing organizational success. *Journal for Business Education and Management, 4*(1), 79–104.

Nandi, A., & Ghatak, I. (2025). Advancing diversity, equity, and inclusion through human resource management practices. *International Journal for Multidisciplinary Research, 7*(1), 1–36. https://doi.org/10.36948/ijfmr.2025.v07i01.36301

Newburry, W., Raskovic, M., Colakoglu, S., Gonzalez-Perez, M., & Minbaeva, D. (2022). Diversity, equity, and inclusion in international business: Dimensions and challenges. *AIB Insights, 22*(3). https://doi.org/10.46697/001c.36582

Okatta, C., Ajayi, F., & Olawale, O. (2024). Enhancing organizational performance through diversity and inclusion initiatives: A meta-analysis. *International Journal of Applied Research in Social Sciences, 6*, 734–758.

Olusanya, E. (2023). Workplace diversity, equity, inclusion. *Journal of Business Diversity, 23*(4). https://doi.org/10.33423/jbd.v23i4.6615

Østergaard, C., Timmermans, B., & Kristinsson, K. (2011). Does a different view create something new? The effect of employee diversity on innovation. *Research Policy, 40*, 500–509. https://doi.org/10.1016/J.RESPOL.2010.11.004

Pawar, V., Magdoom, S., Yadav, P., Jadhav, M., & Vishwakarma, P. (2024). Study of work culture and its impact on employees' productivity working under different organizations. *International Journal of Advanced Multidisciplinary Research and Studies, 4*(3), 1061–1064.

Poppas, A., Albert, M., Douglas, P., & Capers, Q. (2020). Diversity and inclusion. *Journal of the American College of Cardiology, 76*, 1494–1497.

Robinson, E., Jones, C., & Brazeau, G. (2023). Addressing an uncertain future with a culture of psychological safety. *American Journal of Pharmaceutical Education, 87*(7), 100032. https://doi.org/10.1016/j.ajpe.2022.11.005

Rohwerder, B. (2017). *Impact of diversity and inclusion within organizations*. Institute of Development Studies.

Russen, M., & Dawson, M. (2023). Which should come first? Examining diversity, equity, and inclusion. *International Journal of Contemporary Hospitality Management, 36*(1), 25–40.

Sabharwal, M. (2014). Is diversity management sufficient? Organizational inclusion to further performance. *Public Personnel Management, 43*, 197–217.

Sherman, B., Kelly, R., & Payne-Foster, P. (2020). Integrating workforce health into employer diversity, equity and inclusion efforts. *American Journal of Health Promotion, 35*, 609–612. https://doi.org/10.1177/0890117120983288

Shore, L., Cleveland, J., & Sanchez, D. (2017). Inclusive workplaces: A review and model. *Human Resource Management Review*, *28*(2), 176–189.

Shore, L., Randel, A., Chung, B., Dean, M., Ehrhart, K., & Singh, G. (2011). Inclusion and diversity in work groups: A review and model for future research. *Journal of Management*, *37*, 1262–1289.

Silverman, S. (2010). What is diversity? *American Educational Research Journal*, *47*, 292–329.

Sparkman, T. E. (2019). Exploring the boundaries of diversity and inclusion in human resource development. *Human Resource Development Review*, *18*(2), 173–195.

Story, J., Iwai, T., & Tavares, G. (2024). Positive minds, inclusive minds: PsyCap's potential in overcoming resistance to DEI initiatives in organizations. *Organizational Dynamics*, *53*(4), 101087. https://doi.org/10.1016/j.orgdyn.2024.101087

Sung, S., & Choi, J. (2019). Contingent effects of workforce diversity on firm innovation: High-tech industry and market turbulence as critical environmental contingencies. *The International Journal of Human Resource Management*, *32*, 1986–2012.

Tanuwijaya, J., Krisanti, C., & Gunawan, A. (2024). The impact of perceived inclusion climate for leader diversity (PICLD) on organizational justice and its effects on employee engagement, emotional wage, and happiness at work. *Asian Journal of Engineering, Social and Health*, *3*(10). https://doi.org/10.46799/ajesh.v3i10.423

Trochmann, M., Stewart, K., & Ragusa, J. (2023). The impact of employee perceptions of inclusion in a racially diverse agency: Lessons from a state government survey. *Public Personnel Management*, *52*, 543–565. https://doi.org/10.1177/00910260231187544

Unzueta, M., Knowles, E., & Ho, G. (2012). Diversity is what you want it to be. *Psychological Science*, *23*, 303–309.

Van Bommel, H., Hubers, F., & Maas, K. (2023). Prominent themes and blind spots in diversity and inclusion literature: A bibliometric analysis. *Journal of Business Ethics*, *192*, 487–499. https://doi.org/10.1007/s10551-023-05522-w

Wadhwa, S., & Aggarwal, P. (2023). Study on the impact of diversity and inclusion at the workplace. *Journal of Management & Public Policy*, *14*(2), 64–73.

Wang, M., Poulin, O., & McKinney, H. (2024). Aligning employee health and diversity, equity, and inclusion initiatives in the workplace: A call for synchronization. *American Journal of Health Promotion*, *38*(8), 1091–1094.

Westover, J. (2024). Catalysts for growth at work: Unlocking human potential through empowering workplace cultures. *Human Capital Leadership Review*, *9*(1), 1–18.

Woldeyesus, A. (2024). Exploring the management of workplace diversity, inclusion and equality – A glance of workplace diversity management. *Current Trends in Engineering Science (CTES)*. https://doi.org/10.54026/ctes/1070

Chapter 12

The Future of Work: Trends Shaping Happiness and Sustainability

Harsha Mishra

Sant Hirdaram Institute of Management for Women, India

Abstract

The global workplace is undergoing an unparalleled shift, owing to rapid technological breakthroughs, the advent of varied employment models, changing demographics of the workforce, and the widespread influence of climate change. These enormous forces require a new rethinking of how firms manage their human resources (HR). This chapter contends that promoting employee happiness and guaranteeing organisational sustainability are not only desirable results, but also strategic imperatives for innovation, long-term success, and resilience. Businesses that truly understand and intentionally integrate these interwoven elements can move beyond reactive tactics and create work cultures that promote respect, purpose, and human potential. The current chapter describes the conceptual foundations, concrete benefits, inherent hurdles, and actionable solutions for building a holistic and human-centred strategy for the future of work, eventually leading to individual well-being and long-term organisational prosperity.

As we look ahead, the nature of work is experiencing a fundamental transformation – one that has the potential to reshape not only the way we perform on job, but additionally how we live, interact, and flourish. This research study investigates important trends impacting the future of work, with an emphasis on their consequences for employee satisfaction and sustainable practices. It also examines how organisations can create meaningful, long-term jobs while maintaining a thriving and contented workforce.

Keywords: Global workplace; happiness; sustainable employment; thriving; satisfied workforce

Circular Happiness: Building Sustainable Workplaces for the Next Generation, 217–240

Published under exclusive licence by Emerald Publishing Limited
doi:10.1108/978-1-80592-907-920261012

1. Introduction: Navigating a Changing Landscape

The conventional frameworks of work have been redefined in response to swift technological advancements, that is, as advances in technology occur, global priorities change, and places of employment evolve, the future of job has been redefined by trends that focus on and result in expectations of workers and global sustainability issues. Individuals and organisations alike recognise that productivity is not anymore the only metric for success; employee well-being, business ethics, and long-term environmental balance are all equally important. The world's economy is undergoing dramatic upheavals, requiring firms to adapt their methods with regard to personnel management. A combination of powerful outside forces is reshaping old employment paradigms, requiring a more sophisticated and centred around people strategic response from companies.

This section investigates these transformative trends, their effects for the future of work, and their potential to increase happiness and encourage sustainable behaviours.

1.1. Trends Shaping Sustainability and Happiness

The unrelenting march of technological advancement, along with a growing consciousness of our planet's limited resources and human hunger for purpose, is profoundly changing the face of employment. The primary focus is no longer just on productivity and profitability; an entirely novel approach has begun to emerge, one that increasingly combines worker happiness, environmental sustainability, and economic viability.

This chapter digs into the fundamental trends driving this transition, examining how they are set to shape not only what we choose to do, but also why and how we work, eventually influences both human well-being and the destiny of our planet.

1.1.1. Redefining Success from Profit Motive to Purpose-driven Work and Ethical Leadership

Throughout the 20th century, the dominant work paradigm was based on production, efficiency, and maximising profits. However, a significant transition is occurring shortly afterward, as organisations increasingly unite around purpose rather than performance.

This shift towards meaning is more than just ideology; it is strategic. Employees, particularly millennials and Gen Z, are seeking more meaningful employment that contributes to a better society. They are increasingly looking for purpose-driven employment in which their work reflects their ideals. Businesses that value social responsibility, environmental awareness, and ethical leadership attract and retain personnel more successfully. Corporate social responsibility (CSR), activities and sustainability-driven firm missions instil a sense of purpose and satisfaction in workers, reinforcing long-term engagement. Purpose-driven businesses typically have stronger employee involvement, loyal clients, and long-term success. Future workplaces will be assessed not only by output but also by influence on societies, ecosystems, and human well-being.

1.1.2. Is Automation and Technology: A Friend or Foe? The Role of Technology in Sustainable Workplaces

One of the most important factors at work is the increasing prevalence of artificial intelligence (AI) and automation. Automation, AI, and decision-making based on data are changing the way we work, making organisations more efficient and sustainable. The rapid advancement of AI and automation is radically altering job roles and skill needs across many industries. According to estimates, up to 60% of existing jobs will require major alteration as a result of AI integration. More precisely, AI is expected to automate more than half of the work in some entry-level white-collar jobs, such as analysts for market research (53%), and sales reps (67%), in striking contrast to the far lower rates reported for managerial positions.

While AI is predicted to produce 11 million fresh employment opportunities, it is also likely to replace 9 million people, mainly in entry-level roles. While concerns about job displacement are valid, the truth is more complex. The rapid pace of technology change can also lead to work insecurity, requiring employees to constantly adapt by emphasising cognitive flexibility, imaginative thinking, emotional intelligence, and solving problems. While digitalisation may raise work-related anxiety when off-hours digital operations and virtual meetings go beyond specific limitations, technology can also improve job satisfaction, balance between work and life, and employee performance by increasing flexibility, efficiency, and communication.

AI and automation are gradually taking over recurring, physically demanding, and frequently unpleasant activities, while simultaneously providing chances for creative thinking, empathy, solving problems, strategic, and other emotionally intelligent endeavours to thrive. This move has the potential to greatly improve worker satisfaction by minimising burnout and allowing people to focus on work with greater meaning and stimulation of intellect. Consider a future in which data entry task and routine assembly line tasks are largely automated, freeing up human capital to focus on innovation, problem solving, and strengthening human ties both within and outside companies.

AI-powered systems improve resource allocation, minimise waste, and increase energy efficiency. The trick is in how we adjust. Continuous learning will be critical to a long-term career path. However, this change is not without problems. Ensuring a decent and equitable future of employment necessitates proactive steps like reskilling and upskilling efforts. Retraining and upgrading will be essential, not solely for competitiveness in the economy, but also for maintaining respect and relevancy in the workplace. Organisations must proactively seek out future-ready talents and give resources for ongoing learning and education in order to develop strategic capabilities rather than simply filling urgent openings.

Lifelong learning must become embedded in both policy and organisational culture. Governments, educational institutions, and businesses must collaborate to equip individuals with the skills needed to thrive in this evolving landscape. Furthermore, the ethical implications of AI in the workplace, including bias in algorithms and the potential for increased surveillance, must be carefully considered and addressed to safeguard worker well-being and autonomy. Smart workplaces incorporate green technologies such as renewable energy, sustainable materials, and efficient digital collaboration tools, minimising environmental impact while fostering innovation and employee satisfaction.

1.1.3. Virtual and Hybrid Work: The New Normal

Another strong trend altering the future job market is the increasing focus on and flexible working options. The COVID-19 pandemic amplified what was already underway: the emergence of hybrid and remote employment patterns. The typical 9-to-5 workplace structure is giving rise to models that value worker autonomy and work–life balance. The transition to these two novel job paradigms has fundamentally impacted workplace interactions. What exactly began as an absolute necessity has turned into a viable, and frequently preferred, arrangement for millions. The transition advantages for employee happiness are numerous: shorter commuting times, more control over timetables, and the chance to strike a better balance between professional and personal responsibilities. This flexibility can result in less stress, improved mental wellness, and a higher sense of general well-being.

Furthermore, from a sustainability standpoint, mass adoption of work from home has the potential to significantly reduce carbon emissions related to commute and office energy consumption in buildings, as well as decentralise urban congestion. However, remote work comes with its own set of issues, including blurring work-life boundaries, digital fatigue, and the possibility of isolation. Instead of facing these issues, future-ready firms must cultivate digital-first cultures that promote connection, mental wellness, and team cohesion – even when people are physically separated. They are adopting flexible work methods, which not only improve employee well-being but also contribute to sustainability efforts.

1.1.4. Evolving Employment Patterns

The emergence of non-traditional employment patterns, most notably the gig economy, is changing the labour market. According to projections, the worldwide gig workforce will approach 1.6 billion individuals by 2025 (MyGigsters, 2025), with gig labour potentially accounting for more than half of the US employment as of 2027. While this paradigm promotes greater freedom and flexibility, it often poses substantial obstacles to worker well-being. These include financial insecurity owing to uncertain income, a lack of significant advantages such as healthcare and compensated time off, and heightened emotions of isolation, stress, and fatigue. Numerous gig workers claim to feel pressured to continue working despite injuries or illnesses owing to financial constraints and minimal benefits, exposing a crucial vacuum in support networks.

At the same time, the hybrid work paradigm is becoming firmly entrenched in the majority of offices, with 60% of North American enterprises already using it and 75% aiming to do so over the coming 2 years. This paradigm reflects employees' desire for more flexibility and better work–life balance. Additionally, a 4-day week of work is gaining popularity, with studies indicating a 65% reduction in leave for illness (Scientific American, 2022), a 57% decrease in worker turnover, 39% lower stress levels, and 71% less burnout among employees as a result of the shift in working patterns.

1.1.5. The Rise of the Gig Market and Freelance Work

The rise of the gig market and freelance labour signals an important shift in conventional employment structures. While it provides flexibility and liberty to many, it additionally brings up serious concerns about secure employment, benefits, and rights for workers. The future of employment must address these issues to ensure that persons in the gig economy receive equitable treatment and social security systems. At the same time, the gig economy can help to improve sustainability by allowing a wider range of workforces and thus eliminating the need for huge centralised workplaces.

Beyond structural shifts in the manner in which we perform, an essential shift in attitudes and objectives is taking place. There is a greater need for work that reflects personal ideals and contributes to the larger good. This is especially obvious among younger generations, who are increasingly looking for purpose-driven jobs and organisations that value social and environmental responsibility. This trend is encouraging firms to embrace sustainable methods, not just for compliance, but also to recruit and retain people and establish a favourable perception of their brand.

1.1.6. Dynamics of Workforce Demographics

For the very first time in years, five generations are actively working together in the job market, each bringing their own assortment of values, their expectations, and work styles. This needs flexible HR procedures and guidelines that support successful teamwork and efficiency across these diverse age groups, ensuring fair opportunity for workers across all generations. Leaders are motivated to purposefully form multigenerational teams, challenge prejudiced perceptions, and provide individualised training to meet varied learning needs. By the year 2034, Millennials, Gen Z, and the first generation of Gen Alphas are predicted to make up 80% of the workforce in established economies, emphasising the increasing significance of understanding and responding to the requirements of younger generations.

1.1.7. Integrating Sustainability into Key Business Strategies

The incorporation of sustainability into basic company strategy is no longer a novel concept, but rather an increasing necessity. Companies are learning that sustainable development and profitability over the long run are not incompatible.

Adopting circular economy ideas, decreasing trash, investing in energy sources that are renewable, and creating sustainable goods and services have become more common. This shift improves the environment while also improving employee morale and attracting environmentally conscientious talent. Workers feel more sense of fulfilment and pride when they are aware that their employment is helping to create a future that is more sustainable.

Additionally, the future of job is likely to place a larger premium on worker wellness and mental health. Realising that healthy and happy employees are more efficient and engaged, businesses are making greater investments in programmes that promote mental wellness, management of stress, and overall well-being. This includes programmes like mindfulness training, flexible working hours, generous leave policies, as well as access to mental health resources. This emphasis on comprehensive well-being immediately leads to employee happiness and fosters a more inclusive and sustainable workplace.

1.1.8. The Four-day Week of Work and the Rethinking of Productivity

A growing number of research and pilot projects are experimenting with shorter workweeks, with encouraging results such as enhanced productivity, job satisfaction, and burnout reduction. This is an important shift in the way we define and gauge productivity.

The future of employment may prioritise innovation and productivity over hours worked. With psychological well-being as well as sustainability at their core, corporations are evaluating whether the conventional 9-to-5, 5-day work week is still relevant in the 21st century.

1.1.9. Inclusion, Equity, and Diversity as Core Values

A future of employment that promotes pleasure must address historical and societal disparities. Diversity, equality, and inclusiveness (DEI) are increasingly important in modern organisations. Teams with different backgrounds are not only more creative, but also better suited to understanding global markets and solving complicated problems. True sustainability necessitates inclusive behaviours that extend beyond recruiting criteria. Fostering a collaborative culture in which employees feel heard, appreciated, and involved promotes happiness and creativity. Inclusive workplaces promote varied perspectives, resulting in new solutions to sustainability concerns. Companies that prioritise diversity build stronger teams, boost employee morale, and foster a shared sense of purpose in achieving positive change. Thus, the workplaces of the future must be created for everyone, not just a select few.

1.1.10. Psychological Wellness as a Strategic Priority

Mental health, traditionally considered a taboo subject in many organisations, is increasingly taking centre stage. The future of work is being defined by a greater emphasis on psychological health and total well-being in order to create supportive work settings that promote psychological safety. Companies are making investments in wellness initiatives, days dedicated to mental health, meditation sessions, and ergonomic designs to not only recruit but also retain talent.

Wellness in the workplace is no longer just a benefit; it is a performance motivator. A workplace that prioritises psychological well-being promotes happiness, lowers burnout, and increases long-term productivity. Sustainability is more than just protecting the environment; it is also about ensuring that individuals may thrive. Happier workers are happier, more efficient, creative, and loyal. The challenge ahead is to include well-being in all aspects of corporate life as a whole from leadership to workloads to recognition systems.

1.1.11. Sustainable Practices in the Workplace – Climate Change and Green Jobs

Climate change is altering the global labour and economy, analogous to the technological or industrial revolutions. According to the World Economic Forum (2025) Future of Job Report for 2025, climate mitigation is the third most important factor altering businesses around the globe.

The climate problem is affecting every industry, including work. Employees are becoming more mindful of their organisation's environmental footprint. Organisations are expected to implement green practices not only in their products, but also in their business activities, distribution networks, and workplace culture.

From remote work that reduces carbon emissions to green workplace architecture and climate-friendly benefits, ecological sustainability will be a fundamental metric for responsible employment. Future occupations will arise from the green economy, necessitating novel abilities in renewable energy, the circular economy structure, and sustainable agriculture.

1.1.12. Human-centred Designs for the Future of Job

The ultimate vision for the future of the job is one that values humanity – not just as workers, but also as creators, caregivers, aspiring individuals, and changemakers. Technology should enhance rather than replace human potential. Companies should be landscapes that promote human well-being.

Human-centred organisations will promote empathy in leadership, adaptable life-stage policies (e.g. maternity leave, elder care), and interactive areas that connect the digital and physical worlds. As a result, work is transformed from a necessity to a catalyst for identity, progress, and joy.

2. The Transition to a Circular Economy

Conventional linear economic models (extract, use, and discard) are being replaced with circular economy paradigms that prioritise re-use, regeneration, and ethical resource management. In work settings, this tendency is reflected in sustainable company procedures, environmentally friendly distribution networks, and a focus on upskilling personnel for longevity as opposed to disposability. Companies that implement circular economy ideas build a staff that is more environmentally friendly while improving job safety and satisfaction.

3. Conclusion: Building the Future Together

3.1. Pilot Research by Author on "Navigating the Future: Career Aspirations of Gen Z in the Digital Age"

Finally, the future of work is a canvas on which we are painting together, rather than a predetermined destination. A dynamic and changing world impacted by technology breakthroughs, altering values, and a rising recognition of the interdependence of human well-being and global health. Remote work, purpose-driven hiring, ethical leadership, and environmentally friendly company procedures all help to create a more balanced and progressive workforce.

The trends discussed in this chapter – the expansion of AI and automation, the embrace of work that is flexible, the emergence of the gig economy, a priority of purpose and sustainability, the emphasis on employee wellness, and the democratisation of technology, among others – are all major forces driving this transformation.

By embracing these modifications, organisations can create environments that promote individual well-being and a long-term ecological as well as social responsibility – creating an era in which work is not only efficient, but meaningful and sustainable, with a focus on both employee happiness and sustainability of the environment, guaranteeing a more satisfying and viable future for everyone.

As per research conducted by the author on 'Navigating the Future: Career Aspirations of Gen Z in the Digital Age' it was detected that the workforce is witnessing a major transition as Gen Z (born between 1997 and 2012) has begun to dominate professional fields. Unlike their ancestors, Gen Z has been brought up in an era of rapid technological advancement, with the social media, AI and internet impacting their worldview from a young age. Their job goals include not simply financial stability, but also a focus on flexibility, purpose, and creativity. Gen Z professionals are looking for professions that connect with their values, offer opportunity for ongoing learning, and allow them to use their digital expertise to drive progress.

As digital natives, Gen Z has an unrivalled ease with technology, allowing them to easily navigate and adapt to new digital trends. They are naturally drawn to industries like remote work solutions, data analytics, AI, and digital marketing. However, their knowledge goes beyond technical abilities; they also emphasise on entrepreneurship, personal branding, and social influence through digital methods.

3.1.1. Review of Literature: Career Aspirations of Gen Z

The fast-changing digital world is having a huge impact on Gen Z's career aspirations. Several studies indicate Gen Z's distinct job aspirations when compared to prior generations. According to Twenge (2017), Gen Z values work security while also preferring flexibility and personal fulfilment. According to a Deloitte (2021) study, 49% of Gen Z respondents desire occupations that match their beliefs, with a focus on sustainability and social responsibility. Gen Z appreciates job advancement opportunities, with many seeking continuous development of skills via online courses and mentorship programmes.

Numerous studies have shown that Gen Z's employment objectives are altering in comparison to earlier generations. According to Twenge (2017), Gen Z is very entrepreneurial, preferring occupations that allow for independence and self-expression. Unlike Millennials, who emphasised collaboration and teamwork, Gen Z seeks hybrid or remote work environments that promote freedom and work–life balance.

According to Deloitte (2022), Gen Z employees prefer social responsibility, environmental sustainability, and ethical business practices in their employment choices. They want employers who match their beliefs and contribute constructively to society. Furthermore, they place an emphasis on ongoing learning and skill development, choosing employers who provide opportunities for professional advancement (Schroth, 2019).

Understanding the elements that drive Gen Z's employment decisions, the challenges they encounter, and their workplace expectations is critical for modern industries. Below is a summarised conceptual model prepared on the basis of major findings from recent literature (Fig. 12.1):

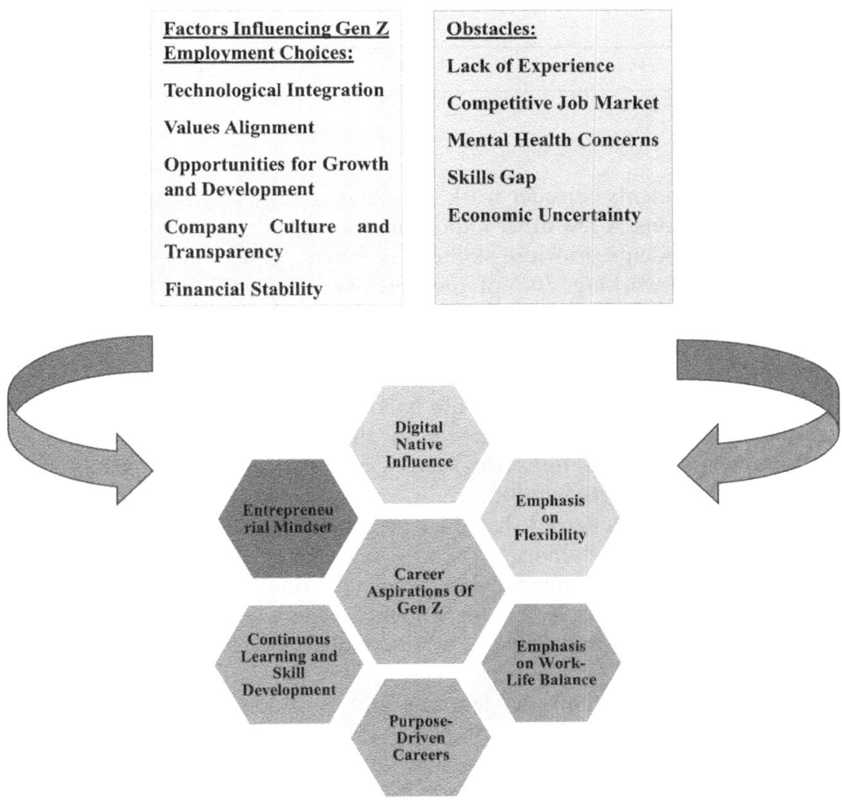

Fig. 12.1. Conceptual Model on Career Aspirations of Gen Z affected by factors and obstacles. *Source*: Author information.

In summary, Gen Z seeks a workplace that reflects their values, embraces technology, encourages flexibility, and provides opportunity for advancement. Organisations that understand and respond to these expectations will have a greater chance of attracting and retaining this valued generation.

Research methodology:
a descriptive research design with a convenience sampling technique was employed to choose 150 students from different educational backgrounds residing in Bhopal which was further categorised into urban, semi-urban, and rural. The respondents were aged between the ages of 18 and 27. Out of the 150 responses in this study, 100 responses were found to be error-free.

The pilot study respondents comprised mainly urban (72%), followed by semi-urban (11%) and rural (17%) backgrounds, with academic distribution including BBA (35%), MBA (35%), IMBA (21%), and others (9%).

Cronbach's alpha test value has provided a green signal for conducting further research (Table 12.1).

Table 12.1. Reliability Statistics.

Cronbach's Alpha	No. of Items
0.72	24

Findings:

- 50% of respondents consider work–life balance extremely important in their career aspirations. A few other important findings are as follows.
- 79% of respondents prioritise skill enhancement, 47% of respondents prefer learning while working, 46% of respondents seek certification programmes, and only 21% of respondents are interested in workshops and conferences.
- 64% of respondents consider financial security the most important factor, 47% of respondents prioritise careers that allow for creativity and innovation, 41% of respondents value work–life balance in their career choices, 28% of respondents are motivated by passion for their field, 22% of respondents prioritise creating a social impact in society, only 10% of respondents are motivated by prestige or recognition.
- 61% of respondents agreed that their personal interests and talent influence their career decision-making.
- 67% of respondents prefer a hybrid work environment, which combines in-office and remote work. 26% of respondents prefer a fully in-office (work from office) work setting, and only 7% of respondents prefer a fully remote work setup.
- 80% of respondents consider learning and development opportunities the most important factor in the workplace, 45% of respondents prioritise leadership and vision in a workplace, 39% of respondents value flexibility and autonomy in their work environment, 27% of respondents prioritise pay and

benefits, and only 18% of respondents consider diversity and inclusion as their priority.

Implications and suggestions:

the study 'Navigating the Future: Career Aspirations of Gen Z in the Digital Age' has major implications for stakeholders. The study suggests a multi-stakeholder approach. Educators should integrate digital skills, foster entrepreneurial mindsets, and emphasise soft skills through guidance and mentorship. Employers are urged to embrace digital transformation, promote purpose-driven inclusive workplaces, and offer flexible work. Policy makers must promote digital literacy, support entrepreneurship, encourage flexible arrangements, and address mental health concerns.

3.1.2. Conclusion

In conclusion, 'Navigating the Future: Career Aspirations of Gen Z in the Digital Age' sheds light on a generation fundamentally impacted by digital immersion and a strong need for purpose-driven work. Their demands for flexibility, continual learning, and technological integration are not only preferences, but rather fundamental principles of their professional goals. The distinct qualities and expectations of this generation as they enter the workplace. Their digital proficiency, value-driven goals, and need for flexibility and continual learning necessitate a paradigm shift in conventional employment methods. According to this report, Gen Z is ready to reinvent the workforce rather than merely entering it.

3.1.3. Implication of the Study in This Chapter

In short, this research work presented the career aspirations of Gen Z which have paved a reason for transforming the future of trends at the workplace. This is just pilot research on Gen Z, but the same aspirations are determined for the coming generations in future too.

4. Real-world Examples

Let's navigate the real-world case studies on companies which are fostering meaningful work, and providing sustainable employment while ensuring a thriving and satisfied workforce. But before that, let us understand common terminologies:

4.1. Impact on Happiness and Well-being

In today's world, building an employee pool that is not simply happy but constantly flourishing is critical to company success. This necessitates a thorough grasp of both contentment and thriving, as well as strategic actions for building culture, leadership, and wellness programmes.

a. Understanding Thriving and Employee Satisfaction: Attributes and Indicators

Understanding the distinctions between employee happiness and thriving is critical to building an effective workforce strategy.

A *thriving workforce* is defined as a dynamic state of mind in which workers experience both a feeling of vitality (being energised, excited, and alive) and a feeling of gaining knowledge (personal growth, continuous growth, and the desire to move forward) at work. This condition is not set, but rather a continuum that is changeable and heavily influenced by the work environment, demonstrating continual development rather than static achievement. Thriving at work has a favourable impact outside the office, increasing an individual's total life happiness and allowing them to reach their fullest potential in their personal and professional lives.

Research has characterised thriving in terms of 37 traits spanning 7 core dimensions, such as work–life integration, emotional, psychological, social, basic necessities, job experience, and health. Thriving workers are distinguished from others by their ability to meet key psychological requirements at work, notably a feeling of connection, meaning, autonomy, and competence.

A *satisfied workforce* (the worker satisfaction) metric assesses employees' level of satisfaction with their jobs and the company. It is a broad, subjective word that includes income, prospects for advancement, stability of employment, job outlook, the current workplace culture, flexibility, the quality of personal connections with peers, and alignment with the company's values and mission. It is a subjective metric for contentment that can vary greatly among people depending on their unique priorities.

Organisations can assess employee happiness using several key indicators (Fig. 12.2):

Although 'employee satisfaction' emphasises happiness and meeting expectations, 'thriving' adds an even more active and dynamic condition that involves 'vitality and learning', 'individual growth and advancement', and 'moving forward'. An employee may be content with their current situation but feel stuck, but a thriving employee is actively involved in self-improvement and contributes dynamically. This distinction is important because mere satisfaction can lead to complacency, whereas flourishing encourages ongoing adaptability, creativity, and sustained high-performance, all of which are required for a long-term organisational dynamism. As a result, firms should aspire beyond simply providing fundamental satisfaction needs and actively cultivate an atmosphere in which employees may actually thrive. This indicates that firms that prioritise building a thriving staff over assuring basic happiness will unleash more human potential. This strategic focus results in a more adaptive, innovative, and resilient staff, better prepared to face future problems and achieve long-term organisational success. It reflects a transition from a static perspective on happiness to a dynamic framework for ongoing individual and organisational growth.

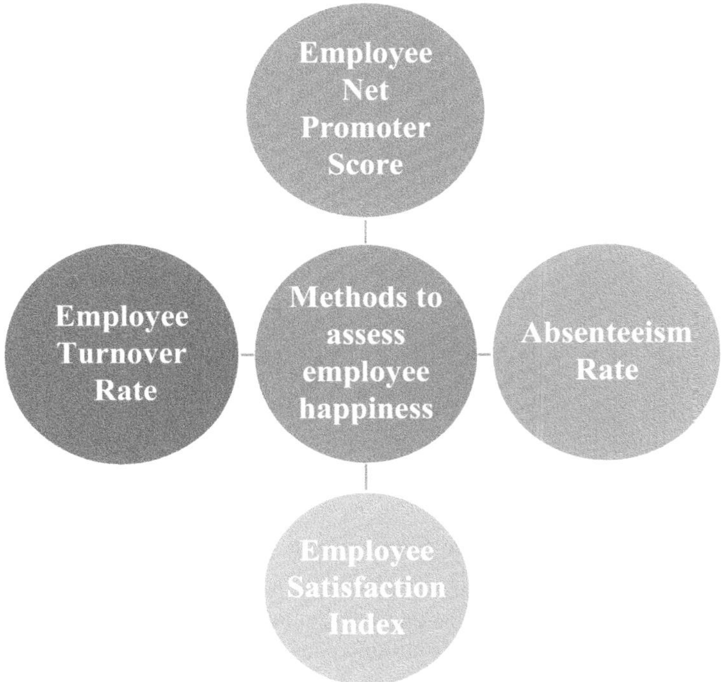

Fig. 12.2. Methods to Assess Employee Happiness. *Source*: Author information.

b. Key Factors Impacting The worker Happiness and Well-being

Organisations must pay strategic attention to a number of crucial aspects that have a substantial impact on staff contentment and overall well-being (see Fig. 12.3).

These factors emphasise the intricate relationship between human well-being and organisational behaviours. Addressing these difficulties proactively is more than just an aspect of employee welfare; it is a strategic priority for keeping a healthy, involved, and productive staff in the face of changing work trends.

4.2. The Impact on Sustainability (Both Organisational and Environmental)

Sustainable employment is a multidimensional concept that is critical to the long-term viability of organisations and societal well-being. It goes beyond typical economic measures to address holistic management of human capital and environmental responsibility.

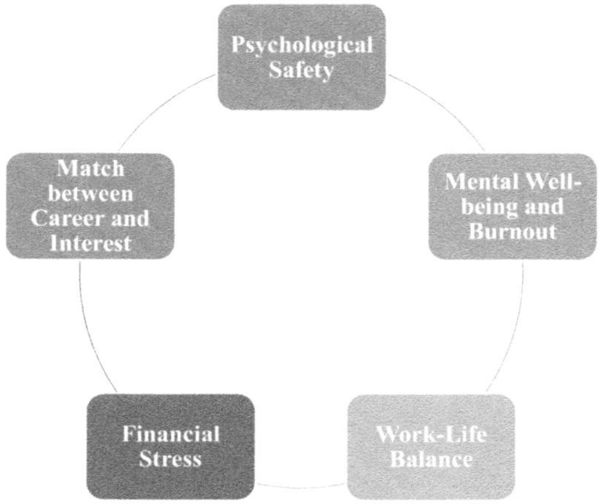

Fig. 12.3. Key Factors Impacting the Worker Happiness and Well-being.
Source: Author information.

Six Key Factors of Sustainable Employment

The underlying goal of sustainable employment is to create and preserve jobs that are stable, gratifying, and flexible enough to adapt to long-term economic and social changes. Its primary goal is making sure that employees are both 'capable and eager to continue working now as well as in the future'. This comprehensive idea goes beyond economic viability to include broader social and environmental factors. The six key elements discovered are:

a. Fair benefits and compensation
   - This is a core component. Fair salaries and extensive secondary benefits are essential for long-term employment. They make employees feel appreciated within an organisation, which reduces staff turnover for businesses. This consists of not only competitive pay, but also perks like health insurance, retirement programmes, and paid time off. Employers should ensure regular wage assessments align with inflation as well as industry norms.
   - Transparent pay structures and practices encourage justice and equity.
   - Comprehensive benefits bundles (e.g. retirement plans, health insurance, paid leave) help employees feel appreciated, reduce turnover, and support their physical and emotional well-being.

   Fair compensation communicates to employees that their hard work is recognised and rewarded, which makes them more unlikely to seek job elsewhere.

b. Safe and healthy working environment
It is an absolute requirement for long-term employment. Employers must prioritise employee health and safety by:

- Adhering to occupational regulations.
- Conducting regular health and safety training programmes.
- Promoting a work–life balance to reduce stress and burnout.

It encompasses the psychosocial, organisational, and physical components of the workplace, which are important in promoting total worker well-being.

c. Ongoing learning and development
The rapid speed of technology change needs ongoing education and skill improvement. Investing in staff development via regular training, professional growth opportunities, and cultivating an environment of lifelong learning is critical. Ongoing learning and development ensure that employees are well-versed in their fields of expertise. They remain at the forefront of ensuring their job security while preventing their talents from stagnating and becoming irrelevant. To ensure sustainability in the workplace, invest in employee growth through:

- Frequent training and career development opportunities.
- Promoting an environment of lifelong learning.

d. An inclusive and varied workplace
Sustainable work requires diversity and inclusion. Diverse employees deliver a wide range of perspectives, encouraging creativity and flexibility. Establishing an environment of diversity delivers a good cultural message to prospective employees, attracting the best talent and leaving all employees feeling comfortable and respected at work. Employers must aim to:

- Prioritise inclusive hiring strategies for attracting a diverse applicant pool.
- Foster an environment of respect and inclusiveness, ensuring all employees feel appreciated.
- Address and prevent harassment and discrimination in the workplace.

e. Employee participation and empowerment

Employees who are engaged and empowered perform better and are more dedicated. Sustainable employment necessitates fostering an environment in which people feel engaged and valued. This can be accomplished by:

- Promoting open door policy and feedback.
- Engaging workers in decision-making processes.
- Recognise and reward efforts and successes.

f. Environmental responsibility
   Incorporating sustainability principles into corporate activities is becoming more significant. Organisations committed for creating sustainable jobs should.

   - Adopt eco-friendly methods and lower their carbon footprint.
   - Promote sustainable behaviours among employees.
   - Support environmental conservation programmes and projects.

Fig. 12.4. Benefits of Sustainable Employment for Organisational Success.
Source: Author information.

5. Meaningful Work

Employees who derive meaning from their job are significantly more inclined to be motivated and engaged. When team members realise the way their individual contributions contribute to the organisation's overall goals, they develop a deeper sense of purpose and devotion to encourage purposeful work, leaders can:

- Clarify the organisation's mission and vision, and link daily duties to these aims.
- Include employees in decision-making so they can understand how their contribution affects outcomes.
- Demonstrate the impact of their efforts, whether by means of testimonials, project results, or team conferences that spotlight individual and collective accomplishments.

5.1. Why Does Meaningful Employment Matter?

Meaningful work is crucial because it correlates with work mindsets, stress indicators, and behaviours. Additionally, meaningful work is significantly associated with increased commitment to the organisation and satisfaction with work, as well as somewhat with increased organisational citizenship behaviour as well as performance at work. Meaningful work is also moderately related with lower turnover intentions and lower levels of burnout, stress, and detrimental work habits (Allan et al., 2018; Hu & Hirsh, 2017).

6. Conclusion:

The examination of meaningful work, sustainable employment, and a thriving, satisfied workforce reveals a profound interconnectedness that is critical for modern businesses navigating an increasingly complex and dynamic global landscape. These are not disparate HR initiatives but rather synergistic components of a holistic human capital strategy.

7. Time to Navigate Real World Examples Promoting Happiness and Sustainability at Workplace

7.1. Case Study: Companies Where Work Trends Shaping Happiness and Sustainability

A case study of organisations that demonstrate favourable work trends that influence happiness and sustainability. Here are a few instances of firms that have effectively cultivated meaningful, long-term employment while maintaining a thriving and contented workforce.

Case Study 1. Patagonia: A model of driven by purpose sustainability.

Company Overview: Patagonia, an outdoor gear and apparel company, is well-known worldwide for its strong dedication to environmental advocacy and ethical business methods. Its creator, Yvon Chouinard, established a new norm for corporate environmental responsibility by donating the business and its future earnings to combat climate change.

Meaningful work initiatives: Patagonia's primary aim to 'save our home planet' gives its employees a deep sense of purpose, connecting their daily work to a bigger cause. This purpose-driven strategy is thoroughly ingrained in the company's activities, from supply chain to product creation. Workers are urged to spend time outside, which reinforces the company's ideals and connects them to the natural environment they are fighting to safeguard.

Sustainable employment procedures: Patagonia has established an extensive social responsibility programme that painstakingly studies and controls the impacts of its operations on employees as well as neighbourhoods throughout its supply chain. The key practices include:

- *Fair labour practices*: more than 90% of their goods are produced in Fair Trade Certified™ manufacturing plants, helping over 85,000 workers. They follow the Fair Labor Association® Programme and use responsible purchasing methods to ensure ethical working conditions.
- *Living wage programmes*: Patagonia promotes living wage programmes for apparel employees, who are generally among the lowest-paid worldwide.
- *Environmental responsibility*: the company aspires to use 100% renewable energy in its global stores, headquarters, and delivery hubs by 2025. By 2025, they aim to use recycled polyester and Regenerative Organic Certified® cotton instead of virgin petroleum. Patagonia intends to achieve net zero by 2040, with a focus on eradicating emissions rather than simply offsetting them.

Thriving and contented workforce: Patagonia shows a great devotion to staff well-being and satisfaction with broad benefits and an environment of support.

- *Comprehensive benefits*: it includes a comprehensive healthcare plan, ample time off, and onsite attractions such as yoga sessions and an organic cafe.
- *Financial support*: Patagonia offers 100% college tuition refund and on-site childcare, reducing financial stress and enabling employees to simply concentrate on their work.
- *Work–life balance*: the company promotes work–life balance by encouraging outdoor activities.

Effects and results: Patagonia's comprehensive strategy for purpose, environmental sustainability and employee wellness has resulted in a staff that is highly engaged and loyal. The strong brand of the employer attracts top individuals who share their beliefs, which contributes to its competitive advantage and continuous advancement in sustainable practices.

Sustainable employment procedures: Patagonia has established an extensive social responsibility programme that painstakingly studies and controls the impacts of its operations on employees as well as neighbourhoods throughout its supply chain. The key practices include:

- *Fair labour practices: more than 90% of their goods are produced in fair-trade Certified™ manufacturing plants, helping over 85,000 workers. They follow the Fair Labor Association® Programme and use responsible purchasing methods to ensure ethical working conditions.*
- *Living wage programmes: Patagonia promotes living wage programs for apparel employees, who are generally among the lowest-paid worldwide.*
- *Environmental responsibility: the company aspires to use 100% renewable energy in its global stores, headquarters, and delivery hubs by 2025. By 2025, they aim to use recycled polyester and Regenerative Organic Certified® cotton instead of virgin petroleum. Patagonia intends to achieve net zero by 2040, with a focus on eradicating emissions rather than simply offsetting them.*

Thriving and contented workforce: Patagonia shows a great devotion to staff well-being and satisfaction with broad benefits and an environment of support.

- *Comprehensive benefits: it includes a comprehensive healthcare plan, ample time off, and onsite attractions, such as yoga sessions and an organic cafe.*
- *Financial support: Patagonia offers 100% college tuition refund and on-site childcare, reducing financial stress and enabling employees to simply concentrate on their work.*
- *Work-life balance: the company promotes work-life balance by encouraging outdoor activities.*

Effects and results: Patagonia's comprehensive strategy for purpose, environmental sustainability and employee wellness has resulted in a staff that is highly engaged and loyal. The strong brand of employer attracts top individuals who share their beliefs, which contributes to their competitive advantage and continuous advancement in sustainable practices.

Case Study 2. Google – innovating for employee well-being and autonomy.

Company overview: Google, a worldwide technology leader, is well-known for its advanced work environment and employee-centric initiatives, in addition to its technological advances.

Purpose-driven work initiatives: Google promotes meaningful work by promoting innovation and giving employees great autonomy.

- *'20% Time' policy*: Google's '20% Time' Policy allows employees to dedicate 20% of their work time to personal projects, resulting in popular products such as Gmail and Google Translate. This autonomy encourages innovation and a feeling of ownership over what they contribute.
- *Social impact initiatives*: Google supports social impact activities that promote racial justice, inclusion of people with disabilities, equal treatment for women and men, the LGBTQ+ community participation, and veteran inclusion, empowering workers to contribute to societal good.

Sustainable employment practices: Google incorporates environmental sustainability into its business activities and supports diversity.

- *Environmental initiatives*: Google is trusted for its environmentally friendly initiatives and practices. Thus, it prioritises environmental sustainability, sourcing 100% of its energy from renewable sources.
- *Diversity and inclusion*: the company encourages diversity and inclusion, creating tools to support minority-owned companies as well as communities. Such dedication to diversity attracts a larger talent pool and develops an inclusive environment.

Contended and thriving workforce: Google is well-known for its robust employee well-being programmes and distinctive office amenities.

- *Complete wellness*: campus amenities include free bikes, massage Salons, on-call surgeons and nurses, laundry, nap rooms, office pets, standing desks, colour-coded nutritious eating places, Lego stations, and Ping-pong, tables.
- *Mental health support*: Google offers mental health services such as self-assessments for depression and anxiety, as well as stress monitoring and mindfulness tools integrated with Fitbit.
- *Psychological safety*: Google's Project Aristotle discovered psychological safety as a key driver of team success, encouraging individuals to speak for themselves with no fear of consequences that are detrimental.

Effects and results: Google's commitment to workforce well-being, autonomy, and a happy work environment has regularly positioned it among the greatest places to work. This approach results in high employee happiness, improved efficiency, and an exceptional capacity to attract and also retain the best talent, which fuels continual innovation.

Case study 3. Salesforce – creating an environment of trust and philanthropy.

Company overview: Salesforce, a renowned customer relationship management (CRM) software firm, is known for its cutting-edge technology and unwavering dedication towards philanthropy, equality, and sustainability (Salesforce Report, 2023a, 2023b).

Purpose-driven work initiatives: Salesforce incorporates purpose into its business model via its '1-1-1 paradigm' of integrated philanthropy.

- *1-1-1 model*: this model devotes 1% of its stock, product, and staff time to philanthropic organisations. This giving culture fosters an intense emotional connection between workers and the organisation, increasing satisfaction and loyalty by connecting work to a larger societal impact.
- *Values-driven culture*: Salesforce's culture prioritises faith, success with clients, creativity, fairness, and environmental sustainability, which are reflected in the company's activities and employee experience.

Sustainable employment practices: Salesforce is committed to equal and fair hiring practices.

- *Pay equality*: the company promotes pay equality and closed gender- or race-related compensation discrepancies in 2015. They continue to monitor pay levels to ensure balance.
- *Professional development*: Salesforce provides extensive professional development opportunities, including tuition reimbursement, job training, and conferences to ensure workers have clear paths for success.

Thriving and satisfied workforce: Salesforce values worker happiness and an encouraging work atmosphere.

- *Flexible work options*: Salesforce's flexible work policy allows workers to do remote work at least once per week, emphasising a healthy balance between work and life and autonomy.
- *Comprehensive benefits*: employees enjoy comprehensive benefits which include health insurance, finance and retirement plans, childcare and leave for parents, and mental health services.
- *Positive work culture*: Salesforce has a positive workplace culture, with 84% of employees reporting a sense of belonging, responsibility, and pride in their job. The organisation prioritises mental wellness assistance through initiatives such as employee help programmes and mindfulness classes.

Effects and results: Salesforce's emphasis on a values-driven culture, pay parity, and extensive well-being initiatives has led to high employee happiness and retention. It consistently rates among the 'Best Organizations to Work For', indicating that its human-centred strategy promotes both staff contentment and corporate success.

Case study 4. Netflix – empowers with freedom and responsibility.

Company overview: Netflix, which is the worldwide entertainment streaming behemoth, is known for its distinct and sometimes contested culture of 'The Freedom & Obligation', which drives its strategy for managing talent and employee empowerment (Hastings & Meyer, 2020).

Purpose-driven work initiatives: Netflix promotes meaningful work by offering employees extensive autonomy and emphasising impact:

- *Context with no control*: managers ought to offer clear context and objectives, allowing teams to make judgments on how to complete tasks without micromanaging. This strategy promotes motivation for oneself, self-awareness, and creativity.
- *'No Rules with regulations' philosophy*: policies such as 'Take holiday' (for holiday) and 'Take action in Netflix's best interest' (regarding costs) allow employees to make their own decisions, encouraging a high level of trust and accountability.
- *Create social impact through content*: Netflix's platform supports social movements and niche audiences, such as the 'Strong Black Lead' channel. Employees can contribute to social causes through their job.

Sustainable employment practices: Netflix's sustainable employment practices are based on strong performance and continual talent evaluation:

- 'Keeper Test': managers can use the 'keeper test' to determine whether they would battle to retain an employee or hire them again. If the response is no, the corporation believes it is more reasonable to change ways promptly, resulting in a high-performing workforce. While this may appear to be a rigorous method, the goal is to retain a workforce in which everybody is a 'star'.
- *Employee rights and benefits*: from a societal perspective, Netflix provides social benefits to staff members and their families.

Thriving and satisfied workforce: Netflix's culture attempts to produce highly motivated and satisfied employees via empowerment and clear expectations, despite its demanding nature.

- *Radical Candor*: the culture values open and honest input, which can promote personal and professional progress constructively.
- *High-performance environment*: Netflix fosters a high-performance culture and offers significant flexibility to attract and keep individuals who thrive in this environment, resulting in an elevated level of engagement and satisfaction.

- *Strong professional bonds*: the company invests in building strong professional bonds that develop the trust and guide people to assume good intentions, which is pivotal for navigating a culture of transparency.

Effects and results: Netflix's distinct culture has allowed the company to retain a highly creative and versatile workforce, which is critical for success in the entertainment and technological industries. The 'The liberty & Responsibility' approach, while not for everyone, fosters an organically inspired, creative, and resilient staff, which drives the organisation's long-term success.

These case studies show various approaches for establishing meaningful, long-term employment and a healthy, satisfied staff, proving that while strategies differ, the core values of meaning, support, and ownership are critical to organisational success.

8. Actionable Recommendations for Businesses

1. *Implement a comprehensive human capital strategy*: moving beyond splintered HR initiatives to create and implement integrated solutions that address all aspects of meaningful work, long-term employment, and worker thriving/satisfaction. Acknowledge that all of these components are interrelated and must be grown together.
2. *Prioritise and emphasise on human-centric job design*: evaluate and restructure employment to increase freedom, skill variety, and task relevance. Empower employees with job crafting efforts that allow individuals to design jobs to their talents and values, resulting in increased internal motivation and purpose.
3. *Invest in holistic well-being ecosystems*: create and promote wellness programmes that cover mental, physical, social well-being and financial. This includes strong psychological support, stress management training, financial literacy initiatives, and flexible working hours that truly promote work–life balance.
4. *Foster ethical and supportive leadership*: offer leadership development programmes that prioritise empathy, openness, and ethical decision-making. Managers should be trained to promote psychological safety, open discussion, and context instead of control, which will help to develop trust and empower teams.
5. *Champion continuous learning and development*: encourage continuous learning and growth by analysing future skill demands and investing in individualised, accessible learning opportunities. Create an atmosphere of perpetual growth that motivates employees to modify their behaviour, upskill, and stay relevant in a continuously changing workplace.
6. *Elevate employee input and recognition*: provide several routes for input and actively involve employees in making decisions that impact their work. Implement recognition and incentive systems that are consistent, timely, and

personalised, recognising contributions and reinforcing desired behaviours while making employees feel appreciated and heard.

9. Conclusion

1. *The human aspect as a strategic asset*: with technological disruption, demographic transitions, and environmental imperatives, the distinctive capabilities and mental health of the human workforce are becoming a key competitive differentiator. Companies need to prioritise the human expertise, knowing that a staff that feels purpose, security, energy, and contentment is naturally more resilient, creative, and productive.
2. *Meaning as a key motivator and a buffer*: meaningful work, resulting from alignment with one's personal beliefs and a sense of their contribution, is a potent internal motivator that can outperform extrinsic incentives. It serves as an important psychological buffer against job stress and burnout, promoting resilience and allowing people to turn obstacles into opportunities for advancement.
3. *Sustainable employment as a foundational ecosystem*: sustainable employment is more than just economic viability; it also includes equitable wages, healthy conditions, continual development, diversity, involvement, and environmental responsibility. These parts form an interconnected ecosystem, with each component reinforcing the others, resulting in an effective structure for long-term workforce sustainability.
4. *The role of leadership and culture in promoting success*: the attitude and deeds of leadership, combined with the prevalent company culture, are the key factors that influence workforce thriving and contentment. Ethical, supportive, and honest leadership, together with a psychologically safe culture, promotes trust, open-door policy, and a culture in which people feel encouraged to learn, grow, and contribute genuinely.

By implementing these suggestions, companies can not only fulfil the shifting demands of the modern workforce but also construct resilient, successful companies capable of long-term profitability and meaningful social impact.

References

Allan, B. A., Batz-Barbarich, C., Sterling, H. M., & Tay, L. (2018). Outcomes of meaningful work: A meta-analysis. *Journal of Management Studies*, *56*(3), 500–528.

Hastings, R., & Meyer, E. (2009, updated 2020). *Netflix culture: Freedom & responsibility*. Netflix Jobs. https://jobs.netflix.com/culture

Hu, J., & Hirsh, J. (2017). The benefits of meaningful work: A meta-analysis. *Academy of Management Proceedings*, *2017*(1), 13866.

Schroth, H. (2019). Are you ready for Gen Z in the workplace? *California Management Review*, *61*(3), 5–18. https://doi.org/10.1177/0008125619841006

Twenge, J. (2017). *iGen: Why today's super-connected kids are growing up less rebellious, more tolerant, less happy—And completely unprepared for adulthood—And what that means for the rest of us*. Atria Books. https://books.google.lt/books?id=HiKaDQAAQBAJ

Reports

For millennials and Gen Zs, social issues are top of mind – Here's how organizations can drive meaningful change.

- The Deloitte Global 2022 Gen Z and millennial survey | Deloitte Global.
- McKinsey & Company (2022). How Gen Z is shaping the future of work.
- 7 Gallup workplace insights: What we learned in 2021.
- Flexible working hours enable remote workers to increase productivity.
- Corporate and social responsibility history – Patagonia.

Websites

Deloitte. (2021). https://www.fm-house.com/wp-content/uploads/2021/07/The-Deloitte-Global-2021Millennial-an-Gen-Z-Survey.pdf

Deloitte. (2022). https://www.deloitte.com/global/en/issues/work/genzmillennialsurvey-2022.html

Google. (2023). *Google diversity annual report*. Google. https://diversity.google/annual-report/

Google Sustainability. (2023). *Our commitments*. Google. https://sustainability.google/commitments/

https://www.patagonia.com/our-footprint/corporate-social-responsibility-history.html

https://www.workday.com/en-us/customer-stories/i-p/patagonia-unifies-its-workforce-todrive-engagement-and-growth.html

Hyderabad startup hires golden retriever as Chief Happiness Officer and the Internet is melting.

MyGigsters. (2025). https://www.mygigsters.com.au/blogs/the-gig-economy-in-2025-10-trends-shaping-the-future-of-work

Salesforce Report. (2023a). *Sustainability at salesforce*. Salesforce. https://www.salesforce.com/company/sustainability/

Salesforce Report. (2023b). *Philanthropy cloud & 1-1-1 model*. Salesforce.org. https://www.salesforce.com/company/philanthropy/

Salesforce Report. (2023b). *Sustainability at salesforce*. Salesforce. https://www.salesforce.com/company/sustainability/

Scientific American. (2022). https://www.scientificamerican.com/article/a-four-day-work-week-reduces-stress-without-hurting-productivity/

World Economic Forum. (2025). https://www.weforum.org/publications/the-future-of-jobs-report-2025/digest/

Chapter 13

Technology's Role in Enhancing Employee Experience

Minie Bhalla, Abhishek Pandey, Ruchi Verma and Sakshi Thakur

Lovely Professional University, India

Abstract

From AI-driven wellness tools to remote collaboration platforms, technological advancements are changing how employees interact, engage, and perform within organisations. In today's rapidly evolving corporate landscape, technology has emerged as a key factor to enhance the overall employee experience (EX). Modern workplaces increasingly rely on digital solutions to support mental and physical well-being, elevate flexibility, and rationalise communication.

Instant communication and uninterrupted communication have been made possible by virtual platforms like Zoom, Slack, and Microsoft Teams. Wearables, smartphone health apps, and mood-tracking software are instances of wellness technology that are being assimilated into normal happenings to boost better lifestyles and avoid burnout. By providing customised learning pathways, systematising tedious jobs, and providing real-time feedback, artificial intelligence (AI) is further improving this environment and boosting performance and job happiness.

Crucially, technology is also fostering to create comprehensive workplaces. Employees from various places and backgrounds will feel appreciated and connected thanks to tools made for digital engagement and transparency. Technology serves as a bridge in remote and hybrid environments, preserving team morale, culture, and transparency. The careful incorporation of

Circular Happiness: Building Sustainable Workplaces for the Next Generation, 241–265

doi:10.1108/978-1-80592-907-920261013

technological innovations will continue to be crucial to employee engagement initiatives as businesses continue to adjust to new work frameworks. Businesses that integrate technological advancements with human-centric concepts may enhance performance and foster long-term employee satisfaction, loyalty, and growth. Technology goes beyond its elementary functions to improve the workplace experience because it is necessary for the nature of work in the future.

Keywords: AI-driven wellness tools; remote collaboration platforms; technological advancements; digital solutions; virtual platforms; wearables; smart phone health-apps

Developing a purposeful and healthy connection with personal technology is known as digital well-being. It's not about abandoning technology; rather, it's about managing it to further your objectives and improve your life rather than taking away from it. Being aware of your digital behaviours, from controlling screen time and notifications to fostering constructive online relationships, is part of this discipline. The main idea is to minimise technology's possible drawbacks, such as distraction, anxiety, and social comparison, while maximising its positive aspects, including connection, information, and ease. It's about making sure your digital life encourages your physical well-being by enabling concentration, presence, and real human connection. Renowned authors and organisations offer specific perspectives:

Cal Newport: in *digital minimalism*, he advocates for 'a philosophy of technology use in which you focus your online time on a small number of carefully selected and optimized activities that strongly support things you value, and then happily miss out on everything else'.

Centre for humane technology: co-founded by Tristan Harris, it frames well-being as the need to 'realign technology with humanity's best interests', moving away from an attention-extractive economy that often works against our well-being.

Jisc (UK): this educational non-profit defines it as 'the impact of technologies and digital services on people's mental, physical, and emotional health'.

1. Digital Well-being and Managing Technologies for Happiness

Technology has emerged as a crucial factor in determining the EX in the modern workplace. Digital tools are changing how businesses engage with their employees, from hiring to retirement. Organisations are increasingly using technology to encourage happiness at work and enhance digital well-being as a result of the rise of employee-centric policies. With an emphasis on digital well-being, managing technological tools for employee satisfaction, and presenting pertinent human resources (HR) solutions with real-world examples and case studies, this essay examines how technology can enhance the EX.

1.1. The Evolution of Employee Experience in the Digital Era

Each relationship that an employee has with a company, including those involving culture, technology, and the physical surroundings, is included in the term 'employee experience' (EX) (Morgan, 2017). EX is becoming more reliant on digital tools and platforms due to the development of remote and hybrid work methods. In order to improve employee engagement, emotional well-being, productivity, and satisfaction, traditional human resource management systems (HRMS) have transformed into intelligent, integrated systems.

1.2. Digital Well-being: A Strategic Priority

The term 'digital well-being' refers to how people's mental, physical, and emotional health are affected by technology. Today's organisations need to use digital tools that promote attention, balance, and overall happiness with intention. The World Economic Forum (2020) states that employees who are overloaded with technology frequently experience weariness, lower productivity, and increased rates of burnout. Currently, a lot of businesses use technology to track and promote the wellbeing of their employees. For example, Microsoft's Viva Insights provides tailored suggestions for wellbeing, like promoting mindfulness breaks, focus time, and disconnecting after work, based on data from Microsoft 365 (Microsoft, 2021). Managers can better assess team stress levels and offer strategies to prevent burnout by examining behavioural patterns.

1.3. Managing Technologies for Employee Happiness

A sense of purpose, acknowledgement, adaptability, and support are all closely related to employee happiness. In such a scenario, technology can be both a facilitator and a hindrance. Constant connectedness can cause stress, but when employed carefully, digital technologies may enhance inclusion, motivation, and teamwork.

To manage technologies effectively for happiness, organisations focus on.

1.3.1. Communication Tools

Clear communication and social interaction are made available by platforms such as Slack, Zoom, and Microsoft Teams, which are crucial for a satisfying work environment for employees who work remotely.

1.3.2. Feedback and Recognition Systems

Real-time feedback collection and recognition are facilitated by tools which include 15Five and Kudos, which raise engagement and morale.

1.3.3. Personalised Learning Platforms

By allowing workers to advance at their own speed and integrating their education with their professional objectives, learning experience platforms (LXPs), such as EdCast and Degreed boost employee happiness.

1.3.4. AI-powered Employee Assistance

Chatbots and virtual assistants, like SAP Success Factors or IBM Watson, give employees instant access to HR services and individualised help.

1.4. HR Tools Enhancing Employee Experience

A wide range of innovative tools is transforming how organisations manage their workforce:

- Workday: a top cloud-based HR software that offers analytics, workforce planning, and employee self-service. Workday offers dashboards to monitor engagement and well-being and integrates with wellness solutions.
- Qualtrics employee XM: allows businesses to gather employee input throughout the lifecycle and utilise AI to find gaps in experience. In this regard, by acting on real-time engagement data, Deloitte uses Qualtrics to enhance organisational culture (Qualtrics, 2021).
- Peakon (by Workday): enables managers with actionable insights to enhance team dynamics and individual happiness by continuously measuring employee sentiment.
- In order to guarantee continuous improvement of EX, Culture Amp integrates feedback and development features with an emphasis on employee engagement and performance.
- Headspace for work: this technology, which is utilised by organisations such as Adobe and LinkedIn, encourages mindfulness and meditation, which relieves stress and enhances mental health.

1.5. Case Studies of Successful Implementation

1.5.1. Unilever's Use of AI for Personalised Career Paths

Employees may discover internal employment, projects, and mentors through Unilever's AI-powered talent marketplace, Flex Experiences. This promotes learning, autonomy, and purpose – all of which are important factors in happiness (Unilever, 2021). The software has increased engagement and retention rates by aligning tasks to users' interests and career goals.

1.5.2. Accenture's Focus on Mental Wellness

Accenture has made investments in digital mental health initiatives, providing mental health chatbots and mobile apps such as Thrive Global. Furthermore, they monitor work–life balance utilising Microsoft Viva. Employee satisfaction increased and stress levels were quantifiably diminished as a result of this initiative (Accenture, 2022).

1.5.3. Google's DNA Project

Data and surveys are analysed in Google's long-running 'gDNA' project to determine how technology affects worker well-being. Initiatives including 'no meeting days', 'work-life harmony policies', and solutions to lessen digital overload were the outcome of the findings (Bock, 2015). Additionally, Google offers gamified internal health tools that foster breaks and meditation.

1.6. Strategies for Choosing the Right Tools

Organisations need to choose technologies that fit their culture, workforce requirements, and level of digital maturity in order to use technology for employee well-being. The following factors should be included in the decision-making process:

- Employee input: to learn about preferences and pain issues, hold focus groups or surveys.
- Integration capabilities: verify that new tools are compatible with current systems, which include ERP or HRIS platforms.
- Security and scalability: choose solutions that safeguard employee data and expand with the company.
- User experience: for high adoption rates, platforms should be simple to use and responsive to mobile devices.

1.7. Challenges in Implementing Digital Well-being Tools

Despite the benefits, businesses still have to deal with issues like a lack of computer knowledge, resistance to change, digital fatigue, and data privacy concerns. Policies that safeguard workers' ability to disconnect, provide training in digital literacy, and guarantee data usage transparency are crucial. Additionally, human empathy should be enhanced by technology, not replaced. Managers continue to be essential in deciphering insights and offering tailored assistance. The most effective approach combines technology and human interaction.

1.8. Future Outlook

Employee experiences will become more tailored in the future as wearable technology, AI, and machine learning advance. Burnout will be identified by predictive analytics, and immersive technologies like virtual reality (VR) can be employed for mental training and stress reduction. Businesses that use digital technologies to encourage happiness and well-being will experience increases in employee engagement, retention, and productivity.

A deliberate focus on digital well-being and the thoughtful use of technology are necessary to improve the work experience in an era in which digital transformation is the norm. Workday, Microsoft Viva, and Culture Amp are just a few of the tools that assist companies in managing their HR and fostering work environments. Real-world examples from businesses such as Google, Accenture, and Unilever show how cautious integration of digital technologies may enhance employee resilience, decrease burnout, and promote happiness. As work continues to change, the future of EX will be determined by the combination of technology and empathy.

2. The Impact of AI on Employee Engagement

Artificial intelligence (AI) has become a disruptive force in the rapidly evolving digital landscape, transforming the EX. AI is being used by businesses more and more to promote employee engagement, which is a key factor in performance, satisfaction, and retention, in addition to automation and efficiency. AI makes it possible for proactive engagement strategies, intelligent insights, and personalised experiences that adapt to the changing demands of employees. With the help of case studies and illustrations of cutting-edge HR technologies now in use by prominent businesses, this essay investigates the effect of AI on employee engagement.

A number of prominent writers and organisations have contributed to the idea of employee engagement, a crucial topic in management and HR. A few renowned definitions are as follows:

William A. Kahn, often credited as the academic father of the concept, Professor William A. Kahn of Boston University provided the foundational definition in 1990. He defines employee engagement as 'The harnessing of organisation members' selves to their work roles; in engagement, people employ and express themselves physically, cognitively, and emotionally during role performances'.

According to Gallup (2013*). State of the American workplace*, 'Engaged employees are those who are involved in, enthusiastic about and committed to their work and workplace'.

Gallup links engagement directly to tangible business outcomes, measuring it through their famous Q12 survey, which assesses the conditions that foster this commitment.

Kevin Kruse, in his bestselling book *Employee Engagement 2.0*, author and entrepreneur offers a concise and impactful definition that is popular with leaders. 'Employee engagement is the emotional commitment the employee has to the organisation and its goals'.

David MacLeod and Nita Clarke, in their influential 2009 UK government report, *Engage for Success*, provided a holistic definition that emphasises the employer's role in creating the right environment.

> Employee engagement is a workplace approach resulting in the right conditions for all members of an organisation to give of their best each day, committed to their organisation's goals and values, motivated to contribute to organisational success, with an enhanced sense of their own well-being (MacLeod & Clarke 2009).

2.1. Understanding Employee Engagement in the Digital Age

The emotional commitment that workers have to their company and its objectives is referred to as employee engagement. In the words of Gallup (2023), engaged workers are more inventive, devoted, and productive. Static intranets, in-person meetings, and yearly surveys are no longer adequate forms of connection. Organisations require real-time, individualised engagement tactics as their workforce grows more diverse, distant, and tech-savvy. AI offers the automation and intelligence critical to move employee engagement from reactive to proactive.

2.2. AI's Role in Enhancing Employee Engagement

AI impacts employee engagement across various dimensions.

2.2.1. Personalised Communication and Support

AI-powered chatbots and virtual assistants enhance corporate communication by offering round-the-clock assistance with company guidelines, onboarding, and HR-related questions. AI-based staff support platforms, such as those provided by Leena AI and Espressive, provide prompt, precise responses, cutting down on wait times and raising customer satisfaction.

To give employees faster access to information and free up HR professionals for more strategic work, Nestlé, for instance, employs Leena AI to handle over 85% of repetitive HR requests (Leena AI, 2022). By fostering a responsive and encouraging work atmosphere, this on-demand assistance increases engagement.

2.2.2. AI-powered Feedback and Sentiment Analysis

For engagement, listening must be ongoing. Natural language processing (NLP) is used by AI products like Qualtrics Employee XM and Peakon (by Workday) to evaluate employee feedback in real time, spot sentiment patterns, and detect possible disengagement hazards.

Vodafone, for example, used Peakon to gather and examine employee input on a weekly basis. HR was able to act with focused tactics once the AI engine identified trends of poor engagement in particular teams. Within a year, Vodafone's team satisfaction ratings improved by 20% as a result (Workday, 2023).

2.2.3. Predictive Analytics for Retention and Well-being

Predictive analytics powered by AI foresee problems before they become significant. Tools such as Visier and Eightfold AI evaluate both past and current data to predict performance declines, burnout, and turnover concerns. With the use of this information, managers can proactively address issues by providing hours that are flexible or learning opportunities.

Based on feedback, absenteeism, and work patterns, Tata Consultancy Services (TCS) employs AI models to detect disengagement indicators. Early interventions made possible by this technology greatly lower attrition and boost employee morale (TCS, 2023).

2.2.4. Personalised Learning and Development (L&D)

AI promotes participation by fostering professional development via platforms for adaptive learning. Machine learning is used by programmes like Degreed, EdCast, and Cornerstone Xplor to suggest learning paths based on the roles, interests, and performance of employees.

Accenture utilises learning technologies driven by AI that select content based on each learner's unique growth objectives. Their technology enhances internal mobility and learning programme participation, which enhances engagement and retention (Accenture, 2022).

2.2.5. Bias-free Performance Management

Conventional performance evaluations frequently have subjectivity and bias. Analytics are used to generate data-driven performance evaluations by AI technologies such as Betterworks and Lattice. These tools assist managers in tracking progress, setting clear objectives, and giving frequent feedback while maintaining equity and inclusivity. For instance, IBM created an in-house AI system that forecasts worker performance and makes tailored career recommendations. By improving performance management's disclosure and equity, the technology raised engagement (IBM, 2021).

2.3. Key HR Tools Leveraging AI

These tools represent the growing convergence of AI and HR management, empowering organisations to make data-driven, employee-centric decisions.

Tool	**AI Function**	**Organisation Using It**
Leena AI	Conversational AI for HR queries and onboarding	Nestlé, Coca-Cola
Peakon	Real-time engagement and sentiment analysis	Vodafone, Capgemini
Eightfold AI	Predictive analytics for retention and talent mobility	T-Mobile, AirAsia
Degreed	AI-based skill development and learning recommendations	Unilever, HSBC
Lattice	AI-powered goal setting and performance tracking	Slack, Reddit
Workday people analytics	Natural language insights into workforce trends	Salesforce, Target

Source: Author's findings.

2.4. Ethical Considerations and Challenges

Although AI holds great potential, using technology for employee engagement raises questions about it.

2.4.1. Privacy

Workers might feel uneasy about AI examining their personal information. Policies for data governance must be transparent. Algorithms educated on skewed data have the potential to reinforce inequality. Human monitoring and ethical AI procedures are crucial.

2.4.2. An Excessive Dependence on Automation

Human interaction should be supplemented by technology, not replaced. Building trust and culture still requires managers to be actively involved.

Organisations must balance AI's efficiency with empathy and ethical responsibility. Ensuring employees understand how AI is used and involving them in the design of these tools can increase trust and adoption.

In today's fast-paced, digitally driven work environment, establishments are progressively identifying the intrinsic association amongst employee wellbeing and productivity. Traditional workplace wellness programmes have evolved into comprehensive strategies that incorporate digital innovations. Customary workplace wellness programmes have evolved into comprehensive strategies that incorporate digital innovations. Among these modernisations, wearable technology and wellbeing apps are playing a critical role. Digital health technologies have become indispensable parts of present-day workplace tactics due to the changing nature of work and the increased focus on holistic employee wellness. In today's fast-paced, technologically advanced workplace, businesses are seeing more and more the direct connection between worker productivity and well-being. Conventional workplace wellness initiatives have developed into all-encompassing plans that use technological improvements. Wearable technology and health applications are at the forefront of these enlargements. These tools are changing how businesses approach employee well being, from tracking stress levels and heart rates to encouraging mental health. In 2020, World Health Organisation (WHO) and United Nations International Children's Emergency Fund (UNICEF) signed a collaborative framework, accelerating public health efforts as well as mental health and psycho-social well being and development. UNICEF Executive Director Henrietta Fore noted that COVID-19 has augmented prevailing inequalities, validating the urgent need to reform health and wellness delivery systems to better serve vulnerable populations.

3. Understanding Wearables and Wellbeing Apps

Wearable devices hold an enormous potential in contributing to an improved global health. The availability, non-intrusive nature, and cost-effectiveness of those systems make them promising candidates to transform the standard of care for health coaching. These wearable devices are now considered as versatile coaching systems (Sqalli & Al-Thani, 2020). Endeavouring to promote both the health and well-being of their workforce and lessening insurance expenditures, many organisations are integrating wearable fitness trackers into their corporate wellness programmes. To improve employees' health and well-being, corporations have expended nearly $100 billion on workplace wellness programs since the 1970s (Giddens, Gonzalez & Leidner, 2016). Fitness-tracking devices offer inimitable features steering at engaging individuals into a healthy lifestyle. By using these devices in tandem with corporate wellness programmes, organisations hope to escalate the efficacy of their wellness initiatives.

Companies including Barclays and Target distribute Fitbits to their employees and offer incentives to applicants to use the devices and share their information (Troiano, 2017). Wearables are cerebral electronic gadgets that are worn on the body with the perseverance of gathering, tracking, and analysing activity and health data in real time. These include smartwatches like the Apple Watch and Samsung Galaxy Watch, widespread fitness trackers like Fitbit, and advanced biosensors built into bands, rings, or apparel. With the use of technical know-how like electrodermal activity sensors, the data can comprise a variety of physiological markers, including heart rate, oxygen saturation, sleep cycles, step count, and even emotional indicators. On the other hand, wellbeing apps are software applications accessible through smartphones, tablets, or computers, specifically designed to promote physical, mental, and emotional health. Examples include Headspace and Calm for meditation and mindfulness, MyFitnessPal for nutrition tracking, Strava for fitness, and Better Help for digital therapy access. Increasingly, these apps are integrating AI and machine learning to create highly personalised health experiences, adapting recommendations based on user habits, biometric inputs, and behavioural patterns.

The combined use of wearables and wellbeing apps marks a fundamental transfer from reactive healthcare to preventive and proactive health management. They encourage individuals to monitor their own health in real time, creating responsiveness around daily behaviours and empowering early intrusions when necessary.

3.1. Wellbeing Apps

Wellbeing apps are mobile-based digital tools envisioned to enhance users' physical, mental, and emotional health. These smartphone-enabled platforms play a crucial role in stimulating holistic health, addressing physical activity, mental clarity, and emotional balance. They range from meditation apps like Headspace and Calm to fitness and nutrition apps like MyFitnessPal and Strava. Many are now incorporating AI and machine learning to provide personalised experiences tailored to individual user behaviours and health trends.

Wellbeing apps have become indispensable in organisations as they endorse healthier lifestyles, moderate stress, and support mental well-being among employees. By proposing features such as activity tracking, guided meditation, hydration reminders, and mood monitoring, these apps endow individuals to take proactive steps towards their health. In the workplace, this means employees feel more energised, take fewer sick days, and enjoy their work more – leading to better performance and a more positive, engaged team environment. The integration of wellness technology aligns with Sustainable Development Goal 3 (SDG 3), which aims to ensure healthy lives and promote well-being for all at all ages. By adopting wellness apps, organisations contribute to creating supportive environments that highlight both physical and mental health, thus evolving global health and sustainability targets.

Companies are gradually integrating these digital technologies into their employee wellness initiatives, which is resulting in lower rates of burnout, improved mental toughness, and fewer absences due to illness. Organisations are directly supporting SDG 3's goals of dropping non-communicable diseases, augmenting mental health, and ensuring that everyone has access to health and well-being, even in high-pressure work environments, by employing know-how to promote preventive healthcare and mental wellness.

Together, wearables and wellbeing apps are not just gadgets or programmes – they're companions in the everyday journey towards better health. By making health data visible and understandable, they help individuals recognise patterns, set meaningful goals, and take small but consistent steps towards positive change. In the workplace, these tools offer more than convenience – they bring a sense of empowerment. Employees gain control over their well being, which can lead to reduced stress, increased energy, and a stronger sense of purpose. For organisations, this means scalable, cost-effective solutions that promote a culture of wellness, encourage self-care, and build a more resilient, motivated workforce. When people feel supported and seen – not just as workers, but as whole individuals – their satisfaction and engagement naturally rise.

3.2. Progressing Role of Wearables and Apps in Promoting Workplace Wellness

3.2.1. Physical Health Monitoring

Employee participation with their personal wellness and fitness regimens has been transformed by the emergence of wearable technologies. Workers can now approach their physical health in a more proactive and customised manner. Step count, heart rate, calorie burn, and sleep quality are just a few of the important health data that can be continuously monitored with devices like fitness trackers and smartwatches. With the help of these insights, people can better understand their daily routines, set healthier exercise goals, and take proactive steps to lead healthier lives. This real-time feedback is used as a guide and a motivation in the workplace. Staff members are urged to prioritise rest and recuperation, make healthy decisions, and increase their level of mobility in their daily routines. Over time, these minor changes lead to increased vitality, better general health, and fewer diseases linked to a particular lifestyle. Workplace vitality, absenteeism, and healthcare costs are all reduced when employees are healthier, which has a substantial cumulative impact on organisations.

Adobe tossed a corporate wellness challenge that encouraged staff members to use Fitbit devices to compete in a step-counting event. During the six weeks, participants' average daily step count climbed substantially. Employees felt more energetic, and many of them had started walking meetings and taking family walks as part of their daily routines. The company data recorded a decrease in short-term sick leave among participating teams during the challenge. The programme encouraged common wellness objectives, which improved team morale and togetherness in addition to physical health. Beyond physical health improvements, the initiative thereby enhances team morale and camaraderie by encouraging shared wellness goals.

3.2.2. Mental Health Support

Digital well being tools are becoming essential allies in supporting employees' mental health. Apps that offer guided meditation, mood tracking, breathing exercises, and stress management techniques enable employees to cope better with workplace pressures. Some wearables can also detect physiological signs of stress and prompt the user to take breaks or breathe deeply.

Global enterprise software provider SAP endorsed the rising needs of its top-performing employees in terms of mental health. In response, they gave staff members the ability to sync their Fitbit wearables and incorporated the meditation software Headspace into their health platform. In order to accentuate that mental health is a shared responsibility, the effort was presented through leadership endorsement, staff webinars, and storytelling. It wasn't just another app release. Employees involved in a high-stakes implementation deadline explained how the tools' integration changed their everyday routine. It was revealed that in the rush to fulfil deadlines, physical cues like a restrained chest and a pounding heart were frequently disregarded. But there was a feeling of care when a Fitbit rang with reminders to take a break or breathe. Breathing techniques were used during stressful states, and mornings started with a 10-minute mindfulness exercise using Headspace.

Team members gradually started adding 'mindful minutes' to meetings, when the first few minutes were devoted to introspection or deep breathing. Employees who used the watch and app together reported better sleep, increased focus, and a 25% decrease in self-reported anxiety during moments of high workload, per internal surveys. SAP's strategy demonstrated how even a little break, bolstered by technology and corporate culture, can transform into a potent self-care gesture.

3.2.3. Behavioural Change

Wearable technology and wellness applications are persistently made to boost healthy living choices by using gamification, frequent reminders, and subtle cues. Employee engagement and consistency in their wellness routines are maintained by features like leader boards, digital badges, and progress tracking, which foster a sense of enjoyment and accomplishment.

At PwC, the 'Move More' campaign progressed into a movement rather than only a way to track steps. Employees together, used a specially premeditated software that censored their sleep and movement habits, converting routine decisions – such as walking or using the stairs – into points-earning chances. The link between individual well-being and community influence implanted new vitality in the workplace. Teams became closer during the eight-week challenge, friendly competition led to laughter in virtual meetings, and daily exercise increased by 20%.

3.2.4. Real-time Feedback

A standout advantage of wearable technology and wellness apps is their ability to deliver immediate insights into health and well being. This real-time feedback loop enables employees to respond proactively – whether that means stretching after a long session at the desk, sipping water to stay hydrated, or stepping away for a mental break.

At Accenture, the adoption of Garmin wearables contributed to employees more than just data; it offered daily guidance. During concentrated coding sprints, movement was often forgotten for hours. Gentle jolts were given by the wearable when posture slumped or hydration dropped. These subtle reminders were perceived as quiet reminders to practice self-care. As a result, improved posture awareness was noted, alertness scores increased, and fatigue complaints were reduced.

By integrating wearables and wellbeing apps into the workplace, organisations are not just adopting new technology – they're embracing a culture of care that supports employees both professionally and personally. On an individual level, these tools empower people to become more aware of their physical and mental health, helping them make informed, proactive choices that lead to better daily habits. For many employees, a simple buzz on the wrist becomes a reminder to breathe, move, or pause – a small gesture that can make a big difference. At the organisational level, the impact multiplies: healthier employees mean lower absenteeism, reduced healthcare costs, and higher productivity. But beyond the metrics, companies that invest in employee well being send a powerful message – that people matter. This commitment fosters loyalty, improves morale, and cultivates a resilient, high-performing workforce that thrives in both the digital and human aspects of work.

The real-world examples emphasise a critical comprehension: when organisations line up employee well being, the benefits encompass beyond individual health to nurture stronger, more engaged workplaces. These initiatives highlight how wearables and wellbeing apps, when instigated thoughtfully, serve not only as tools for health monitoring but as significant components of a universal EX. As the nature of work continues to evolve, investing in digital wellness strategies will remain indispensable to enlightening resilient, high-performing, and people-centric workplaces.

4. Virtual Workplaces and Their Influence on Happiness

The emergence of digital technology and, more recently, the COVID-19 pandemic have caused a momentous change in the nature of work. An influential substitute for the conventional office model is virtual workplaces, where staff members interact, cooperate, and communicate via digital platforms. The rapid expansion of electronic gadgets and the widespread shift brought about by the COVID-19 pandemic have made virtual workplaces a perceptible aspect of modern organisational systems. The attention switched to comprehending how remote work settings impact employee happiness, an acute component accompanied by productivity, creativity, retention, and overall organisational performance, as millions of people began working remotely. With the help of cloud computing, video conferencing, collaboration tools, and asynchronous communication platforms, these settings have completely changed how people engage with their jobs, co-workers, and company culture.

Employee satisfaction may be positively or negatively impacted by virtual workplaces. On the positive side, remote work provides greater autonomy, flexible scheduling, eradication of commute stress, and enhanced work-life balance – all factors known to enhance job satisfaction and overall well-being. Moreover, for many employees, working virtually has led to increased efficacy and the ability to tailor workspaces to personal comfort.

Nevertheless, there are hitches to the virtual model that may negatively impact happiness. Commonly mentioned concerns include digital weariness, social isolation, a lack of casual connections, and distorted work-life boundaries. Lack of physical manifestation might limit mentorship and spontaneous innovation, as well as moderate attitudes of belonging and teamwork. Incongruences in home office configurations and technological approachability can also result in uneven experiences, which further affect happiness and morale.

Organisational strategies such as encouraging virtual team-building activities, offering mental health assistance, certifying regular communication, and respecting boundaries are necessary to endure and educate employee satisfaction in distant work settings. Virtual workplaces provide unparalleled freedom and prospects for increased enjoyment, but accomplishing these benefits need for thoughtful preparation, empathetic leadership, and comprehensive digital policies that emphasise workers' well-being.

5. Positive Influences of Virtual Workplaces on Employee Happiness

With the rapid rise of remote work and the widespread adoption of digital collaboration tools, virtual workplaces are transforming the traditional EX. Employees now have more flexibility, autonomy, and control over their work settings since they are no longer inhibited by physical office premises or strict timetables. When virtual workplaces are considerately designed with clear communication channels, supportive leadership, and wellness integration they do more than just facilitate remote operations; they substitute a culture of trust, inclusivity, and psychological safety. This shift not only improves employee delight and emotional well-being but also augments productivity, engagement, and long-term job satisfaction. As organisations circumnavigate the future of work, prioritising employee-centred virtual ecosystems is becoming indispensable for sustainable growth and workplace accomplishment. Here are some of the most impactful ways virtual workplaces contribute positively to employee well-being and satisfaction.

5.1. Greater Flexibility and Sovereignty

Virtual workplaces endow employees with the liberty to manage their own schedules. Without the restraints of a rigid 9to5 routine or the pressure of physical oversight, individuals can line up their work with their most prolific hours and personal responsibilities. Dell Technologies executed a flexible work policy where employees could choose distant, hybrid, or in-office work. Internal surveys showed that 94% of employees reported better work-life balance and felt more in control of their day. Self-sufficiency nurtures trust, boosts self-esteem, and reduces workplace stress leading to long-term happiness.

5.2. Improved Work-life Balance

Remote work eliminates commuting time and allows employees to spend more time with family, pursue hobbies, or simply rest. This balance between professional and personal life helps recharge emotional reserves and prevents burnout. Tata Consultancy Services (TCS) adopted the '25/25 model', aiming for only 25% of its workforce to work from the office by 2025. Employees in cities like Delhi or Mumbai reported saving up to three hours daily, which they could invest in family or wellness activities. Better balance leads to improved mood, stronger family relationships, and greater job satisfaction.

5.3. Customised and Comfortable Work Environment

Remote setups let employees plan their workspaces to suit their comfort and preferences; be it lighting, noise levels, seating, or even background music. Automattic, the parent company of WordPress, offers a stipend to employees to build personalised home workstations. This not only develops well being but also makes work feel less stressful and more enjoyable. Comfortable ambiances reduce physical strain and boost mental well-being, directly impacting morale and performance.

5.4. Inclusion and Accessibility

Virtual workrooms provide equal prospects to those who may have formerly been excluded due to geography, physical disabilities, or caregiving responsibilities. GitLab, a fully remote company with employees in over 60 countries, makes sure everyone – regardless of location or physical ability – has equal access to tools, meetings, and growth opportunities. When obstacles are removed, people feel more acknowledged and valued, contributing to a more comprehensive and gratifying work experience.

5.5. Increased Focus and Reduced Office Distractions

Deeper concentration is frequently possible with remote systems, particularly for employees who do well in calmer settings. Employees are better able to concentrate when they are not distracted by office gossip, worthless meetings or lengthy discussions. At first, IBM claimed that because there were fewer interruptions in the office, remote workers were more productive. The early results continue to show the benefits of deep-focus work settings, even if they have since reconsidered their remote strategy. Focused work that gives a sense of success boosts motivation, emotional health, and job happiness.

5.6. Better Integration of Wellness and Lifestyle Habits

Virtual work locations make it easier for employees to assimilate wellness habits like midday workouts, healthy meals, or power naps without judgement. Accenture assimilated wellness apps such as Virgin Pulse across its global teams. Employees used the platform to track steps, hydration, and mindfulness, leading to augmented energy levels and reduced stress. When employees feel they can care for their health during the day, they feel reinforced and valued key components of workplace happiness.

5.7. Enhanced Trust and Accountability Culture

In a virtual setup, micromanagement frequently gives way to outcome-based appraisals. Employees are trusted to manage their own time, which builds a sense of accountability and pride. Hub Spot adopted a 'remote-first' approach during the COVID-19 pandemic and shifted towards trust-based performance models. This resulted in higher employee gratification and retention. It rose in confidence, loyalty, and emotional connection to the organisation.

Virtual workplaces can significantly increase employee satisfaction if they are implemented with responsiveness, suppleness, and diversity. From reducing daily stressors like commuting to enabling a deeper sense of autonomy and belonging, the digital workplace supported by tools, trust, and thoughtful leadership – can create a thriving, engaged, and emotionally healthy workforce. As we move into the future of work, happiness will no longer be an afterthought but a strategic priority in virtual work design.

6. Challenges of Virtual Workplaces Leading Adequate Happiness

6.1. Social Loneliness and Loneliness

While remote work offers independence, it also reduces informal interactions and spontaneous bonding that occur in physical offices. In their annual state of remote work report, buffer noted that many employees experienced loneliness as their top challenge. The company responded by implementing virtual team hangouts, coffee chats, and peer-pairing programmes. Lack of social collaborations can cause emotional detachment, eroded trust, and ultimately burnout if left unchecked.

6.2. Distorted Work-life Boundaries

The boundaries between work and home life are normally blurred by remote work. Employees find it difficult to 'switch off' when they are not physically separated, which eventually results in overwork and burnout. A study by Microsoft discovered that remote employees were recording more hours and attending more meetings than before. Employees recounted a rise in stress and difficulty sustaining work-life separation. Continuous connectivity without disruptions can erode well-being and lead to long-term frustration and mental fatigue.

6.3. Digital Fatigue and Communication Overload

Screen fatigue and a decline in cognitive performance might result from an over dependence on digital communication tools like video conferencing. Unexpectedly, 'Zoom fatigue' even affected Zoom staff. In response, the business encouraged asynchronous communication and implemented 'Zoom-free Fridays'. Constant internet engagement depletes mental and emotional resources. Restricted screen time and planned breaks improve clarity and mood.

6.4. Unequal Access to Infrastructure

A quiet workspace, ergonomic furnishings, and a firm internet connection are not available to all employees. Self-esteem and performance are compressed by these differences. Infosys discovered infrastructural deficiencies among junior employees during the changeover to remote work. To inspire efficiency, company provided laptop deliveries and paid for internet costs. Feelings of inadequacy and obstruction are brought on by unequal resources. Reasonable tools increase employees' involvement and satisfaction.

7. Organisational Strategies to Foster Happiness in Virtual Workplaces

7.1. Balanced and Human-centric Communication

Numerous, apparent, and compassionate communication helps in building trust and prevents feeling of isolation. Salesforce hosts weekly town halls, check-ins, and team jumbles to sustain open lines of communication. Emotional safety and transparency are strategic parts of their governance drill.

7.2. Wellness Ingenuities and Emotional Well-being Support

Companies that prioritise emotional and psychological health see higher engagement and retention. Google offers mindfulness classes, virtual remedy, and resilience training. During high-stress periods, they introduced 'reset days' for communal psychological disruptions.

7.3. Recognition, Rewards, and Digital Appreciation

Remote workers can often feel unseen. Consistent appreciation, even in digital forms, boosts morale. Zappos created a 'Peer Bonus' system where employees can reward each other with small digital bonuses and public appreciation through internal platforms.

8. Future of Happitude in the Hybrid-virtual Work Model

Employee contentment will depend on how well flexibility, connectivity, and human needs are handled as businesses exchange more and more towards a hybrid-virtual work paradigm. The impartiality and sovereignty of remote work combined with the community and cooperative atmosphere of real offices are the supreme features of hybrid models, which combine remote and in-office work. However, thoughtful design, comprehensive leadership, and employee-centric strategies are essential to ensure gratification in this changing environment.

8.1. Designing for Flexibility Without Fragmentation

Organisations will need to provide flexible work plans in the future without forgoing team unity. Employees should be free to choose where and when they work best, in spite of sense of belonging towards the company's culture and objectives. Google's hybrid work strategy inspires in-office alliance three days a week while agreeing to remote flexibility, thus maintaining team collaboration without discouraging personal sovereignty. Individually designed flexibility endows employees, builds trust, and pulls down stress, all of which contribute to long-term arrangement and pleasure.

8.2. Digitally Facilitated Well-being

Virtual workrooms of the future will embrace wellness tools in routine operations. Personalised health jolts, mood-tracking dashboards, and AI-powered well-being check-ins will assist in sorting pressures and halting fatigue before it gets out of control. The well-being data in Teams comes from Microsoft's Viva platform, which is responsible in providing helpful statistics on individual productivity, collaboration excess, and concentration time. Active wellness support nurtures emotional resilience, mental clarity, and a stronger feeling of the organisation's concern for its employees.

8.3. Human-centric Governance and Responsive Intelligence

In hybrid environments, enthusiastically intellectual leadership will be critical. Managers will need to stabilise performance expectations with compassion, active listening, and psychosomatic safety. Salesforce trains hybrid managers to lead with responsive intelligence, using regular check-ins, thankful rituals, and mental health leave options. Employees have a more approachable connection to their work and are more encouraged and upbeat when they feel heard, seen, and valued.

8.4. Purpose-driven Hybrid Philosophy

In a hybrid-virtual environment, shared ideals, purpose, and responsive connection will be essential than tangible office facilities. The companies that promote inclusive cultures and fulfilling employment will be illustrious. While indorsing a 'Live and Work Anywhere' concept, Airbnb assured that its culture and vision are upheld through shared experiences, virtual storytelling, and projects with clear perseverance. Long-term contentment depends on having a sense of purpose and belonging, predominantly in situations when physical presence is restricted.

8.5. Redefining Equity and Access in Hybrid Systems

Organisations must ensure equitable access to resources, opportunities, and visibility for all employees, regardless of location, in order to avoid a digital divide or two-tier workforce remote vs in-office. LinkedIn reformed meeting policies to be remote-first confirming that everyone, whether online or in person, has the same level of contribution and acknowledgement. Equivalence, insertion, and equal opportunity build trust and endorse emotional security which are the key drivers of workplace happiness.

9. Designing Happiness in Humanised Digital Future

The extent to which virtual workplaces are built with thoughtfulness determines whether they increase or decrease happiness. Companies that value independence, endorse connectivity, encourage well-being, and place an extraordinary priority on equity are much more likely to have content and driven employees, as demonstrated by Dell, Git Lab, and Infosys.

The hybrid-virtual paradigm exemplifies a change in how we approach work as well as where we work. The aptitude of companies to create systems that are both passionately intellectual and digitally well-organised will determine the future of contentment in this field. True employee happiness will depend on compassion, determination, compliance, and a people-first culture, even while technology continues to advance. Happiness is a pleasant vital indicator of triumph in this new digital world, not an outcome of hard effort.

10. Using Gamification for a Happier Workplace

Technology is frequently seen through the prism of automation and efficiency in the current effort to improve the work experience. But perhaps its greatest influence is found in its capacity to make labour more essentially human – more interesting, inspiring, and fulfilling. Gamification is one of the most effective technology approaches to accomplish this. Gamification, the deliberate use of game design aspects and concepts outside of games, is far from being a pointless endeavour to transform work into a video game. It may revolutionise routine chores, provide a sense of achievement, and create a truly happier workplace when applied carefully.

Gamification makes use of ingrained psychological cues that have contributed to the allure of games for thousands of years. It appeals to our primal needs for control, independence, meaning, and interpersonal relationships. By incorporating tools such as leaderboards, progress bars, badges, and points into work procedures, companies may establish feedback loops that give workers a sense of competence, engagement, and value. As a result, the workforce is not only more productive but also happier.

11. Why Gamification Is Effective: The Psychological Engine

The science of human motivation must be examined in order to comprehend the power of gamification. A fundamental framework is the self-determination theory (SDT), which was put out by psychologists Richard Ryan and Edward Deci. According to SDT, people have three basic psychological needs: relatedness (the need to feel connected to other people), competence (the need to feel successful and skilled), and autonomy (the need to feel in control of one's own activities). People have greater levels of intrinsic motivation, well being, and performance when these requirements are satisfied (Deci & Ryan, 2000). Technology-driven gamification directly serves these needs:

11.1. Autonomy

Gamified systems give workers options for how to approach assignments or follow educational pathways. Branching storylines or extra 'side quests', for example, might be incorporated into a training session to provide employees the freedom to select their own learning path. A strict, one-size-fits-all strategy is significantly less powerful than this sense of control.

11.2. Competence

Gamification may be most effective in this area. Levelling-up systems, badges, and points offer quick and concrete feedback on accomplishments. On a complicated project, a progress bar that is slowly approaching 100% offers a visible confirmation of work. An employee's abilities are reinforced when they effectively resolve a customer issue and receive the 'Problem Solver' badge. A key component of professional happiness is confidence and a sense of mastery, which are developed via this ongoing feedback loop.

11.3. Relatedness

When leader boards are centred on team-based objectives, they can promote camaraderie, but if they are badly structured, they can also occasionally encourage unhealthy competitiveness. Departmental silos can be broken down and a sense of shared purpose can be fostered through collaborative quests that demand cooperation from several departments. Social skills, such as the capacity to offer 'kudos' or points to a helpful co-worker, enhance constructive interactions and fortify relationships between people.

Gamification activates the brain's reward system in addition to SDT. Dopamine is a neurotransmitter linked to motivation and pleasure that is released when a challenge is finished or a badge is earned (Zichermann & Cunningham, 2011). Employees are neurologically rewarded for exhibiting desired behaviours, which results in a positive feedback loop that transforms work from a tedious task to a fulfilling endeavour.

12. Real-world Uses: Where Experience and Technology Collide

Through its useful, tech-enabled applications throughout the whole employee lifecycle, gamification's theoretical potential is brought to life. These are not futuristic ideas; top businesses are already using them with advanced platforms and interfaces.

12.1. Training and on Boarding

A new job's first few weeks might be quite demanding. This experience can be turned from a knowledge dump into an interesting exploration using gamification. A 'Newbie Quest' is a checklist of duties that can be given to new hires in the form of levels to do.

Level 1: Watch introduction films and finish HR documentation.

Level 2: 'Meet Your Guild': Arrange initial meetings with team members to collect points for each relationship formed.

Level 3: Earn a 'Culture Keeper' badge by finishing the first e-learning module on the company's values.

For its leadership academy, Deloitte famously introduced a gamified on boarding approach. Participants discovered that gamification, which uses leader boards and badges, boosted the number of users who returned to the platform by almost 50%, proving its ability to increase learning engagement (Meister, 2013).

12.2. Productivity and Performance

Gamification can increase the transparency and engagement of routine work. With visual fireworks to commemorate each significant deal signed, a sales team's live dashboard can display progress towards a team-based quarterly target. Compared to a static spreadsheet, this is more motivating. A system may provide developers points for resolving issues, closing tickets, and getting good peer reviews on their code. This encourages quality and teamwork in addition to productivity. The laborious process of software localisation testing has been effectively gamified by Microsoft. They developed a game that allowed staff members to compete rather than only designating language specialists to look for mistakes in various Windows versions. Employees were encouraged to identify even the most elusive mistakes in order to win, which not only expedited the process but also significantly enhanced the calibre of input (Kappen & Nacke, 2013).

12.3. Culture and Collaboration

Mutual respect and cooperation are the cornerstones of a strong company culture. This can be facilitated by gamification platforms that are integrated with communication technologies such as Microsoft Teams or Slack. When a co-worker goes above and beyond on a project, an employee might give them a 'kudos' point. These points can be accrued, exchanged for minor incentives, or just put on a 'Wall of Fame'. This formalises and promotes showing gratitude, which is essential to a positive work atmosphere. Interdepartmental collaboration and a feeling of group identity can be promoted through team-based competitions, in which departments compete to accomplish a common corporate objective.

12.4. Employee Wellness

The happiness and well-being of employees are closely related. Businesses can gamify wellness programmes at scale because of technology. Points, streaks, and team challenges are frequently used in corporate wellness apps to promote mindfulness, exercise, and a balanced diet. Maintaining a 'meditation streak' or competing with co-workers in a company-wide 'step challenge' gives personal health goals a fun and social accountability component that directly contributes to a happier and healthier workforce.

13. The Principles and Difficulties of Successful Design

Although gamification is an effective tool, it is not a cure-all. A badly thought-out system may backfire, causing disengagement, anxiety, and cynicism. The secret is to concentrate on designing for genuine incentive rather than using what gamification expert Yu-kai Chou refers to as 'PBLs' (points, badges, and leaderboards) (Chou, 2015). Crucial Elements of Success are as follows.

13.1. Put Intrinsic Motivation First

Improving the work itself should be the main objective. Instead of only providing extrinsic rewards like gift cards, the game aspects should showcase an employee's development and proficiency. Not simply the award, but the sense of achievement should be the reward.

13.2. Assure Fairness and Transparency

The game's rules ought to be understandable, attainable, and seen as equitable. Employee disengagement will occur if they believe the system is biased or promotes inappropriate behaviour. Performance must be transparently and objectively measured by the technology.

13.3. Strike a Balance between Competition and Collaboration

While some rivalry is good for you, focusing too much on individual leader boards can lead to a ruthless atmosphere. Creating team-based competitions or emphasising individual greatest accomplishments are frequently more successful. Flexible configurations that align with the company's culture should be possible with the technology.

13.4. Make it Optional

Fun is rarely enjoyable when it is required. It is desirable for gamified systems to be opt-in. Employee involvement is more genuine when they voluntarily participate.

13.5. Complement Business Goals

Gamification shouldn't be implemented in a vacuum. The actions being rewarded, such as finishing training, working together on a project, or reaching a sales goal, must be closely related to the organisation's strategic objectives. This guarantees that the system has ongoing executive support and generates actual value.

14. Creating a More Fulfilling Work Environment

Gamification stands out in the larger context of technology's influence in the work experience. It supports the notion that work can be re-humanised through technology rather than dehumanised. By utilising basic psychological motivations, it moves the emphasis from completing tasks to a more interesting and fulfilling path of development, success, and connection.

It turns feedback into a constant, uplifting flow of information rather than a dismal yearly evaluation. It transforms education from a required task into an individual pursuit. Additionally, it transforms cooperation into a shared adventure rather than a need. The resulting sense of skill, pride, and camaraderie is very genuine, even though the points and badges may be fictitious. Investing in well-designed gamification technology is not just playing games for companies hoping to create a more contented, resilient, and creative staff; it is a real and effective strategy for creating a better workplace of the future.

When it comes to enlighten the contemporary work experience, technological advancement is both disruptive and indispensable. Improved flexibility, smooth communication, and tailored well-being support have transformed how employees interact with their jobs and companies. Technology acts as an intermediary and a catalyst in detached and hybrid settings, bringing people altogether from different places and reassuring collaboration, inclusivity, and productivity. Likewise, by catering to individual specifications and fostering mental, responsive, and physical health, AI-powered tools and wellness applications are contributing to the humanisation of the digital workplace. But the real stimulus of know-how is found in how well it is incorporated into workplace culture, not merely in how well it works.

References

Accenture. (2022). *How Accenture is using AI for learning and development*. https://www.accenture.com

Bock, L. (2015). *Work rules!: Insights from Inside Google that will transform how you live and lead.* Twelve.

Chou, Y. (2015). *Actionable gamification: Beyond points, badges, and leaderboards*. Octalysis Media.

Deci, E. L., & Ryan, R. M. (2000). The "What" and "Why" of goal pursuits: Human needs and the self-determination of behavior. *Psychological Inquiry*, *11*(4), 227–268.

Dell Technologies. (n.d.). *What are digital assistants?* Dell Technologies InfoHub. https://infohub.delltechnologies.com/en-us/l/design-guide-generative-ai-digital-assistants-in-the-enterprise/what-are-digital-assistants/

Gallup. (2023). *State of the global workplace report*. https://www.gallup.com

Giddens, L., Gonzalez, E., & Leidner, D. (2016). I track, therefore I Am: Exploring the impact of wearable fitness devices on employee identity and wellbeing.

Google. (2025, March 5). *Expanding AI Overviews and introducing AI Mode.* Google Blog. https://blog.google/products/search/ai-mode-search/

Hill, N. S., Axtell, C., Raghuram, S., & Nurmi, N. (2024). Unpacking virtual work's dual effects on employee well-being: An integrative review and future research agenda. *Journal of Management*, *50*(2), 752–792.

IBM. (2021). *AI and the future of performance management at IBM*. https://www.ibm.com/blogs

Kahn, W. A. (1990). *Psychological conditions of personal engagement and disengagement at work*. *Academy of Management Journal*, *33*(4), 692–724.

Kappen, D. L., & Nacke, L. E. (2013). The kaleidoscope of effective gamification: A review of existing gamification design frameworks. *Proceedings of the first international conference on gameful design, research, and applications* (pp. 1–8).

Kruse, K. (2012). *Employee engagement 2.0: How to motivate your team for high performance*. The Kruse Group.

Leena AI. (2022). *How Nestlé streamlined HR support with AI*. https://www.leena.ai

MacLeod, D., & Clarke, N. (2009). *Engaging for success: Enhancing performance through employee engagement*. Department for Business, Innovation and Skills, UK Government.

Meister, J. (2013, April 29). *How Deloitte made learning a game*. *Harvard Business Review*. https://hbr.org/2013/04/how-deloitte-made-learning-a-game

Microsoft. (2021). *Empowering people and teams with Microsoft Viva*. https://www.microsoft.com/en-us/microsoft-viva

Morgan, J. (2017). *The employee experience advantage: How to win the war for talent by giving employees the workspaces they want, the tools they need, and a culture they can celebrate*. Wiley.

Qualtrics. (2021). *Deloitte case study*. https://www.qualtrics.com/customers/deloitte/

Sqalli, M. T., & Al-Thani, D. (2020). Evolution of wearable devices in health coaching: Challenges and opportunities. *Frontiers in Digital Health*, *2*, 545646. https://www.unicef.org/press-releases/who-and-unicef-recommit accelerating%C2%A0health-and-well-being-all-ages

Tata Consultancy Services. (2023). *AI for proactive employee engagement*. https://www.tcs.com

Troiano, A. (2017). Wearables and personal health data: Putting a premium on your privacy. *Brooklyn Law Review*, *82*(4), 6.

Unilever. (2021). *Flex experiences: Unilever's AI-powered talent marketplace*. https://www.unilever.com/news/news-search/2021/flex-experiences/

Wang, Y., & Haggerty, N. (2011). Individual virtual competence and its influence on work outcomes. *Journal of Management Information Systems*, *27*(4), 299–334.

Werbach, K., & Hunter, D. (2012). *For the win: How game thinking can revolutionize your business*. Wharton Digital Press.

Workday. (2023). *Vodafone case study – Employee engagement with Peakon*. https://www.workday.com

World Economic Forum. (2020). *The future of jobs report*. https://www.weforum.org/reports/t

Wortley, D., An, J.-Y., & Nigg, C. R. (2017). Wearable technologies, health and well-being: A case review. *Digital Medicine*, *3*(1), 11–17.

Zichermann, G., & Cunningham, C. (2011). *Gamification by design: Implementing game mechanics in web and mobile apps*. O'Reilly Media, Inc.

Chapter 14

A Framework for Circular Happiness: A Systematic Literature Review and Future Research Agenda

Manoj Bansal[a], *Bharath S.*[b] *and Asmita Choudhary*[a]

[a]*University School for Graduate Studies, Chaudhary Devi Lal University, India*
[b]*Brindavan College, India*

Abstract

The main aim of this chapter is to prepare a systematic literature review and a bibliometric on a framework for circular happiness. Employee's productivity will increase when they are happy; happiness leads to more productivity in an organisation. Happiness means a good life, and how a good life can be lived at the workplace. A systematic literature review has been done from past studies with the help of MS Excel. VOSviewer software has been used for bibliometric analysis. The data has been taken from the Scopus database. Future research agenda has been found with the help of the rotated component matrix. The clustering of variables into components provides a framework to identify thematic areas such as methodology, emotional well-being, employee roles, and organisational impact. Implications are discussed that are important for marketers and policy-makers. In the end, a future research agenda was also found for future research studies. This study provides a framework for circular happiness. The results and findings, and their future applications, are very beneficial for policy-makers of the organisation, and creating more improvements in the domain of 'Circular Happiness'.

Keywords: Happiness at workplace; circular happiness; systematic literature review; employee productivity; workplace well being; organizational sustainability

Circular Happiness: Building Sustainable Workplaces for the Next Generation, 267–286

Published under exclusive licence by Emerald Publishing Limited
doi:10.1108/978-1-80592-907-920261014

Introduction

Happiness is defined as a holistic experience – cognitive, emotional, psychological, and social that influences not just productivity but also overall quality of life. As the Dalai Lama once said, 'The purpose of life is to be happy', an attitude that has been profoundly ingrained in company ethos, leadership philosophies, and national well-being indicators.

In the 21st century, market domination and financial prosperity are no longer the only indicators of an organisation's success. Employee happiness, workplace culture, and mental health are examples of intangible assets that are increasingly recognised as critical factors in long-term sustainability. Happiness at work has arisen as a significant characteristic of humanoid capital management. As firms adapt to digital disruptions, demographic shifts, global uncertainties, and post-epidemic recalibrations of life goals, ensuring employee happiness has evolved from a minor worry to a critical strategic significance.

Happier workforces incline to be extra creative, involved, in addition pleased with their jobs, which pays to organisational achievement by deteriorating turnover and taming loyalty. Businesses can realise prominent gains in employee retention and company success by cultivating a healthy work environment where staff members feel cherished and inspired (Caraballo-Arias et al., 2024). Job happiness is allied to better performance, stronger relationships, and more community participation (Boehm & Lyubomirsky, 2008; Grossmeier et al., 2019).

Sustenance from coworkers and superiors, organisational fairness, chances for individual development, and a strong corporate culture are all factors that subsidise to workplace satisfaction (Caraballo-Arias et al., 2024). Important factors that affect pleasure at work include job fulfilment, job rendezvous, workplace safety, strain management, and self-assurance (Jain & Sharma, 2019; Rahmi, 2019). A happy workplace is significantly influenced by autonomy, enjoyment, and the capacity to make decisions, accentuating the significance of organisational culture and psychological well-being (Mittal, 2023). To learn happiness at work, Various theoretical contexts have been used counting the job demand-resources (JD-R) model, social exchange theory, and broaden-and-build theory. There is a call for exploring fewer prevalent theories, like flow theory and the positive emotions, engagement, relationships, meaning, and accomplishment (PERMA) model for future research (Jaswal et al., 2024). Happiness at the office is energetic and uninterruptedly budding, demanding continuing negotiations crossways through numerous research stages (Saritha & Mukherjee, 2024). Work engagement, job gratification, and affective organisational assurance are the measures of individual-level contentment (Fisher, 2010). A happy employee would be more efficient than an unfortunate one, and those free from anxiety would quintessentialise their efforts on their work instead of other spheres of their life, including their financial situation (Sharifzadeh & Almaraz, 2014). The positive correlation between work instability and trepidation of COVID-19 was protected by employee mindfulness. An optimistic association between job diffidence and frontline employees' emotive fatigue is supported by perceived structural support (Chen & Eyoun, 2021). Since organisational virtuousness is the only factor that is considered a source of job success in Japan, particular well-being is relatively more important there since it enhances job performance (Magnier-Watanabe et al., 2020). Workplace happiness comprises, but is far supplementary than, job fulfilment. Work rendezvous, job fulfilment, and affective organisational assurance are included in a full amount of individual-level happiness (Fisher, 2010).

Recent bibliometric and systematic reviews have consolidated the happy–productive worker thesis by examining its conceptual evolution, measurement approaches, and productivity outcomes Costa et al. (2024). The idea that job satisfaction boosts efficiency is empirically reinforced by a number of research. For example, a natural experimentation carried out at a telecom business showed that positive affect, obstructed by outside variables like the weather, greatly enhanced sales success by raising worker efficiency (Bellet et al., 2019). Likewise, studies conducted in a piece-rate framework exposed that happy individuals were around 12% more productive, guiding to an unswerving association between performance and happiness (Oswald et al., 2015). The broaden-and-build theory and attitude-behaviour models are two of the theoretical frameworks that underpin the happy-productive worker thesis. According to these frameworks, people who experience pleasant emotions are able to think and act more creatively, which improves performance (García-Buades et al., 2019). The link amidst job demands and performance results can also be facilitated by well-being, as explained by the job-demands-resources model (García-Buades et al., 2019). Studies from numerous settings, including one from Laos, emphasise the unique influence of emotional states on output. Happiness was shown to be suggestively and favourably associated with productivity more than any other emotional state, highlighting the necessity for businesses to take emotional well-being into account when developing their operational plans (Kadoya et al., 2020). Although the happy-productive relationship is generally accepted, some research finds different outlines, including happy-unproductive and unhappy-productive situations. According to a study on young Spanish workers, these trends are influenced by organisational and personal factors like over-qualification and job self-efficacy (Ayala et al., 2017).

The central premise of this chapter is that happiness is more than a feel-good construct or a luxury reserved for successful businesses; rather, it is a fundamental element that governs how people engage with their roles, relate to encounters, and modernise under pressure. In this situation, happiness is demarcated as an all-inclusive experience, cognitive, emotional, psychological, and social that influences not just productivity but also overall quality of life. Circular happiness is a sustainable, regenerative model of workplace well-being that has gained popularity as researchers and practitioners look for comprehensive frameworks that combine social benefit, corporate productivity, and individual desire.

Even with the increasing amount of conceptual and empirical studies on workplace happiness, the literature is still dispersed and ill-integrated. Several studies have looked at discrete factors like autonomy, engagement, and job satisfaction without properly capturing how intertwined and circular workplace happiness is. Furthermore, there is a dearth of fusion that unifies current ideas into a cohesive system, even if they offer essential insights. Examples of these theories are the JD-R model, social exchange theory, and broaden – and – build theory. Words alike 'employee happiness', 'well being', and 'positive affect' are frequently used indiscriminately, which makes information accumulation more difficult and hinders the development of theories. To further investigate how the research environment has changed over time, what themes are prevalent, and where important knowledge gaps still exist, few studies use bibliometric and systematic review approaches. These drawbacks highlight how urgently a systematised method is needed that not only examines preceding research but also charts the conceptual landscape, pinpoints subject clusters, and suggests a research plan for 'circular happiness' in the future.

The present knowledge of workplace happiness is based on several significant hypotheses. According to the JD-R model, social support, autonomy, and feedback are examples of work resources that can increase employee satisfaction by lowering burnout and increasing engagement. Positive emotions extend cognitive and behavioural repertoires, which improve creativity and resilience, as stated by Fredrickson's broaden and build hypothesis. Furthermore, as the nitty-gritties of happiness, optimistic emotions, rendezvous, associations, meaning, and triumph are all included in the multifaceted framework provided by Seligman's PERMA model. Empirical studies back up these theories with evidence showing that contented employees are more resilient, productive, and devoted.

By combining and broadening the disparate literature on workplace happiness, this piece advances both academic research and managerial practice. Initially, it creates an integrative framework for circular pleasure, providing a means of comprehending how happiness operated as a dynamic, linked system rather than a linear input–output process. Second, for managers and policymakers looking to match corporate objectives with human-centric values, the study offers evidence-based insights. Thirdly, it highlights new areas of study, such as how well-being and sustainability are entwined, digital workplaces and intercultural viewpoints.

Research questions

(i) How happiness leads to productivity at workplace?
(ii) Which are the co-occurrence terms that have impact on happiness at workplace studies?
(iii) What are the key factors that are helpful for future research?

Research methodology: a datasheet downloaded from the Scopus database using the keyword 'Employee's happiness'. In the first 1,127 records were identified, 14 papers were removed due to some other reasons like abstract not found, not related with employee's happiness, etc. At last, 1,113 records were analysed. All PRISMA standards have been followed while penetrating and screening the data.

Prisma Chart

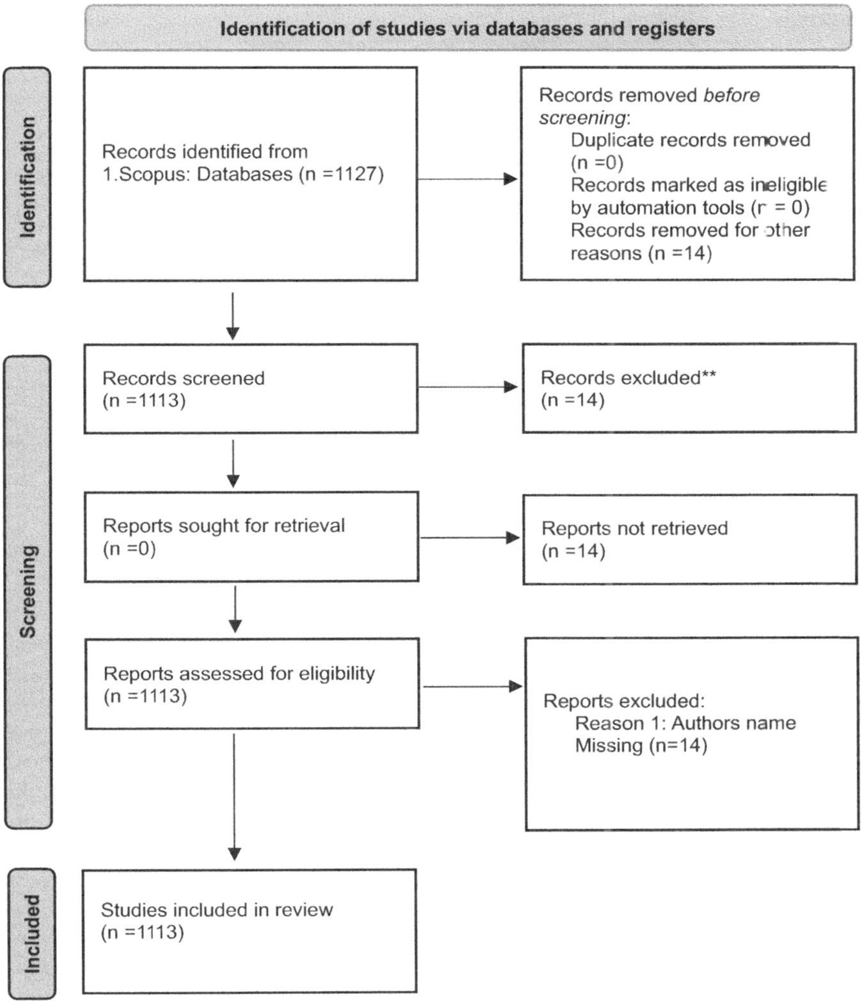

Main Findings

The top 10 journals and top 10 authors in this area are discussed below.

Top 10 Cited Journals

The citation data highlights the academic influence and relevance of the listed journals, communally accounting for a total of 6,224 citations (Table 14.1). Leading the list is the *Journal of Management* with 1,108 citations, showcasing its strong influence in management research. Following closely are the *Journal*

Table 14.1. Top 10 Journals.

Journals	Citations
Journal of Management	1,108
Journal of Happiness Studies	854
Journal of Occupational Health Psychology	815
International Journal of Management Reviews	592
Academy of Management Perspectives	553
Journal of Labor Economics	548
American Economic Review	498
International Journal of Environmental Research and Public Health	478
Journal of Business Venturing	394
Journal of Business Ethics	384
Total	6,224

Source: Authors' own work.

of Happiness Studies (854 citations) and the *Journal of Occupational Health Psychology* (815 citations), reflecting a growing academic interest in well-being and workplace health. Moderately cited journals, such as the *International Journal of Management Reviews* (592 citations) and the *Academy of Management Perspectives* (553 citations), validate their consistent contribution to management discourse. Additionally, the *Journal of Labor Economics* (548 citations) and the *American Economic Review* (498 citations) underline the importance of economic studies. Meanwhile, niche-focused journals like the *International Journal of Environmental Research and Public Health* (478 citations) highlight the rising recognition of environmental and public health issues. The *Journal of Business Venturing* (394 citations) and the *Journal of Business Ethics* (384 citations) contribute significantly to entrepreneurial and ethical business studies, though they exhibit comparatively lower citation counts. Overall, the data accentuates the varying levels of influence across these journals, with management, well-being, and occupational health topics commanding greater academic attention. Researchers can use this insight to strategically select journals for submissions, aiming for maximum reach and impact in their respective fields.

Top 10 Cited Authors

The citation data for authors reflects their academic influence based on the total citations of their works, which collectively amount to 5,489 citations (Table 14.2). Among the authors, Youssef, C. M., and Luthans, F. lead with 1,108 citations, signifying their substantial contribution to the field, principally in areas likely related to organisational behaviour or psychological capital. Following them are Wright, T. A., and Cropanzano, R., with 829 citations, showcasing their significant influence in workplace well-being and related domains.

Table 14.2. Top 10 Authors.

Authors	Citations
Youssef, C. M., and Luthans, F.	1,108
Wright, T. A., and Cropanzano, R.	829
Van De Voorde, K., Paauwe, J., and Van Veldhoven, M.	592
Grant, A. M., Christianson, M. K., and Price, R. H.	553
Oswald, A. J., Proto, E., and Sgroi, D.	548
Card, D., Mas, A., Moretti, E., and Saez, E.	498
Cropanzano, R., and Wright, T. A.	348
Hofmann, W., Wisneski, D. C., Brandt, M. J., and Skitka, L. J.	346
Boehm, J. K., and Lyubomirsky, S.	343
Oakman, J., Kinsman, N., Stuckey, R., Graham, M., and Weale, V.	324
Total citation	5,489

Source: Authors' own work.

The trio Van De Voorde, K., Paauwe, J., and Van Veldhoven, M. have garnered 592 citations, indicating the impact of their research, possibly on human resource management or organisational performance. Similarly, Grant A. M., Christianson, M. K., and Price, R. H. achieved 553 citations, reflecting their remarkable contributions, potentially in leadership and organisational health. The group Oswald, A. J., Proto, E., and Sgroi, D. has 548 citations, emphasising their role in economic and psychological studies.

Other distinguished contributors include Card, D., Mas, A., Moretti, E., and Saez, E., whose works collectively received 498 citations, suggesting influence in labour economics. Additionally, Cropanzano, R., and Wright, T. A. reappear with 348 citations, reinforcing their prominence in academic discourse. Authors like Hofmann, W., Wisneski, D. C., Brandt, M. J., and Skitka, L. J. (346 citations), as well as Boehm, J. K., and Lyubomirsky, S. (343 citations), reflect significant contributions in moral psychology and happiness studies, respectively. Lastly, Oakman J. and collaborators received 324 citations, highlighting their impact in professional health and ergonomics.

This data exemplifies the varied yet impactful charities of these authors across various fields, providing valuable insights for researchers looking to engage with influential studies or authors in their respective areas.

The study is divided into five sections: introduction, review of literature, research methodology, findings and conclusion, and future investigation agenda covering all aspects of good research.

Meta Analysis

From the analysis of 20,665 terms extracted from 1,127 Scopus papers using the keyword employee happiness, a threshold of a minimum occurrence of 137 was applied to filter the most frequently occurring terms. This process identified

21 terms that met the occurrence criteria, ensuring their relevance and prominence in the literature. However, two terms, namely research and paper, were excluded from the list due to their generic nature and lack of contextual significance. This enhancement resulted in a final selection of 19 key terms, which are considered highly relevant to the thematic analysis of employee happiness. The exclusion of overly broad terms like research and paper enhances the focus on meaningful concepts and ensures that the analysis remains centred on the core themes and variables within the literature. These selected terms provide a robust foundation for further bibliometric analysis, enabling researchers to discover trends, relationships, and clusters within the academic discourse on employee happiness.

The analysis further reveals the visualisation of term relationships based on their co-occurrence patterns. Thin lines in the picture indicate less frequent co-occurrence between terms, highlighting weaker connections or less momentous relationships. In contrast, thick lines represent more frequent co-occurrence, indicating stronger associations and greater significance in the academic discourse.

Additionally, the clusters provide an instinctive representation of thematic groupings. Each one corresponds to a specific cluster of terms that are closely interrelated, reflecting discrete themes or areas of focus within the field of employee happiness. This clustering helps in identifying key areas of research and their interconnections, offering insights into the edifice and depth of the literature.

Such visual representations not only enhance the understanding of the data but also provide a foundation for identifying gaps, trends, and future directions in the study of employee happiness (Fig. 14.1).

Table 14.3 offers the consequences of the PCA, highlighting the amount of variance explained by each component before and after rotation. Here's an interpretation of the findings:

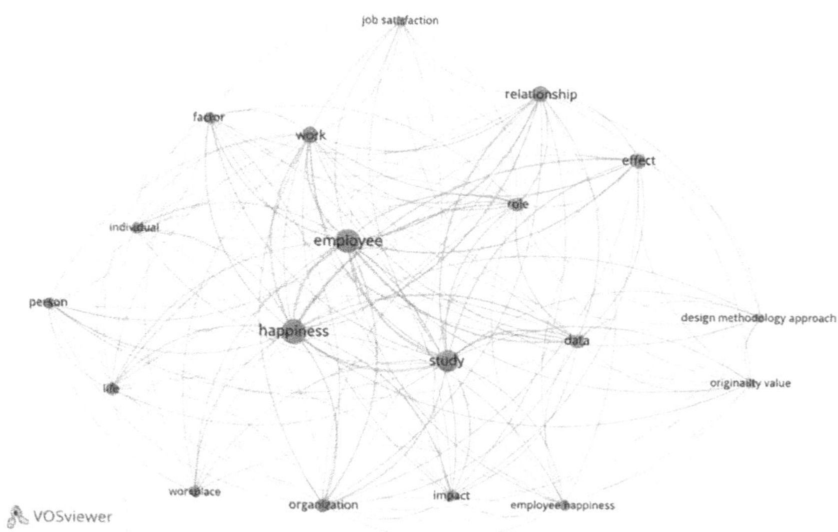

Fig. 14.1. Terms of Relativity. *Source*: Authors' original work.

Table 14.3. Total Variance Explained.

Component	Initial Eigenvalues			Extraction Sums of Squared Loadings			Rotation Sums of Squared Loadings		
	Total	% of Variance	Cumulative %	Total	% of Variance	Cumulative %	Total	% of Variance	Cumulative %
1	3.526	18.557	18.557	3.526	18.557	18.557	2.313	12.176	12.176
2	2.001	10.532	29.089	2.001	10.532	29.089	2.043	10.752	22.928
3	1.739	9.153	38.242	1.739	9.153	38.242	1.973	10.383	33.311
4	1.445	7.604	45.846	1.445	7.604	45.846	1.599	8.414	41.724
5	1.217	6.406	52.252	1.217	6.406	52.252	1.507	7.932	49.656
6	1.097	5.776	58.027	1.097	5.776	58.027	1.469	7.732	57.388
7	1.015	5.341	63.368	1.015	5.341	63.368	1.136	5.980	63.368
8	0.969	5.102	68.470						
9	0.889	4.677	73.147						
10	0.832	4.379	77.526						
11	0.768	4.041	81.567						
12	0.711	3.743	85.310						
13	0.645	3.394	88.704						
14	0.587	3.091	91.796						
15	0.560	2.946	94.742						
16	0.545	2.866	97.609						
17	0.454	2.391	99.999						
18	0.000	0.001	100.000						
19	−1.002E−013	−1.013E−013	100.000						

Extraction method: principal component analysis (PCA).
Source: Authors' original work.

1. Initial eigenvalues
   - The eigenvalues represent the amount of variance accounted for by each component. Components with eigenvalues of a matrix greater than 1 are considered significant based on the Kaiser criterion.
   - The first 7 components have eigenvalues greater than 1, collectively explaining 63.368% of the total alteration in the data.

2. Cumulative variance
   - The collective variance indicates how much of the total variance is enlightened as components are added.
   - The first constituent explains 18.557% of the variance, while the second and third components contribute an additional 10.532% and 9.153%, respectively. Together, the first three components explain 38.242% of the variance.
   - Adding more components gradually increases the cumulative variance, reaching 63.368% by the seventh component.

3. Extraction sums of squared loadings
   - These values represent the variance explained by each component after extraction but before rotation. They remain the same as the initial eigenvalues for the first seven components, as no additional components were extracted.

4. Rotation sums of squared loadings
   - After the revolution, the variance is reordered among the apparatuses for better interpretability.
   - The variance explained by individual apparatuses is to some extent adjusted, but the cumulative variance remains the same (63.368%).
   - For example, the first component's contribution decreases from 18.557% to 12.176%, while the contributions of other components, such as the second and third, are more evenly distributed.

5. Key insights
   - The first seven components elucidate an extensive serving of the variance, making them sufficient for capturing the causal construction of the data.
   - The rotated solution improves interpretability by distributing variance more evenly, ensuring that each component captures a distinct aspect of the data.
   - Components beyond the seventh have eigenvalues less than 1 and contribute minimal variance, indicating they are not significant.

The PCA results suggest that the first seven components effectively summarise the data while capturing its most significant patterns. The rotation further enhances clarity, aiding in the identification of key themes or factors related to the dataset. This analysis provides a robust basis for further exploration, such as identifying the specific variables loading on each component and interpreting their thematic implications (Fig. 14.2 and Table 14.4).

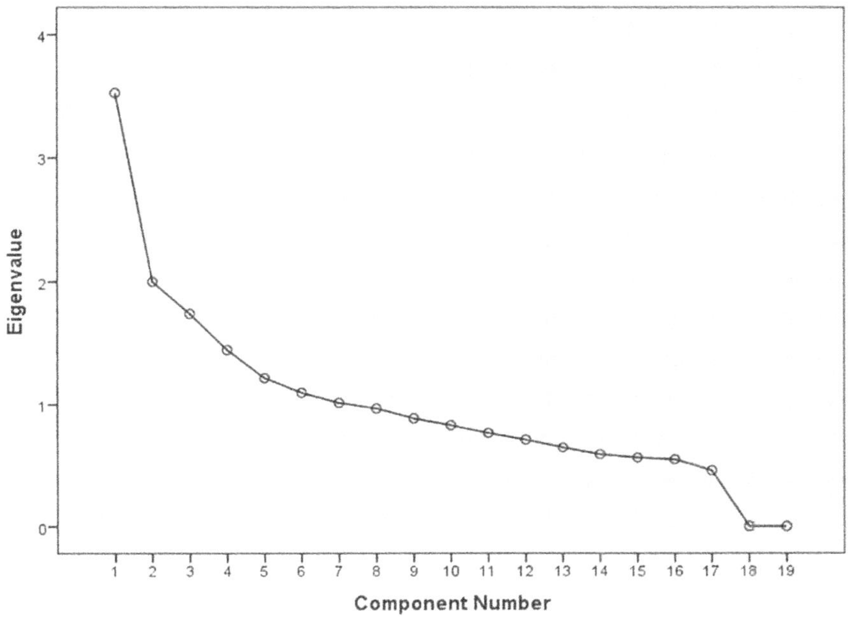

Fig. 14.2. Scree Plot. *Source*: Authors' own work.

Table 14.4. Rotational Matrix Table from Statistical Package for the Social Sciences (SPSS).

Rotated Component Matrix[a]							
	Component						
	1	2	3	4	5	6	7
VAR00001	0.282	−0.035	−0.123	0.293	0.252	0.497	0.209
VAR00002	0.210	0.955	−0.044	0.071	0.016	0.101	0.067
VAR00003	0.195	0.053	0.026	0.588	0.180	0.407	−0.072
VAR00004	0.147	−0.070	0.635	0.081	−0.156	−0.032	0.156
VAR00005	0.200	0.002	−0.852	0.050	0.008	−0.054	0.106
VAR00006	0.158	−0.304	−0.026	−0.636	0.044	0.217	0.075
VAR00007	−0.044	−0.010	0.831	−0.038	0.010	−0.082	−0.006
VAR00008	0.109	−0.012	−0.211	−0.131	0.667	0.172	−0.135
VAR00009	−0.484	−0.139	−0.060	0.019	−0.037	−0.021	−0.012
VAR00010	0.228	−0.148	−0.071	−0.069	0.001	−0.012	−0.876
VAR00011	−0.724	−0.035	0.113	−0.147	0.029	0.013	0.162
VAR00012	0.204	−0.108	−0.209	−0.347	−0.444	−0.172	0.356

(Continued)

Table 14.4. (*Continued*)

Rotated Component Matrix[a]							
	Component						
	1	**2**	**3**	**4**	**5**	**6**	**7**
VAR00013	0.215	0.955	−0.050	0.070	0.015	0.093	0.072
VAR00014	−0.735	−0.148	0.105	−0.118	−0.023	−0.034	0.149
VAR00015	0.454	0.057	0.065	0.354	−0.024	0.307	0.085
VAR00016	0.284	−0.103	−0.072	0.618	0.034	0.067	0.162
VAR00017	0.570	0.056	−0.022	−0.144	0.467	0.163	0.167
VAR00018	−0.009	0.001	0.004	−0.187	−0.721	0.091	−0.092
VAR00019	0.016	−0.160	0.030	0.039	−0.001	−0.886	0.076

Extraction method: PCA.
[a]Rotation method: Varimax with Kaiser normalisation. Rotation converged in 22 iterations.

The rotated component matrix, consequential from the PCA, delivers understandings into the assemblage of variable stars (terms) across seven components (Table 14.5). The varimax rotation with Kaiser normalisation was applied to attain a stronger structure by maximising the alteration clarified by each constituent. Below is the interpretation of the key findings:

Table 14.5. Rotational Matrix Analysis Table after Analysis.

Rotated Component Matrix[a]							
	Component						
	1	**2**	**3**	**4**	**5**	**6**	**7**
Data						0.497	
Design methodology approach		0.955					
Effect				0.588			
Employee			0.635				
Employee happiness	0.200						
Factor						0.217	
Happiness			0.831				
Impact					0.667		
Individual				0.019			
Job satisfaction	0.228						

Table 14.5. (*Continued*)

Rotated Component Matrix[a]							
	Component						
	1	**2**	**3**	**4**	**5**	**6**	**7**
Life							0.162
Organisation							0.356
Originality value		0.955					
Person							0.149
Relationship	0.454						
Role				0.618			
Study	0.570						
Work						0.091	
Workplace							0.076

Source: Authors' own work.
[a]Rotation method: Varimax with Kaiser normalisation. Rotation converged in 22 iterations.
Extraction method: PCA.

The future of circular happiness at the workplace: with the help of components, we can find a future research agenda for circular happiness.

1. Component loadings:
   The matrix highlights the strength of the association between a piece variable and the components. Higher loadings (close to ±1) indicate a stronger association between a term and a specific component. For instance: Design methodology tactic and originality value load highly on component 2 (0.955 each). Happiness shows a strong loading on component 3 (0.831). Employee loads significantly on component 2 (0.635).

2. Key variables across components:
   Component 1: variables such as study (0.570) and relationship (0.454) have moderate loadings, suggesting a focus on general research relationships.
   Component 2: this component includes terms like design methodology approach (0.955) and originality value (0.955), indicating its connotation with methodological rigour and innovation.
   Component 3: strongly associated with happiness (0.831) and role (0.618), highlighting themes around emotional well-being and roles.
   Component 4: variables like impact (0.667) dominate, pointing to the significance of outcome-driven studies.
   Components 5, 6, and 7: these have relatively weaker associations with terms like organisation (0.356) and factor (0.217), indicating potential peripheral themes.

3. Convergence:
   The rotation congregated in 22 repetitions, illustrating a well-fitted explanation, where the components effectively capture the variance construction of the data.

Implications

The factor analysis of circular happiness at the workplace reveals important insights that hold both managerial and theoretical significance. The high loadings of design methodology approach and originality value on component 2 emphasise that innovation and methodological rigour are central to sustaining happiness at work. For managers, this implies the necessity of integrating creativity and design-driven strategies into organisational practices by fostering participatory approaches, encouraging originality in problem-solving, and embedding employee-centric methods into workplace structures. At the same time, these findings contribute to theory by bridging methodological sophistication with employee well-being, extending the existing literature to highlight how innovation-oriented processes can shape workplace happiness in novel ways.

Similarly, the strong association of happiness and role with component 3 underscores the importance of role clarity, meaningful work design, and emotional well-being. Practically, managers can enhance happiness by aligning tasks with employees' intrinsic motivations and ensuring that job roles are structured to provide purpose and fulfilment. Theoretically, this reinforces role theory by positioning workplace happiness not merely as an affective construct but as one deeply embedded in structural and functional alignment within organisations. Component 4, which is strongly linked to impact, suggests that happiness is closely tied to outcome-oriented recognition. In practice, this highlights the need for organisations to value employees not just for their tasks but also for the broader contributions they make. From a theoretical standpoint, this finding enhances models of happiness by incorporating an outcome-based perspective, where the perceived societal or organisational impact of one's work becomes a vital source of well-being.

Although components 5, 6, and 7 display relatively weaker associations, their connections to terms such as organisation and factor point towards peripheral yet meaningful influences. Managerially, this signals the role of supportive organisational culture and contextual assessment in sustaining happiness. Theoretically, it opens pathways for future research into indirect and context-specific determinants of well-being, particularly across industries, cultural settings, and administrative frameworks.

Taken together, these findings propose a comprehensive framework where innovation, role alignment, emotional well-being, and impact creation operate in a circular manner to reinforce happiness at the workplace. The convergence of managerial and theoretical perspectives underscores the dual contribution of this study: providing actionable strategies for organisations to cultivate circular happiness and advancing scholarly discourse by reframing happiness as a cyclical and interconnected construct. This integrated understanding not only strengthens present practices but also sets a vibrant schema for upcoming research aimed at examining how methodological rigour, role clarity, and outcome-driven recognition collectively sustain workplace happiness in dynamic organisational contexts.

Societal Implications

At the social level, the study presents a bigger narrative: happy workplaces generate positive externalities that benefit the entire communities. Organisations that focus on employee well-being promote greater mental health, lower workplace stress, and more civic participation among employees. This endorses augmented social stability, healthier family relationships, and communal cohesiveness.

Furthermore, the study emphasises the link between economic productivity and emotional and psychological health, which has policy implications. Governments and labour ministries might develop public policies to encourage employee's well-being efforts, such as tax benefits for firms that have excellent happiness and health programmes or national happiness indices that integrate work-life indicators.

The larger viewpoints are consistent with the worldwide drive towards 'Beyond GDP' measurements and sustainable development goals (SDGs) that promote quality of life and well-being. In essence, encouraging workplace happiness becomes a public good with benefits that reach beyond the bounds of individual businesses and into a country's socioeconomic fabric.

Steps for Organisation to Implement Circular Happiness

Integrated sustainability and circular happiness principles with employee fostering the circular happiness in an organisation. The following steps we can implement for circular happiness.

- *Step 1: concept understandability*: recycling, reusing, renewing resources of economy with principles of mental, emotional, bodily health, and job gratification reflects circular happiness. The main purpose should be to Create structures where materials circulate competently, and people find persistence, have their place, and pleasure.
- *Step 2: vision and leadership*: vision should be clear, and it must be aligned with the employee well-being and society's benefit. While applying, the happiness charter must be prepared.
- *Step 3: assess the current state*: well-being audit, environmental audit, and stakeholder engagement are important aspects to measure the current state.
- *Step 4: set clear areas*: employee happiness, circular economy and community impact are major areas where an organisation must work and measure from time to time that employees are happy, sustainable sources are passable and social impact is effective.
- *Step 5: design circular systems*: an organisation must develop a design circular system, like recycling loops, remanufacturing, prevention of harm and waste, and a regenerative system.

- *Step 6: integrate well-being at work*: an organisation must have an organised wellness programme for employees, prospects for learning, a culture of gratitude and recognition for the well-being of the employees.
- *Step 7: monitor and measure impact*: for measuring the impact, use key performance indicators (KPI) like resource efficiency, employees' net promoter score, community rendezvous metrics, etc.
- *Step 8: education and communication*: training sessions, success stories, and progress updates are important steps for circular happiness. They can help in communicating and educating the employees so that they can perform better.
- *Step 9: foster partnerships*: alliances with social enterprises, NGO, and government foster the partnership with other articles. Circular economy networks and well-being conditions help employees to learn more from other organisations.
- *Step 10: continuous improvement*: lastly, adopt policies and practices and update them strategically. Celebrating your achievement is also a very important aspect of it. We should align our achievements with the values for the future path shown to our employees.

Creating Sustainable Work Culture for Next Generation

Environmental sustainability, social well-being and meaningful work are important aspects for creating a sustainable work culture for future generations. Circular happiness is a thought of reconstructing and balancing the system.

For future generations, thinking about regeneration is necessary, not only is sustainability enough. It is important to understand that happiness is not a perk; it is a key to productivity. Design of policies should be according to the future generation, keeping in mind.

While designing the policies, open-minded thoughts and feedback were also considered so that suggestions can be inculcated into policies.

While preparing work culture for the next generation, company goals must be aligned with climate conditions and social impact. Sustainability literacy and emotional intelligence are also important factors to consider for upskilling the employees. Organisation also underscores on value maximisation instead of profit maximisation.

Marketers and managers must be focused on the above-mentioned aspects for creating a sustainable work culture for the next generation.

Summarising the key learning: this study uses a wide-ranging literature review and bibliometric analysis to inspect the important association amidst worker fulfilment and workplace productivity. The findings confirm that the happiness is a strategic factor of individual performance and organisational success, rather than a subjective or incidental feature of work life. Drawing studies and modern bibliometric tactics the study finds significant topics such as emotional well-being, job satisfaction, employee roles, and organisational effect, emphasising the multidimensional character of workplace happiness.

The findings give strong theoretical support for existing models such as the JD-R model and the broadened build theory, while also promoting the use of developing frameworks like the PERMA model and the flow theory. The study highlights the necessity of fostering psychologically secure, supportive, and engaging work environments to increase productivity. On a social level, it emphasises the larger economic and community benefits of addressing workplace well-being.

However, the study recognises its limitations, such as database breadth, methodological limits, and a lack of source data, which open the way for future research. Cross-cultural comparisons, longitudinal research, qualitative investigations, and the use of technology to quantify happiness in real time are all proposed directions.

In summary, this study confirms that examining employee satisfaction is not just ethical, but also economically beneficial. As companies negotiate increasingly complicated work settings, a focus on holistic well-being and emotional health will be critical for long-term productivity and organisational resilience.

Future Scope/Future Research Directions

Building on the discoveries and accepting the study's restrictions, many options for forthcoming research are projected to deepen and broaden our understanding of employee satisfaction and its influence on productivity:

1. Diversifying data sources and terminology: future research should investigate combining other databases, such as Web of Science, ProQuest, Google Scholar, and discipline-specific repositories, to capture a more complete and varied body of literature. Furthermore, expanding the search keywords to include synonyms and similar notions such as 'subjective well-being', 'positive organizational behavior', 'job engagement', and 'emotional wellness' would enhance the study.
2. Cross-cultural and sector-specific investigations: more empirical research should investigate how cultural environment, industry type, and organisational structure influence the happiness–productivity link. Longitudinal research associating western and eastern viewpoints on workplace satisfaction, as well as commercial and public sector enterprises, might give more nuanced findings.
3. Longitudinal and causal research designs: the majority of current research is cross-sectional or correlational. To more rigorously prove causation, future research should use longitudinal, experimental, or quasi-experimental approaches. Interventions aimed at increasing happiness (for example, wellness programmes, mindfulness trainings, or positive leadership efforts) might be assessed for their long-term impact on employee performance.
4. Inclusion of underrepresented populations: much of the present literature is geared towards white collar or knowledge professionals. Future studies should look at blue-collar, gig-economy, remote, and frontline workers to see how happiness emerges in different job contexts. This can assist customise happiness boosting tactics to different demographics and socioeconomic groupings.
5. Integration of qualitative approaches: more qualitative research, such as interviews, focus groups, and ethnographies that investigate employees' lived

experiences with workplace happiness are required. Such techniques can unearth deeper motivations, beliefs, and quantitative investigations that are frequently overlooked.

6. Measurement standardisation and innovation: future research should concentrate on creating and verifying reliable, context-sensitive instruments for assessing workplace pleasures. Exploring the use of real-time data gathering approaches (e.g., ecological momentary assessment, wearable technologies, or mood tracking applications) might give more dynamic and precise insights into how happiness swings during the workday.
7. Exploring digital and hybrid models: given the prevalence of remote and hybrid work, future research should look into how digital communication, flexibility, and work–life balancing technologies impact employee happiness and productivity. This involves investigating how virtual team dynamics, digital fatigue, and autonomy affect the happiness–productivity relationship.
8. Policy and organisational strategy integration: researchers should also investigate how government policies, labour laws, and organisational governance models might be harmonised with the happiness productivity paradigm. Investigating macro-level variables that promote or impede employee well-being across regions and economies can help shape public policy and company strategy.

Limitations

Though this learning delivers an appreciated understanding of the association between employee happiness and productivity through a systematic literature review and bibliometric analysis, numerous boundaries must be accredited. First, the investigation trusted exclusively on the Scopus database and employed the single keyword 'employee happiness' as the primary search term. Although Scopus is a highly reputable and comprehensive source, it may not incorporate all pertinent studies available in other databases such as Web of Science, Google Scholar, or domain-specific repositories. In addition, limiting the search to a single keyword may have inadvertently excluded studies that examined related concepts using alternative terms such as well-being, job engagement, or positive affect at work. Second, the review considered only English-language publications, which introduces linguistic bias by excluding possibly pertinent studies issued in other languages. Moreover, prioritising peer-reviewed journal articles may have resulted in publication bias, as important contributions from grey literature, conference proceedings, or organisational reports were not included.

Third, there are inherent methodological limitations in the bibliometric and statistical tools employed in this study. The use of VOSviewer and Microsoft Excel, while effective in identifying word co-occurrence and mapping clusters, offers limited capacity to capture contextual complexity, qualitative nuances, or causal linkages between variables. As a result, the ability to fully interpret complex social and psychological dynamics underlying employee happiness is constrained. Fourth, the learning is constructed exclusively on secondary data and does not involve the collection of primary empirical evidence through methods such as surveys, interviews, or experiments. Consequently, the findings remain dependent on existing literature and cannot be directly tested or quantified within specific organisational contexts.

Fifth, the study is subject to temporal limitations, as the dataset only includes research published up to a defined point in time. Given the rapidly evolving nature of workplace dynamics – particularly in the post-COVID era – emerging trends, technologies, and shifts in employee expectations may not be fully captured. Finally, the synthesis of global literature poses challenges for generalisation. The determinants of happiness and productivity are often shaped by cultural, industrial, and institutional contexts, meaning that insights derived from international studies may not be universally applicable. For instance, factors influencing employee happiness may vary significantly between nations, industries such as technology versus manufacturing, or across community and cloistered sector organisations. These limitations highlight the need for future research that is more inclusive, context-specific, and methodologically diverse to deliver a deeper understanding of the intricate association between employee happiness and productivity.

References

Ayala, Y., Silla, J., Tordera, N., Lorente, L., & Yeves, J. (2017). Job satisfaction and innovative performance in young Spanish employees: Testing new patterns in the happy-productive worker thesis – A discriminant study. *Journal of Happiness Studies*, *18*, 1377–1401. https://doi.org/10.1007/S10902-016-9778-1

Bellet, C., Neve, J., & Ward, G. (2019). Does employee happiness have an impact on productivity? *Political Methods: Experiments & Experimental Design e Journal*. https://doi.org/10.2139/ssrn.3470734

Bellet, C., De Neve, J. E., & Ward, G. (2020). *Does employee happiness have an impact on productivity? CEP Discussion Papers dp1655*. Centre for Economic Performance, London School of Economics. Saïd Business School, WP 2019-13.

Boehm, J., & Lyubomirsky, S. (2008). Does happiness promote career success? *Journal of Career Assessment*, *16*, 101–116. https://doi.org/10.1177/1069072707308140

Caraballo-Arias, Y., Milani, S., & Feola, D. (2024). O-266 a state-of-the art of happiness at work. *Occupational Medicine*, *74*(Suppl. 1). https://doi.org/10.1093/occmed/kqae023.1098

Chen, H., & Eyoun, K. (2021). Do mindfulness and perceived organizational support work? Fear of COVID-19 on restaurant frontline employees' job insecurity and emotional exhaustion. *International Journal of Hospitality Management*, *94*, 102850. https://doi.org/10.1016/j.ijhm.2020.102850

Costa, N., Ferreira, P., & Oliveira, C. (2024). *A bibliometric approach to the thesis of the happy-productive worker – A journey through the concepts and measurement*. Sage Open. https://doi.org/10.1177/21582440241249549

Fisher, C. D. (2010). Happiness at work. *International Journal of Management Reviews*, *12*(4), 384–412. https://doi.org/10.1111/j.1468-2370.2009.00270.x

García-Buades, M., Peiró, J., Montañez-Juan, M., Kozusznik, M., & Ortiz-Bonnin, S. (2019). Happy-productive teams and work units: A systematic review of the 'happy-productive worker thesis'. *International Journal of Environmental Research and Public Health*, *17*(1), 69. https://doi.org/10.3390/ijerph17010069

Grossmeier, J., Viswanath, K., Kubzansky, L., Black, H., Greenberg, S., Saulsgiver, K., Sinar, E., Reece, A., Carr, E., Kellerman, G., Heap, L., Wheaton, R., Gassmann, J., & O'Brien, N. (2019). Editor's desk: The why and how of addressing employee happiness. *American Journal of Health Promotion*, *33*, 1209–1226. https://doi.org/10.1177/0890117119878277

Iwasaki, K. (2021, January). *Happiness makes workers more productive: Evidence from large-scaled experiments*. Paper presented at the Allied Social Science Associations (ASSA) annual meeting, online. https://www.aeaweb.org/conference/2021/preliminary/paper/bGddFeha

Jain, S., & Sharma, V. (2019). What determines workplace happiness? *Research Journal of Humanities and Social Sciences*, *10*(2), 495–502. https://doi.org/10.5958/2321-5828.2019.00082.2

Jaswal, N., Sharma, D., Bhardwaj, B., & Kraus, S. (2024). Promoting well-being through happiness at work: A systematic literature review and future research agenda. *Management Decision*, *62*(13), 332–369. https://doi.org/10.1108/md-08-2023-1492

Kadoya, Y., Khan, M., Watanapongvanich, S., & Binnagan, P. (2020). Emotional status and productivity: Evidence from the special economic zone in Laos. *Sustainability*, *12*(4), 1544. https://doi.org/10.3390/su12041544

Magnier-Watanabe, R., Uchida, T., Orsini, P., & Benton, C. F. (2020). Organizational virtuousness, subjective well-being, and job performance: Comparing employees in France and Japan. *Asia-Pacific Journal of Business Administration*, *12*(2), 115–138. https://doi.org/10.1108/APJBA-11-2019-0214

Mittal, D. (2023). Happiness at workplace: A psychological perspective. *International Journal of Science and Research (IJSR)*, *12*(4), 1374–1376. https://doi.org/10.21275/sr23422161340

Oswald, A., Proto, E., & Sgroi, D. (2015). Happiness and productivity. *Journal of Labor Economics*, *33*, 789–822. https://doi.org/10.1086/681096

Peiró, J., Montesa, D., Soriano, A., Kozusznik, M., Villajos, E., Magdaleno, J., Djourova, N., & Ayala, Y. (2021). Revisiting the happy-productive worker thesis from a eudaimonic perspective: A systematic review. *Sustainability*, *13*(6), 3174. https://doi.org/10.3390/SU13063174

Pratiwi, A., & Setiyowati, A. (2024). Individual happiness and well-being as a strategy to increase productivity. *Psychology, Evaluation, and Technology in Educational Research*, *7*(1), 74–81. https://doi.org/10.33292/petier.v7i1.237

Rahmi, F. (2019). Happiness at workplace. In *International conference of mental health, neuroscience, and cyber-psychology* (pp. 32–40). Fakultas Ilmu Pendidikan.

Saritha, S. R., & Mukherjee, U. (2024). Happiness at workplace – A systematic literature review. *International Journal of Research in Engineering, Science and Management*, *7*(5), 38–44. https://www.ijresm.com

Sharifzadeh, M., & Almaraz, J. (2014). Happiness and productivity in the workplace. *American Journal of Management*, *14*(4), 19–26.

Zelenski, J., Murphy, S., & Jenkins, D. (2008). The happy-productive worker thesis revisited. *Journal of Happiness Studies*, *9*, 521–537. https://doi.org/10.1007/S10902-008-9087-4

Zertuche Pérez, L. V., & Dávila Figueroa, R. (2021). Happiness and labour productivity. *Academia Letters*, 2.

Printed and bound by CPI Group (UK) Ltd, Croydon, CR0 4YY

27/04/2026

14869510-0004